T0375296

A Four-column Parallel and Chronological Harmony of the Gospels of Matthew, Mark, Luke and John:

Using the modern World English Bible, Translated from the Greek Majority Text, and Ordering historical events in the life of Jesus of Nazareth on the basis of the priority of Matthew over Mark

Robert M. Sutherland

Order this book online at www.trafford.com
or email orders@trafford.com

Most Trafford titles are also available at major online book retailers.

Print information available on the last page.

ISBN: 978-1-6987-0174-5 (sc)
ISBN: 978-1-6987-0173-8 (e)

Library of Congress Control Number: 2020911032

Trafford rev. 06/26/2020

www.trafford.com

North America & international
toll-free: 1 888 232 4444 (USA & Canada)
fax: 812 355 4082

This book is dedicated to my wife
Cindy Sutherland.

CONTENTS

INTRODUCTION

1. THE BASIC QUESTION TO BE ASKED AND ANSWERED

The biblical gospels of Matthew, Mark, Luke and John tell the greatest story ever told. The second divine person of the triune God of love came to earth in the person of Jesus of Nazareth to demonstrate the height, breadth and depth of the love of God, and to offer and effect a personal transformation in and through that love, in this life and the next life, for all who would trust in and and surrender to him.

These four biblical gospels of Matthew, Mark, Luke and John assert three things. (1) Jesus of Nazareth claimed to be divine. (2) He died for that claim. (3) He rose again from the dead to establish the truth of that claim. These are purely historical matters, knowable and provable on a balance of probabilities in the court of public opinion.

2. THIS BOOK'S INTRODUCTORY NATURE

This book is as an introductory interpretive aid, to all students of all ages, interested in knowing for themselves something of the objective historical truth of those claims and their biblical foundation.

I say introductory for at least three reasons.

First, this book is simply how I would format the testimonial evidence of the various gospel writers as a first step to an examination as to their individual and collective credibility and reliability, and the reader will likely find it helpful. This book does not indicate why certain other evidence is necessarily excluded on the grounds of irrevelance and immateriality. This book does not contain my assessment of the evidence in terms of analysis of the credibility and reliability of certain events and their authors, which would include material beyond the testimonial accounts themselves. This book does not contain my judgements in the areas of the totality of the evidence, the strength of the evidence, and the sufficiency of the evidence in meeting the historical standard of proof on a balance of probabilities. Those three things are the subject of a later book.

Second, a philosophical check is a necessary and reflective check on any historical conclusions reached, and this book does not provide that. History is in the realm of the possible: what is said to have happened in the past. Philosophy sets out the range of the possible, what can happen: past, present or future. While philosophy can be a handmaiden to theology, it is equally true that philosophy is a traffic cop to history. If any one of these five things: (1) the existence of God, (2) the Trinity, (3) the Incarnation, (4) the Resurrection or (5) the Final Judgement is logically impossible, then any historical claim that Jesus rose from the dead in fulfillment of a truth claim to be divine is necessarily false, regardless of how good the historical evidence is in its favour. Suffice to say at this point, I find that, on that evidence, that the existence of God, the Trinity, the Incarnation, the Resurrection and the Final Judgment is either logically probable or necessary, and thus, any historical claim that Jesus rose from the dead in fulfillment of a truth claim to be divine as might be found in the historical testimony of the gospel writers is corroborated philosophically. That evidence in those five areas is the subject of a later book.

Third, knowledge is but a pre-ample to faith. The knowledge that might be afforded by historical inquiry certainly commends itself to the mind for acceptance as truth, at least until such time as further evidence or better ways of weighing the evidence become available. But knowledge is not faith. It is said in the scriptures themselves that the devils themselves know the historical truth of things, but remain damned. Why? Because they have not taken the second step from knowledge to faith. Knowledge is an intellectual act. Faith is a certain type of volitional act, a personal and passionate choice and committment, sometimes based on knowledge, sometimes not. As a relational concept, faith is always expressed as the oneness of three things: gratitude for, surrender to and love of a particular person. The gospel writers of Matthew, Mark, Luke and John present the knowledge of Jesus of Nazareth that they do, for the purpose of enjoining their readers to make a personal and passionate committment to him. (1) They enjoin a faith in Jesus that is a personal gratitude to Jesus for what he has done for you, especially on the cross, and will do for you personally, especially in this life and at the time of the Final Judgement. (2) They enjoin a faith in Jesus that is a personal surrender to Jesus as your rightful lord and saviour here in this life. (3) They enjoin a faith in Jesus that is an on-going personal transformation by the love of God in and through Jesus actually living in you. Faith is different from knowledge, as any act of the will is different from any act of the intellect. But faith is related to the knowledge of the truth. A faith in Jesus is only a saving faith, if two things are historically and philosophically true. (1) Jesus is who he claimed to be: God incarnate, and (2) Jesus can and will do what he claimed he will do: grant eternal salvation to all who trust in him and only him.

In that respect, the knowledge provided in this book may be helpful for readers, either prompting a personal choice in faith to invite Jesus into your life or reinforcing a choice already made.

3. THIS BOOK'S AUTHOR

I suspect the reader will want to know who I am.

First, I am a Canadian defense lawyer with 34 years at the bar. I hold a four-year Honours B.A. in the History of Ideas from University of Toronto (1977-1981). I hold a three-year L.L.B. in Law from Osgoode Hall Law School (1981). My law school criminal law and criminal procedure professor was Louise Arbour, who would later become a Supreme Court of Canada justice, sit on the World Court in the Hague and is currently the United Nations Human Rights commissioner. I have practised criminal law, child protection law and family law for 34 years in five provinces: Ontario (1986-2005), Alberta (2005-2007), Newfoundland-Labrador (2007-2010), Nova Scotia (2010-2017), Manitoba (2017-2018), Nova Scotia (2018-2020). In the course of my career, I have some notable successes, changing the law nationally and provincially at various points in time. Throughout my career, my legal work has been focused on the representation of the poor and those otherwise in dire need of help.

Second, I am a philosophically moderate realist and a natural law thinker, in the tradition of the three great Western thinkers: Aristotle, Thomas Aquinas and Mortimer J. Adler. The last of the three was one of my mentors. Mortimer J. Adler was a prominent 20th century American philosopher of common sense, a former law school professor from the University of Chicago, the head of the Institute for Philosophical Research, and for many decades the Chairman of the Board of Editors of the Encyclopedia Britannica, responsible for its publication of the 62 volume *Great Books* (1952, expanded 1992) series. I first discovered his writings in 1988, was quickly transformed by them, joining his American Chicago-based think-tank *The Mortimer J. Adler Center for the Study of the Great Ideas* (http://www.thegreatideas.org), serving as its Canadian director for a number of years, having communications with Dr. Adler through its director Max Weismann. I would strongly recommend to the readers six of Mortimer J. Adler's books: *How to Read a Book* (1972), *How to Think About the Great Ideas* (2020), *Six Great Ideas* (1997) *Ten Philosophical Mistakes* (1997), *We Hold These Truths* (1987), and *Truth in Religion* (1990), and four of Dr. Edward Feser's books: *Aquinas: A Beginner's Guide* (2009), *Philosophy of Mind: A Beginner's Guide* (2006), *Five Proofs for the Existence of Go*d (2017), *Aristotle's Revenge: The Metaphysical Foundations of Physical and Biological Science* (2019) for their own philosophical check on those historical claims and conclusions arising from the gospels themselves.

Third, I am an evangelical Christian, theologically traditional, in most areas, but Baptist in my rejection of the doctrine of original sin and its inherited transmission of damnation. I was not raised Christian and had no childhood religious upbringing. In my high school years (1972-1977), I read virtually all the writings of an English Calvinist poet John Milton, a Scottish Presbyterian theologian William Barclay, a German philosopher Friedrich Nietzsche, and an Austrian pyscho-analyst Eric Fromm, and those readings were preparatory to my ultimate religious conversion. I trace my spiritual journey back to a powerful "born-again" experience on August 20, 1976. I was aged 18 years old, alone in a tent in middle of the backwoods of Prince Edward Island. I had just finished listening to a Christian sharing his testimony to others around a campfire outside my tent. He was not reaching them, but he was reaching me. He never knew it, and he never knew I was there. I have always regarded it as a profound reminder that you never know the influence you can have on others. In 1981, I was simultaneously accepted into the "Wycliffe" seminary at the Toronto School of Theology and the Osgoode Law School. I choose the law school over the seminary. And it was not a choice I have ever regretted. My legal training and career have afforded me the time, talent and treasure to pursue my religious interests in the direction and depth that I wanted. In 2004, I published a book *Putting God on Trial: The Biblical Book of Job*, a revolutionary contribution to Job studies that has been a course text in several Canadian, American and Indian universities. Over the years, I have been blessed with many blessings. The most important blessing is my closest friend and selfless wife Cindy Sutherland, whom I cherish beyond life itself. My hope and prayer is that the reader would find such a companion as she on their journey. In the meantime, the spiritual blessings that I can recommend to readers include any of Dr. Malcolm Guite's "You-Tube" videos on *Love*, *Light*, *Coleridge*, *Lewis* and *Tolkien* and Dr. Charles Mathewes' two audiobooks *City of God* and *Why Evil Exists*, the latter being a profoundly deep examination of the meaning of good and evil in Western civilization through its very best thinkers, religious and otherwise, from 4500 B.C. to the present day. Everyone everywhere should wrestle with the questions that book raises and with the range of options it offers. I currently fellowship in and am a member of my local church down the street, a part of the United Church of Canada.

4. THIS BOOK'S USE OF THE WORLD ENGLISH BIBLE

I have used the World English Bible (WEB) for this work, integrating some of its notes in brackets into the text, for two reasons.

First, I would note the *World English Bible* (WEB) is a modern translation in the *King James Version* (KJV) tradition: elegant, readable and fairly literal. It is actually an evangelical revision of the 1901 *American Standard Version* (ASV), which itself was a kind of KJV update. I have chosen it over the KJV or ASV, because the language is more modern. No translation can ever be or should be completely literal, for simple reason that it would cease to be a translation. And yet, there are real advantages in aiming, as this translation does, at a formal rather than a dynamic equivalence in the translation of Hebrew or Greek into English. The reader does not have to believe in the inerrancy of the scriptures in order to read the texts closely, attentive to what is actually said.

Second, I would note that the *World English Bible* (WEB) has the decisive advantage of being free from all copyright and attendant royalties. Virtually all modern English translations are copyrighted. If I were to use any popular modern translation, then my reproducing all four gospels in parallel columns for analysis would be virtually impossible financially. The owner of the copyright to those modern translations would normally require an up-front royalty of at least $10,000 and on-going royalties of at least $10 for each individual sale. I choose to make this work affordable and available to all free of charge.

5. THIS BOOK'S USE OF THE GREEK MAJORITY TEXT

I note that the World English Bible (WEB) is translated from the Greek Majority Text (MT), which some might think a problem, but I do not.

First, all New Testament (NT) translations necessarily build on some particular reconstructed Greek text.

(1) The original autographs do not survive.

(2) Out of the 5865 ancient manuscripts or fragments of the Greek NT that do survive, no two documents agree 100% with each other. The printing press would not be invented until 1454 AD.

(3) For the approximate 138,000-142,000 Greek New Testament words, depending on the reconstructed Greek text chosen for the NT, there are about 500,000 variant readings, though they do seem to divide into families of textual variants, where a family is defined as its members sharing, at least 60% of the time, common textual readings for a passage.

(4) A textual variant or textual reading is any place in the text where there is a difference in language from a base text. You might call it an error or a corruption, but you need not. It is just a difference. Those differences can be simple differences in spelling (as there was no standardized ancient spelling of a word), in word order (as there was no standardized ancient grammar and there were various ways to convey a single thought with no loss in meaning), or in additions or omissions of words (sometimes accidental, sometimes intentional). This is what generates the high number of 500,000 textual variants.

(5) What is important is not the number of textual variants, but their nature or kind. About 99.5% are not meaningful or viable. They don't change the meaning even in a slight way. They are so late or rare in the manuscript stream that they could not possibly represent the original reading. About 0.5% are meaningful and viable. They do change the meaning, sometimes slightly, sometimes more so. They are viable in that they could possibly represent the original reading. That reduces the 500,000 textual variants down to about 2,000 textual variants, for the New Testament as a whole, only a portion of which is in the gospels, that might be worth discussing, but they all are resolvable. My resolution of that portion of the 2000 textual variants dealing with the four gospels is the subject of a later book.

Second, textual criticism is the method of historical inquiry by which textual variants are resolved. The basic principle is "one should choose the reading that best explains the rise of the others." It begins, using a base text, with an assessment of credibility (believability) asking: what was an original author likely to have written, and what was a scribe likely to have written, in order to arrive at a plausible and reliable story as to what happened in textual transmission.

(1) To sort out the New Testament variations, the *King James Version* (KJV) basically uses the *Received Text* (RT): essentially Erasmus' 1522 reconstructed Greek text (3rd edition) as amended by Stephanus' 1589-1590 reconstructed Greek text (5th edition). The editors of the *Received Test* based their work on only 7 Byzantine Greek manuscripts, none earlier than the 11th century A.D., though they had access to the rival Catholic *Complutensian Polygot* which referenced the 4th century Alexandrian manuscript *Vaticanus*, but they rejected it and its tradition as an inaccurate representation of the Greek original. The same editors had extensive knowledge of the early Church fathers' quotations of New Testament readings going back to the 2nd century A.D. It is kind of a regional variation on the *Majority Text* (MT), not using best and most representative Greek texts within that tradition, which were then not known to them. The resulting *Revised Text* (RT) is about 142,000 Greek words in length; that is to say, about 2000 Greek more than the *Majority Text* (MT) and about 4000 Greek words more than the *Nestle Aland-United Bible Societies Text* (NU).

(2) To sort out the New Testament variations, the *World English Bible* (WEB) basically uses the 1885 *Majority Text* (MT), as amended by Robinson and Pierpont' 1991 and 2005 reconstructed Greek text. The editors of the Majority Text base their work on about 1000 or so complete Byzantine Greek manuscripts, none early than the 5th century AD. The same editors had extensive knowledge of the early Church fathers' quotations of New Testament readings going back to the second century A.D. The resulting *Majority Text* contains about 140,000 Greek words; that is to say, about 2000 Greek words less than the *Revised Text* (RT) and about 2000

Greek words more than the *Nestle Aland-United Bible Societies Text* (NU). The *Majority Text* (MT) and the *Revised Text* (RT) agree on the readings about 98.5 % of the time.

(3) To sort out the New Testament variations, virtually all the major modern translations: the *Revised Standard Version* (RSV), the *New Revised Standard* (NRSV), the *New International Version* (NIV), the *English Standard Version* (ESV), the *New English Translation* (NET), and the *Jerusalem Bible* (JB) use the latest edition of the *Nestle Aland-United Bible Societies Text* (NU) reconstructed Greek text, now in the 28th edition. The editors of that text base their work primarily on two early Alexandrian Greek manuscripts: *Vaticanus* and *Sinaiticus*, none earlier than the 4th century A.D., and even earlier Alexandrian Greek manuscript fragments going back to the 2nd century A.D. While the editors of that text have extensive knowledge of the early Church fathers' quotations of New Testament readings going back to the second century AD, they never use any of those readings to seriously challenge or overturn an Alexandrian reading. This is surprising and uncritical. The resulting *Nestle Aland-United Bible Societies Text* (NU) contains about 138,000 Greek words; that is to say, about 4000 Greek words less than the *Received Text* (RT), and about 2000 Greek words less than the *Majority Text*. The NU and MT agree on reading for a passage about 87% of the time.

Third, in my judgement on the evidence, the *Majority Text* is just the better Greek text, better in the sense that it, more likely than not, best represents what was in the original Greek New Testament. Admittedly, this is a minority viewpoint in modern scholarship, but I nonetheless believe it to be the correct one for a number of reasons.

(1) Antiquity does not equate with accuracy. All textual scholars now acknowledge this point.

(2) Both Alexandrian and Byzantine readings can be found in the early manuscript fragments and in the writings of the early church fathers, whose importance cannot be overstated.

(3) The reason that early Alexandrian manuscripts survive and early Byzantine ones do not is sheer historical accident. All manuscripts from the early period were written on papyrus rather than vellum, which made those manuscripts highly corruptible through moisture in the air. The only place they would be preserved is ancient Egypt which has an extremely dry climate, and indeed all scholars acknowledge that is where the major manuscripts of *Vaticanus* and *Sinaiticus* and earlier manuscript fragments come from.

(4) Accidental scribal error is much more likely than intentional scribal error. That is true even when the latter was pious. The reason is common sense. The scribe's job is to copy the text before them, rather than make up a new text. And it is more probable than not to believe that a scribe would at least attempt to do the job given to them. Indeed, the best and simplest causal explanation for the textual variation that exists is accidental scribal error, contracting a longer original Greek text (the MT) into a shorter one (the NU), rather than intentional scribal error, expanding a shorter original Greek text (the NU) into a longer Greek text (the MT). NU scholarship's preference for intentional scribal error often results in unnecessesary, counter-intuitive, and counter-productive changes, counter to the very purpose for which the scribe was posited to make the change.

(5) The dramatic disappearance of Alexandrian manuscripts and textform from the textual stream in the 6th century A.D. and their dramatic replacement by Byzantine manuscripts and textform in the textual stream in the same period seriously undermines the NU's assumption of an original universally circulating and universally accepted Alexandrian textform. Neither imperial decree, nor ecclesiastic pronouncement mandating a particular form, both of which did not occur, nor Islamic expansion, which did occur but did not result in the stopping of Christian manuscript production, adequately explains this disappearance of the Alexandrian manuscripts and textform and their replacement by the Byzantine manuscripts and textform. It is strong evidence that the so-called original universal Alexandrian textform may have been nothing more than a regional textual variant, flourishing for a time, but dying out under the pressures of an original universally accepted Byzantine textform.

Fourth, for those interested in pursuing matters of textual criticism, I would strongly commend:

(1) Dr. Maurice A. Robinson's article "*New Testament Textual Criticism: The Case for Byzantine Priority*" (2001) http://rosetta.reltech.org/TC/v06/Robinson2001.html.

(2) James Snapp Jr.'s website *The Text of the Gospels* http://www.thetextofthegospels.com/and especially his published works: (a) *Authentic: The Case for Mark 16:9-20* (2016) and (b) *A Fresh Analysis of John 7:53-8:11: With a Tour of the External Evidence* (2015) will be extremely helpful for students. Some of his seminal articles on *Equitable Eclecticism - Part 1* (October 26, 2017) *Equitable Eclecticism - Part 2* (October 27, 2017), *The Text of Reasoned Eclecticism: Is It Reasonable and Eclectic? Parts One of a Four-Part Response to Dan Wallace* (January 30, 2015); *The Text of Reasoned Eclecticism: Is It Reasonable and Eclectic? Parts Two of a Four-Part Response to Dan Wallace* (January 30, 2015); *The Text of Reasoned Eclecticism: Is It Reasonable and Eclectic? Parts Three of a Four-Part Response to Dan Wallace* (January 30, 2015) *The Text of Reasoned Eclecticism: Is It Reasonable and Eclectic? Part Four of a Four-Part Response to Dan Wallace* (January 30, 2015) are very informative on the NU-MT controvery. His website has a tool in the upper left box that allows the reader to search for any textual varant and can be extremely helpful.

(3) Dr. R.E. Elliot's online summary of *The Encyclopedia of New Testament Textual Criticism* https://www.holybibleinstitute.com/files/Encyclopedia_Textual_Criticism.pdf is very good.

(4) Dr. Wilbur Pickering's books *The Identity of the New Testament Text* (1981) and *The Greek New Testament According to Family 35* (2017) are good.

(5) Wieland Willker's in-depth online textual commentaries, each 400 plus pages in length,

A Textual Commentary on the Greek Gospels Vol. 1 Matthew (2015),
http://www.willker.de/wie/TCG/TC-Matthew.pdf

A Textual Commentary on the Greek Gospels Vol. 2 Mark (2015)
http://www.willker.de/wie/TCG/TC-Mark.pdf

A Textual Commentary on the Greek Gospels Vol. 3 Luke (2015)
http://www.willker.de/wie/TCG/TC-Luke.pdf

A Textual Commentary on the Greek Gospels Vol. 4 John" (2015)
http://www.willker.de/wie/TCG/TC-John.pdf,

all of which are downloadable free of charge in PDF format, are very helpful to advanced text-critical students, or students seeking to become the same.

The student of textual criticism should never despair and always remember that there is an "abudance of riches", as Dr. Dan Wallace puts it, available to the modern New Testament historians in their field that is not available to modern Greek and Roman historians in their fields.

First, there is solid base for any reliability check on a theory of textual transmission in the ancient Greek NT manuscripts themselves. "As many as 12 manuscripts can be dated to the second century or thereabouts, and by the end of the fourth century as many as 121." (Personal conversation with Dr. Dan Wallace, Dallas Theological Seminary, April 23, 2018) And that number rises to as many as: 179 by end of the 5th century AD, 258 by the end of the 6nd century AD, 302 by the end of 7th century AD, 370 by the end of the 8th century AD, 565 by the end of the 9th century AD and 967 by the end of the tenth century AD, 999 AD. Contrast this fact with that fact that within 900 years of the average classical Greek or Roman author's writings, 0 manuscripts survive.

Here is my list of some of the most important manuscripts or fragments used in text critical arguments.

P66- late 2nd century A.D.;
P75- early 3rd century A.D.;
P46- 3rd century A.D.;
03, B, Majuscule Vaticanus- 4th century A.D.;
01, א, Majuscule Sinaiticus- 4th century A.D.;
04, C- Majuscule Ephraemi Rescriptus- 5th century A.D.;
032, W, Majuscule Washingtonias- 5th century A.D.;
02, A, Majuscule Alexandrinus- 5th century A.D.;
05, D, Majuscule Bezae- 6th century A.D.;
02, N, Majuscule Petropolitanus Purpureus- 6th century A.D.;
23, O, Majuscule Sinopensis- 6th century A.D.;
041, Ξ Majuscule – 6th century A.D.;
042, Σ, Majuscule Rossanensis- 6th century A.D.;
043, Φ, Majuscule Beratinus- 6th century A.D.;
07, E, Majuscule Basilensis- 8th century A.D.;
09, F, Majuscule Boreelianus- 8th century A.D.;
019, L- Majuscule Regius- 8th century A.D.;
047, unnamed- 8th century A.D.;

011, G^e, Majuscule Seidelianus I- 9th century A.D.;
013, H^e, Majuscule Seidelianus II- 9th century A.D.;
O45, Ω, Majuscule Athous Dionysiou- 9th century A.D.;
017, K, Majuscule Cyprius- 9th century A.D.;
021, M, Majuscule Campianus- 9th century A.D.;
030, U, Majuscule Nanianus- 9th century A.D.;
33, miniscule- 9th century A.D.;
37, Δ, Majuscule Sangellensis- 9th century A.D.;
38, Θ, Majuscule Koridethi- 9th century A.D.;
41, Π, Majuscule Petropolitanus- 9th century A.D.;
44, Ψ, Majuscule Athous Laurae- a 9th century A.D.;
565, minuscule- 9th century A.D.;
21, M, Majuscule Monacensis- 10th century A.D.;
028, S, Majuscule Vaticanus 354 aka Guelpherbytanus B - 10th century A.D.;
1739, minuscule- 10th century A.D.;
2193, miniscule- 10th century A.D.;
F^{35} a family of minuscules- 11th century A.D.;
664, miniscule- 12th century A.D.;
579, minuscule- 13th century A.D.;
F^1 a family of minuscules- 12-14th centuries A.D.;
F^{13} a family of minuscules- 11-15th centuries A.D.;
69, Codex Leicestrensis, miniscule- 15th century A.D.;

And second, there is a solid base for any reliability check on a theory of textual transmission in the ancient church fathers themselves. There are about 1,000,000 direct or indirect quotations of New Testament passages, some discussions of the variant readings known to them, and occasionally their resolutions of the same. Indeed, "the New Testament can be almost entirely reconstructed many times over from the Fathers' writings alone." (Personal conversation with Dr. Dan Wallace, Dallas Theological Seminary, April 23, 2018)

Here is my list of some important church fathers cited in text critical arguments and their respective geographical locations.

First century AD
Clement of Rome (ca.? - 99 AD)- Italy
Ignatius of Antioch (ca.35-107 AD)- Syria

Second century AD
Papias (ca.60-138 AD)- Turkey,
Polycarp (ca.69-155 AD)- Turkey
Justin Martyr (ca.100-165 AD)- Turkey, Rome,
Melito of Sardis (ca.?-180 AD)- Turkey
Hegesippus of Palestine (ca.110-180 AD)- Israel, Rome
Theophilus of Antioch (ca.?-180 AD)- Syria
Tatian (ca.120-173 AD)- Syria

Irenaeus (ca.115-180 AD)- France,

Third century AD
Clement of Alexandria (ca.150-215 AD)- Egypt, Israel,
Tertullian (ca.155-220 AD)- Libya,
Sextus Julius Africanus (ca.160-240 AD)- Israel, Greece, Italy, Egypt,
Hippolytus of Rome (ca.170-235 AD)- unknown, Egypt, Israel, Turkey, Italy
Origen (ca.185-253 AD)- Egypt, Israel,
Cyprian of Carthage (ca.200-258)- Libya

Fourth century AD
Lucian of Antioch (ca.240-312 AD)- Syria
Lactantius (ca.250-325 AD)- Algeria
Eusebius (ca.260-340 AD)- Turkey,
Athanasius of Alexandria (ca.296-373 AD)- Egypt
Isidore of Pelusium (ca.?-350 AD)- Egypt
Lucifer of Caligari (ca.?-371 AD)- Sardinia, Italy
Ephrem the Syrian (ca.306-373 AD)- Turkey
Cyril of Jerusalem (ca.313-386 AD)- Israel
Didymus the Blind (ca.313-398 AD)- Egypt
Epiphanius of Salamis (ca.320- 403 AD- Cyprus
Gregory of Nazianzus (ca.329-390 AD)- Turkey
Gregory of Nyssa (ca.335-395 AD)- Turkey
Ambrose of Milan (ca.340-397 AD)- Italy
Basil of Caesaria (ca.329-379 AD)- Turkey
John Chysostom (ca.349-407 AD)- Turkey
Jerome (ca.342-420 AD)- Rome, Israel
Alexander 1 of Alexandria (ca.?-428 AD)- Egypt

Fifth century AD
Augustine (354-430 AD)- Libya, Italy.
Cyril of Alexandria (ca.376-444 AD)- Egypt
Peter of Chrysologus (ca.380-450 AD)- Italy
Leo 1 the Great (ca.400-461AD)- Italy

Sixth century AD
Gregory 1 (ca.540-604 AD)- Italy
Isadore of Sevile (ca.560-636 AD)- Spain

Eighth century AD
John of Damascus (ca.675-749 AD)- Syria

6. THIS BOOK'S USE OF THE PRIORITY OF MATTHEW OVER MARK

This book orders the events in the life of Jesus of Nazareth chronologically on basis of the priority of Matthew not the priority of Mark for a number of reasons. Admittedly, this is a minority viewpoint in modern scholarship, but nonetheless, I believe it to be correct one for a number of reasons.

First, the custodians of the documents, the ancient and traditional church itself, was unanimous in its position that the gospel of Matthew was written and published "prior" to when the gospel of Mark was written and published. And hence, the gospel of Matthew most likely preserves the correct chronological order of those events.

Second, my reconstruction of the dating of the four gospels is as follows.

(1) The gospel of Matthew was most probably written and published in Greek in the early 40s A.D.: 41-45 A.D., about 8-12 years after Jesus' death and resurrection in 33 A.D.

The gospel of Matthew reflected the joint recollection of all the apostles and was written with their concurrence and ratification in Israel. At that time, Herod Agrippa II and the Sanhedrin were conducting a persecution of Christians in the Holy Land. It was deemed expedient that a number of the leading apostles leave Jerusalem for their own safety and for evangelization abroad. A copy of the gospel of Matthew was left with the church in Jerusalem. Each departing apostle took a copy of the gospel of Matthew with them interpreting and expounding on it as best they could. Peter went to Rome with his copy of the gospel of Matthew.

(2) The gospel of Luke was most probably written and published in the later 50s A.D.: 58-60 A.D., about 25-27 years after Jesus' death and resurrection in 33 A.D.

At the time, the apostle Paul was imprisoned in Jerusalem, later in Caesarea, awaiting Roman trial on trumped up Jewish religious charges. It was claimed Paul had taken a Gentile into parts of Jewish temple where they were prohibited from going and the charge carried with it the death penalty. In preparing his gospel, Luke had extensively interviewed a number of remaining apostles and others in the Jerusalem area, and consulted the Jerusalem church's copy of the gospel of Matthew, taking and making notes from it. The gospel of Luke was intended as a kind of pre-trial brief for any Roman court that might hear Paul's case. As Paul grew increasingly wary of the impartiality of his likely trial judge Roman governor Felix in Israel, Paul invoked his absolute right, as a Roman citizen, to be tried on a capital charge in Rome. And so, a change of venue was ordered: the apostle was sent in chains to Rome 60 A.D., with Luke accompanying him. With a backlog in cases in Rome delaying the hearing of Paul's case, Luke would complete his companion work the Acts of the Apostles there in Rome: 60-62 A.D. Both the gospel of Luke and the Acts of the Apostles were intended as a kind of pre-trial brief, an amicus curie, intended to be filed with Paul's trial court in Rome. It would be subsequently published and circulated widely in Greece (Achaia).

(3) The gospel of Mark was most probably written early 60s A.D.: likely 60-62 A.D., about 27-29 years after Jesus' death and resurrection in 33 A.D.

The apostles Peter, Paul and Luke were in Rome at the same time. With time on his hands as his Roman trial had been delayed, the apostle Paul sought and obtained the apostle Peter's public ratification of the legitimacy of the gospel of Luke and the Gentile mission. Peter did so through a series of public speeches. The speeches, likely five in number, were delivered to a Roman Jewish audience, with a number of high-ranking Roman officials, equites, judges in attendance, and with Mark recording Peter's words. Perhaps one in attendance was the one who would ultimately hear Paul's case. Christianity was setting the world on fire and everyone in Rome wanted to hear as much about it as they could. Peter delivered those public speeches by reading from the gospels of Matthew and Luke in tandem, summarizing some sections in each and adding his personal recollections. Peter had his assistants put in front of him the two scrolls: one containing the gospel of Matthew, the other, the gospel of Luke and unroll each as needed, to pre-selected points in their narratives of events. Peter would go back and forth between the two scrolls as he spoke, following the chronology of events in one and then the other, creating a unique zig-zag effect in his ordering of events. At no time did Peter ever turn back to relate events in one gospel that he had passed over by his following events in the other gospel; he was always proceeding forward. Peter's account was oral, somewhat off-the-cuff, deeply personal, lacking in the polish of the gospels of Matthew and Luke he was using. Peter stops with an affirmation of the resurrection of Jesus (Mark 16:8) and does not include Jesus' post-resurrection appearances to the apostles and others, because Peter never intended to create a third gospel, just an official recognition of the legitimacy of Luke' gospel. His Roman Jewish audience already knew of those post resurrection appearances. And Peter was satisfied the gospels of Matthew and Luke had already accurately covered those items off. Peter' ending is not unlike Luke's ending of the Acts of the Apostles. Having heard the evidence of Jesus' public ministry, his death and resurrection, Peter leaves it for listeners to make their decision. At that point, they themselves are on trial: What do you personally make of Jesus of Nazareth? Is he who he claimed to be? Is he the incarnation of the second divine person of the triune God of love? Is he your personal lord and saviour? The talks were a huge success. Some in Peter's audience sought personal copies of the same from Mark, who had transcribed the speeches. Mark consulted Peter, and Peter authorized such limited publication of the version ending at Mark 16:8. The apostle Paul would ultimately be acquitted at trial in Rome. The apostles Peter and Paul would ultimately die in Rome, sometime during Nero' brutal persecution of the Christians 64-67 A.D., ironically for literally setting Rome on fire. Mark would ultimately survive that persecution. After Peter's death and on his own authority, Mark authorized a broader publication to the churches as a whole. It was a publication of that very same record of Peter's public speeches, this time with Mark adding a brief section dealing with the resurrection (Mark 16:9-20). This fuller version would become the modern gospel of Mark, though copies of the earlier version remained in circulation. Hence for the gospel of Mark, there were, in effect, two originals. The shorter one shows up in the Alexandrian textform; the longer one shows up in the Byzantine textform.

(4) The gospel of John was most probably written last, at the turn of the century: 101 A.D., 68 years after Jesus' death and resurrection in 33 A.D. And it was intended as a kind of

supplementary and complimentary addition to the three gospels of Matthew, Luke and Mark already in existence and circulation.

Third, I am sustained in this view that Matthew intended a chronological presentation, through my reading of Papias, an early second century A.D. Christian historian.

Ecclesiatical History 3.39.15. "*This also the presbyter said: Mark,* having become the interpreter of Peter, *wrote down accurately, though not in order, whatsoever he remembered of the things said or done by Christ.* For he neither heard the Lord nor followed him, but afterward, as I said, he followed Peter, who adapted his teaching to the needs of his hearers, but *with no intention of giving a connected account of the Lord's discourses,* so that *Mark committed no error while he thus wrote some things as he remembered them. For he was careful of one thing, not to omit any of the things which he had heard, and not to state any of them falsely." These things are related by Papias concerning Mark.*

(1) In other words, Papias indictes there was a factual problem with the chronology of events set out in the gospel of Mark when it first was published: they were "not in [their proper] order".

(2) Papias' answer to the problem, and it likely was the early church's answer, was that there was no fraud involved, because with Mark's gospel, it was never an intention of Peter and Mark to set out an accurate chronology: "no intention of giving a [properly] connected account of the Lord's discourses". The actual events described in the gospel of Mark were accurately described. "Mark committed no [intentional] error while he thus wrote some things as he remembered them. For he was careful of one thing, not to omit any of the things which he had heard, and not to state any of them falsely." In today's language, we would say the gospel of Mark was written topically to make the same point. Papias' answer is a fair answer in so far as it goes, but that's not the complete answer.

(3) Why was there a factual problem with the chronology of events in the first place? Papias doesn't explicitly answer that question. But Papias' comments on the very existence of such a controversy implicitly provides the answer to that question. Papias' comments necessarily entail the prior existence of an accepted chronology or order of events from which the chronology or order of events in the gospel of Mark differed and for which an explanation was required. Moreover, Papias' comments very strongly indicate the existence of prior written gospel, a gospel prior to Mark, that set out that accepted chronology or order of events. A definitive chronology as to what happened and when it happened is not something that an oral transmission of events would be or should be expected to generate. Something more is required: a written chronology of those events. And according the ancient and traditional church, that's the gospel of Matthew, the first gospel written.

(4) This does not mean Matthew's chronology of events was correct in all respects. It too has some elements that appear topical. It just means that Matthew's chronology was the earliest accepted chronology of events and therefore more likely to have been historically accurate, at least more likely so than Mark's chronology. Events happen much slower in Matthew and with

better causation than they do in Mark and Luke, where they often occur out of the blue. Mark and Luke are much more topical than Matthew is, though Matthew can be topical.

Fourth, most modern harmonies or commentaries assume, but do not prove, the priority of Mark. That is to say, they adopt the uniquely modern position that the gospel of Mark was written and published "prior" to when the gospels of Matthew and Luke were written and published. And hence for moderns, the gospel of Mark most likely preserves the correct chronological order of those events. This is pure modern literary speculation. It builds on the shortness of Mark's gospel and the possibility Matthew's and Luke's gospels are later longer expansions of it. But this is built on an historical error. The unanimous witness of the ancient and traditional church is that the gospel of Matthew was written first, and there is strong evidence from that same church that the gospel of Luke was written second and the gospel of Mark was written third (Clement of Alexandria, Tertullian, Eusebius). Mark's gospel is simply Peter's public reading of the longer gospels of Matthew and Luke, in tandem, through a series of five sermons delivered to a dual audience of Jewish Christian believers interested in the Gentile mission and Roman judges interested in the facts behind Paul's then pending trial in Rome 60-62 A.D. with slight additions.

Fifth, in the chronology of this book, I follow Beattie's quite helpful, reconstructed, Jewish-Roman calendar www.cgsf.org/dbeattie/calendar/, assigning specific dates where probable. At this point, I wish to add two important points on my presentation of Matthew's chronology as integrated into John's overall chronology.

(1) I find there to have been two cleansings of the Temple, one at the beginning of his ministry recorded in John and one at the end of his ministry recorded in Matthew, Mark and Luke. Jesus' Jewish trial for blasphemy becomes readily understandable if there were two cleansings. The witnesses understandably merely misremember events from three years earlier. They would not have made the mistakes they did at Jesus' Jewish trial if events they described had happened only four days earlier, the time of Matthew's, Mark's and Luke' second cleansing.

(2) I find the crucifixion date to have been April 3, 33 A.D., not April 5, 30 A.D. On the traditional chronology, Jesus is baptized in the fall of 26 A.D. and crucified on April 5, 30 A.D. On a more modern evangelical chronology, Jesus is baptized in the fall of 29 A.D. and crucified April 3, 33 A.D. While both chronologies fit the evidence, the latter chronology better fits the evidence. Jesus' Roman trial becomes morely readily understandable if it involved that later crucifixion date. There are two things about Jesus' Roman trial before Roman governor Pontius Pilate that shout out for explanation. Pilate is acting seriously out of character, from what we know about him from first century A.D. Jewish historian Josephus. He is vacillating and capitulating. Moreover, the Jewish authorities use the seemingly obligue term "not a friend of Caesar" to bring about that capitulation. What's happening here? The answer is Roman power politics. Pilate's anti-semetic Roman patron Sejanus no longer had Pilate's back. Pilate most likely got his appointment as governor by marriage into Sejanus' extended family. Sejanus was the de-facto emperor in Tiberias' place for almost a decade and had blocked prior provincial complaints against Pilate for excessive use of force, and probably even approved of the same, because they both were anti-semnites. Sejanus had not long earlier been deposed from power

by Tiberias himself and summarily executed: October 31, 31 A.D. And from that time on, Tiberias oversaw a political purge of supporters or suspected supporters of Sejanus throughout Italy and beyond. Pilate's actions are now readily understandable in terms of simple naked self-interest. Given his historically close ties to Sejanus, Pilate is fearful of being reported to Tiberias as a friend of Sejanus. He would face criminal charges carrying the death penalty, where conviction was routinely obtained with little or no evidence. The political crime that followers and suspected followers of Sejanus were prosecuted under and executed for is what is called "lese majesty", "disrespect for the dignity of the office of Caesar", popularly termed by Romans themselves as "not being a friend of Caesar". The Jewish religious authorities knew that fact and used that fact against Pilate. Such motivation would not have been available to Pilate, nor such opportunity to his opponents on April 5, 30 A.D., but it would have been available to both on April 3, 33 A.D. and it certainly renders Jesus' Roman trial readily understandable.

Sixth, for those who are interested in exploring more deeply the priority of Matthew over Mark, I would strongly commend:

(1) William Barclay's *Introduction to the First Three Gospels* (1975),

(2) Bernard Orchard's and Harold Riley's *The Order of the Synoptics: Why Three Synoptic Gospels* (1989),

(3) Bernard Orchard's *Matthew, Luke & Mark: The Griesbach Solution to the Synoptic Question* (1977),

(4) Mark Goodacre's *The Case Against Q: Studies in Markan Priority and the Synoptic Problem* (2002).

7. HELPFUL METHODOLOGIES

As the reader works through this work, methodogy is important. Consequently, I intend below to provide the reader with some basic methodologies for understanding (1) truth, (2) the natural moral law and (3) a proper historical methology. These three things may assist the reader as they proceed through this harmony assessing the evidence found therein.

8. A PROPER METHODOLOGY FOR UNDERSTANDING THE TRUTH

An understanding of the truth is helpful.

1. The definition of truth

Philosophically, truth is the perfect correspondence of thought with one of three things: reality, right desire or fulfilled purpose. It is important to understand five things here.

(1) First, by "perfect correspondence", what is meant is two things. The correspondence is agreement. And the perfection of that correspondence or agreement is its being that which is

appropriate to or fitted for the subject matter in question. Where the subject matter consists of the self-evident truths which are the foundational first principles of all bodies of knowledge involving reality (facts) or right desires (values) or fulfilled purpose (mixed questions of facts and values), this perfection of correspondence or agreement is absolute certainty. Where the subject matter consists of reasoned truths which are secondary principles of knowledge deduced or derived from those foundational first principles, this perfection of correspondence or agreement is probability.

(2) Second, by "thought", what is meant is an assertive declaration that something is true. That declaration exists first in the human mind as an affirmative thought, unconsciously or consciously held, but one which can be expressed propositionally in a verbal or written statement or statements for analysis.

(3) Third, by "reality", what is meant is that which exists totally independently of the human mind. Reality is what it is and has the character it has, whether or how we think about it. Reality is sensible, and intelligible, and therefore potentially knowable by the human mind. Perfect correspondence with reality is an external check on certain propositions of thought (facts) posited to be true.

(4) Fourth, by "right desire", what is meant is what ought to be desired, whether or not it is actually desired at a particular time and place. Perfect correspondence with right desire is an external check on certain propositions of thought (values) posited to be true.

(5) Fifth, by "fulfilled purpose", what is meant is the successful actualization of the potentialities that define the being of a thing, the purpose for which it exists or was made. Perfect correspondence with fulfilled purpose is an external check on certain propositions of thought (mixed facts and values) posited to be true.

2. The three types of truth

That basic three-in-one definition of truth in terms of reality, right desire and fulfilled purpose is often framed in terms of truth, goodness and beauty, the basic ideas by which we judge. That distinction may assist the reader in understanding the further three-fold distinction in the types or branches of truth: descriptive truth (often simply called truth), prescriptive truth (often simply called goodness) and ontological truth (often simply called beauty) which follows.

(1) Descriptive truth

First, descriptive truth deals with the reality external to the human mind through variations on the verb "is". It describes what it "is" now in the present, what "was" in the past, or what "could be" or "will be" in the future. Its range is extremely broad, covering all matters of fact, whether they be physical or non-physical, material or immaterial, and whether they come to us through one or more of the major branches of knowledge: science, philosophy or religion. The language commonly used in connection with such statements of descriptive truth is the language of "true" as opposed to "false".

The basic questions that can be asked here are at least four in number.

(1) Does what Jesus is said to have said or done perfectly correspond to or agree with the reality of what actually happened in the present of his day: what he actually said and did?

(2) Does what Jesus is said to have said about what had happened in that past of his day or what would happen in the future of his day perfectly correspond to or agree with the reality of what actually had or has happened?

(3) Does what his opponents are said to have said and done perfectly correspond to or agree with the reality of what actually happened in the present of his day: what they actually said and did?

(4) Does what Jesus is said to have said about who he was and is perfectly correspond to or agree with the reality of who he was and is?

(2) Prescriptive truth

Second, prescriptive truth deals with right desires in the human person through variations on the verb "ought" or "should". It prescribes what "ought" to be desired, what is "really good". Its range is extremely broad, covering all matters of value. The language commonly used in connection with such statements of prescriptive truth is the language of "right or, good" as opposed to "wrong, or evil."

The basic questions that can be asked here are at least three in number.

(1) Is what Jesus is said to have said is the underlying reason or first principle why things are rightly desired, why they ought to be desired, perfectly correspond to or agree with the reason why something is rightly desired, why something ought to be desired?

(2) Is what Jesus is said to have said about what objects of desire are really good for human beings perfectly correspond to or agree with what is rightly desired, what is really good for human beings?

(3) Is what Jesus is said to have said about what is the total or complete good for human beings perfectly correspond to or agree with what is really good for human beings?

(3) Ontological truth

Third, ontological truth deals with purpose rooted in the being of persons or things through variations on the verbs of "realize", "actualize" and "fulfill". It is two-fold. It is partly descriptive, in that it judges whether a purpose exists in a person or thing. In this respect, it differs from descriptive truth, in that the focus is on purpose within being, not the mere existence of being. It is partly prescriptive, in that it judges whether that particular purpose is successfully realized in a particular person or thing. In this respect, it differs from prescriptive truth, in that the focus in on the actualization of potential, not on the mere potential for action that is obligation. It is a judgment that someone or something, at a particular state in their development, pleases upon being seen, because they or it are well-formed, well-developed or beautiful, they or it have a kind of unity, proportionality and clarity to their developed potentialities. Its range is extremely broad, covering a wide variety of matters of mixed fact and value. The language commonly used in connection with such statements of ontological truth is the language of "real, true, authentic, faithful, genuine, mature, complete, whole, perfect, beautiful" as opposed to "imitation, false, inauthentic, faithless, counterfeit, fraudulent, immature, incomplete, broken, imperfect, ugly."

The basic questions that can be asked here are at least five in number.

(1) Is what Jesus is said to have said about the purpose for which human beings exist perfectly correspond to or agree with the purpose for which they do exist?

(2) Is what Jesus is said to have said about the extent to which human beings have realized or actualized their potentials to be what they are perfectly correspond to or agree with what would be reasonably expected of them?

(3) Is what Jesus is said to have said about the purpose for which certain human institutions and practices exist perfectly correspond to or agree with the purpose for which they did or do exist?

(4) Is what Jesus is said to have said about the extent to which those human institutions and practises have fulfilled the purpose for which they exist or are used perfectly correspond to or agree with what would be reasonably expected of them?

(5) Is what Jesus is said to said about what would happen to those human beings, human institutions and practises that have not met their purpose perfectly correspond to or agree with what might reasonably be expected to happen to them?

3. The primacy of knowledge

In any search for truth, knowledge is primary.

Philosophically, a mind has a firm grasp on the truth when it is in the possession of knowledge as opposed to mere opinion in a matter, because only then does the mind understand how and why something is true. In understanding the mind's grasp on the truth, it is helpful to understand how and why knowledge and opinion are related to three things: to truth, to doubt, and to the mind in the way they are.

(1) Knowledge in relationship to opinion

First, knowledge and opinion are related to the truth in a particular way.

(1) Knowledge is always knowledge of the truth. There is no such thing as false or wrong knowledge. If it were known to be false or wrong, it would not be knowledge.

(2) The same is not the case with respect to opinion. Opinion can be either true or false, either right or wrong, and still be opinion.

(2) Knowledge in relationship to doubt

Second, knowledge and opinion related to doubt in a particular way.

(1) Knowledge is always accompanied by the absence of doubt.

(2) The same is not the case with respect to opinion. Opinion is always accompanied by the presence of doubt, the three types of doubt being: (a) purely theoretical or possible doubt, (b) reasonable doubt, or (c) substantial doubt.

However, that's not the full picture. Well-reasoned opinion and mere opinion are related to substantial doubt in a particular and clarifying way.

(1) Well-reasoned opinion is always accompanied by probability. It is the absence of such a substantial doubt that would overturn it and show it to be improbable. Well-reasoned opinion always possesses a predominance of the evidence in its favor. Hence, well-reasoned opinion is always and legitimately called knowledge. But this is a different sense of the word knowledge than previously used, a lesser sense of knowledge, but still legitimately knowledge.

(2) The same is not the case with mere opinion. Mere opinion is always accompanied by the lack of good reasons in its favor, or indeed by no reasons at all. At this point, there can be seen to be three types of mere opinion. (a) There are opinions having some reasons in their favour, but those reasons establish only possibility not probability. (b) There are right opinions held on the basis of authority alone, but the holder of such right opinions lacks the understanding of how and why they are true and is unable to advance reasons in their favour, even when such reasons do exist. (c) There are opinions that are nothing more than preferences, or prejudices, having absolutely no reasons in their favor and incapable of ever obtaining such. Hence, mere opinion is never called knowledge.

That being said, the initial three statements above in this section: ("knowledge is always accompanied by the absence of doubt", "the same is not the case with opinion" and "opinion is always accompanied by the presence of doubt") requires amendment, clarification and restatement.

(1) Knowledge is properly described as always accompanied by the management of doubt. (a) In cases of the strong sense of word knowledge, it is the recognition that no doubt exists in the matter. (b) In cases of the less strong sense of the word knowledge, it is the recognition that while possible, reasonable, or substantial doubt might continue to exist concerning a matter, one viewpoint predominates over all others on a balance of probabilities. That kind of knowledge or truth may have a future to it and may require revision or abandonment as new evidence or new methods of weighing the evidence become available.

(2) The same is not the case with mere opinion. Mere opinion is always accompanied by the presence of such substantial doubt that a viewpoint on a balance of probabilities does not exist.

(3) Knowledge in relationship to the mind

Third, knowledge and opinion are related to the human mind in a particular way.

(1) Knowledge always necessitates its acceptance by the mind. The mind is never free to reject it.

(2) The same is not the case with opinion. Opinion never necessitates its acceptance by the mind. The mind is always free to accept or reject the alleged truth that opinion presents to the mind for consideration.

That being said, the initial five statements above in this section ("knowledge always necessitates its acceptance by the mind", "the mind is never free to reject it, "the same is not the case with opinion" and "opinion never necessitates its acceptance by the mind" and "the mind is always free to accept or reject the alleged truth that opinion presents to the mind for consideration") again require amendment, clarification and restatement.

(1) Knowledge in the strong sense of the word always necessitates its acceptance by the mind, because it involves the presentation of self-evident truths to the mind. The mind is not free to accept or reject the truth that kind of knowledge presents to the mind. It might be rightly said that the truth that knowledge expresses makes the decision for the mind itself.

A self-evident truth is knowledge that is "immediately, not mediately known- not known through the mediation of reasoning from other propositions that serve as its grounds or premises," as Adler puts it. It is directly known and it is known with certitude. Its denial involves a contradiction.

There are at least two types of self-evident truth, and possibly a third.

(a) There are the directly known self-evident truths of perception which involve certitude. Aritotle calls them axioms.

The first unique thing about perception is this. Perception is qualitatively different from all other acts of mind such as memory, imagination, conceptualization, reasoning, desiring and feeling.

In very act of perception, the reality of a world external to the mind, the reality of the things in it, is directly known, to the mind, and fused with the mind's judgement that what is perceived really exists. There is no process of reasoning from one thing to another involved in the matter. At the moment something is perceived, there is never any doubt in the mind that the object perceived really exists external to the mind. In that timeless moment, the question of existence, whether what is perceived really exists, is never asked and indeed, never comes up for consideration. That is what makes it a self-evidently known truth, an axiomatic truth: it is immediately known to be true.

In all other acts of mind such as memory, imagination, conceptualization or desire, the reality of a world external to the mind, the reality of things in it, is not directly known to the mind, and not fused with mind's judgement that what is remembered, imagined, conceptualized or desired really exists or had existed or could exist. There is always a process of reasoning from one thing to another involved in those matters. At the moment of contemplation, when something is remembered, imagined, conceptualized or desired, there is always a doubt in the mind that the object remembered, imagined, conceived or desired really exists external to the mind. In the time-bound, reflective moment of remembering, imagining, conceiving or desiring, the question of existence: whether the object remembered, imagined, conceptualized or desired really existed, exists now, had existed or could exist, is always asked and central to that contemplation. That is what makes those other things not self-evidently known truths, not axiomatic truths: the objects they involve are not immediately known to be true.

Perception is always a perception of reality, and always is understood as such. Its opposite, illusion or hallucination, is never a perception of reality, and always is understood as such. We have very good tools in psychology, psychiatry and law to sort out when and why such rare instances of illusion or hallucination might have happened and how to remedy those conditions. But the really interesting thing to note here is that even when we perform those corrections, the definition of a perception as a perception of reality remains the same and the definition of an illusion or hallucination as a not a perception of reality remains the same. And herein again lies reality's independence from the individual human mind.

This self-evident truth of perception is the first foundational principle for all descriptive truth. and the first of the two foundational principles for all ontological truth.

The second unique thing about perception is this. Perception results in objective, public experience, and not subjective, private experiences.

Now the objective is that which is the same for me, for you and for everyone else.

And the subjective is two-fold: that which differs from one individual to another or that which is in the exclusive possession of one individual and of no one else.

A public experience such as perception is an experience that is common to two or more individuals. It may not be actually common to all, but it must be at least potentially so.

And a private experience is an experience that belongs to one individual alone and cannot possibly be experienced directly by anyone else at the same time it is being experienced by the one individual alone. Certain things such as my emotions and my bodily feelings (my anger, my toothache, my heartburn, and the like) are uniquely subjective and private experiences for me alone. To the extent that others have had similar private experiences, we can talk about them. But at the instant I perceive them, they are in my possession and in no one else's possession. They are subjective in the second sense of that term. No other person is directly experiencing my emotions and my bodily feelings. Loosely speaking, we might say such emotions or bodily feelings are objects of consciousness for those experiencing them. But strictly speaking, they have no objectivity about them, because they are not common experiences.

The objects of perception however have objectivity and intelligibility, precisely because, as objects of consciousness, they can be immediately and simultaneously experienced by two or more individuals. That is why we can talk to one another about them as things we are experiencing in common. If this were not the case, then language and communication would not exist. And we know this with certitude.

These points cannot be overstated in its importance. This is the foundational first principle for all facts, in that it is descriptive not prescriptive in character, the first foundational principle for all descriptive truth and one of the two first foundational principles for all ontological truth.

(b) There are directly known self-evident truths of the understanding, certain propositions which involve certitude. Aristotle calls them self-evident truths and per se nota propositions.

The unique thing about these self-evident truths of understanding, these tautologies and more importantly, per se nota propositions, is this. These propositions are qualitively different from all other propositions.

At the instance of knowing these propositions to be true, there is no reasoning involved. The truth is directly known though an understanding of meaning of the terms themselves, a meaning existing independently and objectively of the individual human minds that understand those terms.

Let me illustrate. Sometimes in a proposition, the terms for the subject and the object are identical, as in the case of definitions or tautologies. For example, "a triangle is a three-sided figure." Here the object is the definition of the subject. At the instance of knowing this proposition to be true, there is no reasoning involved. The truth is directly known though an understanding of the meaning of the terms themselves, a meaning existing independently and objectively of the individual human minds that understand those terms.

Let's go deeper. Sometimes in a proposition, the terms for subject and the object are not identical, but are related to each other in a unique way, as in "per se nota" propositions, or "commensurate universals". For example, "the part is always less than the whole." Here the terms for subject "part" and the object "whole" are not identical, but they are related to each other in a unique and inescapable way. Both are such basic or universal terms that cannot be defined except in so far as the way in which they are related to each other, the way in which they are commensurate with each other. The part is always a section of the whole; the whole is always the sum of the parts. It is impossible to define the part without making reference to the whole, and vis-versa. At the instance of knowing this proposition to be true, there is no reasoning involved. The truth is directly known though an understanding of meaning of the terms themselves, a meaning existing independently and objectively of the individual human minds that understand those terms.

Let's go even deeper. Here are two further per se nota propositions. "The desirable is the good." "The good is the desirable." Whenever we speak of something as good (really good or apparently good), it always has the aspect of the desirable about it (intrinsically desirable or instrumentally desirable). Whenever we speak of something as desirable (intrinsically desirable or instrumentally desirable), it always has the aspect of the good about it (really good or apparently good). Both are such basic or universal terms that they cannot be defined except in so far as the way in which they are related to each other, the way in which they are commensurate with each other. The desirable is the potential for goodness; goodness is the actualization of desire. It is impossible to define the good without making reference to desire, and vis-versa. At the instance of knowing this proposition to be true, there is no reasoning involved. The truth is directly known though an understanding of meaning of the terms themselves, a meaning existing independently and objectively of the individual human minds that understand those terms. It may seem trite, a self-evident truth that is is purely descriptive and undeniable, but it lays the foundation for our next example which is truly revolutionary and transformative, because that next example is purely prescriptive and undeniable.

Let's now go really deep. And this is the crucial, most morally significant, per se nota proposition. "You ought to desire that which is really good and nothing else." Let's unpack it. Whenever we speak of something as really good, it has the aspect of the ought to desired about it. Whenever we speak of something as that which ought to be desired, it has the aspect of the really good about it. Like part and whole, like desire and goodness, "ought to be desired" and "really good" are such basic or universal terms that they cannot be defined except in so far as the way in which they are related to each other, the way in which they are commensurate with each other. The phrase "what ought to be desired" goes by the other name "right desire". Right desire is the potential for real goodness; real goodness is the actualization of right desire. It is impossible to define right desire without making reference to real goodness, and vis-versa.

This point cannot be overstated in its importance. This is the foundational first principle for all values, all ethics and morality, in that it is prescriptive not descriptive in character, the first foundational principle for all prescriptive truth and one of the two first foundational principles for all ontological truth.

(c) There may be a directly and immediately known, self-evident truth of religious understanding, namely, an experience of God himself.

That self-evident truth is said to be a supernatural gift from God, whereby a penitent knows with certitude that God exists, that God is directly before them, and that God loves them personally. It is a kind of spiritual union between God and a human being, difficult to explain to those who have not had it, but perhaps not impossibly so.

A helpful human parallel is the spiritual union of a man and woman in orgasm, again something difficult to explain to those who have not had an orgasm, but perhaps not impossibly so.

In both, the experience is a transforming experience of truth and love, wherein one is lifted out of themselves, into the immediate presence of and union with another person, and knows without doubt, at least in that experience, that they are loved.

Normally, the natural powers of the human intellect to apprehend immaterial ideas allow a human being to know God's existence and God's love for them is through a process of reasoning and inference. This is knowledge in the lesser sense of the term. And that is called natural knowledge.

However, this particular capacity for knowledge of God is of a higher order. This knowledge in the sense of direct awareness is said to be con-natural knowledge, because it can be given to a particular mind at a particular time as a gift, existing alongside, which is the meaning of word "con" in the term con-natural knowledge, the natural human capacity to know God through reasoning and inference. Such an infusion of knowledge is premised on three ideas. God creates each and every human intellect. God intends an intimate personal relationship with each and every human being. And God sets up the communication channel whereby that is possible, even for the simple and unlearned in things. This experience is one of certainty without any trace of doubt or deception at the instant of the experience. This is knowledge in the higher sense of the term.

While this potential experience of knowledge and love is open to all, it is only actualized by some, because it has to be asked for, and is granted only to the truly penitent. It has been called the "born again" experience, because of its power to radically reshape human lives or directions within those lives. This was what I was talking about earlier when I said "Faith is a certain type of volitional act, a personal choice and committment, sometimes based on knowledge, sometimes not." When I said "sometimes not", I meant this kind of knowledge, this kind of direct immediate experience that bypasses historical inquiry, goes beyond it, but is not contrary to it.

If this self-evident truth exists, then it is the foundation for a very special religious truth that is a human union with God in this life or the next. It is a kind of supra-descriptive, supra-prescriptive and supra-ontological truth all rolled into one.

To summarize, in all these three types of self-evident truth, the sheer act of knowing, the knowing that you know you know, happens instantaneously, in no time at all.

As Socrates once famously asked: where does the mind go when it knows, knows in the sense of self-evidently knows? His answer was eternity. And on that point, I believe Socrates was right.

The sheer act of knowing takes no time at all. The poetic language of space and time, the language of a bang, a flash, an eureka moment, might be used to describe this act of knowledge, but strictly speaking, this sheer act of knowing is not an act in space and time. There may be a sequential process of reasoning in space and time preceding that instantaneous experience. There may be a sequential process of explaining things in space and time following that instantaneous experience. But the experience of knowing, and knowing that you know, is not an experience in space and time. It is the human mind touching the mind of God, or, in some cases, the mind of God touching the human mind.

As creatures in space and time, all human beings stand at the fence of eternity, and peer over onto the other side. The experience of knowing is that experience. All human beings, fallen or unfallen, have had the experience of knowing, and knowing that they know. But not all take the time to reflect on the timelessness of their knowing, its meaning, the consequent gratitude that needs to be expressed, and to whom it must be expressed. The deep sin of atheism or agnostism is, after all, ingratitude and indifference. That secondary reflection can have a profound significance on a person's understanding of their origin as a child of God, and of their potential destiny as a child with that loving parent in all eternity.

(2) Knowledge in the lesser sense of the word always strongly commends its acceptance to mind, because it involves the presentation of a probable truth to the mind. The mind is not entirely free to reject it, certainly not to reject it out of hand.

That strong commendation has a kind of conditional necessity to it, conditional on the state of the evidence, and conditional on the methods of weighing the evidence at a particular time and place.

But the commendation itself can be very strong. Some well reasoned truths of science such as the earth goes around the sun may have started as possible truths, become probable truths, possessing the minimal requirement of knowledge; namely, knowledge on a balance of probabilities, but they have been so frequently confirmed, in so many ways, that the very word opinion is just too weak a word to express the kind of knowledge these truths express. They do however still remain probable knowledge, probable truths, but the levels of knowledge they describe can approach certainty.

Virtually all secondary matters of fact or value, whether they be descriptive, prescriptive or ontological in character, fall into this category.

9. A PROPER METHODOLOGY FOR UNDERSTANDING THE NATURAL MORAL LAW

1. **Defining the natural moral law**

Philosophically, there is a self-evidently true, objective and universal moral framework to reality. It is called the natural moral law. It is the duty of every human being to lead a good human life, to be truly and fully human. It is the reason behind all the rules. It is what justifies and explains all the rules. It is same for all persons regardless of time or place. It is what allows individuals, customs or institutions to be justly criticized and changed, where and when needed.

This natural moral law can be stated as follows.

(1) Major premise: "you ought to seek what really good for you and nothing else."

(2) Minor premise: "what's really good is what fulfills a natural human need."

(3) Conclusion: "therefore, you ought to pursue and possess

(a) all the real goods that every human being needs by nature" (natural needs, real goods),

(b) "properly ordered and proportioned so that each good is really good for you as a human being" (moral virtue),

(c) "all the apparent innocuous or harmless goods that you yourself might want, as an individual," (exercises of the real good liberty),

(d) "provided your pursuit and possession of those apparent goods does not interfere with your or anyone else's pursuit and possession of all the real goods every human being needs by nature" (right desire, justice).

2. **How is the major premise known to be true?**

It is known to be true through understanding the terms "ought to desire" and "real goodness" and their relationship to each other.

First, "ought to desire" and "real goodness" are such basic terms, like part and whole, that can only be defined in terms of each other.

Second, whenever you think about what you desire, that object always has a certain aspect of goodness connected to it:

(1) good as useful,

(2) good as pleasurable,

(3) good as valuable in and of itself.

Third, whenever you think about the goodness, that object always has certain the aspect of desire about it:

(1) desired as "apparently good" or

(2) desired as "really good".

Fourth, this means surprisingly that all persons actually desire goodness. The good is the desirable and the desirable is the good. Specifically, desire is the always the dispositional potential for goodness. Goodness is always actualized desire. Evil is always enframed by goodness. Now, some persons may be seriously mistaken in their choices, because they posit apparent goods as real goods when they are not or they pursue real goods to an extent greater or lesser than they should. But even such persons always justify themselves with the claim: it seemed good to me at the time, because evil is already enframed by goodness.

Fifth, right desire crucially adds the term "ought" to the terms "want" or "need", making statements about right desire categorical propositions not hypothetical propositions.

Sixth, right desire is simply another way to saying "what you ought to desire". Right desire is always the dispositional potential for real goodness. Real goodness is always actualized right desire.

Seventh, how does this make the major premise true? The answer is simple: any denial of the major premise would involve a contradiction. And there are only two possible denials

(1) "you ought *not* to desire that which is really good" or

(2) "you ought to desire *what is really bad*".

Because both denials are self-evidently false, misunderstanding the relationship between right desire and real goodness, that fact makes the major premise to be self-evidently true.

And that fact is how the major premise can be known to be self-evidently true.

3. **How is the minor premise known to be true?**

It is through understanding the term "natural human needs".

First, desire divides into wants and needs.

Second, wants are rooted in nurturing.

Third, natural needs are rooted in human nature.

Fourth, all animals, including humankind, have a nature or essence. It is what separates one kind of animal from another kind of animal.

Fifth, a nature is a set of species-specific characteristics or potentialities for development with a certain direction and within a certain range, aimed at a certain end: human fulfillment. Human beings are metaphysically purposeful, goal-directed creatures. All defective expositions of human nature, used historically to justify tyranny, slavery or sexism, focus on deficient nurtured actualizations of potentials, and not on the potentials themselves. Another name for these human species-specific characteristics or potentialities for development toward a specific end is natural needs. They have three qualities about them.

(1) They are universal within the human species, in the sense that all members, without exception, have them. They are possessed either actually when known, virtually or eminently otherwise.

(2) They are non-eradicable within the human species, in the sense that all members, without exception, have them at all points in their life, and they cannot be eradicated.

(3) They are irresistible within the human species, in the sense that they are constantly seeking fulfillment; they never really go away.

Sixth, there are not many natural needs that meet the three-fold criteria of universality, eradicability and irresistibility, but twelve do.

(1) There is the natural desire for life, growth and health.

(2) There is the natural desire for food and drink.

(3) There is the natural desire for shelter.

(4) There is the natural the desire to be free.

(5) There is the natural desire to work and creatively express one's self.

(6) There is the natural desire for pleasure.

(7) There is the natural desire for justice,

(8) There is the natural desire to know the truth.

(9) There is the natural desire to seek goodness.

(10) There is the natural desire to enjoy beauty.

(11) There is the natural desire to love and be loved.

(12) There is the natural desire for God.

Seventh, certain real goods fulfill these natural desires.

(1) There are the biological goods which include life, health and vigor.

(2) There are the economic goods which include a decent supply of the means of subsistence, living and working conditions that are conducive to health, medical care, opportunities for access to the pleasures of sense, the pleasures of play, aesthetic pleasures, opportunities for access to the goods of the mind through educational facilities in youth and adult life and enough free time from subsistence work, both in youth and adult life, to take full advantage of these opportunities.

(3) There are the political goods which include liberty, peace, both civil and external, the political liberties of citizenship, voting and holding office, together with the protection of individual freedom by the prevention of violence, aggression, coercion, or intimidation, and justice.

(4) There are the social goods which include equality of status, equality of opportunity and equality of treatment in all matters affecting the dignity of the human person.

(5) There are the psychological goods which include the goods of personal association (family, friendship, and love), the goods of character (the cardinal virtues of prudence, temperance, courage, and justice and the theological virtues of faith, hope and love), and the goods of the mind (the contemplation of the beautiful, creativity, knowledge, understanding, and wisdom).

(6) There are the religious goods include awe and wonder, repentance and forgiveness, and the gratitude, surrender, and love involved in a personal relationship with God.

All of these real goods are matters of objective fact. Reasonable people reflecting on what it is to be human would agree that these are things people need for a good and complete human life.

Eighth, only wants can be wrong:

(1) wanting the wrong thing, or

(2) wanting the right thing in the wrong way, such as wanting it to an excess or wanting it not enough.

Ninth, there can never be a wrong natural need. The very idea of a wrong natural need is incoherent and unthinkable. Try thinking of one; it's impossible to do so. Why? The reason is simple: if it were wrong, then you would not, as a matter of nature, really need it.

And that fact is how the minor premise can be known to be self-evidently true.

4. **How is the conclusion known to be true?**

First, as a matter of logic, a prescriptive major premise (a statement of value), as we have here, followed by a descriptive minor premise (a statement of fact), as we have here, logically leads to a prescriptive conclusion (a further statement of value), as we have here.

Second, as a matter of truth, when the two premises are self-evidently true, as we have here, the conclusion is inescapable and self-evidently true.

And that is how you can know this conclusion is self-evidently true.

10. A PROPER METHODOLOGY FOR UNDERSTANDING HISTORICAL INQUIRY

An exposition of a proper historical methodology is helpful.

The traditional methodology, one that has been used and refined over the centuries by professionals in the field such as professional historians, lawyers and judges, consists of three things. First, it involves two basic principles for the admissibility of evidence; namely, relevance and materiality. Second, it involves three basic principles for the assessment of that evidence; namely, neutrality, credibility, and reliability. Third, it involves three basic principles for any judgement on the evidence; namely, totality, weight, and proof on a balance of probabilities. It is essential that the reader understand the meaning and usage of these critical terms.

1. **Basic principles for the admissibility of evidence**

The basic principles for the admissibility of evidence are two in number: relevance and materiality.

(1) Relevance

First, relevance is the tendency of something to make something else more probable. It may be a piece of evidence making a fact more probable. It may be a fact or a set of facts making another fact more probable. It may be a fact or a set of facts making a conclusion more probable. It may be a conclusion or set of conclusions making another conclusion more probable. Relevance is always a relationship between two things. That initial something may be a something a person has said about what was said or done; in which case, it is called testimonial evidence. That initial something may be a something physical such an object; in which case, it is called real evidence. The focus is always on tendency. The important point to remember is that relevance is not an inherent characteristic of any piece of evidence, but is rather a characteristic of the relationship of that piece of evidence to other matters: facts, inferences and conclusions. Relevance is primarily a function of two things: the closeness in time of the evidence to the events in question, and/or the carefulness with which the evidence has been preserved. A particular piece of evidence close in time to the events in question tends to make certain things more probable. And a particular piece of evidence not close in time to the events in question, but which was carefully preserved, tends to make certain things more probable. Relevance is a two-edged sword. Positively, it justifies the admission of certain things into consideration. All relevant evidence is admissible evidence; that is to say, it is worthy of consideration. It does not mean the evidence is true. It merely means the evidence is worthy of assessment and judgement as to whether or not it is true. Negatively, all irrelevant evidence is inadmissible evidence; that is to say, it is not worthy of consideration. It means the evidence is not capable of being true. Indeed, it means the evidence is likely to mislead.

Any serious trier-of-fact should assess information found in the following sources of information as they are worthy of consideration:

(1) the Biblical gospel of Matthew,

(2) the Biblical gospel of Mark,

(3) the Biblical gospel of Luke and

(4) the Biblical gospel of John.

The reason is simple. They are comprehensive accounts of Jesus' public ministry written by his immediate followers within one to two generations of his death. The circumstances under which that evidence was obtained, preserved and presented indicates its worthiness for consideration.

Those gospels provide valuable eye-witness and hearsay evidence to the events in question. The evidence in those gospels is relevant, because it proves or tends to prove certain things about the life of Jesus of Nazareth.

Any serious trier-of-fact should assess information found in the following sources of information as they are worthy of consideration:

(1) ancient Christian documents such as the Acts of the Apostles, and the epistles of Paul;

(2) ancient Christian writings from early church fathers such as Papias, Justin Martyr, Irenaeus, Tertullian, Clement of Alexandria, Origen, Eusebius, Jerome and Augustine;

(3) ancient Jewish documents such as the Book of Jubilees, the Book of Parables (a part of the larger Book of 1 Enoch), 1 and 2 Maccabees, the Dead Sea Scrolls, the Targums, the Mishnah, the Tosefta, the Mekilta, the Sifres, the Babylonian and Jerusalem Talmuds and the Midrashs;

(4) ancient Jewish writers such as Josephus and Philo;

(5) ancient Roman administrative documents dealing with governance; and

(6) ancient Roman writers such as Tacitus, Seutonius, Pliny the Younger.

The reason is simple. All of those other sources contain important background information that is either close in time to the events in question or was carefully preserved or both. As such, this information and tends proves or makes more probable certain things about the life of Jesus of Nazareth.

Any serious trier-of-fact should not access information found in the following sources of information:

(1) the so-called Gospel of Thomas,

(2) the so-called Gospel of Peter,

(3) the so-called Gospel of the Hebrews,

(4) the so-called Gospel of the Egyptians,

(5) the so-called Secret Gospel of Mark,

(6) the so-called Gospel of Judas,

(7) the so-called Gospel of Mary Magdalene and

(8) the so-called Infancy Gospels.

The reason is simple. All of these works are fanciful sources, known to have been written centuries after the events in question by parties having no connection to the events in question and no interest in accurately preserving earlier evidence. Nevertheless, I touch on these apocryphal or false gospels if only to indicate they have been debunked, lest the serious readers be misled by them or by commentaries based on them.

(2) Materiality

Second, materiality is the tendency of a proven fact or a proven conclusion to prove the ultimate issue under discussion. A proven fact or a proven conclusion is material if it tends to decide a particular issue. The focus is again on tendency. Materiality is a particular type of relevance: the relevance of something to decide a question under consideration. The important point to remember is materiality is not an inherent characteristic of any fact or conclusion, but is rather a characteristic of the relationship of those proven facts or conclusions to the ultimate issues in question.

Any serious trier-of-fact should be especially attentive to information in the following fields of evidence:

(1) the existence of a serious Unitarian-Trinitarian controversy in ancient Judaism;

(2) the Biblical titles either claimed or accepted by Jesus such as the Son of Man, the Son of God, the Son of the Most High, the Lord, the I AM, Messiah or Christ, and and the ontological status of the person or persons they denote or connote, whether they be human, angelic or divine;

(3) the actions performed by Jesus such as his cleansing of the Temple twice, his healings and exorcisms especially on the Sabbath, his forgiving the sins of others and at the same time declaring their salvation, his invitation to others to rely on him exclusively for their salvation, his calling God his personal and unique Father, and the unprecedented authority by which he purported to justify those actions;

(4) the Jewish criminal law on blasphemy, on sabbath violation, on sorcery, on leading the people astray, and the death penalties involved therein;

(5) the Jewish theological expectations on the time of the resurrection of the dead, and the time of God's establishment of his rule of earth;

(6) the Jewish theocratic state power vested in the high priest and the Pharisees to define the faith and enforce uniformity of thought through force;

(7) the Roman criminal law on sedition (actual rebellion) and on "lese majesty" (disrespect for the dignity of the office of Caesar), and the death penalties involved therein.

The reason is simple. This assessment of these pieces of relevant evidence tends to decide the three material issues of whether Jesus claimed to be divine, whether those hearing those claims would have sought his death, and whether his resurrection from the death would have been seen at the time as confirmation of his divinity. This evidence is therefore worthy of very special consideration.

2. **Basic principles for the assessment of the evidence.**

The basic principles for the assessment of evidence are three in number: neutrality, credibility and reliability.

(1) Neutrality

First, neutrality is openness. It is the state of mind that must exist in any trier of fact before they approach and assess the evidence. It is a prerequisite for any legitimate consideration of the evidence. Neutrality is primarily a function of two things: the absence of bias and, the presence of impartiality.

(1) Bias is a predisposition towards a particular result in advance. The absence of bias means four things. First, a trier-of-fact cannot presume that a particular witness is telling the truth. Second, a trier-of-fact cannot presume that a particular witness is not telling the truth. Third, a trier-of-fact must set aside any conservative belief in inspiration and inerrancy, which amounts to the bias that a witness should be presumed to be telling the truth until proven false. Fourth, a trier-of-fact must set aside any sceptical belief in inauthenticity, which amounts to the bias that a witness should be presumed to be lying until proven to be telling the truth. The case must be decided on the evidence, not any bias that the trier-of-fact might bring to the case.

(2) Impartiality is a fearless willingness to follow the evidence where it leads, even if it leads to supernatural or immaterial causation. The presence of impartiality means four things. First, a trier-of-fact must set aside any prior belief in a purely physical and material world and consider the historical evidence for a supernatural or immaterial explanation, at least on some occasions. Second, a trier-of-fact should only adopt a supernatural or immaterial source of causation if a physical or material explanation will not suffice. Third, a trier-of-fact should not adopt a divine source of causation if an angelic source, including a demonic source, will suffice. Fourth, a trier-of-fact should only adopt a divine source of causation if that is the explanation that best explains the evidence. This is the historical procedure that must be adopted for any judgement on the historical evidence. The case must be decided on the evidence, not on any partiality against the supernatural that the trier-of-fact might bring to case.

(2) Credibility

Second, credibility is believability or truthfulness, either of a story, a witness, or both.

Credibility is a function of two things: the inherent plausibility of the story presented and the honesty with which that story is presented.

(1) Inherent plausibility relates to believability or truthfulness in that it focuses on what might reasonably be in the mind of a witness, because it is the kind of thing that could have happened in reality.

(2) Honesty delivery relates to believability or truthfulness in that it focuses on the faithful expression of what is actually in the mind of a witness, because it is the kind of thing they believe happened in reality.

The witness' story appears believable or truthful and therefore could and should be accepted as true, because their story is plausible and honestly held.

a. Inherent plausibility

Inherent plausibility is intelligibility or understandability; there is an internal logic to story, namely, the existence of causal factors that create a plausible story as to what happened and why.

(1) A plausible or reasonable story is a story with a discernible and understandable plot. Plot is character. Character is interest. Interest is motivation. The motivation may be religious, psychological, social, political or economic or any combination of the same. The participants in the story may or may not act "reasonably", in the sense that they do not act as an "objective reasonable man" would in such situations before them. But they act intelligibly, in the sense that they are motivated to act in the way they do in the situation before them. They act for "reasons" they think appropriate, whether or not they really are appropriate.

(2) Motivation is important, because "[w]hat is caused in history are not natural events, but the actions of 'conscious and responsible' agents...Causing a man to act, in this sense, 'means affording him a motive for doing it.'...The force of causes in this sense [is] a rational one. It is through the agent's recognition of the claim, in reason, which they make upon him to act, that they achieve what we call their effects. It follows that a 'cause' in the historical sense, might have failed to have an effect. For it to be effective, the agent has to 'accept' it as his cause, to 'make' it his cause."[1]

(3) Motivation divides into necessary and sufficient motivation. Necessary motivation means the participants in the story had a good reason to act. Their actions were necessary in the practical sense that, without it, they "would not" have had any reason to act. Their actions were not necessary in the philosophical sense that without it, they "could not" have acted at all.[2] Sufficient motivation means the participants in the story had good reason not only to act, but a good reason to act when and how they did. Their actions were sufficient in the practical sense that "it renders the course of action in question 'rationally required'. Their actions were not sufficient in the philosophical sense that "given it, that action "would necessarily have been performed"[3]

1 Dray, W.H., *Philosophy of History* (Prentice Hall, Englewood Cliffs, 1964) pp. 43-44.

2 Dray, W.H., *Philosophy of History* (Prentice Hall, Englewood Cliffs, 1964) pp. 44.

3 Dray, W.H., *Philosophy of History* (Prentice Hall, Englewood Cliffs, 1964) pp. 44.

(4) Motivation and intention are related, but not the same. Intention is a person's mental state concerning what is to be done. Motive is a person's mental state concerning why it is to be done. The difference is between what and why. More often than not, people are motivated to act in their interests rather than contrary to them. They intend things that line up with their interests, rather than are contrary to them. In both acts, motivations and intentions can and are inferred from their known interests and actions, inferred from something in the story or known from outside.

(5) Inherent plausibility does not reduce to the commonality or frequency of an event. Many well-established historical events are unique and were unique at the time they were performed. Such incidents include Hannibal's crossing the Alps, Caesar's crossing the Rubicon, Washington's crossing the Delaware. They all meet this test of uniqueness. Yet, then and now, those events are completely intelligible and understandable in terms of their motivations which are inferred from their known interests and actions.

Any serious trier-of-fact should assess the interests or motivations of the participants in the basic story line:

(1) John the Baptist's interest in presenting an end-times national religious revival focused on a kind of repentance that put Jews and Gentiles on an equal standing before God and on the immanent arrival of God on earth and John's identification of that person;

(2) Jesus' interest in presenting, promoting and prolonging a particular type of Trinitarian religious ministry, one focused on inviting and challenging others to discover for themselves his inherent divinity, and to trust in him and him alone for their eternal salvation;

(3) the Sadducees' interest in promoting and preserving the smooth operation of the Jerusalem Temple and their attendant privileges, in preserving the integrity of the Jewish faith as they understood it: a form of Unitarian monotheism, in quashing what they regarded as blasphemy, leading the people astray, or potentially revolutionary activity;

(4) the Pharisees' interest in preserving the oral law, in preserving the integrity of the Jewish faith, as they understood it: a form of Unitarian monotheism, in quashing what they regarded as blasphemy, leading the people astray, or potentially revolutionary activity;

(5) the Zealots' interest in fomenting revolution, and in co-opting or using Jesus to that end;

(6) the Romans' interest in preserving the status quo, collecting taxes, suppressing real or imagined revolutionary discontent, and preventing grave robbing;

(7) Pilate's professional interest in preserving the peace, and personal interest in preserving his own political position, especially in light of his patron Sejanus' fall from power in Rome in October 31 A.D. and the subsequent prosecutorial use of the term "not a friend of Caesar" for a particular kind of criminal charge of sedition known as "lese majesty";

(8) Herod Antipas' professional interest in preserving the peace, and personal interest in preserving his own political position; and

(9) the disciples' interest in accurately preserving and promoting Jesus' message, and in preserving their own lives.

The reason is simple. Controversy is at the heart of the story line in the gospels of Matthew, Mark, Luke and John. The religious, psychological, political, social and economic interests of the participants in that story set up their motivations to act: why, how and when they do act. A plausible story is a potentially credible story. It describes a thought that could correspond to reality.

b. Honest delivery

Honest delivery is sincerity or genuineness in presentation. It is an inference from two things about how the witness has presented their story.

(1) There is a straightforwardness to the presentation. The witness does hesitate to confront difficult matters. The witness does not exaggerate or overstate matters. The witness does not present himself or participants in the story as better or worse than they actually were.

(2) There is a frankness to the presentation. The witness actually presents embarrassing details about either themselves or other participants in the story they favour. The witness actually presents positive details about participants in the story they do not favour. The witness does not have a discernible motive to lie.

Honest delivery is not the absence of perspective. The mere fact that a witness has a perspective on the events observed and has made judgements on the morality of the participants in their story is not inconsistent with the witness attempting to be historically accurate to the extent their memory permits, provided of course they are not overstating the goodness or badness of the participants in the story. The mere fact that a witness might rearrange the order of events from a chronological order to a topical order, might add events others do not cover, might omit events others do cover, might excerpt, summarize, or reword statements of participants in the story does not detract from the historicity of the story. Reporters do that all the time in presenting news reports and we do not accuse them of inaccuracy in their doing so. The reason is simple. It is not perspective, but the deliberate distortion of data, that makes for dishonest delivery.

Honest delivery is not the absence of all error, but the only the absence of a particular kind of error. An error is simply a mistake, a misrepresentation of a fact. The error may be an innocent misrepresentation of a fact. The witness simply got the facts wrong. The error may be a negligent misrepresentation of a fact. The witness was not as attentive or as critical as they should have been. The error may be a fraudulent misrepresentation of a fact. The witness here had two facts in their mind: one true, one false, yet presents the false fact to be true, while at the same time knowing it to be false. In other words, only a person who knows can actually lie. The existence of innocent or even the negligent error in presentation does not make for a dishonest delivery. Only the deliberate and fraudulent distortion of the evidence in presentation makes for dishonest delivery.

Any serious trier-of-fact should assess the following lines of evidence:

(1) the allegedly embellished details of the disciples' ignorance, the Pharisees' legalism and hypocrisy, and the Jewish crowd's acceptance before Pilate of blood guilt for Jesus' death; and

(2) the allegedly embarrassing details of Jesus' sinfulness, Jesus' subordination to John the Baptist, Jesus' ignorance in certain spiritual matters, Jesus' false prophesy concerning the end of the world, and Jesus' despair on the cross.

The reason is simple. Embarrassment and embellishment are at the heart of honest delivery. An honestly delivered story is is a potentially credible story. It describes a thought that could correspond to reality.

(3) Reliability

Third, reliability is accuracy, either of a story, a witness, or both.

Reliability is a function of five things: (1) a witness in the know, (2) possessing intelligence, maturity and seriousness, (3) possessing good powers of observation, recall and precision in statement, (4) corroborated in their testimony, either in whole or in part and (5) not seriously contradicted in their testimony, either internally or externally. All these five things are external checks on the basic storyline: an inherently plausible story honestly delivered.

Reliability supplements credibility in the sense that it adds to the probability of a plausible story honestly delivered being true by reference to things external to the story itself and its presentation. Remember descriptive truth is a correspondence of thought with reality. Credibility deals with the thought itself: the inherent plausibility of the basic storyline and its honest delivery. Reliability deals with reality itself, something technically external to the content of the thought and its presentation in reality: namely, the position, character and memory of a particular witness in relationship to the events described, the relationship of that testimony to other witnesses and other things in the world.

a. Position of a witness

The first criterion of reliability deals with the position of the witness in relation to the events they describe.

(1) Being an eye-witness puts a witness in the know in the first place. An eye-witness is a person who actually observed the events in question. They possess first hand information and are in an ideal position to pass on accurate information.

(2) Being a hearsay witness put a witness in the know in the first place. A hearsay witness is a person who reports what an eye witness to an event actually observed. They possess second hand information of the events in question and are in a good position to pass on accurate information. This is especially so when that hearsay information is "necessary" and "reliable". That hearsay information will be considered necessary when it is the best available evidence. That hearsay information will be considered reliable when it was apparent or can reasonably inferred (a) that that information came from a eye-witness who attempting to truthfully and accurately communicate that information, (b) that the hearsay witness was attentive to that information, and (c) that the eye witness had no apparent reason to lie, and even if they had, the hearsay witness could readily have discovered the lie. Even in legal inquiries with its quite strict rules of evidence which sometimes prevent the acquisition of the truth, hearsay information is fairly routinely admitted for its truth value, as an exception of the hearsay rule, when it meets the aforementioned circumstantial indicia of reliability. Circumstantial indicia of reliability merely add to its weight.

The reason is simple. A witness needs to be in a position to receive accurate information about the events in question.

Any serious trier-of-fact should assess the position of a witness in terms of the following lines of evidence:

(1) the unanimous ancient church's evidence on the authorship of the biblical gospels of Matthew, Mark, Luke and John, as coming from persons in the know, and the consistency of that attribution with the gospels themselves;

(2) the extent to which each of these authors were either eye witnesses or hearsay witnesses to the events in question; and

(3) the extent to which these authors used hearsay information which was necessary and reliable.

The reason is simple. A witness in the know is a potentially reliable witness. It adds accuracy to the story.

b. Character of the witness

The second criterion of reliability deals with the character of the witness in relation to the moral obligation to tell the truth about the events they described. Intelligence, maturity and seriousness are important here.

(1) Being intelligent, they recognized the importance of the matters they described.

(2) Being mature, they recognized that others might rely on what they had to say and they needed to tell the truth, even though they themselves were not under a formal legal obligation to tell the truth.

(3) Being serious, they recognized that others might hold them accountable for what they had to say and they needed to tell the truth, even though they themselves were not under a formal caution such that anything they said could and would be used against them.

The reason is simple. A witness needs to be willing to pass on accurate information about the events in question.

Any serious trier-of-fact should assess the character of a witness in terms of the following lines of evidence:

(1) the extent to which Jesus placed a premium on truth and truth telling;

(2) the extent to which a witness accepted that teaching;

(3) the extent to which a witness was prepared to suffer or die for what they believed to be true.

The reason is simple. An intelligent, mature and serious witness is a potentially reliable witness. It adds accuracy to the story.

c. Memory of a witness

The third criterion of reliability deals with the memory of the witness in relation to the events in question. Good powers of observation, recall and statement are important here.

(1) Possessing good powers of observation, they formed solid memories of the events they relate which could be preserved over time.

(2) Possessing good powers of recall, and precision in statement, they were able to repeat the content of their memories in a form that was readily analyzable.

The reason is simple. A witness needs to be capable of communicating accurate information about the events in question.

Any serious trier-of-fact should assess the memory of the witness in terms of the following lines of evidence:

(1) the Jewish educational system and its premium on rote memorization;

(2) Jesus' status as a rabbi and the premium rabbis placed on rote memorization;

(3) the disciples' status as students of a rabbi and the premium students placed on rote memorization and note taking;

(4) the availability of tools for note-taking in 1st century A.D. Israel;

(5) Jesus' deliberate use of rhythmic and metaphoric language to facilitate solid memory formation in the disciples;

(6) Jesus' deliberate use of drama and controversy to facilitate solid memory formation in the disciples;

(7) Jesus' deliberate use of repetition of key themes to facilitate solid memory formation in the disciples,

(8) Jesus' sending of the disciples on evangelistic missions during his public ministry to facilitate memory reinforcement in the disciples and the standardization of Jesus' message;

(9) the disciples' constant repetition of his message in and out of the Temple in the time following Jesus public ministry as a vehicle of memory reinforcement in the disciples and the standardization of Jesus's message; and

(10) the apostolic control and oversight of manuscript production and distribution following Jesus' public ministry.

The reason is simple. A witness with a clearly formed memory, repeating and reinforcing that memory over time is a potentially reliable witness. It adds accuracy to the story.

d. Corroboration of a witness

The fourth criterion of reliability is corroboration, either in whole in in part.

Corroboration is evidence from another source that actually confirms or at least tends to confirm the accuracy of a witness' testimony, either in whole or in part. To the extent that other source is a person, that corroborative evidence is called "testimonial" evidence. To the extent that other source is a thing of any sort, that corroborative evidence is called "real" evidence.

(1) The test for corroboration of a witness by another witness is only relative not complete independence of the testifying witness from the corroborating witness. This reflects the human reality that eyewitnesses to important events want to and do share and discuss their observations and experiences of those events with other eyewitnesses to those same events. In purely legal inquiries where deprivations of liberty and money are in play, our legal system tends to separate witnesses one from another, lest they contaminate each other's testimony. But historical inquiry has no such requirement.

(2) The ultimate test for ensuring the absence of real contamination of one witness' testimony by another witness' testimony is the simple presence of disagreement between the two witnesses. And it is the same test whether the inquiry is a legal or historical one. A witness is independent of other witnesses to the same events if they disagree on minor or major points of fact or interpretation, the greater the degree of disagreement, the greater the degree of independence. Disagreement always establishes independence and it does so decisively.

(3) How one handles "adopted testimony" has become a problem for some, but it need not be one. There is no requirement that that a witness never repeat in whole or in part the language of another witness giving testimony. It is common and natural for a witness to common events to have adopted portions of each other witnesses' testimonies given, because that witness agrees with its factual content and believes he himself could not have expressed it better. As before, a witness remains independent of another witness to the same events if they still disagree on minor or major points of fact or interpretation. Disagreement always establishes independence and it does so decisively, the greater the degree of disagreement, the greater the degree of independence.

(4) It is only "colluded evidence" that is not independent evidence, and cannot constitute corroborating evidence. Colluded evidence is a special type of fabricated evidence involving two things: (a) virtually identical evidence from two witness on "all" matters, coupled with (b) a discernible motive in both witnesses to lie. Their testimony is so unexpectedly similar or identical, on matters where a detached observer would have expected at least some disagreement, that a detached observer can only conclude that such complete agreement could not have arisen, but for, the existence of a common plan between the two witness to manipulate and deceive a trier-of-fact. Colluded evidence is extremely rare, but readily discernable when it exists. Adopted evidence should never be confused with colluded evidence. Disagreement also and always establishes the absence of collusion and it does so decisively, the greater the degree of disagreement, the greater the proof of non-collusion.

Any serious trier-of-fact should assess a witness' corroboration in whole or in part in terms of the following lines of evidence:

(1) any substantial correspondence of their testimony with the testimony of another or others;

(2) any correspondence of their testimony with the reality of the Jesus' religious controversies with his opponents over issues of Sabbath, purity and blasphemy, and the seriousness of those controversies;

(3) any correspondence of their testimony with the known religious, psychological, social, political and economic realities of 1st century A.D. Israel; and

(4) any correspondence of their testimony with the known geographical and topographical realities of 1st century A.D. Israel.

The reason is simple. Corroboration is the heart of reliability. A witness who is corroborated on matters is a potentially reliable witness. It adds great accuracy to the story.

e. Contradiction of a witness

The fifth criterion of reliability is the witness' lack of contradiction, meaning serious real contradiction from either inside or outside of their testimony.

Contradiction is evidence that actually establishes a witness to be inaccurate in a fact or conclusion they claim to be true. It may internal or external to a witness's testimony. It may be minor or major. The key wording here is "actually establishes". It is different from key words used in explaining relevance or materiality where the wording is "tends to make more probable" or "tends to establish".

(1) Assessing contradiction begins with assessing difference, but it does not end there.

(2) Difference is not contradiction. The distinction is something that is often ignored, especially by laypersons. Most differences in witness testimony are simple matters of differences in perspective or phrasing, readily reconcilable as such. Witnesses are expected to disagree. Witnesses are even expected to make mistakes. Most mistakes are innocent or negligent. Very few are fraudulent. It is actually a sign of one's reliability that one makes mistakes.

(3) Real contradiction divides into minor and major contradiction. It is only major contradiction that is important and can be serious.

(4) Major contradiction divides into two types: real and apparent contradictions.

(5) Apparent contradictions are unexpected differences which are contextually explained or capable of being explained.

(6) Real contradictions are unexpected differences which are not contextually explained or not likely to be explained.

(7) Real contradictions divide into two types: minor and serious. Only real contradictions count as serious contradictions. Only serious real contradictions have the potential to undermine or destroy the credible testimony of a witness who has already been determined to be reliable through corroboration, because only they "actually establish" inaccuracy. Anything less is merely difference and, to be technical, not really contradiction at all.

Any serious trier-of-fact should assess a witness' contradiction in terms of following lines of evidence:

(1) the disagreement of Jewish first century A.D. historian Josephus with Matthew and Luke on the whether a census occurred on or about the time of Jesus' birth requiring Mary and Joseph to journey to Bethlehem, the former not mentioning it; the latter two mentioning it;

(2) the disagreement of Roman archival material with Luke's testimony on whether Quirinius was ever actually governor of Syria; the former denying it; the latter asserting it;

(3) the disagreement of John with Matthew, Mark and Luke on what immediately followed Jesus' baptism by John: Jesus' journey with his disciples to Cana or Jesus' journey alone into the wilderness to be tempted; John asserting the former; Matthew, Mark and Luke, the latter;

(4) the disagreement of John with Matthew, Mark and Luke on whether Jesus' cleansing of the Temple occurred at the beginning of his public ministry or at its end; John asserting the former; Matthew, Mark and Luke, the latter;

(5) the disagreement of Matthew with Mark and Luke on whether Jesus' journey across the Sea of Galilee to heal demoniacs there preceded or followed Jesus' healing of a paralyzed man and forgiving his sins; Matthew asserting the former; Mark and Luke, the latter;

(6) the disagreement of Matthew with Mark and Luke on whether Jesus healed two or one Gergesene/Gadarene demoniacs; Matthew asserting two; Mark and Luke one;

(7) the disagreement of Matthew with Luke on whether Jesus' healing of the centurion's servant is at his own personal request, the centurion being immediately before Jesus or is at the request of a group of Jews speaking on his behalf, the centurion being at home; Matthew asserting the former; Luke, the latter;

(8) the disagreement of John with Matthew and Mark on whether the woman smashing an alabaster flask of ointment over Jesus' feet in preparation for his coming death occurred six days or two days before his execution: John asserting the former; Matthew and Mark, the latter;

(9) the disagreement of John with Matthew, Mark and Luke on whether the Passover in the year of Jesus' execution fell on a Friday or a Thursday; John asserting the former; Matthew, Mark and Luke, the latter.

The reason is simple. The absence of condiction, meaning serious real contradiction, is at the heart of reliability. A witness who is not seriously and really contradicted is a potentially reliable witness. It adds accuracy to the story.

A cautionary note

The failure of a trier-of-fact to understand, preserve, and apply the distinction between credibility and reliability can have disastrous consequences.

(1) In the 1950s, courts used to decide cases primarily on the basis of credibility alone. They had gotten lazy. They would pay lip service to reliability, but cases were ultimately decided on a narrow definition of credibility: plausible story. The classic case in that regard was *Faryna v. Chorney* [1952] 2 D.L.R. 353 at page 356 (British Columbia Court of Appeal).

"The credibility of interested witnesses, particularly in cases of conflict of evidence, cannot be gauged solely by the test of whether the personal demeanour of the particular witness carried conviction of the truth. *The test must reasonably subject his story to an examination of its consistency with the probabilities that surround the currently existing conditions. In short, the real test of the truth of the story of a witness in such a case must be its harmony with the preponderance of the probabilities which a practical and informed person would readily recognize as reasonable in that place and in those conditions.*"

There was an internal logic to the storyline. That was all was needed. There was no rigorous analysis of reliability.

(2) In the early and mid 1990s, things changed dramatically. DNA analysis had enabled outsiders to identify clear cases of miscarriages of justice. At various judicial conferences in that time period, a range of social scientists presented a large number of fact situations to the judges assembled. The fact situations were real. In all cases, the correct outcomes were known in advance of the presentation. They asked the judges how they would have decided the respective fact situations if those cases had come before them. The results were astounding. They found the judges got the answers wrong 40% of the time. They reviewed the reasons the judges gave for wrongly deciding the cases the way they did, and they found the erroneous judges were deciding cases on a narrow definition of credibility, that is plausible story, and not stressing the equal importance of reliability.

(3) In 1995, the case of *R. v. Morrisey* (1995) 97 CCC (3d) 193 at p. 205 or para 33, cf 1995 CanLII 3498 (ON CA), 80 O.A.C. 161; 22 O.R. (3d) 514 (C.A.), at 526 [O.R.] (Ontario Court of Appeal) evidences a reflection on the content and conclusion of those conferences. It clearly sets out the equal importance of credibility (believability) and reliability (accuracy).

"*Testimonial evidence can raise* veracity and *accuracy concerns.* The former relate to the witness's sincerity, that is, his or her willingness to speak the truth as the witness believes it to be. The latter concerns relate to the actual accuracy of the witness's testimony. *The accuracy of a witness's testimony involves considerations of the witness's ability to accurately observe, recall and recount the events in issue.* When one is concerned with a witness's veracity, one speaks of the witness's credibility. *When one is concerned with the accuracy of a witness's testimony, one speaks of the reliability of that testimony.* Obviously a witness whose evidence on a point is not credible cannot give reliable evidence on that point. *The evidence of a credible, that is, honest witness, may, however, still be unreliable.*"

(4) The point to be made here is a simple one. Just because something sounds correct does not make it correct. The trier-of-fact needs to remember judgements in the area of plausible story alone can be wrong 40% of the time, as it was with the erroneous judges at those conferences. Even professionals can get things wrong, when they get sloppy.

3. Basic principles for any judgment on the evidence

The basic principles for the judgement on the evidence are three in number: totality, weight and proof on a balance of probabilities.

(1) Totality

First, totality is the integration of all the evidence into a single whole. Judgement is a judgement on the whole of that evidence.

Totality is similar to neutrality in that it is a kind of perspective the trier-of-fact must bring to the analysis. The reason is simple. Individual pieces of evidence find their weight not in their isolation from, but in their connection with, all the other pieces of evidence. This is especially the case when there are multiple witnesses to an event. On important points, the testimony of each witness must be known and stated individually. But that testimony must be integrated collectively, to the extent that is humanly possible, never forcing the matter when integration is impossible, but never flinching from the task because of its difficulties.

The normal legal and historical term for this process is integration and for its product, it's a totality. The normal layman's term for this process is harmonization and for its product, it's a harmony. For certain New Testament scholars, that process and product, harmonization and harmony has fallen into disrepute. But, in my judgment, this is a serious mistake. When such scholar makes it, they are apt to be weighing the evidence piecemeal. And that is a fundamental mistake no competent jurist or historian would ever endorse.

Any serious trier-of-fact should assess totality in terms of the following lines of evidence:

(1) the creation of a basic chronology for Jesus' early life and public ministry, into which the evidence can be integrated;

(2) the noting of any disagreements in the chronology of events;

(3) the noting of multiple descriptions of the same event within that ministry;

(4) the noting of any disagreements in those descriptions of events.

The reason is simple. A basic chronology enables a trier-of-fact to more clearly understand how causation operates: how interest and motivations play out over time, how one event leads into another event.

(2) Weight

Second, weight is the strength of the evidence as a whole, the degree of credibility and reliability that attaches to it.

The simplest way to describe degrees of credibility and reliability is in terms of the degrees of confidence with which the trier-of-fact holds the evidence to be credible and reliable.

(1) If it is more than 5% but less than 50% confidence, the evidence is said to describe a mere possibility not a probability. It is "somewhat" credible and reliable; it has an air of reality to it.

(2) If it is more than 50% confidence but less than certitude, the evidence is said to describe a probability. It "is" probable; it is more likely true than not, but significant doubt still remains in the matter.

(3) If it is more than 67% but less than 95% confidence, the evidence is said to describe a high probability, eliminating or virtually eliminating substantial doubt in the matter.

(4) If it is more than 95% confidence but less than certitude, the evidence is said to describe a very high probability, eliminating reasonable doubt in the matter.

Any serious trier-of-fact, whether it be this author or his readers, should attempt to weigh the cumulative evidence from Matthew, Mark, Luke and John bearing in mind the following.

(1) In the area of plausible story (the first component of credibility), probability is established through the identification of interests or motives for action (why it occurs).

(2) High or very high probability is established through the identification of necessary and sufficient motivation for action (how and when it occurs).

(3) In the area of honest delivery (the second component of credibility), probability is established through straightforwardness and frankness.

(4) High or very high probability, is established through the presentation of embarrassing details and the lack of embellishment.

(5) In the area of a witness being in the know (the first component of reliability), probability is established through a single eye witness, even one supplementing their testimony with necessary and reliable hearsay on matters they did not personally witness.

(6) High or very high probability is established through the existence of multiple eye witnesses or hearsay witnesses, even ones similarly supplementing their testimonies with necessary and reliable hearsay on matters they did not personally witness.

(7) In the area of a witness possessing reasonable intelligence along with maturity and seriousness (the second component of reliability), possessing good powers of observation, memory and recall (the third component of reliability), probability is established through evidence for such features in the testimony of a single witness.

(8) High or very high probability is established through evidence of such features in the testimony of multiple witnesses.

(9) That high or very high probability is still further increased to the extent that it can be shown that there existed available tools or techniques for memory preservation prior to their actual testimony and it is known or reasonably inferable that those witnesses used those techniques.

(10) In the area of a witness being corroborated (the fourth component of reliability), probability is established with a confirmation of the Jesus' claim of divinity, the seriousness and lethality of the controversies such claims would have created, and high or very high probability is through multiple witnesses presenting the same or similar testimony in the same area.

(11) In the area of a witness not being contradicted (the fifth component of reliability), probability is established with the absence of any serious challenge, and high or very high probability, with the absence of any challenge at all.

The reason is simple. The overall strength of a story is a function of the combined plausibility of stories delivered by a single or multiple witnesses, their honesty delivery of those stories, their being in the know in the first place, their possessing intelligence, maturity and seriousness, their possessing good powers of observation, memory and recall, their being corroborated, their not being seriously contradicted. This overall strength of a story does not preclude individual judgements on individual witnesses: some witnesses being stronger than others in certain areas and at certain times, some witnesses being weaker than others in certain areas and at certain times.

(3) Standard of proof

Third, the standard of proof is the sufficiency of the evidence as a whole in answering the ultimate questions for consideration on a balance of probabilities.

It is a plausible story honestly delivered by witnesses in the know, witnesses who are possessed of reasonable intelligence, good powers of observation, memory and recall, precision in statement, witnesses who are corroborated or capable of being corroborated with in whole or in part, witnesses who are not seriously contradicted in the story they tell. It is a story that is more likely true than not.

It is a story that a trier-of-fact can hold with at least a 51 percent degree of confidence that it is true. There may or may not exist reasonable doubt or substantial doubt in the matter, but such doubts do not make an alternative finding more likely true than not. In other words, such doubts do not overturn a judgement that one explanation of what happened is preferable to all others, on the evidence.

Satisfying a standard of proof is a function of two things:

(1) the explanatory power of a particular judgement (its simplicity, its breadth and its depth, its comprehensiveness and its coherence) and

(2) its superiority to all other positions as an explanation of the evidence.

Any serious trier-of-fact, whether it be this author or his readers, should consider the cumulative weight of evidence from Matthew, Mark, Luke and John in relationship to follow items for consideration;

(1) the explanatory power of "Jesus' claims to divinity" as a means to explain six things: (a) the existence of, the nature of, and the scope of Jesus' public ministry, (b) his execution, (c) his alleged resurrection, (d) the empty tomb, (e) the transformation of his disciples and (f) the creation of the early church, and the extent to which such an explanation requires secondary modifications;

(2) the explanatory power of "religious misunderstanding and political expediency" as a means of to explain six things: (a) the existence of, the nature of, the and scope of Jesus' public ministry, (b) his execution, (c) his alleged resurrection, (d) the empty tomb, (e) the transformation of his disciples and (f) the creation of the early church, and the extent to which such an explanation requires secondary modifications;

(3) the explanatory power of "fraud and deception" as a means of to explain six things: (a) the existence of, the nature and the scope of Jesus' public ministry, (b) his execution, (c) his alleged resurrection, (d) the empty tomb, (e) the transformation of his disciples and (f) the creation of the early church, and the extent to which such an explanation requires secondary modifications; and

(4) the possibility that "none of the above" explanations or variations thereon meet the standard of proof on a balance of probabilities or that "two explanations are so equally balanced" such that no explanation has a preponderance of the evidence in its favour.

The reason is simple. A judgement that is probable is a judgement that is superior to all other judgements on the evidence. Until new evidence becomes available or new methods of evaluating the evidence become available, a historical proof on a balance of probabilities is a proof that demands rational acceptance as truth.

For average reader of this book who is grappling with the testimony of the gospel writers, I would commend the following works:

(1) Dr. Joel Natan's books *Jewish Trinity: When Rabbis Believed in the Father, Son and Holy Spirit* (2003), and *The Jewish Trinity Sourcesbook: Trinitarian Readings from the Old Testament* (2003);

(2) Craig Blomberg's books *The Historical Reliability of the Gospels* (1987), *The Historical Reliability of John's Gospel: Issues and Commentary* (2001); and *Jesus and the Gospels: An Introduction and Survey* (2009);

(3) Daniel Bock's book *Blasphemy and Exaltation in Judaism: The Charge Against Jesus in Mark 14:53_65 (2000), Studying the Historical Jesus: A Guide to Sources and Methods* (2002), and *Jesus According to Scripture: Restoring the Portrait from the Gospels* (2002);

(4) R.E. Brown's book *The Death of the Messiah: Volume 1 and 2* (1994);

(5) Inter Varsity's book *Dictionary of Jesus and the Gospels: A Compendium of Contemporary Biblical Scholarship* Edit. J.B. Green, S. McKnight and I.H. Marshall (1992);

(6) Josh McDowell and Sean McDowell's book *The Evidence that Demands A Verdict: Life-Changing Truth for a Skeptical World* (2017);

(7) J. Warner Wallace's book *Cold Case Christianity: A Homicide Detective Investigates the Claims of the Gospels* (2013);

(8) William Lane Craig's book *Reasonable Faith: Christian Truth and Apologetics* (2008). His website https://www.reasonablefaith.org/ has three superb short videos, about five minutes each, accessible on the left side of the front page of the website in a drop down column: (a) *Who Did Jesus Think He Was?*, (b) *Did Jesus Rise from the Dead?: The Facts*, and (c) *Did Jesus Rise from the Dead?: The Explanation*, which are so good I would almost recommend the reader consult them even before commencing reading this account of the gospel evidence. They are that good.

Otherwise, any major biblical commentary or, indeed, the materials referenced in my Bibliography that would be part of my later book in the area will be of assistance to the reader.

11. AN IMPROPER METHODOLOGY FOR UNDERSTANDING HISTORICAL INQUIRY

The so-called "Search for the Historical Jesus" methodology is neither historically nor methodologically sound. It emerges in the mid to late 1980s, but it is built on decades of New Testament "form criticism" and "source criticism" which started in the 1920s. Not all New Testament scholars endorse it and use it, but too many do.

That methodology involves a single governing principle (inauthenticity) and ten subsidiary interpretative principles, which divide into two groupings: five primary principles: (1) double dissimilarity, (2) embarrassment, (3) multiple attestation, (4) consistency and (5) rejection and existence, and five secondary principles: (6) traces of Aramaic, (7) Palestinian environment, (8) vividness in narration, (9) tendencies within the synoptic tradition and (10) historical presumption. That methodology involves no philosophical check on any historical findings.

Inauthenticity

The single governing principle is inauthenticity.

Inauthenticity is the assertion that any word or deed attributed to Jesus must be presumed to be false until proven true. Inauthenticity means not real, not corresponding to reality.

The essence of inauthenticity is the presumption of falsehood.

As a principle for the admissibility of evidence, inauthenticity is deeply flawed. It presumes, without proving, the relevant and material unanimous witness of the early Christian church is entirely false. That witness is that the gospels of Matthew, Mark, Luke, and John came from persons in the know, persons either directly or indirectly connected with Jesus' public ministry. In doing so, it places the apocryphal gospels on an equal footing with the canonical gospels. The relevant and material unanimous witness of the early Christian church is that the apocryphal gospels came from persons unconnected with Jesus' public ministry, centuries after the fact. They were excluded from the canon of scripture for precisely that reason. Inauthenticity is further historically flawed, precisely because it is the rejection of relevance and materiality as it is normally understood. In inauthenticity, the emphasis is on "actually proves". In relevance and materiality, the emphasis is on "tends to make probable" and "tends to prove" respectively.

As a principle for the assessment of evidence, inauthenticity is deeply flawed. It illicitly imports a philosophical position of extreme scepticism into a historical inquiry. Historical inquiry requires open mindedness and thoughtful consideration of the evidence. Inauthenticity is historically flawed, precisely because it is the rejection of neutrality as it is normally understood. Indeed, this presumption of falsehood is identifiable bias.

As a principle for any judgement on the evidence, inauthenticity is deeply flawed.

(1) It weighs the evidence piecemeal in that the presumption of falsehood is applied to not only to each and every aspect of a witness' testimony, but to each and every very word. This might not be apparent at first glance from how the principle is formulated. It merely states "a presumption of falsehood". It is how "falsehood" is understood and applied in practice that brings out this dimension implicit in the principle. So understood, inauthenticity is historically flawed, precisely because it is the rejection of totality as it is normally understood. Meaning is found not in individual pieces of evidence, but in the interrelationship one with another.

(2) It adopts what, at times, appears to be the legal standard of proof beyond a reasonable doubt, and, at other times, appears to be a philosophical standard of proof beyond all possible doubt, rather than the normal historical standard of proof on a balance of probabilities. This might not be apparent at first glance from how the principle is formulated. The principle itself merely states "until proven true". It is how "proves is understood and applied in practice that brings out this dimension implicit in the principle. So understood, inauthenticity is historically flawed, precisely because it is the rejection of the normal historical standard of proof. To require certainty in matters of probability is to make a category mistake of the first order. It requires a historian to reject, as unproven, any credible and reliable story as to what happened that has a preponderance of the evidence in its favour, a story which better explains the evidence than any other story, merely because that story contains some doubt: possible doubt, reasonable doubt or substantial doubt, even though such doubt in the matter is manageable and not so strong as to overturn the fact that one explanation for what happened is distinctly better than all other explanations of the evidence. No competent historian endorses such a standard. Simple probability is all that is required.

The principle of inauthenticity is corrupt and corrupting. It corrupts most of the ten principles that follow. Many of those principles contain valuable insights, but those insights are rendered unusable, because of the procrustean framework of inauthenticity in which they are embedded. Inauthenticity is unsalvageable. Some of the other principles are salvageable. When reformulated and incorporated into a proper historical methodology, some of those ten principles can be quite valuable.

(1) Double dissimilarity

The first of those ten principles is double dissimilarity, occasionally called double discontinuity, is the assertion that the early Christian church was "highly unlikely" or "very highly unlikely" to have fabricated those words or deeds attributed to Jesus that have no parallels in the Judaism that preceded him and no parallels in the Christianity that followed him. Those words or deeds of Jesus are "dissimilar" or "discontinuous", meaning "unconnected", with both the Judaism that preceded him and Christianity that followed him.

The essence of double dissimilarity is the identification of a piece of evidence that is unconnected to interest.

(1) Obviously, the early Christian church had no selfish interest or motivation to preserve certain words or deeds of Jesus that did not serve their interest, motivation or agenda in promoting

themselves as either the rightful successors of Jesus or as the rightful successors of the Judaism that preceded him. The only reason those particular words or deeds unconnected with interest were preserved in the first place is that they were thought to be truly spoken or done by Jesus.

(2) The reader will note that agenda of the early Christian church is not only understood to be false; it is understood to be fraudulent. This is identifiable bias playing out through an actual assessment of the evidence.

As a principle for the assessment of evidence, double dissimilarity is good in some respects, but deeply flawed in other respects.

(1) Double dissimilarity correctly describes an important piece of evidence. It is clear evidence of honest delivery. Any statement that is unconnected to a witness' real or suspected interest in promoting an agenda is evidence of straightforwardness or frankness in a matter. The presenters of that evidence sincerely and genuinely believed it to be true and preserved it for that reason. Honest delivery is the second component of credibility. But double dissimilarity does not exhaust the definition of honest delivery. Double dissimilarity is narrower than what is needed.

(2) Double dissimilarity is not designed to identify any causal factors in the interests of Jesus or his opponents that could create a plausible story resulting in Jesus' execution. As such, double dissimilarity cannot and should not open any proper discussion of methodology. Honest delivery is clearly a secondary principle of credibility not the primary principle of credibility which is plausible story. The "Search for the Historical Jesus" methodology gives it a primacy it does not deserve.

(3) Double dissimilarity captures only that which unique to Jesus, with no parallels to the Judaism that preceded him or the Christianity that followed him. What is unique to Jesus may or may not be important. It may or may not designate an interest or motivation in Jesus towards certain action. It may be merely something eccentric to him.

(4) Double dissimilarity is too broadly framed.

(a) Single dissimilarity would suffice to establish probability. Any single statement that is completely unconnected to a witness' real or suspected interest in promoting an agenda is evidence of straightforwardness or frankness in a matter. It does not have to be double. It does not have show both that the early church is the successor to Jesus and the successor to the Judaism that preceded him. It can be "either or". It need not be "both and". Double dissimilarity merely raises the degree of credibility from probability to high or very high probability. Probability is already established through single dissimilarity.

(b) Indeed, even single incomplete significant dissimilarity would suffice to establish probability. Any single statement that is significantly unconnected to a witness' real or suspect interest in promoting an agenda that the early church is the successor to Jesus and the successor to the Judaism that preceded him is evidence of straightwordness or frankness in the matter, precisely because the statement was not embellished to provide a greater fit with a real or suspected agenda. It does not have to be complete. It can be "incomplete" and "significant". It can be "either or". Double dissimilarity or complete single dissimilarity merely raises the degree of credibility from probability to high or very high probability. Probability is already established through single incomplete significant dissimilarity.

As a principle for any judgment on the evidence, the principle of double dissimilarity is deeply flawed in that it entails a standard of proof other than proof on a balance of probabilities.

(1) The negative phraseology of "'highly unlikely false" or "very highly unlikely false" is the equivalent of the positive phraseology of "highly likely true" or "very highly likely true." That positive phraseology entails a standard of proof that is, at the very least, proof beyond a reasonable doubt. This standard of proof which was only implicit in the principle of inauthenticity is now made explicit in the principle of double dissimilarity.

(2) It requires a historian to reject, as unproven, any credible and reliable story as to what happened that has a preponderance of the evidence in its favour, a story which better explains the evidence than any other story, merely because that story contains some doubt: possible doubt, reasonable doubt or substantial doubt, even though such doubt in the matter is manageable and not so strong as to overturn the fact that one explanation for what happened is distinctly better than all other explanations of the evidence. No competent historian endorses such a standard. Simple probability is all that is required.

(3) This is identifiable bias playing out through a judgement on the evidence.

(2) Embarassment

The second of those ten principles is embarrassment. It is assertion that the early church was "highly unlikely" or "very highly unlikely" to have fabricated those words or deeds of Jesus that embarrassed them in their promotion of Jesus and in their arguments with the Jewish authorities.

The essence of embarrassment is the identification of a piece of evidence that is contrary to interest.

(1) Obviously, the early Christian church had no selfish interest or motivation to preserve certain words or deeds of Jesus that were actually contrary to their interest, motivation or agenda in promoting themselves as either the rightful successors of Jesus or as the rightful successors of the Judaism that preceded him. The only reason those particular words or deeds unconnected with interest were preserved in the first place is that they were thought to be truly done or spoken by Jesus.

(2) The reader will note that agenda of the early Christian church is not only understood to be false; it is understood to be fraudulent. This is identifiable bias playing out through an actual assessment of the evidence.

As a principle for the assessment of evidence, embarrassment is solid.

(1) Embarrassment correctly describes an important piece of evidence. It is clear evidence of honest delivery. Any statement that is contrary to a witness' real or suspected interest in promoting an agenda is both evidence of straightforwardness or frankness in a matter and the absence of fabrication in the matter. The presenters of that evidence sincerely and genuinely believed it to be true and preserved it for that reason. Honest delivery is the second component of credibility. But embarrassment does come close to exhausting the definition of honest delivery.

(2) The relationship between double dissimilarity and embarrassment merits comment.

(a) Embarrassment is a much stronger form of honest delivery than dissimilarity. A statement contrary to interest is always weightier than a statement unconnected to interest.

(b) Single significant incomplete dissimilarity alone will normally establish probability in the matter of honest delivery, but it will not eliminate reasonable or substantial doubt in that area. Single complete dissimilarity will eliminate substantial doubt in the area of honest delivery. "Double dissimilarity" will eliminate both substantial doubt and reasonable doubt in the area of honest delivery.

(c) "Embarrassment" alone will normally establish probable credibility in the area of honest delivery. Substantial embarrassment will go even further and eliminate both substantial doubt and reasonable doubt in that area of honesty delivery.

As a principle for any judgment on the evidence, the principle of "embarrassment" is deeply flawed in that it entails a standard of proof other than proof on a balance of probabilities.

(1) The negative phraseology of "highly unlikely false" or "very highly unlikely false" is the equivalent of the positive phraseology of "highly likely true" or "very highly likely true." That positive phraseology entails a standard of proof that is, at the very least, proof beyond a reasonable doubt. This standard of proof which was only implicit in the principle of inauthenticity is now made explicit in the principle of embarassment.

(2) It requires a historian to reject, as unproven, any credible and reliable story as to what happened that has a preponderance of the evidence in its favour, a story which better explains the evidence than any other story, merely because that story contains some doubt: possible doubt, reasonable doubt or substantial doubt, even though such doubt in the matter is manageable and not so strong as to overturn the fact that one explanation for what happened is distinctly better than all other explanations of the evidence. No competent historian endorses such a standard. Simple probability is all that is required.

(3) This is identifiable bias playing out through a judgement on the evidence.

(3) Multiple Attestation

The third of those ten principles is multiple attestation. It is the principle that the early church is "highly unlikely" or "very highly unlikely" to have created those words or deeds of Jesus that are recorded in multiple independent sources.

The essence of multiple attestation is (a) the determination of a core external reality to Jesus' public ministry through the identification of multiple pieces of evidence that are independent of and co-incidental to interest, (b) to which the words and deeds of Jesus previously identified as doubly dissimilar (things unconnected with interest) or embarrassing (things contrary to interest) might correspond, and (c) from which they might acquire corroboration.

The essence of multiple attention is the indentification of a piece of evidence that is co-incidental to interest.

There is a real quirkiness to this multiple attestation.

(1) Multiple attestation is not multiple corroboration through multiple instances of eye-witness or hearsay testimony as one might think. Attestation here does not mean eye-witness or hearsay testimony. The discerning reader should know the literary speculation behind the Search for the Historical Jesus methodology, a certain understanding of Markan priority, posited the gospels were not written by persons in the know, not written by eye-witness or hearsay witnesses.

(2) By attestation, what is meant is corroboration through particular things not persons. To be precise, what I mean by things are not documents, but fragments within documents. The discerning reader should know that the literary speculation behind the Search for the Historical Jesus methodology, a certain understanding of Markan priority, posited certain fragments of the external reality of Jesus' public ministry circulated after his death. Over time, these fragments were incorporated into five independent sources of information, some of which were reduced to or incorporated into the biblical gospel documents or sources that lead to those documents:

(a) Q (material in Matthew and Luke not in Mark),

(b) Mark,

(c) M (material in Matthew distinct from Matthew's adoption of portions of Mark and Q),

(d) L (material in Luke distinct from Luke's adoption of portions of Mark and Q), and

(e) John,

but none of the fragments involved eye-witness or hearsay testimony. These fragments are understood to be differing literary forms that circulated without context or narrative such as:

(a) pronouncement stories,

(b) miracle stories,

(c) legend stories where Jesus is not the centrepiece of the story,

(d) simple sayings, whether they be wisdom sayings, prophetic sayings, apocalyptic sayings, or "I" sayings,

(e) parables.

(3) By independence, what is meant is complete independence. The discerning reader should know the literary speculation behind the Search for the Historical Jesus methodology, a certain understanding of Markan priority, posited the five sources of information: Q, Mark, M, L and John were independent of one another, but all believing communities. This understanding of complete independence adds a further dimension. The fragments embedded in these community sources of information were independent to the communities themselves. It is precisely the co-incidental nature of the literary forms that makes them something other than the creation of those communities. They are unintentional, almost accidental, things and therefore incidental to any interest of the early communities in promoting Jesus. The fragments testify to an external historical reality behind Jesus' public ministry. The community sources of information that went into the gospels themselves and the gospel documents themselves are not reliable sources, but certain fragments embedded within them are reliable, and therefore subject to the tests of correspondence and corroboration. So the story goes.

(4) This principle is so quirky that at times it looks like just a form of honesty delivery, the second principle of credibility, but at other times it looks like just a form of corroboration, the fourth principle of reliability. In my judgment, the emphasis on independence makes it a principle of corroboration.

As a principle for the assessment of the evidence, multiple attestation is deeply flawed.

(1) Complete independence is not a requirement for corroboration. Corroboration is evidence from another source that actually confirms or at least tends to confirm the accuracy of a witness' testimony, either in whole or in part. The emphasis is on other not independent. The test for corroboration of a witness by another witness is only relative not complete independence of the testifying witness from the corroborating witness. This reflects the human reality that eyewitnesses to important events want to and do share and discuss their observations and experiences of those events with other eyewitnesses to those same events. In purely legal inquiries where deprivations of liberty and money are in play, our legal system tend to separate witnesses one from another, lest they contaminate each other's testimony. But historical inquiry has no such requirement. Disagreement establishes any relative independence that might be required. Disagreement always establishes independence and it does so decisively.

(2) Moreover, multiple attestation seriously misunderstands "adopted testimony", where a witness repeats in whole or in part the language of another witness giving testimony. It is natural for witnesses to common events have adopted portions of each other's testimonies given orally or in

writing, because that witness agrees with its factual content and believes he himself could not have expressed it better. As before, a witness remains independent of another witness to the same events if they still disagree on minor or major points of fact or interpretation. Disagreement always establishes independence and it does so decisively, the greater the degree of disagreement, the greater the degree of independence. Adopted testimony is corrobating testimony.

As a principle for any judgment on the evidence, the principle of multiple attestation is deeply flawed in that it entails a standard of proof other than proof on a balance of probabilities.

(1) The negative phraseology of "highly unlikely false" or "very highly unlikely false" is the equivalent of the positive phraseology of "highly likely true" or "very highly likely true." That positive phraseology entails a standard of proof that is, at the very least, proof beyond a reasonable doubt. This standard of proof which was only implicit in the principle of inauthenticity is now made explicit in the principle of multiple attestation.

(2) It requires a historian to reject, as unproven, any credible and reliable story as to what happened that has a preponderance of the evidence in its favour, a story which better explains the evidence than any other story, merely because that story contains some doubt: possible doubt, reasonable doubt or substantial doubt, even though such doubt in the matter is manageable and not so strong as to overturn the fact that one explanation for what happened is distinctly better than all other explanations of the evidence. No competent historian endorses such a standard. Simple probability is all that is required.

(3) This is identifiable bias playing out through a judgement on the evidence.

(4) Consistency

The fourth of those ten principles is consistency. It is the assertion that a trier-of-fact might attribute further words or deeds to Jesus if they cohere with or are consistent with the initial portrait built up through the principles of double dissimilarity, embarrassment, and multiple attestation.

The essence of consistency is coherence: a creation of plausible story coherent with and derived not deduced from what has been already determined to be highly true or very highly, because it is unconnected to interest, contrary to interest and co-incidental to interest.

As a principle for the assessment, consistency is deeply flawed, because it is a poor and sloppy attempt to articulate plausible story. It is unfocused, failing to advise the trier-of-fact of the importance of interests and motivation that serves as the causal basis for actions and plot.

As a principle for any judgement on the evidence, consistency is deeply flawed. It assumes too narrow a basis for integration, necessarily resulting in only a partial integration of the evidence. It ignores the most important feature of credibility: plausible story.

(5) Rejection and execution

The fifth of those ten principles is rejection and execution. It is the assertion that some words and deeds of Jesus had to be threatening, disturbing or infuriating, because he met a violent end at the hands of Roman officials. It can be understood as a principle of assessment and judgement.

The essence of "rejection and execution" is a plausible story that explains the reason for Jesus' death on the cross at the hands of the Roman occupying force.

As a principle for the assessment of evidence, rejection and execution is good, but not great. It identifies part of the key causal element: the motivation that sets up plausible story. That motivation in Jesus' opponents must result in Jesus' execution. Within the framework of the Search for the Historical Jesus methodology, this principle functions a kind of plausible story. Plausible story is first criteria of credibility. This principle functions as a necessary check on any evidence, an initial historical portrait of Jesus built up through double dissimilarity (that which is unconnected with interest), embarrassment (that which is contrary to interest), multiple attestation (that which is co-incidental to interest) and consistency (that which is coherent with all three, derived not deduced from all three). The only flaw is this principle is not given a greater primacy and expanded to include Jesus' motivations within this improper historical methodology; it is relegated to the status of a fifth principle, occurring almost as an afterthought.

(6) Traces of Aramaic

The sixth of those ten principles is traces of Aramaic. It asserts that the early church which was Greek is "unlikely" to have created words of Jesus which indicate an Aramaic vocabulary, grammar, syntax, rhythm or rhyme.

As a principle for the assessment of evidence, traces of Aramaic is good, but not great.

(1) First, traces of Aramaic correctly identify the importance of an honest delivery, the secondary component of credibility. Certain words and phrases of Jesus were simply so important during his public ministry that no attempt was made to even translate those words or phrases into more contemporary language. They evidence a faithful repetition.

(2) Second, traces of Aramaic correctly identify the importance of capacity to remember, the second component of reliability. Certain words and phrases of Jesus were simply so closely associated with a particular event in his public ministry that the clear memory of one implies the clear memory of the other. The events in question burnt the words and phrases into the disciples' memories.

As a principle for any judgement on the evidence, traces of Aramaic is without flaw. Traces of Aramaic evidences an enhanced degree of credibility in the area of honest delivery and an enhanced degree of reliability in the area of capacity to remember. Weight attaches to both.

The only real flaw here is the distinctly subordinate nature of the principle. Unlike the principles of double dissimilarity, embarrassment and multiple attestation which employ the terminology of "very highly unlikely" to describe the early churches' use of such materials, the principle of traces of Aramaic uses the terminology of mere "unlikely" to describe the same. Since the governing principle of "inauthenticity" requires evidence that is "very highly unlikely" false evidence to rebut the presumption of falsehood, a principle such as vividness in narration which involves only "unlikely" false evidence has no real importance within the overall methodology. And indeed, practitioners hardly ever use or make comment on it.

(7) Palestianian environment

The seventh of those ten principles is Palestinian environment. It asserts that the early church which was non-Palestinian is "unlikely" to have created words or deed of Jesus that accurately reflect the geographic, economic, political, social and religious conditions of first century A.D. Palestine rather than the Roman world outside of Palestine in which the gospels were written.

As a principle for the assessment of evidence, Palestinian environment is without flaw.

(1) Palestinian environment correctly identifies the importance of plausible story, the primary component of credibility.

(2) Palestinian environment correctly identifies the importance of a capacity to remember and an accuracy in statement, the second and third components of reliability.

As a principle for any judgment on the evidence, Palestinian environment is without flaw. Palestinian environment correctly identifies the importance of corroboration, a component of weight.

The only real flaw here is the distinctly subordinate nature of the principle. Unlike the principles of double dissimilarity, embarrassment and multiple attestation which employ the terminology of "very highly unlikely" false to describe the early churches' use of such materials, the principle of Palestinian environment uses the terminology of merely "unlikely" false to describe the same. Since the governing principle of "inauthenticity" requires evidence that is "very highly unlikely" false to rebut the presumption of falsehood, a principle such as traces of Aramaic which involves only "unlikely" false evidence has no real importance within the overall methodology. And indeed, practitioners hardly ever use of it or make comment on it.

(8) Vividness in narration

The eighth of those ten principles is vividness in narration. It asserts that the early church is "unlikely" to have created certain vividness of their narration of events, especially when that vividness serves no apparent purpose in the narrative, and especially when that same narrative does not exploit those elements that would have otherwise greatly contributed to the narrative's purpose. It can be understood as a principle of assessment and judgment.

As a principle for the assessment of evidence, vividness in narration is without flaw.

(1) Vividness in narration correctly identifies the importance of honest delivery, the second component of credibility, especially when the testimony does not vividly exploit elements that might have contributed to a person's purpose, if they had been intent on embellishing the facts.

(2) Vividness in narration correctly identifies the importance of the importance of the capacity to remember, the second component of reliability.

The only real flaw here is the distinctly subordinate nature of the principle. Unlike the principles of double dissimilarity, embarrassment and multiple attestation which employ the terminology of "very highly unlikely" false to describe the early churches' use of such materials, the principle of vividness in narration uses terminology of merely "unlikely" false to describe the same. Since the governing principle of "inauthenticity" requires evidence that is "very highly unlikely" false to rebut the presumption of falsehood, a principle such as traces of Aramaic which involves only "unlikely" false evidence has no real importance within the overall methodology. And indeed, practitioners hardly ever use of it or make comment on it.

(9) Tendencies within the synoptic tradition

Tendencies with the synoptic tradition asserts that a gospel writer is "unlikely: to have created and inserted words or deeds of Jesus that run contrary to his editorial focus. The term "synoptic" comes from a Greek work meaning "seeing things together". Scholars use it to describe the writings of Matthew, Mark and Luke because they adopt a relatively similar position towards the chronology of events in Jesus' public ministry and the description of those events.

As a principle for the assessment of evidence, tendencies within the synoptic tradition is without flaw, to extent that it is properly conceived.

(1) First, tendencies within the synoptic tradition correctly identifies the importance of honesty delivery, the second component of credibility; the first being plausible story. Any statement that is unconnected to a witness' interest is invariably an expression of honesty delivery. Tendencies within the synoptic tradition, like double dissimilarity, evidences the absence of any motive for fabrication. The only difference between the two is the nature and scope of the witness' interest. Double dissimilarity addresses the general interests of Christianity as a whole. Tendencies within the synoptic tradition addresses the particular interests of a gospel writer as an individual.

(2) Second, tendencies within the synoptic tradition is flawed to the extent that it speculates as to the existence of communities shaping and distorting a witness' original message. Communities do not create traditions; witnesses do. Communities merely perpetuate the tradition. And the continuing presence of the witnesses to the life of Jesus in those early Christian communities is a sufficient check on the creation of new traditions not in accordance with the carefully preserved existing tradition.

Other than the last point dealing with downplaying of the importance of eyewitnesses, the only real flaw here is the distinctly subordinate nature of the principle. Unlike the principles of double dissimilarity, embarrassment and multiple attestation which employ the terminology of "very highly unlikely" false to describe the early churches' use of such materials, the principle of tendencies within the gospel tradition uses terminology of merely "unlikely" false to describe the same. Since the governing principle of "inauthenticity" requires evidence that is "very highly unlikely" false to rebut the presumption of falsehood, a principle such as tendencies within the gospel tradition which involves only "unlikely" false evidence has no real importance with the overall methodology. And indeed, practitioners hardly ever use of it or make comment on it.

(10) Historical presumption

Historical presumption asserts that the burden of proof for the historicity of any word or action attributed to Jesus lies on the person asserting its historicity. It can be understood as a principle of judgement.

As a principle for any judgement on the evidence, the "historical presumption" violates totality. Historical presumption violates totality in that it assumes each word or action must be weighed piecemeal. Historical presumption is really nothing more than inauthenticity approached from a different angle.

But quite frankly, the principle of historical presumption is really nothing more that a narrower and sloppier formulation of the principle of inauthenticity. The errors of the principle of inauthenticity are equally the errors of historical presumption.

Summarizing thoughts

In summary, "the search for the historical Jesus" methodology is a fundamentally flawed historical methodology.

(1) The governing principle of inauthenticity is irredeemably flawed and must be rejected entirely. That basic framework must go. Since all the ten principles of historical interpretation that are set within that basic framework, they must find a different setting. The setting I articulated earlier in my exposition of the normal historical methodology is the only real setting in which they might provide some kind of life to them, to the extent they are redeemable.

(2) The principle of double dissimilarity requires serious revision. Double dissimilarity guarantees at best the recovery of a partial portrait of Jesus revealing his eccentricities, eccentricities from the Judaism that preceded his public ministry and the Christianity that followed it. Double dissimilarity needs to be narrowed to single incomplete significant dissimilarity rather than complete dissimilarity. Its further life is most likely to be found within the area of honest delivery, the secondary component of credibility, but I would anticipate some growth into the area of plausible story, the primary component of credibility.

(3) The principle of embarrassment requires no serious revision. Its life and future are, most likely, to be found within the area of honest delivery, the secondary component of credibility.

(4) The principles of multiple attestation and consistency so poorly understand what constitutes corroboration that both probably have no life or future.

(5) The principle of rejection and execution so poorly understands what constitutes plausibly story that it probably has no life or future. Remember it only functions as a goal, an end not the means to an end.

(6) The principles of traces of Aramaic, Palestinian background, vividness in narration are readily redeemable and have a life and future in areas of powers of memory and recall and corroboration, the secondary and tertiary components of reliability.

(7) Tendencies within the synoptic tradition and historical presumption are just poorer formulations of earlier principles.

All in all, one would have expected more from New Testament scholars in this area.

At this point, I merely enjoin the reader to read on and profit.

A CHRONOLOGICAL PRESENTATION OF THE GOSPEL EVIDENCE

Event 1: Authorial Introductions

MATTHEW 1:1	MARK 1:1	LUKE 1:1-4	JOHN 1:1-14; 16-18
1:1 The book of the genealogy of Jesus Christ [Messiah (Hebrew) or Christ (Greek) means "Anointed One"], the son of David, the son of Abraham.	1:1 The beginning of the Good News of Jesus Christ [Messiah (Hebrew) or Christ (Greek) means "Anointed One"], the Son of God.	1:1 Since many have undertaken to set in order a narrative concerning those matters which have been fulfilled among us, 1:2 even as those who from the beginning were eyewitnesses and servants of the word delivered them to us, 1:3 it seemed good to me also, having traced the course of all things accurately from the first, to write to you in order, most excellent Theophilus; 1:4 that you might know the certainty concerning the things in which you were instructed.	1:1 In the beginning was the Word, and the Word was with God, and the Word was God. 1:2 The same was in the beginning with God. 1:3 All things were made through him. Without him was not anything made that has been made.
			1:4 In him was life, and the life was the light of men. 1:5 The light shines in the darkness, and the darkness hasn't overcome it. [The "katelaben" here translated "overcome" can also be translated "comprehended. It refers to getting a grip on an enemy to defeat him.]

			1:6 There came a man, sent from God, whose name was John. 1:7 The same came as a witness, that he might testify about the light, that all might believe through him. 1:8 He was not the light, but was sent that he might testify about the light. 1:9 The true light that enlightens everyone was coming into the world.
			1:10 He was in the world, and the world was made through him, and the world didn't recognize him. 1:11 He came to his own, and those who were his own didn't receive him. 1:12 But as many as received him, to them he gave the right to become God's children, to those who believe in his name: 1:13 who were born not of blood, nor of the will of the flesh, nor of the will of man, but of God.
			1:14 The Word became flesh, and lived among us. We saw his glory, such glory as of the one and only Son of the Father, full of grace and truth.

			1:15 John testified about him. He cried out, saying, "This was he of whom I said, 'He who comes after me has surpassed me, for he was before me.'" 1:16 From his fullness we all received grace upon grace. 1:17 For the law was given through Moses. Grace and truth came through Jesus Christ. 1:18 No one has seen God at any time. The one and only Son [NU has instead of Son, "God"], who is in the bosom of the Father, he has declared him.

Event 2: Jesus' genealogy

MATTHEW 1:2-17	LUKE 3:23-38
	3:23 Jesus himself, when he began to teach, was about thirty years old,
1:1 The book of the genealogy of Jesus Christ, the son of David, the son of Abraham.	
1:2 Abraham became the father of Isaac. Isaac became the father of Jacob. Jacob became the father of Judah and his brothers. 1:3 Judah became the father of Perez and Zerah by Tamar. Perez became the father of Hezron. Hezron became the father of Ram. 1:4 Ram became the father of Amminadab. Amminadab became the father of Nahshon. Nahshon became the father of Salmon. 1:5 Salmon became the father of Boaz by Rahab. Boaz became the father of Obed by Ruth. Obed became the father of Jesse. 1:6 Jesse became the father of David the king.	

David became the father of Solomon by her who had been the wife of Uriah. 1:7 Solomon became the father of Rehoboam. Rehoboam became the father of Abijah. Abijah became the father of Asa. 1:8 Asa became the father of Jehoshaphat. Jehoshaphat became the father of Joram. Joram became the father of Uzziah. 1:9 Uzziah became the father of Jotham. Jotham became the father of Ahaz. Ahaz became the father of Hezekiah. 1:10 Hezekiah became the father of Manasseh. Manasseh became the father of Amon. Amon became the father of Josiah. 1:11 Josiah became the father of Jechoniah and his brothers, at the time of the exile to Babylon.	
1:12 After the exile to Babylon, Jechoniah became the father of Shealtiel. Shealtiel became the father of Zerubbabel. 1:13 Zerubbabel became the father of Abiud. Abiud became the father of Eliakim. Eliakim became the father of Azor. 1:14 Azor became the father of Sadoc. Sadoc became the father of Achim. Achim became the father of Eliud. 1:15 Eliud became the father of Eleazar. Eleazar became the father of Matthan. Matthan became the father of Jacob. 1:16 Jacob became the father of Joseph, the husband of Mary, from whom was born Jesus, who is called Christ.	
1:17 So all the generations from Abraham to David are fourteen generations; from David to the exile to Babylon fourteen generations; and from the carrying away to Babylon to the Christ, fourteen generations.	
	being the son (as was supposed) of Joseph, the son of Heli, 3:24 the son of Matthat, the son of Levi, the son of Melchi, the son of Jannai, the son of Joseph, 3:25 the son of Mattathias, the son of Amos, the son of Nahum, the son of Esli, the son of Naggai, 3:26 the son of Maath, the son of Mattathias, the son of Semein, the son of Joseph, the son of Judah, 3:27 the son of Joanan, the son of Rhesa, the son of Zerubbabel, the son of Shealtiel,

	the son of Neri, 3:28 the son of Melchi, the son of Addi, the son of Cosam, the son of Elmodam, the son of Er, 3:29 the son of Jose, the son of Eliezer, the son of Jorim, the son of Matthat, the son of Levi, 3:30 the son of Simeon, the son of Judah, the son of Joseph, the son of Jonan, the son of Eliakim, 3:31 the son of Melea, the son of Menan, the son of Mattatha, the son of Nathan, the son of David,
	3:32 the son of Jesse, the son of Obed, the son of Boaz, the son of Salmon, the son of Nahshon, 3:33 the son of Amminadab, the son of Aram [NU has instead of Aram, "Admin, the son of Arni"], the son of Hezron, the son of Perez, the son of Judah, 3:34 the son of Jacob, the son of Isaac, the son of Abraham,
	the son of Terah, the son of Nahor, 3:35 the son of Serug, the son of Reu, the son of Peleg, the son of Eber, the son of Shelah, 3:36 the son of Cainan, the son of Arphaxad, the son of Shem, the son of Noah, the son of Lamech, 3:37 the son of Methuselah, the son of Enoch, the son of Jared, the son of Mahalaleel, the son of Cainan, 3:38 the son of Enos, the son of Seth, the son of Adam, the son of God.

Event 3: The angel's revelation to Zechariah and his response
Time: sometime 6-4 B.C.
Place: Jerusalem, Judea

LUKE 1:5-25
1:5 There was in the days of Herod, the king of Judea, a certain priest named Zacharias, of the priestly division of Abijah. He had a wife of the daughters of Aaron, and her name was Elizabeth. 1:6 They were both righteous before God, walking blamelessly in all the commandments and ordinances of the Lord.
1:7 But they had no child, because Elizabeth was barren, and they both were well advanced in years.
1:8 Now it happened, while he executed the priest's office before God in the order of his division, 1:9 according to the custom of the priest's office, his lot was to enter into the temple of the Lord and burn incense. 1:10 The whole multitude of the people were praying outside at the hour of incense.
1:11 An angel of the Lord appeared to him, standing on the right side of the altar of incense.
1:12 Zacharias was troubled when he saw him, and fear fell upon him.

1:13 But the angel said to him, "Don't be afraid, Zacharias, because your request has been heard, and your wife, Elizabeth, will bear you a son, and you shall call his name John. 1:14 You will have joy and gladness; and many will rejoice at his birth. 1:15 For he will be great in the sight of the Lord, and he will drink no wine nor strong drink. He will be filled with the Holy Spirit, even from his mother's womb. 1:16 He will turn many of the children of Israel to the Lord, their God. 1:17 He will go before him in the spirit and power of Elijah, 'to turn the hearts of the fathers to the children,' and the disobedient to the wisdom of the just; to make ready a people prepared for the Lord."
1:18 Zacharias said to the angel, "How can I be sure of this? For I am an old man, and my wife is well advanced in years."
1:19 The angel answered him, "I am Gabriel, who stands in the presence of God. I was sent to speak to you, and to bring you this good news. 1:20 Behold, you will be silent and not able to speak, until the day that these things will happen, because you didn't believe my words, which will be fulfilled in their proper time."
1:21 The people were waiting for Zacharias, and they marveled that he delayed in the temple.
1:22 When he came out, he could not speak to them, and they perceived that he had seen a vision in the temple. He continued making signs to them, and remained mute. 1:23 It happened, when the days of his service were fulfilled, he departed to his house.
1:24 After these days Elizabeth, his wife, conceived, and she hid herself five months, saying, 1:25 "Thus has the Lord done to me in the days in which he looked at me, to take away my reproach among men."

Event 4: The angel's revelation to Mary and her response
Time: sometime 6-4 B.C.
Place: Nazareth, Galilee

LUKE 1:26-56
1:26 Now in the sixth month, the angel Gabriel was sent from God to a city of Galilee, named Nazareth, 1:27 to a virgin pledged to be married to a man whose name was Joseph, of the house of David. The virgin's name was Mary.
1:28 Having come in, the angel said to her, "Rejoice, you highly favored one! The Lord is with you. Blessed are you among women!"
1:29 But when she saw him, she was greatly troubled at the saying, and considered what kind of salutation this might be.
1:30 The angel said to her, "Don't be afraid, Mary, for you have found favor with God. 1:31 Behold, you will conceive in your womb, and bring forth a son, and will call his name 'Jesus.' 1:32 He will be great, and will be called the Son of the Most High. The Lord God will give him the throne of his father, David, 1:33 and he will reign over the house of Jacob forever. There will be no end to his Kingdom."
1:34 Mary said to the angel, "How can this be, seeing I am a virgin?"

1:35 The angel answered her, "The Holy Spirit will come on you, and the power of the Most High will overshadow you. Therefore also the holy one who is born from you will be called the Son of God. 1:36 Behold, Elizabeth, your relative, also has conceived a son in her old age; and this is the sixth month with her who was called barren. 1:37 For everything spoken by God is possible."
1:38 Mary said, "Behold, the handmaid of the Lord; be it to me according to your word."
1:39 Mary arose in those days and went into the hill country with haste, into a city of Judah, 1:40 and entered into the house of Zacharias and greeted Elizabeth.
1:41 It happened, when Elizabeth heard Mary's greeting, that the baby leaped in her womb, and
Elizabeth was filled with the Holy Spirit. 1:42 She called out with a loud voice, and said, "Blessed are you among women, and blessed is the fruit of your womb! 1:43 Why am I so favored, that the mother of my Lord should come to me? 1:44 For behold, when the voice of your greeting came into my ears, the baby leaped in my womb for joy! 1:45 Blessed is she who believed, for there will be a fulfillment of the things which have been spoken to her from the Lord!"
1:46 Mary said, "My soul magnifies the Lord. 1:47 My spirit has rejoiced in God my Savior, 1:48 for he has looked at the humble state of his handmaid. For behold, from now on, all generations will call me blessed. 1:49 For he who is mighty has done great things for me. Holy is his name. 1:50 His mercy is for generations of generations on those who fear him. 1:51 He has shown strength with his arm. He has scattered the proud in the imagination of their heart. 1:52 He has put down princes from their thrones. And has exalted the lowly. 1:53 He has filled the hungry with good things. He has sent the rich away empty. 1:54 He has given help to Israel, his servant, that he might remember mercy, 1:55 As he spoke to our fathers, to Abraham and his seed forever."
1:56 Mary stayed with her about three months, and then returned to her house.

Event 5: The angel's revelation to Joseph and his response
Time: sometime 6-4 B.C.
Place: Nazareth, Galilee

MATTHEW 1:18-25
1:18 Now the birth of Jesus Christ was like this; for after his mother, Mary, was engaged to Joseph, before they came together, she was found pregnant by the Holy Spirit.
1:19 Joseph, her husband, being a righteous man, and not willing to make her a public example, intended to put her away secretly.
1:20 But when he thought about these things, behold, an angel of the Lord appeared to him in a dream, saying, "Joseph, son of David, don't be afraid to take to yourself Mary, your wife, for that which is conceived in her is of the Holy Spirit. 1:21 She shall bring forth a son. You shall call his name Jesus, for it is he who shall save his people from their sins."
1:22 Now all this has happened, that it might be fulfilled which was spoken by the Lord through the prophet, saying, 1:23 "Behold, the virgin shall be with child, and shall bring forth a son. They shall call his name Immanuel;" which is, being interpreted, "God with us." [Isaiah 7:14]
1:24 Joseph arose from his sleep, and did as the angel of the Lord commanded him, and took his wife to himself; 1:25 and didn't know her sexually until she had brought forth her firstborn son. He named him Jesus. [Jesus means in Hebrew, "Salvation"]

Event 6: The birth of John the Baptist and Zechariah's response
Time: sometime 6-4 B.C.
Place: Jerusalem, Judea

LUKE 1:57-80
1:57 Now the time that Elizabeth should give birth was fulfilled, and she brought forth a son. 1:58 Her neighbors and her relatives heard that the Lord had magnified his mercy towards her, and they rejoiced with her.
1:59 It happened on the eighth day, that they came to circumcise the child; and they would have called him Zacharias, after the name of the father. 1:60 His mother answered, "Not so; but he will be called John."
1:61 They said to her, "There is no one among your relatives who is called by this name." 1:62 They made signs to his father, what he would have him called.
1:63 He asked for a writing tablet, and wrote, "His name is John."
They all marveled.
1:64 His mouth was opened immediately, and his tongue freed, and he spoke, blessing God.
1:65 Fear came on all who lived around them, and all these sayings were talked about throughout all the hill country of Judea. 1:66 All who heard them laid them up in their heart, saying, "What then will this child be?" The hand of the Lord was with him.
1:67 His father, Zacharias, was filled with the Holy Spirit, and prophesied, saying,
1:68 "Blessed be the Lord, the God of Israel, for he has visited and worked redemption for his people; 1:69 and has raised up a horn of salvation for us in the house of his servant David 1:70 (as he spoke by the mouth of his holy prophets who have been from of old), 1:71 salvation from our enemies, and from the hand of all who hate us; 1:72 to show mercy towards our fathers, to remember his holy covenant, 1:73 the oath which he spoke to Abraham, our father, 1:74 to grant to us that we, being delivered out of the hand of our enemies, should serve him without fear, 1:75 in holiness and righteousness before him all the days of our life.
1:76 And you, child, will be called a prophet of the Most High, for you will go before the face of the Lord to make ready his ways, 1:77 to give knowledge of salvation to his people by the remission of their sins, 1:78 because of the tender mercy of our God, whereby the dawn from on high will visit us, 1:79 to shine on those who sit in darkness and the shadow of death; to guide our feet into the way of peace."
1:80 The child was growing, and becoming strong in spirit, and was in the desert until the day of his public appearance to Israel.

Event 7: Caesar's census and the birth of Jesus
Time: sometime 5-4 B.C.
Place: all of Israel

LUKE 2:1-7
2:1 Now it happened in those days, that a decree went out from Caesar Augustus that all the world should be enrolled.

2:2 This was the first enrollment made when Quirinius was governor of Syria.
2:3 All went to enroll themselves, everyone to his own city.
2:4 Joseph also went up from Galilee, out of the city of Nazareth, into Judea, to the city of David, which is called Bethlehem, because he was of the house and family of David; 2:5 to enroll himself with Mary, who was pledged to be married to him as wife, being pregnant.
2:6 It happened, while they were there, that the day had come that she should give birth. 2:7 She brought forth her firstborn son, and she wrapped him in bands of cloth, and laid him in a feeding trough, because there was no room for them in the inn.

Event 8: The angel's revelation to the Bethlehem shepherds and their discovery of Jesus
Time: sometime 5-4 B.C.
Place: Bethlehem, Judea

LUKE 2:8-20
2:8 There were shepherds in the same country staying in the field, and keeping watch by night over their flock.
2:9 Behold, an angel of the Lord stood by them, and the glory of the Lord shone around them, and they were terrified.
2:10 The angel said to them, "Don't be afraid, for behold, I bring you good news of great joy which will be to all the people. 2:11 For there is born to you, this day, in the city of David, a Savior, who is Christ the Lord. 2:12 This is the sign to you: you will find a baby wrapped in strips of cloth, lying in a feeding trough."
2:13 Suddenly, there was with the angel a multitude of the heavenly army praising God, and saying, 2:14 "Glory to God in the highest, on earth peace, good will toward men."
2:15 It happened, when the angels went away from them into the sky, that the shepherds said one to another, "Let's go to Bethlehem, now, and see this thing that has happened, which the Lord has made known to us."
2:16 They came with haste, and found both Mary and Joseph, and the baby was lying in the feeding trough.
2:17 When they saw it, they publicized widely the saying which was spoken to them about this child.
2:18 All who heard it wondered at the things which were spoken to them by the shepherds.
2:19 But Mary kept all these sayings, pondering them in her heart.
2:20 The shepherds returned, glorifying and praising God for all the things that they had heard and seen, just as it was told them.

Event 9: Jesus and Mary at the Temple, Simeon and Anna's response
Time: sometime 6-4 B.C.
Place: Jerusalem, Judea

LUKE 2:21-38
2:21 When eight days were fulfilled for the circumcision of the child, his name was called Jesus, which was given by the angel before he was conceived in the womb.
2:22 When the days of their purification according to the law of Moses were fulfilled, they brought him up to Jerusalem, to present him to the Lord 2:23 (as it is written in the law of the Lord, "Every male who opens the womb shall be called holy to the Lord"), [Exodus 13:2,12] 2:24 and to offer a sacrifice according to that which is said in the law of the Lord, "A pair of turtledoves, or two young pigeons." [Leviticus 12:8]
2:25 Behold, there was a man in Jerusalem whose name was Simeon. This man was righteous and devout, looking for the consolation of Israel, and the Holy Spirit was on him. 2:26 It had been revealed to him by the Holy Spirit that he should not see death before he had seen the Lord's Christ. ["Christ" (Greek) and "Messiah" (Hebrew) both mean "Anointed One"]
2:27 He came in the Spirit into the temple.
When the parents brought in the child, Jesus, that they might do concerning him according to the custom of the law, 2:28 then he received him into his arms, and blessed God, and said, 2:29 "Now you are releasing your servant, Master, according to your word, in peace; 2:30 for my eyes have seen your salvation, 2:31 which you have prepared before the face of all peoples; 2:32 a light for revelation to the nations, and the glory of your people Israel."
2:33 Joseph and his mother were marveling at the things which were spoken concerning him,
2:34 and Simeon blessed them, and said to Mary, his mother, "Behold, this child is set for the falling and the rising of many in Israel, and for a sign which is spoken against. 2:35 Yes, a sword will pierce through your own soul, that the thoughts of many hearts may be revealed."
2:36 There was one Anna, a prophetess, the daughter of Phanuel, of the tribe of Asher (she was of a great age, having lived with a husband seven years from her virginity, 2:37 and she had been a widow for about eighty-four years), who didn't depart from the temple, worshipping with fastings and petitions night and day.
2:38 Coming up at that very hour, she gave thanks to the Lord, and spoke of him to all those who were looking for redemption in Jerusalem.
2:39 When they had accomplished all things that were according to the law of the Lord, they returned into Galilee, to their own city, Nazareth.

Event 10: Wise men journey from the east and their discovery of Jesus
Time: sometime 5-4 B.C.
Place: Bethlehem, Judea

MATTHEW 2:1-12
2:1 Now when Jesus was born in Bethlehem of Judea in the days of Herod the king, behold, wise men from the east came to Jerusalem, saying, 2:2 "Where is he who is born King of the Jews? For we saw his star in the east, and have come to worship him."
2:3 When Herod the king heard it, he was troubled, and all Jerusalem with him.

2:4 Gathering together all the chief priests and scribes of the people, he asked them where the Christ would be born.
2:5 They said to him, "In Bethlehem of Judea, for thus it is written through the prophet, 2:6 'You Bethlehem, land of Judah, are in no way least among the princes of Judah: for out of you shall come forth a governor, who shall shepherd my people, Israel.'" [Micah 5:2]
2:7 Then Herod secretly called the wise men, and learned from them exactly what time the star appeared. 2:8 He sent them to Bethlehem, and said, "Go and search diligently for the young child. When you have found him, bring me word, so that I also may come and worship him."
2:9 They, having heard the king, went their way; and behold, the star, which they saw in the east, went before them, until it came and stood over where the young child was. 2:10 When they saw the star, they rejoiced with exceedingly great joy.
2:11 They came into the house and saw the young child with Mary, his mother, and they fell down and worshiped him. Opening their treasures, they offered to him gifts: gold, frankincense, and myrrh.
2:12 Being warned in a dream that they shouldn't return to Herod, they went back to their own country another way.

Event 11: Joseph, Mary and Jesus flee into Egypt and return
Time: sometime 5-3 B.C.
Place: Bethlehem, Judea; Egypt; Nazareth, Galilee

MATTHEW 2:13-23
2:13 Now when they had departed, behold, an angel of the Lord appeared to Joseph in a dream, saying, "Arise and take the young child and his mother, and flee into Egypt, and stay there until I tell you, for Herod will seek the young child to destroy him."
2:14 He arose and took the young child and his mother by night, and departed into Egypt, 2:15 and was there until the death of Herod; that it might be fulfilled which was spoken by the Lord through the prophet, saying, "Out of Egypt I called my son." [Hosea 11:1]
2:16 Then Herod, when he saw that he was mocked by the wise men, was exceedingly angry, and sent out, and killed all the male children who were in Bethlehem and in all the surrounding countryside, from two years old and under, according to the exact time which he had learned from the wise men. 2:17 Then that which was spoken by Jeremiah the prophet was fulfilled, saying, 2:18 "A voice was heard in Ramah, lamentation, weeping and great mourning, Rachel weeping for her children; she wouldn't be comforted, because they are no more." [Jeremiah 31:15]
2:19 But when Herod was dead, behold, an angel of the Lord appeared in a dream to Joseph in Egypt, saying, 2:20 "Arise and take the young child and his mother, and go into the land of Israel, for those who sought the young child's life are dead."
2:21 He arose and took the young child and his mother, and came into the land of Israel. 2:22 But when he heard that Archelaus was reigning over Judea in the place of his father, Herod, he was afraid to go there.
Being warned in a dream, he withdrew into the region of Galilee, 2:23 and came and lived in a city called Nazareth; that it might be fulfilled which was spoken through the prophets: "He will be called a Nazarene."

Event 12: Jesus' early life in Nazareth
Time: sometime between 3 B.C. to 8-9 A.D.
Place: Nazareth, Galilee

LUKE 2:39-40
2:39 When they had accomplished all things that were according to the law of the Lord, they returned into Galilee, to their own city, Nazareth.
2:40 The child was growing, and was becoming strong in spirit, being filled with wisdom, and the grace of God was upon him.

Event 13: Jesus' trip to Jerusalem at age 12
Time: sometime 8-9 A.D.
Place: Jerusalem, Judea

LUKE 2:41-51
2:41 His parents went every year to Jerusalem at the feast of the Passover.
2:42 When he was twelve years old, they went up to Jerusalem according to the custom of the feast,
2:43 and when they had fulfilled the days, as they were returning, the boy Jesus stayed behind in Jerusalem.
Joseph and his mother didn't know it, 2:44 but supposing him to be in the company, they went a day's journey, and they looked for him among their relatives and acquaintances. 2:45 When they didn't find him, they returned to Jerusalem, looking for him.
2:46 It happened after three days they found him in the temple, sitting in the midst of the teachers, both listening to them, and asking them questions.
2:47 All who heard him were amazed at his understanding and his answers.
2:48 When they saw him, they were astonished, and his mother said to him, "Son, why have you treated us this way? Behold, your father and I were anxiously looking for you."
2:49 He said to them, "Why were you looking for me? Didn't you know that I must be in my Father's house?"
2:50 They didn't understand the saying which he spoke to them.
2:51 And he went down with them, and came to Nazareth. He was subject to them, and his mother kept all these sayings in her heart.

Event 14: Jesus's early life in Nazareth continued
Time: sometime between 8-9 A.D. to 29 A.D.
Place: Nazareth, Galilee

LUKE 2:52
2:52 And Jesus increased in wisdom and stature, and in favor with God and men.

Event 15: John the Baptist baptizes Jesus
Time: between September 27- October 6, 29 A.D.
Place: Judea

MATTHEW 3:1-17	MARK 1:2-11	LUKE 3:1-22	JOHN 1:6-34
		3:1 Now in the fifteenth year of the reign of Tiberius Caesar, Pontius Pilate being governor of Judea, and Herod being tetrarch of Galilee, and his brother Philip tetrarch of the region of Ituraea and Trachonitis, and Lysanias tetrarch of Abilene, 3:2 in the high priesthood of Annas and Caiaphas,	
3:1 In those days, John the Baptizer came, preaching in the wilderness of Judea,		the word of God came to John, the son of Zacharias, in the wilderness. 3:3 He came into all the region around the Jordan,	1:6 There came a man, sent from God, whose name was John.
			1:7 The same came as a witness, that he might testify about the light, that all might believe through him. 1:8 He was not the light, but was sent that he might testify about the light.
			1:9 The true light that enlightens everyone was coming into the world.
			1:10 He was in the world, and the world was made through him, and the world didn't recognize him.

			1:11 He came to his own, and those who were his own didn't receive him.
			1:12 But as many as received him, to them he gave the right to become God's children, to those who believe in his name: 1:13 who were born not of blood, nor of the will of the flesh, nor of the will of man, but of God.
			1:14 The Word became flesh, and lived among us. We saw his glory, such glory as of the one and only Son of the Father, full of grace and truth.
Saying, 3:2 "Repent, for the Kingdom of Heaven is at hand!"		preaching the baptism of repentance for remission of sins.	
	1:2 As it is written in the prophets, "Behold, I send my messenger before your face, who will prepare your way before you. [Malachi 3:1]		
3:3 For this is he who was spoken of by Isaiah the prophet, saying,		3:4 As it is written in the book of the words of Isaiah the prophet,	
"The voice of one crying in the wilderness, make ready the way of the Lord. Make his paths straight." [Isaiah 40:3]	1:3 The voice of one crying in the wilderness, 'Make ready the way of the Lord! Make his paths straight!'" [Isaiah 40:3]	"The voice of one crying in the wilderness, 'Make ready the way of the Lord. Make his paths straight.	

		3:5 Every valley will be filled. Every mountain and hill will be brought low. The crooked will become straight, and the rough ways smooth.	
		3:6 All flesh will see God's salvation.'" [Isaiah 40:3-5]	
	1:4 John came baptizing in the wilderness and preaching the baptism of repentance for forgiveness of sins.		
3:4 Now John himself wore clothing made of camel's hair, with a leather belt around his waist. His food was locusts and wild honey.			
3:5 Then people from Jerusalem, all of Judea, and all the region around the Jordan went out to him.	1:5 All the country of Judea and all those of Jerusalem went out to him.		
3:6 They were baptized by him in the Jordan, confessing their sins.	They were baptized by him in the Jordan river, confessing their sins.		
	1:6 John was clothed with camel's hair and a leather belt around his waist. He ate locusts and wild honey.		
3:7 But when he saw many of the Pharisees and Sadducees coming for his baptism, he said to them,		3:7 He said therefore to the multitudes who went out to be baptized by him,	

"You offspring of vipers, who warned you to flee from the wrath to come?		"You offspring of vipers, who warned you to flee from the wrath to come?	
3:8 Therefore bring forth fruit worthy of repentance!		3:8 Bring forth therefore fruits worthy of repentance,	
3:9 Don't think to yourselves, 'We have Abraham for our father,' for I tell you that God is able to raise up children to Abraham from these stones.		And don't begin to say among yourselves, 'We have Abraham for our father;' for I tell you that God is able to raise up children to Abraham from these stones!	
3:10 "Even now the axe lies at the root of the trees. Therefore, every tree that doesn't bring forth good fruit is cut down, and cast into the fire.		3:9 Even now the axe also lies at the root of the trees. Every tree therefore that doesn't bring forth good fruit is cut down, and thrown into the fire."	
		3:10 The multitudes asked him, "What then must we do?"	
		3:11 He answered them, "He who has two coats, let him give to him who has none. He who has food, let him do likewise."	
		3:12 Tax collectors also came to be baptized, and they said to him, "Teacher, what must we do?"	
		3:13 He said to them, "Collect no more than that which is appointed to you."	
		3:14 Soldiers also asked him, saying, "What about us? What must we do?"	

		He said to them, "Extort from no one by violence, neither accuse anyone wrongfully. Be content with your wages."	
		3:15 As the people were in expectation, and all men reasoned in their hearts concerning John, whether perhaps he was the Christ,	1:19 This is John's testimony, when the Jews sent priests and Levites from Jerusalem to ask him, "Who are you?"
			1:20 He confessed, and didn't deny, but he confessed, "I am not the Christ."
			1:21 They asked him, "What then? Are you Elijah?"
			He said, "I am not."
			"Are you the prophet?"
			He answered, "No."
			1:22 They said therefore to him, "Who are you? Give us an answer to take back to those who sent us. What do you say about yourself?"
			1:23 He said, "I am the voice of one crying in the wilderness, 'Make straight the way of the Lord,' as Isaiah the prophet said." [Isaiah 40:3]
			1:24 The ones who had been sent were from the Pharisees. 1:25 They asked him, "Why then do you baptize, if you are not the Christ, nor Elijah, nor the prophet?"

	1:7 He preached, saying,	3:16 John answered them all,	1:26 John answered them,
3:11 I indeed baptize you in water for repentance, but he who comes after me is mightier than I, whose shoes I am not worthy to carry.	"After me comes he who is mightier than I, the thong of whose sandals I am not worthy to stoop down and loosen.	"I indeed baptize you with water, but he comes who is mightier than I, the latchet of whose sandals I am not worthy to loosen.	"I baptize in water, but among you stands one whom you don't know. 1:27 He is the one who comes after me, who is preferred before me, whose sandal strap I'm not worthy to loosen."
			1:15 John testified about him. He cried out, saying, "This was he of whom I said, 'He who comes after me has surpassed me, for he was before me.'" 1:16 From his fullness we all received grace upon grace. 1:17 For the law was given through Moses. Grace and truth came through Jesus Christ. 1:18 No one has seen God at any time. The one and only Son who is in the bosom of the Father, he has declared him.
	1:8 I baptized you in water,		
He will baptize you in the Holy Spirit.	But he will baptize you in the Holy Spirit."	He will baptize you in the Holy Spirit	
[TR and NU add "and with fire"]		and fire,	
3:12 His winnowing fork is in his hand, and he will thoroughly cleanse his threshing floor. He will gather his wheat into the barn, but the chaff he will burn up with unquenchable fire."		3:17 whose fan is in his hand, and he will thoroughly cleanse his threshing floor, and will gather the wheat into his barn; but he will burn up the chaff with unquenchable fire."	

		3:18 Then with many other exhortations he preached good news to the people,	
			1:28 These things were done in Bethany beyond the Jordan, where John was baptizing.
		3:19 but Herod the tetrarch, being reproved by him for Herodias, his brother's [TR has "brother Philip's] wife, and for all the evil things which Herod had done, 3:20 added this also to them all, that he shut up John in prison.	
3:13 Then Jesus came from Galilee to the Jordan to John, to be baptized by him.	1:9 It happened in those days, that Jesus came from Nazareth of Galilee, and was baptized by John in the Jordan.		1:29 The next day, he saw Jesus coming to him, and said, "Behold, the Lamb of God, who takes away the sin of the world! 1:30 This is he of whom I said, 'After me comes a man who is preferred before me, for he was before me.' 1:31 I didn't know him, but for this reason I came baptizing in water: that he would be revealed to Israel."
3:14 But John would have hindered him, saying, "I need to be baptized by you, and you come to me?"			

3:15 But Jesus, answering, said to him, "Allow it now, for this is the fitting way for us to fulfill all righteousness."			
Then he allowed him.			
3:16 Jesus, when he was baptized, went up directly from the water:	1:10 Immediately coming up from the water,	3:21 Now it happened, when all the people were baptized, Jesus also had been baptized, and was praying.	1:32 John testified, saying,
and behold, the heavens were opened to him. He saw the Spirit of God descending as a dove, and coming on him.	he saw the heavens parting, and the Spirit descending on him like a dove.	The sky was opened, 3:22 and the Holy Spirit descended in a bodily form as a dove on him;	"I have seen the Spirit descending like a dove out of heaven, and it remained on him. 1:33 I didn't recognize him, but he who sent me to baptize in water, he said to me, 'On whomever you will see the Spirit descending, and remaining on him, the same is he who baptizes in the Holy Spirit.'
3:17 Behold, a voice out of the heavens said, "This is my beloved Son, with whom I am well pleased."	1:11 A voice came out of the sky, "You are my beloved Son, in whom I am well pleased."	and a voice came out of the sky, saying "You are my beloved Son. In you I am well pleased."	1:34 I have seen, and have testified that this is the Son of God."

Event 16: Jesus meets Andrew, Peter, Phillip and Nathanael
Time: one day after Jesus's baptism between September 27- October 6, 29 A.D.
Place: Jordan River area

JOHN 1:35-51
1:35 Again, the next day, John was standing with two of his disciples, 1:36 and he looked at Jesus as he walked, and said, "Behold, the Lamb of God!"
1:37 The two disciples heard him speak, and they followed Jesus.
1:38 Jesus turned, and saw them following, and said to them, "What are you looking for?"
They said to him, "Rabbi" (which is to say, being interpreted, Teacher), "where are you staying?"
1:39 He said to them, "Come, and see."

They came and saw where he was staying, and they stayed with him that day. It was about the tenth hour. [4:00 pm]
1:40 One of the two who heard John, and followed him, was Andrew, Simon Peter's brother. 1:41 He first found his own brother, Simon, and said to him, "We have found the Messiah!" (which is, being interpreted, Christ). ["Messiah" (Hebrew) and "Christ" (Greek) both mean "Anointed One"] 1:42 He brought him to Jesus.
Jesus looked at him, and said, "You are Simon the son of Jonah. You shall be called Cephas" (which is by interpretation, Peter).
1:43 On the next day, he was determined to go out into Galilee, and he found Philip.
Jesus said to him, "Follow me." 1:44 Now Philip was from Bethsaida, of the city of Andrew and Peter.
1:45 Philip found Nathanael, and said to him, "We have found him, of whom Moses in the law, and the prophets, wrote: Jesus of Nazareth, the son of Joseph."
1:46 Nathanael said to him, "Can any good thing come out of Nazareth?"
Philip said to him, "Come and see."
1:47 Jesus saw Nathanael coming to him, and said about him, "Behold, an Israelite indeed, in whom is no deceit!"
1:48 Nathanael said to him, "How do you know me?"
Jesus answered him, "Before Philip called you, when you were under the fig tree, I saw you."
1:49 Nathanael answered him, "Rabbi, you are the Son of God! You are King of Israel!"
1:50 Jesus answered him, "Because I told you, 'I saw you underneath the fig tree,' do you believe? You will see greater things than these!" 1:51 He said to him, "Most certainly, I tell you, hereafter you will see heaven opened, and the angels of God ascending and descending on the Son of Man."

Event 17: Jesus and his friends go to a wedding in Cana
Time: the third day after Jesus' baptism between September 27- October 6, 29 A.D.
Place: Cana, Galilee

JOHN 2:1-12
2:1 The third day, there was a marriage in Cana of Galilee. Jesus' mother was there. 2:2 Jesus also was invited, with his disciples, to the marriage.
2:3 When the wine ran out, Jesus' mother said to him, "They have no wine."
2:4 Jesus said to her, "Woman, what does that have to do with you and me? My hour has not yet come."
2:5 His mother said to the servants, "Whatever he says to you, do it."
2:6 Now there were six water pots of stone set there after the Jews' manner of purifying, containing two or three metreres [about 75-115 litres, 20-30 US gallons, 16-25 imperial gallons] apiece. 2:7 Jesus said to them, "Fill the water pots with water." They filled them up to the brim. 2:8 He said to them, "Now draw some out, and take it to the ruler of the feast." So they took it.

2:9 When the ruler of the feast tasted the water now become wine, and didn't know where it came from (but the servants who had drawn the water knew), the ruler of the feast called the bridegroom, 2:10 and said to him, "Everyone serves the good wine first, and when the guests have drunk freely, then that which is worse. You have kept the good wine until now!"
2:11 This beginning of his signs Jesus did in Cana of Galilee, and revealed his glory; and his disciples believed in him.

Event 18: Jesus goes to Capernaum with family and friends
Time: October 29 A.D.
Place: Capernaum, Galilee

JOHN 2:12
2:12 After this, he went down to Capernaum, he, and his mother, his brothers, and his disciples; and they stayed there a few days.

Event 19: Jesus is tempted by the devil in the wilderness
Time: sometime October- November 29 A.D.
Place: the Wilderness east of Jerusalem, Judea

MATTHEW 4:1-11	MARK 1:12-13	LUKE 4:1-13
4:1 Then Jesus was led up by the Spirit into the wilderness to be tempted by the devil.	1:12 Immediately the Spirit drove him out into the wilderness.	4:1 Jesus, full of the Holy Spirit, returned from the Jordan, and was led by the Spirit into the wilderness
4:2 When he had fasted forty days and forty nights, he was hungry afterward.	1:13 He was there in the wilderness forty days tempted by Satan. He was with the wild animals; and the angels were serving him.	4:2 for forty days, being tempted by the devil. He ate nothing in those days. Afterward, when they were completed, he was hungry.
4:3 The tempter came and said to him,		4:3 The devil said to him,
"If you are the Son of God, command that these stones become bread."		"If you are the Son of God, command this stone to become bread."
4:4 But he answered, "It is written,		4:4 Jesus answered him, saying, "It is written,
'Man shall not live by bread alone, but by every word that proceeds out of the mouth of God.'" [Deuteronomy 8:3]		'Man shall not live by bread alone, but by every word of God.'" [Deuteronomy 8:3]
4:5 Then the devil took him into the holy city. He set him on the pinnacle of the temple, 4:6 and said to him,		4:9 He led him to Jerusalem, and set him on the pinnacle of the temple, and said to him,

"If you are the Son of God, throw yourself down, for it is written, 'He will put his angels in charge of you.' and, 'On their hands they will bear you up, so that you don't dash your foot against a stone.'" [Psalm 91:11-12]		"If you are the Son of God, cast yourself down from here, 4:10 for it is written, 'He will put his angels in charge of you, to guard you;' 4:11 and, 'On their hands they will bear you up, lest perhaps you dash your foot against a stone.'" [Psalm 91:11-12]
4:7 Jesus said to him, "Again, it is written,		4:12 Jesus answering, said to him, "It has been said,
'You shall not test the Lord, your God.'" [Deuteronomy 6:16]		'You shall not tempt the Lord your God.'" [Deuteronomy 6:16]
4:8 Again, the devil took him to an exceedingly high mountain, and showed him all the kingdoms of the world, and their glory.		4:5 The devil, leading him up on a high mountain, showed him all the kingdoms of the world in a moment of time.
4:9 He said to him, "I will give you all of these things, if you will fall down and worship me."		4:6 The devil said to him, "I will give you all this authority, and their glory, for it has been delivered to me; and I give it to whomever I want. 4:7 If you therefore will worship before me, it will all be yours."
4:10 Then Jesus said to him, "Get behind me [TR and NU have instead "Go Away], Satan!		4:8 Jesus answered him, "Get behind me Satan!
For it is written, 'You shall worship the Lord your God, and you shall serve him only.'" [Deuteronomy 6:13]		For it is written, 'You shall worship the Lord your God, and you shall serve him only.'" [Deuteronomy 6:13]
4:11 Then the devil left him, and behold, angels came and served him.		4:13 When the devil had completed every temptation, he departed from him until another time.

Event 20: Jesus cleanses the Jerusalem Temple for the first time
Time: sometime between March 29- April 5, 30 A.D.
Place: Jerusalem, Judea

JOHN 2:13-25
2:13 The Passover of the Jews was at hand, and Jesus went up to Jerusalem.

2:14 He found in the temple those who sold oxen, sheep, and doves, and the changers of money sitting. 2:15 He made a whip of cords, and threw all out of the temple, both the sheep and the oxen; and he poured out the changers' money, and overthrew their tables.
2:16 To those who sold the doves, he said, "Take these things out of here! Don't make my Father's house a marketplace!" 2:17 His disciples remembered that it was written, "Zeal for your house will eat me up." [Psalm 69:9]
2:18 The Jews therefore answered him, "What sign do you show us, seeing that you do these things?"
2:19 Jesus answered them, "Destroy this temple, and in three days I will raise it up."
2:20 The Jews therefore said, "Forty-six years was this temple in building, and will you raise it up in three days?"
2:21 But he spoke of the temple of his body. 2:22 When therefore he was raised from the dead, his disciples remembered that he said this, and they believed the Scripture, and the word which Jesus had said.
2:23 Now when he was in Jerusalem at the Passover, during the feast, many believed in his name, observing his signs which he did. 2:24 But Jesus didn't trust himself to them, because he knew everyone, 2:25 and because he didn't need for anyone to testify concerning man; for he himself knew what was in man.

Appendix: one cleansing or two?

MATTHEW 21:12-17	MARK 11:15-19	LUKE 19:45-48	JOHN 2:13-22
			2:13 The Passover of the Jews was at hand, and Jesus went up to Jerusalem.
21:12 Jesus entered into the temple of God, and drove out all of those who sold and bought in the temple, and overthrew the money changers' tables and the seats of those who sold the doves.	11:15 They came to Jerusalem, and Jesus entered into the temple, and began to throw out those who sold and those who bought in the temple, and overthrew the tables of the money changers, and the seats of those who sold the doves.	19:45 He entered into the temple, and began to drive out those who bought and sold in it,	2:14 He found in the temple those who sold oxen, sheep, and doves, and the changers of money sitting. 2:15 He made a whip of cords, and threw all out of the temple, both the sheep and the oxen; and he poured out the changers' money, and overthrew their tables.
	11:16 He would not allow anyone to carry a container through the temple.		

21:13 He said to them, "It is written, 'My house shall be called a house of prayer,' [Isaiah 56:7] but you have made it a den of robbers!" [Jeremiah 7:11]	11:17 He taught, saying to them, "Isn't it written, 'My house will be called a house of prayer for all the nations?' [Isaiah 56:7] But you have made it a den of robbers!" [Jeremiah 7:11]	19:46 saying to them, "It is written, 'My house is a house of prayer,' [Isaiah 56:7] but you have made it a 'den of robbers'!" [Jeremiah 7:11]	2:16 To those who sold the doves, he said, "Take these things out of here! Don't make my Father's house a marketplace!"
			2:17 His disciples remembered that it was written, "Zeal for your house will eat me up." [Psalm 69:9]
			2:18 The Jews therefore answered him, "What sign do you show us, seeing that you do these things?
			2:19 Jesus answered them, "Destroy this temple, and in three days I will raise it up."
			2:20 The Jews therefore said, "Forty six years was this temple in building, and will you raise it up in three days?" 2:21 But he spoke ot the temple of his body. 2:22 When therefore he was raised from the dead, his disciples remembered that he said this, and they believed the Scripture, and the word which Jesus had said.
21:14 The blind and the lame came to him in the temple, and he healed them.			

21:15 But when the chief priests and the scribes saw the wonderful things that he did, and the children who were crying in the temple and saying, "Hosanna to the son of David!" they were indignant, 21:16 and said to him, "Do you hear what these are saying?"			
Jesus said to them, "Yes. Did you never read, 'Out of the mouth of babes and nursing babies you have perfected praise?'" [Psalm 8:2]			
	11:18 The chief priests and the scribes heard it, and sought how they might destroy him. For they feared him, because all the multitude was astonished at his teaching.	19:47 He was teaching daily in the temple, but the chief priests and the scribes and the leading men among the people sought to destroy him. 19:48 They couldn't find what they might do, for all the people hung on to every word that he said.	
21:17 He left them, and went out of the city to Bethany, and lodged there.	11:19 When evening came, he went out of the city.		

Event 21: Jesus meets with Nicodemus the Pharisee that night
Time: sometime beween March 29- April 5, 30 A.D.
Place: Jerusalem, Judea

JOHN 2:23-3:15
2:23 Now when he was in Jerusalem at the Passover, during the feast, many believed in his name, observing his signs which he did. 2:24 But Jesus didn't trust himself to them, because he knew everyone, 2:25 and because he didn't need for anyone to testify concerning man; for he himself knew what was in man.

3:1 Now there was a man of the Pharisees named Nicodemus, a ruler of the Jews. 3:2 The same came to him by night, and said to him, "Rabbi, we know that you are a teacher come from God, for no one can do these signs that you do, unless God is with him."
3:3 Jesus answered him, "Most certainly, I tell you, unless one is born anew [the word "anothen" translated here "anew" also means "again" and "from above"], he can't see the Kingdom of God."
3:4 Nicodemus said to him, "How can a man be born when he is old? Can he enter a second time into his mother's womb, and be born?"
3:5 Jesus answered, "Most certainly I tell you, unless one is born of water and spirit, he can't enter into the Kingdom of God! 3:6 That which is born of the flesh is flesh. That which is born of the Spirit is spirit. 3:7 Don't marvel that I said to you, 'You must be born anew.' [the word "anothen" translated here "anew" also means "again" and "from above"] 3:8 The wind [The same Greek word (pneuma) means wind, breath, spirit] blows where it wants to, and you hear its sound, but don't know where it comes from and where it is going. So is everyone who is born of the Spirit."
3:9 Nicodemus answered him, "How can these things be?"
3:10 Jesus answered him, "Are you the teacher of Israel, and don't understand these things? 3:11 Most certainly I tell you, we speak that which we know, and testify of that which we have seen, and you don't receive our witness. 3:12 If I told you earthly things and you don't believe, how will you believe if I tell you heavenly things? 3:13 No one has ascended into heaven, but he who descended out of heaven, the Son of Man, who is in heaven. 3:14 As Moses lifted up the serpent in the wilderness, even so must the Son of Man be lifted up, 3:15 that whoever believes in him should not perish, but have eternal life. 3:16 For God so loved the world, that he gave his one and only Son, that whoever believes in him should not perish, but have eternal life. 3:17 For God didn't send his Son into the world to judge the world, but that the world should be saved through him. 3:18 He who believes in him is not judged. He who doesn't believe has been judged already, because he has not believed in the name of the one and only Son of God. 3:19 This is the judgment, that the light has come into the world, and men loved the darkness rather than the light; for their works were evil. 3:20 For everyone who does evil hates the light, and doesn't come to the light, lest his works would be exposed. 3:21 But he who does the truth comes to the light, that his works may be revealed, that they have been done in God."

Event 22: Jesus instructs his disciples and they baptize
Time: sometime summer to late fall or winter 30 A.D.
Place: Judea

JOHN 3:22-36
3:22 After these things, Jesus came with his disciples into the land of Judea. He stayed there with them, and baptized. 3:23 John also was baptizing in Enon near Salim, because there was much water there. They came, and were baptized. 3:24 For John was not yet thrown into prison.
3:25 There arose therefore a questioning on the part of John's disciples with some Jews about purification. 3:26 They came to John, and said to him, "Rabbi, he who was with you beyond the Jordan, to whom you have testified, behold, the same baptizes, and everyone is coming to him."
3:27 John answered, "A man can receive nothing, unless it has been given him from heaven.

3:28 You yourselves testify that I have said, 'I am not the Christ,' but, 'I have been sent before him.' 3:29 He who has the bride is the bridegroom; but the friend of the bridegroom, who stands and hears him, rejoices greatly because of the bridegroom's voice. This, my joy, therefore is made full. 3:30 He must increase, but I must decrease. 3:31 He who comes from above is above all. He who is from the Earth belongs to the Earth, and speaks of the Earth. He who comes from heaven is above all. 3:32 What he has seen and heard, of that he testifies; and no one receives his witness. 3:33 He who has received his witness has set his seal to this, that God is true. 3:34 For he whom God has sent speaks the words of God; for God gives the Spirit without measure. 3:35 The Father loves the Son, and has given all things into his hand. 3:36 One who believes in the Son has eternal life, but one who disobeys [The same word can be translated "disobeys" or "disbelieves" in this context] the Son won't see life, but the wrath of God remains on him."

Event 23: John is arrested and Jesus leaves for Galilee
Time: sometime late fall or early winter 30 A.D.
Place: Judea

MATTHEW 4:12	MARK 1:14	LUKE 4:14	JOHN 4:1-3
4:12 Now when Jesus heard that John was delivered up,	1:14 Now after John was taken into custody,		4:1 Therefore when the Lord knew that the Pharisees had heard that Jesus was making and baptizing more disciples than John 4:2 (although Jesus himself didn't baptize, but his disciples),
he withdrew into Galilee.	Jesus came into Galilee	4:14 Jesus returned in the power of the Spirit into Galilee, and news about him spread through all the surrounding area.	4:3 he left Judea, and departed into Galilee.

Event 24: Jesus meets the Samaritan woman at the well
Time: January 31, A.D.
Place: Samaria

JOHN 4:4-43
4:4 He needed to pass through Samaria. 4:5 So he came to a city of Samaria, called Sychar, near the parcel of ground that Jacob gave to his son, Joseph.
4:6 Jacob's well was there. Jesus therefore, being tired from his journey, sat down by the well. It was about the sixth hour [12:00 pm].
4:7 A woman of Samaria came to draw water. Jesus said to her, "Give me a drink." 4:8 For his disciples had gone away into the city to buy food.

4:9 The Samaritan woman therefore said to him, "How is it that you, being a Jew, ask for a drink from me, a Samaritan woman?" (For Jews have no dealings with Samaritans.)
4:10 Jesus answered her, "If you knew the gift of God, and who it is who says to you, 'Give me a drink,' you would have asked him, and he would have given you living water."
4:11 The woman said to him, "Sir, you have nothing to draw with, and the well is deep. From where then have you that living water? 4:12 Are you greater than our father, Jacob, who gave us the well, and drank of it himself, as did his children, and his livestock?"
4:13 Jesus answered her, "Everyone who drinks of this water will thirst again, 4:14 but whoever drinks of the water that I will give him will never thirst again; but the water that I will give him will become in him a well of water springing up to eternal life."
4:15 The woman said to him, "Sir, give me this water, so that I don't get thirsty, neither come all the way here to draw."
4:16 Jesus said to her, "Go, call your husband, and come here."
4:17 The woman answered, "I have no husband."
Jesus said to her, "You said well, 'I have no husband,' 4:18 for you have had five husbands; and he whom you now have is not your husband. This you have said truly."
4:19 The woman said to him, "Sir, I perceive that you are a prophet. 4:20 Our fathers worshiped in this mountain, and you Jews say that in Jerusalem is the place where people ought to worship."
4:21 Jesus said to her, "Woman, believe me, the hour comes, when neither in this mountain nor in Jerusalem, will you worship the Father. 4:22 You worship that which you don't know. We worship that which we know; for salvation is from the Jews. 4:23 But the hour comes, and now is, when the true worshippers will worship the Father in spirit and truth, for the Father seeks such to be his worshippers. 4:24 God is spirit, and those who worship him must worship in spirit and truth." 4:25 The woman said to him, "I know that Messiah comes," (he who is called Christ). "When he has come, he will declare to us all things."
4:26 Jesus said to her, "I am he, the one who speaks to you."
4:27 At this, his disciples came. They marveled that he was speaking with a woman; yet no one said, "What are you looking for?" or, "Why do you speak with her?"
4:28 So the woman left her water pot, and went away into the city, and said to the people, 4:29 "Come, see a man who told me everything that I did. Can this be the Christ?" 4:30 They went out of the city, and were coming to him.
4:31 In the meanwhile, the disciples urged him, saying, "Rabbi, eat."
4:32 But he said to them, "I have food to eat that you don't know about."
4:33 The disciples therefore said one to another, "Has anyone brought him something to eat?"
4:34 Jesus said to them, "My food is to do the will of him who sent me, and to accomplish his work.
4:35 Don't you say, 'There are yet four months until the harvest?' Behold, I tell you, lift up your eyes, and look at the fields, that they are white for harvest already. 4:36 He who reaps receives wages, and gathers fruit to eternal life; that both he who sows and he who reaps may rejoice together. 4:37 For in this the saying is true, 'One sows, and another reaps.' 4:38 I sent you to reap that for which you haven't labored. Others have labored, and you have entered into their labor."

4:39 From that city many of the Samaritans believed in him because of the word of the woman, who testified, "He told me everything that I did." 4:40 So when the Samaritans came to him, they begged him to stay with them.
He stayed there two days.
4:41 Many more believed because of his word. 4:42 They said to the woman, "Now we believe, not because of your speaking; for we have heard for ourselves, and know that this is indeed the Christ, the Savior of the world."
4:43 After the two days he went out from there and went into Galilee.

Event 25: Jesus arrives in Galilee
Time: spring 31 A.D.
Place: Galilee

MATTHEW 4:12-17	MARK 1:14-15	LUKE 4:14-15	JOHN 4:43-45
4:12 Now when Jesus heard that John was delivered up, he withdrew into Galilee.	1:14 Now after John was taken into custody, Jesus came into Galilee,	4:14 Jesus returned in the power of the Spirit into Galilee,	4:43 After the two days he went out from there and went into Galilee.
4:13 Leaving Nazareth, he came and lived in Capernaum, which is by the sea, in the region of Zebulun and Naphtali, 4:14 that it might be fulfilled which was spoken through Isaiah the prophet, saying, 4:15 "The land of Zebulun and the land of Naphtali, toward the sea, beyond the Jordan, Galilee of the Gentiles, 4:16 the people who sat in darkness saw a great light, to those who sat in the region and shadow of death, to them light has dawned." [Isaiah 9:1-2]			

-		and news about him spread through all the surrounding area. 4:15 He taught in their synagogues, being glorified by all.	4:44 For Jesus himself testified that a prophet has no honor in his own country. 4:45 So when he came into Galilee, the Galileans received him, having seen all the things that he did in Jerusalem at the feast, for they also went to the feast.
4:17 From that time, Jesus began to preach, and to say, "Repent! For the Kingdom of Heaven is at hand."	preaching the Good News of the Kingdom of God, 1:15 and saying, "The time is fulfilled, and the Kingdom of God is at hand! Repent, and believe in the Good News."		

Event 26: Jesus heals a royal official's son
Time: spring A.D.
Place: Cana, Galilee

JOHN 4:46-54
4:46 Jesus came therefore again to Cana of Galilee, where he made the water into wine. There was a certain nobleman whose son was sick at Capernaum.
4:47 When he heard that Jesus had come out of Judea into Galilee, he went to him, and begged him that he would come down and heal his son, for he was at the point of death. 4:48 Jesus therefore said to him, "Unless you see signs and wonders, you will in no way believe."
4:49 The nobleman said to him, "Sir, come down before my child dies."
4:50 Jesus said to him, "Go your way. Your son lives."
The man believed the word that Jesus spoke to him, and he went his way. 4:51 As he was now going down, his servants met him and reported, saying "Your child lives!" 4:52 So he inquired of them the hour when he began to get better. They said therefore to him, "Yesterday at the seventh hour [1:00 pm], the fever left him." 4:53 So the father knew that it was at that hour in which Jesus said to him, "Your son lives." He believed, as did his whole house.
4:54 This is again the second sign that Jesus did, having come out of Judea into Galilee.

Event 27: Jesus calls Peter, Andrew, James and John a second time
Time: spring March 31 A.D.
Place: seashore Sea of Galilee, Galilee

MATTHEW 4:18-22	MARK 1:16-20	LUKE 5:1-11
4:18 Walking by the sea of Galilee,	1:16 Passing along by the sea of Galilee,	5:1 Now it happened, while the multitude pressed on him and heard the word of God, that he was standing by the lake of Gennesaret.
he [TR instead has "Jesus"] saw two brothers: Simon, who is called Peter, and Andrew, his brother, casting a net into the sea; for they were fishermen.	he saw Simon and Andrew the brother of Simon casting a net into the sea, for they were fishermen.	5:2 He saw two boats standing by the lake, but the fishermen had gone out of them, and were washing their nets. 5:3 He entered into one of the boats, which was Simon's, and asked him to put out a little from the land. He sat down and taught the multitudes from the boat.
		5:4 When he had finished speaking, he said to Simon, "Put out into the deep, and let down your nets for a catch."
		5:5 Simon answered him, "Master, we worked all night, and took nothing; but at your word I will let down the net." 5:6 When they had done this, they caught a great multitude of fish, and their net was breaking. 5:7 They beckoned to their partners in the other boat, that they should come and help them. They came, and filled both boats, so that they began to sink.
		5:8 But Simon Peter, when he saw it, fell down at Jesus' knees, saying, "Depart from me, for I am a sinful man, Lord." 5:9 For he was amazed, and all who were with him, at the catch of fish which they had caught;

4:19 He said to them, "Come after me, and I will make you fishers for men."	1:17 Jesus said to them, "Come after me, and I will make you into fishers for men."	Jesus said to Simon, "Don't be afraid. From now on you will be catching people alive.
		5:10 and so also were James and John, sons of Zebedee, who were partners with Simon.
4:20 They immediately left their nets and followed him.	1:18 Immediately they left their nets, and followed him.	5:11 When they had brought their boats to land, they left everything, and followed him.
4:21 Going on from there, he saw two other brothers, James the son of Zebedee, and John his brother, in the boat with Zebedee their father, mending their nets. He called them.	1:19 Going on a little further from there, he saw James the son of Zebedee, and John, his brother, who were also in the boat mending the nets.	
4:22 They immediately left the boat and their father, and followed him.	1:20 Immediately he called them, and they left their father, Zebedee, in the boat with the hired servants, and went after him.	

Event 28: Jesus delivers a Capernaum sermon and exorcism
Time: spring 31 A.D.
Place: Capernaum, Galilee

MARK 1:21-28	LUKE 4:31-37
1:21 They went into Capernaum, and immediately on the Sabbath day he entered into the synagogue and taught.	4:31 He came down to Capernaum, a city of Galilee. He was teaching them on the Sabbath day,
1:22 They were astonished at his teaching, for he taught them as having authority, and not as the scribes.	4:32 and they were astonished at his teaching, for his word was with authority.
1:23 Immediately there was in their synagogue a man with an unclean spirit,	4:33 In the synagogue there was a man who had a spirit of an unclean demon,
and he cried out, 1:24 saying, "Ha! What do we have to do with you, Jesus, you Nazarene? Have you come to destroy us? I know you who you are: the Holy One of God!"	and he cried out with a loud voice, 4:34 saying, "Ah! what have we to do with you, Jesus of Nazareth? Have you come to destroy us? I know you who you are: the Holy One of God!"
1:25 Jesus rebuked him, saying, "Be quiet, and come out of him!"	4:35 Jesus rebuked him, saying, "Be silent, and come out of him!"
1:26 The unclean spirit, convulsing him and crying with a loud voice, came out of him.	When the demon had thrown him down in their midst, he came out of him, having done him no harm.

1:27 They were all amazed, so that they questioned among themselves, saying, "What is this? A new teaching? For with authority he commands even the unclean spirits, and they obey him!"	4:36 Amazement came on all, and they spoke together, one with another, saying, "What is this word? For with authority and power he commands the unclean spirits, and they come out!"
1:28 The report of him went out immediately everywhere into all the region of Galilee and its surrounding area.	4:37 News about him went out into every place of the surrounding region.

Event 29: Jesus delivers the Sermon on the Mount
Time: spring 31 A.D.
Place: Galilee

MATTHEW 4:23-7:29
4:23 Jesus went about in all Galilee, teaching in their synagogues, preaching the Good News of the Kingdom, and healing every disease and every sickness among the people. 4:24 The report about him went out into all Syria. They brought to him all who were sick, afflicted with various diseases and torments, possessed with demons, epileptics, and paralytics; and he healed them. 4:25 Great multitudes from Galilee, Decapolis, Jerusalem, Judea and from beyond the Jordan followed him.
5:1 Seeing the multitudes, he went up onto the mountain. When he had sat down, his disciples came to him. 5:2 He opened his mouth and taught them, saying,
5:3 "Blessed are the poor in spirit, for theirs is the Kingdom of Heaven. [Isaiah 57:15; 66:2] 5:4 Blessed are those who mourn, for they shall be comforted. [Isaiah 61:2; 66:10,13] 5:5 Blessed are the gentle, for they shall inherit the earth. [Psalm 37:11] 5:6 Blessed are those who hunger and thirst after righteousness, for they shall be filled. 5:7 Blessed are the merciful, for they shall obtain mercy. 5:8 Blessed are the pure in heart, for they shall see God. 5:9 Blessed are the peacemakers, for they shall be called children of God. 5:10 Blessed are those who have been persecuted for righteousness' sake, for theirs is the Kingdom of Heaven.
5:11 "Blessed are you when people reproach you, persecute you, and say all kinds of evil against you falsely, for my sake. 5:12 Rejoice, and be exceedingly glad, for great is your reward in heaven. For that is how they persecuted the prophets who were before you.
5:13 "You are the salt of the earth, but if the salt has lost its flavor, with what will it be salted? It is then good for nothing, but to be cast out and trodden under the feet of men. 5:14 You are the light of the world. A city located on a hill can't be hidden. 5:15 Neither do you light a lamp, and put it under a measuring basket, but on a stand; and it shines to all who are in the house. 5:16

Even so, let your light shine before men; that they may see your
good works, and glorify your Father who is in heaven.

5:17 “Don’t think that I came to destroy the law or the prophets. I didn’t come to
destroy, but to fulfill. 5:18 For most certainly, I tell you, until heaven and earth pass
away, not even one smallest letter or one tiny pen stroke shall in any way pass away
from the law, until all things are accomplished. 5:19 Whoever, therefore, shall break
one of these least commandments, and teach others to do so, shall be called least in the
Kingdom of Heaven; but whoever shall do and teach them shall be called great in the
Kingdom of Heaven. 5:20 For I tell you that unless your righteousness exceeds that of
the scribes and Pharisees, there is no way you will enter into the Kingdom of Heaven.

5:21 “You have heard that it was said to the ancient ones, ‘You shall not murder;’
and ‘Whoever shall murder shall be in danger of the judgment.’ [Exodus 20:13]
5:22 But I tell you, that everyone who is angry with his brother without a cause
[NU lacks “without cause] shall be in danger of the judgment; and whoever shall
say to his brother, ‘Raca!’ [empty-headed] shall be in danger of the council; and
whoever shall say, ‘You fool!’ shall be in danger of the fire of Gehenna. [Hell]

5:23 “If therefore you are offering your gift at the altar, and there remember that your brother
has anything against you, 5:24 leave your gift there before the altar, and go your way. First
be reconciled to your brother, and then come and offer your gift. 5:25 Agree with your
adversary quickly, while you are with him in the way; lest perhaps the prosecutor deliver you
to the judge, and the judge deliver you to the officer, and you be cast into prison. 5:26 Most
certainly I tell you, you shall by no means get out of there, until you have paid the last penny.

5:27 “You have heard that it was said [TR adds “to the ancients”], ‘You shall not commit
adultery;’ [Exodus 20:14] 5:28 but I tell you that everyone who gazes at a woman to
lust after her has committed adultery with her already in his heart. 5:29 If your right
eye causes you to stumble, pluck it out and throw it away from you. For it is more
profitable for you that one of your members should perish, than for your whole body
to be cast into Gehenna. [Hell] 5:30 If your right hand causes you to stumble, cut
it off, and throw it away from you. For it is more profitable for you that one of your
members should perish, than for your whole body to be cast into Gehenna. [Hell]

5:31 “It was also said, ‘Whoever shall put away his wife, let him give her a
writing of divorce,’ [Deuteronomy 24:1] 5:32 but I tell you that whoever puts
away his wife, except for the cause of sexual immorality, makes her an adulteress;
and whoever marries her when she is put away commits adultery.

5:33 “Again you have heard that it was said to them of old time, ‘You shall not make
false vows, but shall perform to the Lord your vows,’ 5:34 but I tell you, don’t swear
at all: neither by heaven, for it is the throne of God; 5:35 nor by the earth, for it is the
footstool of his feet; nor by Jerusalem, for it is the city of the great King. 5:36 Neither
shall you swear by your head, for you can’t make one hair white or black. 5:37 But let your
‘Yes’ be ‘Yes’ and your ‘No’ be ‘No.’ Whatever is more than these is of the evil one.

5:38 “You have heard that it was said, ‘An eye for an eye, and a tooth for a tooth.’ [Exodus 21:24;
Leviticus 24:20; Deuteronomy 19:21] 5:39 But I tell you, don’t resist him who is evil; but whoever
strikes you on your right cheek, turn to him the other also. 5:40 If anyone sues you to take away
your coat, let him have your cloak also. 5:41 Whoever compels you to go one mile, go with him
two. 5:42 Give to him who asks you, and don’t turn away him who desires to borrow from you.

5:43 "You have heard that it was said, 'You shall love your neighbor [Leviticus 19:18], and hate your enemy.' [Qumran Manual of Discipline 60:21-26] 5:44 But I tell you, love your enemies, bless those who curse you, do good to those who hate you, and pray for those who mistreat you and persecute you, 5:45 that you may be children of your Father who is in heaven. For he makes his sun to rise on the evil and the good, and sends rain on the just and the unjust. 5:46 For if you love those who love you, what reward do you have? Don't even the tax collectors do the same? 5:47 If you only greet your friends, what more do you do than others? Don't even the tax collectors do the same?

5:48 Therefore you shall be perfect, just as your Father in heaven is perfect.

6:1 "Be careful that you don't do your charitable giving before men, to be seen by them, or else you have no reward from your Father who is in heaven. 6:2 Therefore when you do merciful deeds, don't sound a trumpet before yourself, as the hypocrites do in the synagogues and in the streets, that they may get glory from men. Most certainly I tell you, they have received their reward. 6:3 But when you do merciful deeds, don't let your left hand know what your right hand does, 6:4 so that your merciful deeds may be in secret, then your Father who sees in secret will reward you openly.

6:5 "When you pray, you shall not be as the hypocrites, for they love to stand and pray in the synagogues and in the corners of the streets, that they may be seen by men. Most certainly, I tell you, they have received their reward. 6:6 But you, when you pray, enter into your inner chamber, and having shut your door, pray to your Father who is in secret, and your Father who sees in secret will reward you openly. 6:7 In praying, don't use vain repetitions, as the Gentiles do; for they think that they will be heard for their much speaking. 6:8 Therefore don't be like them, for your Father knows what things you need, before you ask him.

6:9 Pray like this: 'Our Father in heaven, may your name be kept holy. 6:10 Let your Kingdom come. Let your will be done, as in heaven, so on earth. 6:11 Give us today our daily bread. 6:12 Forgive us our debts, as we also forgive our debtors. 6:13 Bring us not into temptation, but deliver us from the evil one. For yours is the Kingdom, the power, and the glory forever. Amen.' [NU lacks "For yours is the Kingdom, the power, and the glory forever. Amen"]

6:14 "For if you forgive men their trespasses, your heavenly Father will also forgive you. 6:15 But if you don't forgive men their trespasses, neither will your Father forgive your trespasses.

6:16 "Moreover when you fast, don't be like the hypocrites, with sad faces. For they disfigure their faces, that they may be seen by men to be fasting. Most certainly I tell you, they have received their reward. 6:17 But you, when you fast, anoint your head, and wash your face; 6:18 so that you are not seen by men to be fasting, but by your Father who is in secret, and your Father, who sees in secret, will reward you.

6:19 "Don't lay up treasures for yourselves on the earth, where moth and rust consume, and where thieves break through and steal; 6:20 but lay up for yourselves treasures in heaven, where neither moth nor rust consume, and where thieves don't break through and steal; 6:21 for where your treasure is, there your heart will be also.

6:22 "The lamp of the body is the eye. If therefore your eye is sound, your whole body will be full of light. 6:23 But if your eye is evil, your whole body will be full of darkness. If therefore the light that is in you is darkness, how great is the darkness!

6:24 "No one can serve two masters, for either he will hate the one and love the other; or else he will be devoted to one and despise the other. You can't serve both God and Mammon. 6:25 Therefore, I tell you, don't be anxious for your life: what you will eat, or what you will drink; nor yet for your body, what you will wear. Isn't life more than food, and the body more than clothing? 6:26 See the birds of the sky, that they don't sow, neither do they reap, nor gather into barns. Your heavenly Father feeds them. Aren't you of much more value than they?

6:27 "Which of you, by being anxious, can add one moment to his lifespan? 6:28 Why are you anxious about clothing? Consider the lilies of the field, how they grow. They don't toil, neither do they spin, 6:29 yet I tell you that even Solomon in all his glory was not dressed like one of these. 6:30 But if God so clothes the grass of the field, which today exists, and tomorrow is thrown into the oven, won't he much more clothe you, you of little faith?

6:31 "Therefore don't be anxious, saying, 'What will we eat?', 'What will we drink?' or, 'With what will we be clothed?' 6:32 For the Gentiles seek after all these things, for your heavenly Father knows that you need all these things. 6:33 But seek first God's Kingdom, and his righteousness; and all these things will be given to you as well. 6:34 Therefore don't be anxious for tomorrow, for tomorrow will be anxious for itself. Each day's own evil is sufficient.

7:1 "Don't judge, so that you won't be judged. 7:2 For with whatever judgment you judge, you will be judged; and with whatever measure you measure, it will be measured to you. 7:3 Why do you see the speck that is in your brother's eye, but don't consider the beam that is in your own eye? 7:4 Or how will you tell your brother, 'Let me remove the speck from your eye;' and behold, the beam is in your own eye? 7:5 You hypocrite! First remove the beam out of your own eye, and then you can see clearly to remove the speck out of your brother's eye.

7:6 "Don't give that which is holy to the dogs, neither throw your pearls before the pigs, lest perhaps they trample them under their feet, and turn and tear you to pieces.

7:7 "Ask, and it will be given you. Seek, and you will find. Knock, and it will be opened for you. 7:8 For everyone who asks receives. He who seeks finds. To him who knocks it will be opened. 7:9 Or who is there among you, who, if his son asks him for bread, will give him a stone? 7:10 Or if he asks for a fish, who will give him a serpent? 7:11 If you then, being evil, know how to give good gifts to your children, how much more will your Father who is in heaven give good things to those who ask him! 7:12 Therefore whatever you desire for men to do to you, you shall also do to them; for this is the law and the prophets.

7:13 "Enter in by the narrow gate; for wide is the gate and broad is the way that leads to destruction, and many are those who enter in by it. 7:14 How narrow is the gate, and restricted is the way that leads to life! Few are those who find it.

7:15 "Beware of false prophets, who come to you in sheep's clothing, but inwardly are ravening wolves. 7:16 By their fruits you will know them. Do you gather grapes from thorns, or figs from thistles? 7:17 Even so, every good tree produces good fruit; but the corrupt tree produces evil fruit. 7:18 A good tree can't produce evil fruit, neither can a corrupt tree produce good fruit. 7:19 Every tree that doesn't grow good fruit is cut down, and thrown into the fire. 7:20 Therefore, by their fruits you will know them.

7:21 Not everyone who says to me, 'Lord, Lord,' will enter into the Kingdom of Heaven; but he who does the will of my Father who is in heaven.

7:22 Many will tell me in that day, 'Lord, Lord, didn't we prophesy in your name, in your name cast out demons, and in your name do many mighty works?' 7:21 Then I will tell them, 'I never knew you. Depart from me, you who work iniquity.'

7:24 "Everyone therefore who hears these words of mine, and does them, I will liken him to a wise man, who built his house on a rock. 7:25 The rain came down, the floods came, and the winds blew, and beat on that house; and it didn't fall, for it was founded on the rock. 7:26 Everyone who hears these words of mine, and doesn't do them will be like a foolish man, who built his house on the sand. 7:27 The rain came down, the floods came, and the winds blew, and beat on that house; and it fell—and great was its fall."

7:28 It happened, when Jesus had finished saying these things, that the multitudes were astonished at his teaching, 7:29 for he taught them with authority, and not like the scribes.

Event 30: Jesus heals a leper
Time: spring 31 A.D.
Place: Galilee

MATTHEW 8:1-4	MARK 1:40-45	LUKE 5:12-16
8:1 When he came down from the mountain, great multitudes followed him.		5:12 It happened, while he was in one of the cities,
8:2 Behold, a leper came to him and worshiped him, saying, "Lord, if you want to, you can make me clean."	1:40 A leper came to him, begging him, kneeling down to him, and saying to him, "If you want to, you can make me clean."	behold, there was a man full of leprosy. When he saw Jesus, he fell on his face, and begged him, saying, "Lord, if you want to, you can make me clean."
8:3 Jesus stretched out his hand, and touched him, saying, "I want to. Be made clean."	1:41 Being moved with compassion, he stretched out his hand, and touched him, and said to him, "I want to. Be made clean.".	5:13 He stretched out his hand, and touched him, saying, "I want to. Be made clean."
Immediately his leprosy was cleansed.	1:42 When he had said this, immediately the leprosy departed from him, and he was made clean.	Immediately the leprosy left him.
8:4 Jesus said to him, "See that you tell nobody, but go, show yourself to the priest, and offer the gift that Moses commanded, as a testimony to them."	1:43 He strictly warned him, and immediately sent him out, 1:44 and said to him, "See you say nothing to anybody, but go show yourself to the priest, and offer for your cleansing the things which Moses commanded, for a testimony to them."	5:14 He commanded him to tell no one, "But go your way, and show yourself to the priest, and offer for your cleansing according to what Moses commanded, for a testimony to them."
	1:45 But he went out, and began to proclaim it much, and to spread about the matter, so that Jesus could no more openly enter into a city, but was outside in desert places: and they came to him from everywhere.	5:15 But the report concerning him spread much more, and great multitudes came together to hear, and to be healed by him of their infirmities. 5:16 But he withdrew himself into the desert, and prayed.

Event 31: Jesus heals a centurion's servant
Time: spring 31 A.D.
Place: Capernaum, Galilee

MATTHEW 8:5-13	LUKE 7:1-10
8:5 When he came into Capernaum,	7:1 After he had finished speaking in the hearing of the people, he entered into Capernaum.
a centurion came to him, asking him, 8:6 and saying, "Lord, my servant lies in the house paralyzed, grievously tormented."	7:2 A certain centurion's servant, who was dear to him, was sick and at the point of death. 7:3 When he heard about Jesus, he sent to him elders of the Jews, asking him to come and save his servant. 7:4 When they came to Jesus, they begged him earnestly, saying, "He is worthy for you to do this for him, 7:5 for he loves our nation, and he built our synagogue for us."
8:7 Jesus said to him, "I will come and heal him."	7:6 Jesus went with them.
8:8 The centurion answered, "Lord, I'm not worthy for you to come under my roof. Just say the word, and my servant will be healed. 8:9 For I am also a man under authority, having under myself soldiers. I tell this one, 'Go,' and he goes; and tell another, 'Come,' and he comes; and tell my servant, 'Do this,' and he does it."	When he was now not far from the house, the centurion sent friends to him, saying to him, "Lord, don't trouble yourself, for I am not worthy for you to come under my roof. 7:7 Therefore I didn't even think myself worthy to come to you; but say the word, and my servant will be healed. 7:8 For I also am a man placed under authority, having under myself soldiers. I tell this one, 'Go!' and he goes; and to another, 'Come!' and he comes; and to my servant, 'Do this,' and he does it."
8:10 When Jesus heard it, he marveled, and said to those who followed, "Most certainly I tell you, I haven't found so great a faith, not even in Israel. 8:11 I tell you that many will come from the east and the west, and will sit down with Abraham, Isaac, and Jacob in the Kingdom of Heaven, 8:12 but the children of the Kingdom will be thrown out into the outer darkness. There will be weeping and gnashing of teeth."	7:9 When Jesus heard these things, he marveled at him, and turned and said to the multitude who followed him, "I tell you, I have not found such great faith, no, not in Israel."
8:13 Jesus said to the centurion, "Go your way. Let it be done for you as you have believed." His servant was healed in that hour.	7:10 Those who were sent, returning to the house, found that the servant who had been sick was well.

Event 32: Jesus raises from the dead the son of the widow of Nain
Time: spring 31 A.D.
Place: Nain, Galilee

LUKE 7:11-17
7:11 It happened soon afterwards, that he went to a city called Nain. Many of his disciples, along with a great multitude, went with him.
7:12 Now when he drew near to the gate of the city, behold, one who was dead was carried out, the only son of his mother, and she was a widow. Many people of the city were with her.
7:13 When the Lord saw her, he had compassion on her, and said to her, "Don't cry."
7:14 He came near and touched the coffin, and the bearers stood still. He said, "Young man, I tell you, arise!"
7:15 He who was dead sat up, and began to speak. And he gave him to his mother.
7:16 Fear took hold of all, and they glorified God, saying, "A great prophet has arisen among us!" and, "God has visited his people!"
7:17 This report went out concerning him in the whole of Judea, and in all the surrounding region.

Event 33: Jesus heals Peter's mother-in-law and others
Time: spring 31A.D.
Place: Capernaum, Galilee

MATTHEW 8:14-17	MARK 1:29-31	LUKE 4:38-39
	1:29 Immediately, when they had come out of the synagogue, they came into the house of Simon and Andrew, with James and John.	4:38 He rose up from the synagogue, and entered into Simon's house.
8:14 When Jesus came into Peter's house, he saw his wife's mother lying sick with a fever.	1:30 Now Simon's wife's mother lay sick with a fever, and immediately they told him about her.	Simon's mother-in-law was afflicted with a great fever, and they begged him for her.
8:15 He touched her hand, and the fever left her.	1:31 He came and took her by the hand, and raised her up. The fever left her,	4:39 He stood over her, and rebuked the fever; and it left her.
She got up and served him. [TR has "Jesus" not him]	and she served them.	Immediately she rose up and served them.
8:16 When evening came, they brought to him many possessed with demons.	1:32 At evening, when the sun had set, they brought to him all who were sick, and those who were possessed by	4:40 When the sun was setting, all those who had any sick with various diseases brought them to him; and he

	demons. 1:33 All the city was gathered together at the door. 1:34 He healed many who were sick with various diseases, and cast out many demons.	laid his hands on every one of them, and healed them.
He cast out the spirits with a word,	He didn't allow the demons to speak, because they knew him.	4:41 Demons also came out from many, crying out, and saying, "You are the Christ, the Son of God!" Rebuking them, he didn't allow them to speak, because they knew that he was the Christ.
and healed all who were sick; 8:17 that it might be fulfilled which was spoken through Isaiah the prophet, saying: "He took our infirmities, and bore our diseases." [Isaiah 53:4]		
		4:42 When it was day, he departed and went into an uninhabited place, and the multitudes looked for him, and came to him, and held on to him, so that he wouldn't go away from them. 4:43 But he said to them, "I must preach the good news of the Kingdom of God to the other cities also. For this reason I have been sent." 4:44 He was preaching in the synagogues of Galilee.

Event 34: Jesus crosses the Sea of Galilee and calms the Sea
Time: spring 31 A.D.
Place: Sea of Galilee

MATTHEW 8:18-27	MARK 4:35-41	LUKE 8:22-26
8:18 Now when Jesus saw great multitudes around him, he gave the order to depart to the other side.		
8:19 A scribe came, and said to him, "Teacher, I will follow you wherever you go."		

8:20 Jesus said to him, "The foxes have holes, and the birds of the sky have nests, but the Son of Man has nowhere to lay his head."		
8:21 Another of his disciples said to him, "Lord, allow me first to go and bury my father."		
8:22 But Jesus said to him, "Follow me, and leave the dead to bury their own dead."		
8:23 When he got into a boat, his disciples followed him.	4:35 On that day, when evening had come, he said to them, "Let's go over to the other side." 4:36 Leaving the multitude, they took him with them, even as he was, in the boat. Other small boats were also with him.	8:22 Now it happened on one of those days, that he entered into a boat, himself and his disciples, and he said to them, "Let's go over to the other side of the lake." So they launched out.
8:24 Behold, a violent storm came up on the sea, so much that the boat was covered with the waves, but he was asleep.	4:37 A big wind storm arose, and the waves beat into the boat, so much that the boat was already filled.	8:23 But as they sailed, he fell asleep. A wind storm came down on the lake, and they were taking on dangerous amounts of water.
8:25 They came to him, and woke him up, saying, "Save us, Lord! We are dying!"	4:38 He himself was in the stern, asleep on the cushion, and they woke him up, and told him, "Teacher, don't you care that we are dying?"	8:24 They came to him, and awoke him, saying, "Master, master, we are dying!"
8:26 He said to them, "Why are you fearful, O you of little faith?" Then he got up, rebuked the wind and the sea, and there was a great calm.	4:39 He awoke, and rebuked the wind, and said to the sea, "Peace! Be still!" The wind ceased, and there was a great calm. 4:40 He said to them, "Why are you so afraid? How is it that you have no faith?"	He awoke, and rebuked the wind and the raging of the water, and they ceased, and it was calm. 8:25 He said to them, "Where is your faith?"
8:27 The men marveled, saying, "What kind of man is this, that even the wind and the sea obey him?"	4:41 They were greatly afraid, and said to one another, "Who then is this, that even the wind and the sea obey him?"	Being afraid they marveled, saying one to another, "Who is this, then, that he commands even the winds and the water, and they obey him?"
		8:26 They arrived at the country of the Gadarenes, which is opposite Galilee.

Event 35: Jesus heals two Gergesene/Gadarene demoniacs
Time: spring 31 A.D.
Place: east side of the Sea of Galilee

MATTHEW 8:28-9:1	MARK 5:1-20	LUKE 8:26-39
8:28 When he came to the other side, into the country of the Gergesenes,	5:1 They came to the other side of the sea, into the country of the Gadarenes.	8:26 They arrived at the country of the Gadarenes, which is opposite Galilee.
two people possessed by demons met him there, coming out of the tombs, exceedingly fierce, so that nobody could pass that way.	5:2 When he had come out of the boat, immediately there met him out of the tombs a man with an unclean spirit,	8:27 When Jesus stepped ashore, a certain man out of the city who had demons for a long time met him.
	5:3 who had his dwelling in the tombs. Nobody could bind him any more, not even with chains, 5:4 because he had been often bound with fetters and chains, and the chains had been torn apart by him, and the fetters broken in pieces. Nobody had the strength to tame him. 5:5 Always, night and day, in the tombs and in the mountains, he was crying out, and cutting himself with stones.	He wore no clothes, and didn't live in a house, but in the tombs.
8:29 Behold, they cried out, saying, "What do we have to do with you, Jesus, Son of God? Have you come here to torment us before the time?"	5:6 When he saw Jesus from afar, he ran and bowed down to him, 5:7 and crying out with a loud voice, he said, "What have I to do with you, Jesus, you Son of the Most High God? I adjure you by God, don't torment me."	8:28 When he saw Jesus, he cried out, and fell down before him, and with a loud voice said, "What do I have to do with you, Jesus, you Son of the Most High God? I beg you, don't torment me!"
	5:8 For he said to him, "Come out of the man, you unclean spirit!"	8:29 For Jesus was commanding the unclean spirit to come out of the man. For the unclean spirit had often seized the man. He was kept under guard, and bound with chains and fetters. Breaking the bands apart, he was driven by the demon into the desert.

	5:9 He asked him, "What is your name?"	8:30 Jesus asked him, "What is your name?"
	He said to him, "My name is Legion, for we are many." 5:10 He begged him much that he would not send them away out of the country.	He said, "Legion," for many demons had entered into him. 8:31 They begged him that he would not command them to go into the abyss.
8:30 Now there was a herd of many pigs feeding far away from them. 8:31 The demons begged him, saying, "If you cast us out, permit us to go away into the herd of pigs."	5:11 Now there was on the mountainside a great herd of pigs feeding. 5:12 All the demons begged him, saying, "Send us into the pigs, that we may enter into them."	8:32 Now there was there a herd of many pigs feeding on the mountain, and they begged him that he would allow them to enter into those.
8:32 He said to them, "Go!"	5:13 At once Jesus gave them permission.	He allowed them.
They came out, and went into the herd of pigs: and behold, the whole herd of pigs rushed down the cliff into the sea, and died in the water.	The unclean spirits came out and entered into the pigs. The herd of about two thousand rushed down the steep bank into the sea, and they were drowned in the sea.	8:33 The demons came out from the man, and entered into the pigs, and the herd rushed down the steep bank into the lake, and were drowned.
8:33 Those who fed them fled, and went away into the city, and told everything, including what happened to those who were possessed with demons.	5:14 Those who fed them fled, and told it in the city and in the country.	8:34 When those who fed them saw what had happened, they fled, and told it in the city and in the country.
8:34 Behold, all the city came out to meet Jesus.	The people came to see what it was that had happened. 5:15	8:35 People went out to see what had happened.
	They came to Jesus, and saw him who had been possessed by demons sitting, clothed, and in his right mind, even him who had the legion; and they were afraid.	They came to Jesus, and found the man from whom the demons had gone out, sitting at Jesus' feet, clothed and in his right mind; and they were afraid.
	5:16 Those who saw it declared to them how it happened to him who was possessed by demons, and about the pigs.	8:36 Those who saw it told them how he who had been possessed by demons was healed.
When they saw him, they begged that he would depart from their borders.	5:17 They began to beg him to depart from their region.	8:37 All the people of the surrounding country of the Gadarenes asked him to depart from them, for they were very much afraid.

	5:18 As he was entering into the boat, he who had been possessed by demons begged him that he might be with him.	He entered into the boat, and returned. 8:38 But the man from whom the demons had gone out begged him that he might go with him,
	5:19 He didn't allow him, but said to him, "Go to your house, to your friends, and tell them what great things the Lord has done for you, and how he had mercy on you."	but Jesus sent him away, saying, 8:39 "Return to your house, and declare what great things God has done for you."
	5:20 He went his way, and began to proclaim in Decapolis how Jesus had done great things for him, and everyone marveled.	He went his way, proclaiming throughout the whole city what great things Jesus had done for him.
9:1 He entered into a boat, and crossed over, and came into his own city.		

Event 36: Jesus heals a paralyzed man and forgives sins
Time: spring 31 A.D.
Place: Capernaum, Galilee

MATTHEW 9:1-8	MARK 2:1-12	LUKE 5:17-26
9:1 He entered into a boat, and crossed over, and came into his own city.	2:1 When he entered again into Capernaum after some days, it was heard that he was in the house.	
	2:2 Immediately many were gathered together, so that there was no more room, not even around the door; and he spoke the word to them.	5:17 It happened on one of those days, that he was teaching; and there were Pharisees and teachers of the law sitting by, who had come out of every village of Galilee, Judea, and Jerusalem. The power of the Lord was with him to heal them.

9:2 Behold, they brought to him a man who was paralyzed, lying on a bed.	2:3 Four people came, carrying a paralytic to him. 2:4 When they could not come near to him for the crowd, they removed the roof where he was. When they had broken it up, they let down the mat that the paralytic was lying on.	5:18 Behold, men brought a paralyzed man on a cot, and they sought to bring him in to lay before Jesus. 5:19 Not finding a way to bring him in because of the multitude, they went up to the housetop, and let him down through the tiles with his cot into the midst before Jesus.
Jesus, seeing their faith, said to the paralytic, "Son, cheer up! Your sins are forgiven you."	2:5 Jesus, seeing their faith, said to the paralytic, "Son, your sins are forgiven you."	5:20 Seeing their faith, he said to him, "Man, your sins are forgiven you."
9:3 Behold, some of the scribes said to themselves, "This man blasphemes."	2:6 But there were some of the scribes sitting there, and reasoning in their hearts, 2:7 "Why does this man speak blasphemies like that? Who can forgive sins but God alone?"	5:21 The scribes and the Pharisees began to reason, saying, "Who is this that speaks blasphemies? Who can forgive sins, but God alone?"
9:4 Jesus, knowing their thoughts, said, "Why do you think evil in your hearts?	2:8 Immediately Jesus, perceiving in his spirit that they so reasoned within themselves, said to them, "Why do you reason these things in your hearts?	5:22 But Jesus, perceiving their thoughts, answered them, "Why are you reasoning so in your hearts?
9:5 For which is easier, to say, 'Your sins are forgiven;' or to say, 'Get up, and walk?'	2:9 Which is easier, to tell the paralytic, 'Your sins are forgiven;' or to say, 'Arise, and take up your bed, and walk?'	5:23 Which is easier to say, 'Your sins are forgiven you;' or to say, 'Arise and walk?'
9:6 But that you may know that the Son of Man has authority on earth to forgive sins..." (then he said to the paralytic), "Get up, and take up your mat, and go up to your house."	2:10 But that you may know that the Son of Man has authority on earth to forgive sins"—he said to the paralytic— 2:11 "I tell you, arise, take up your mat, and go to your house."	5:24 But that you may know that the Son of Man has authority on earth to forgive sins" (he said to the paralyzed man), "I tell you, arise, and take up your cot, and go to your house."
9:7 He arose and departed to his house.	2:12 He arose, and immediately took up the mat, and went out in front of them all;	5:25 Immediately he rose up before them, and took up that which he was laying on, and departed to his house, glorifying God.
9:8 But when the multitudes saw it, they marveled and glorified God, who had given such authority to men.	so that they were all amazed, and glorified God, saying, "We never saw anything like this!"	5:26 Amazement took hold on all, and they glorified God. They were filled with fear, saying, "We have seen strange things today."

Event 37: Jesus meets his future disciple Matthew and dines with sinners
Time: spring 31 A.D.
Place: Capernaum, Galilee

MATTHEW 9:9-17	MARK 2:13-22	LUKE 5:27-39
9:9 As Jesus passed by from there, he saw a man called Matthew sitting at the tax collection office. He said to him, "Follow me." He got up and followed him.	2:13 He went out again by the seaside. All the multitude came to him, and he taught them. 2:14 As he passed by, he saw Levi, the son of Alphaeus, sitting at the tax office, and he said to him, "Follow me." And he arose and followed him.	5:27 After these things he went out, and saw a tax collector named Levi sitting at the tax office, and said to him, "Follow me!" 5:28 He left everything, and rose up and followed him.
9:10 It happened as he sat in the house, behold, many tax collectors and sinners came and sat down with Jesus and his disciples.	2:15 It happened, that he was reclining at the table in his house, and many tax collectors and sinners sat down with Jesus and his disciples, for there were many, and they followed him.	5:29 Levi made a great feast for him in his house. There was a great crowd of tax collectors and others who were reclining with them.
9:11 When the Pharisees saw it, they said to his disciples, "Why does your teacher eat with tax collectors and sinners?"	2:16 The scribes and the Pharisees, when they saw that he was eating with the sinners and tax collectors, said to his disciples, "Why is it that he eats and drinks with tax collectors and sinners?"	5:30 Their scribes and the Pharisees murmured against his disciples, saying, "Why do you eat and drink with the tax collectors and sinners?"
9:12 When Jesus heard it, he said to them, "Those who are healthy have no need for a physician, but those who are sick do.	2:17 When Jesus heard it, he said to them, "Those who are healthy have no need for a physician, but those who are sick.	5:31 Jesus answered them, "Those who are healthy have no need for a physician, but those who are sick do.
9:13 But you go and learn what this means: 'I desire mercy, and not sacrifice,' [Hosea 6:6]		
for I came not to call the righteous, but sinners to repentance." [NU lacks "to repentance]	I came not to call the righteous, but sinners to repentance."	5:32 I have not come to call the righteous, but sinners to repentance."
9:14 Then John's disciples came to him, saying, "Why do we and the Pharisees fast often, but your disciples don't fast?"	2:18 John's disciples and the Pharisees were fasting, and they came and asked him, "Why do John's disciples and the disciples of the Pharisees fast, but your disciples don't fast?"	5:33 They said to him, "Why do John's disciples often fast and pray, likewise also the disciples of the Pharisees, but yours eat and drink?"

9:15 Jesus said to them, "Can the friends of the bridegroom mourn, as long as the bridegroom is with them? But the days will come when the bridegroom will be taken away from them, and then they will fast.	2:19 Jesus said to them, "Can the groomsmen fast while the bridegroom is with them? As long as they have the bridegroom with them, they can't fast. 2:20 But the days will come when the bridegroom will be taken away from them, and then will they fast in that day.	5:34 He said to them, "Can you make the friends of the bridegroom fast, while the bridegroom is with them? 5:35 But the days will come when the bridegroom will be taken away from them. Then they will fast in those days."
		5:36 He also told a parable to them.
9:16 No one puts a piece of unshrunk cloth on an old garment; for the patch would tear away from the garment, and a worse hole is made. 9:17 Neither do people put new wine into old wineskins, or else the skins would burst, and the wine be spilled, and the skins ruined. No, they put new wine into fresh wineskins, and both are preserved."	2:21 No one sews a piece of unshrunk cloth on an old garment, or else the patch shrinks and the new tears away from the old, and a worse hole is made. 2:22 No one puts new wine into old wineskins, or else the new wine will burst the skins, and the wine pours out, and the skins will be destroyed; but they put new wine into fresh wineskins."	"No one puts a piece from a new garment on an old garment, or else he will tear the new, and also the piece from the new will not match the old. 5:37 No one puts new wine into old wineskins, or else the new wine will burst the skins, and it will be spilled, and the skins will be destroyed. 5:38 But new wine must be put into fresh wineskins, and both are preserved. 5:39 No man having drunk old wine immediately desires new, for he says, 'The old is better.'"

Event 38: Jesus heals a hemorrhaging woman and raises Jairus' daughter from the dead
Time: spring 31 A.D.
Place: Galilee

MATTHEW 9:18-26	MARK 5:22-43	LUKE 8:40-56
9:18 While he told these things to them,	5:21 When Jesus had crossed back over in the boat to the other side, a great multitude was gathered to him; and he was by the sea.	8:40 It happened, when Jesus returned, that the multitude welcomed him, for they were all waiting for him.
behold, a ruler came and worshiped him, saying, "My daughter has just died, but come and lay your hand on her, and she will live."	5:22 Behold, one of the rulers of the synagogue, Jairus by name, came; and seeing him, he fell at his feet, 5:23 and begged him much, saying,	8:41 Behold, there came a man named Jairus, and he was a ruler of the synagogue. He fell down at Jesus' feet, and begged him to come into his

	“My little daughter is at the point of death. Please come and lay your hands on her, that she may be made healthy, and live.”	house, 8:42 for he had an only daughter, about twelve years of age, and she was dying.	
9:19 Jesus got up and followed him, as did his disciples.	5:24 He went with him, and a great multitude followed him, and they pressed upon him on all sides.	But as he went, the multitudes pressed against him.	
9:20 Behold, a woman who had an issue of blood for twelve years came behind him, and touched the fringe of his garment; 9:21for she said within herself, “If I just touch his garment, I will be made well.”	5:25 A certain woman, who had an issue of blood for twelve years, 5:26 and had suffered many things by many physicians, and had spent all that she had, and was no better, but rather grew worse, 5:27 having heard the things concerning Jesus, came up behind him in the crowd, and touched his clothes. 5:28 For she said, “If I just touch his clothes, I will be made well.”	8:43 A woman who had a flow of blood for twelve years, who had spent all her living on physicians, and could not be healed by any, 8:44 came behind him, and touched the fringe of his cloak,	
	5:29 Immediately the flow of her blood was dried up, and she felt in her body that she was healed of her affliction.	and immediately the flow of her blood stopped.	
	5:30 Immediately Jesus, perceiving in himself that the power had gone out from him, turned around in the crowd, and asked, “Who touched my clothes?”	8:45 Jesus said, “Who touched me?”	
	5:31 His disciples said to him, “You see the multitude pressing against you, and you say, ‘Who touched me?’”	When all denied it, Peter and those with him said, “Master, the multitudes press and jostle you, and you say, ‘Who touched me?’”	
	5:32 He looked around to see her who had done this thing.	8:46 But Jesus said, “Someone did touch me, for I perceived that power has gone out of me.”	
	5:33 But the woman, fearing and trembling, knowing what had been done to her, came	8:47 When the woman saw that she was not hidden, she came trembling, and falling down before him declared to	

	and fell down before him, and told him all the truth.	him in the presence of all the people the reason why she had touched him, and how she was healed immediately.
9:22 But Jesus, turning around and seeing her, said, "Daughter, cheer up! Your faith has made you well." And the woman was made well from that hour.	5:34 He said to her, "Daughter, your faith has made you well. Go in peace, and be cured of your disease."	8:48 He said to her, "Daughter, cheer up. Your faith has made you well. Go in peace."
	5:35 While he was still speaking, they came from the synagogue ruler's house saying, "Your daughter is dead. Why bother the Teacher any more?"	8:49 While he still spoke, one from the ruler of the synagogue's house came, saying to him, "Your daughter is dead. Don't trouble the Teacher."
	5:36 But Jesus, when he heard the message spoken, immediately said to the ruler of the synagogue, "Don't be afraid, only believe."	8:50 But Jesus hearing it, answered him, "Don't be afraid. Only believe, and she will be healed."
9:23 When Jesus came into the ruler's house, and saw the flute players, and the crowd in noisy disorder, 9:24 he said to them, "Make room,	5:37 He allowed no one to follow him, except Peter, James, and John the brother of James. 5:38 He came to the synagogue ruler's house, and he saw an uproar, weeping, and great wailing.	8:51 When he came to the house, he didn't allow anyone to enter in, except Peter, John, James, the father of the child, and her mother. 8:52 All were weeping and mourning her,
because the girl isn't dead, but sleeping."	5:39 When he had entered in, he said to them, "Why do you make an uproar and weep? The child is not dead, but is asleep."	but he said, "Don't weep. She isn't dead, but sleeping."
They were ridiculing him.	5:40 They ridiculed him.	8:53 They were ridiculing him, knowing that she was dead.
9:25 But when the crowd was put out, he entered in,	But he, having put them all out, took the father of the child and her mother and those who were with him, and went in where the child was lying.	8:54 But he put them all outside,
took her by the hand,	5:41 Taking the child by the hand, he said to her, "Talitha cumi;" which means, being interpreted, "Girl, I tell you, get up."	and taking her by the hand, he called, saying, "Child, arise!"
and the girl arose.	5:42 Immediately the girl rose up, and walked, for she was twelve years old.	8:55 Her spirit returned, and she rose up immediately.

9:26 The report of this went out into all that land.	They were amazed with great amazement. 5:43 He strictly ordered them that no one should know this, and commanded that something should be given to her to eat.	He commanded that something be given to her to eat. 8:56 Her parents were amazed, but he commanded them to tell no one what had been done.

Event 39: Jesus heals two blind men
Time: spring 31 A.D.
Place: Galilee

MATTHEW 9:27-31
9:27 As Jesus passed by from there, two blind men followed him, calling out and saying, "Have mercy on us, son of David!"
9:28 When he had come into the house, the blind men came to him. Jesus said to them, "Do you believe that I am able to do this?"
They told him, "Yes, Lord."
9:29 Then he touched their eyes, saying, "According to your faith be it done to you." 9:30 Their eyes were opened. Jesus strictly commanded them, saying, "See that no one knows about this." 9:31 But they went out and spread abroad his fame in all that land.

Event 40: Jesus heals a mute demoniac
Time: spring 31 A.D.
Place: Galilee

MATTHEW 9:32-34
9:32 As they went out, behold, a mute man who was demon possessed was brought to him. 9:33 When the demon was cast out, the mute man spoke. The multitudes marveled, saying, "Nothing like this has ever been seen in Israel!"
9:34 But the Pharisees said, "By the prince of the demons, he casts out demons."

Event 41: Jesus does a Galilean tour
Time: spring 31A.D.
Place: Galilee

MATTHEW 9:35-38
9:35 Jesus went about all the cities and the villages, teaching in their synagogues, and preaching the Good News of the Kingdom, and healing every disease and every sickness among the people. 9:36 But when he saw the multitudes, he was moved with compassion for them, because they were harassed [TR has instead "weary"] and scattered, like sheep without a shepherd. 9:37 Then he said to his disciples, "The harvest indeed is plentiful, but the laborers are few. 9:38 Pray therefore that the Lord of the harvest will send out laborers into his harvest."

Event 42: Jesus chooses 12 disciples for a Jewish ministry
Time: spring 31 A.D.
Place: Galilee

MATTHEW 10:1-42	MARK 3:13-19 MARK 6:6-23	LUKE 6:12-19 LUKE 8:1-3 LUKE 9:1-6
	3:13 He went up into the mountain,	6:12 It happened in these days, that he went out to the mountain to pray, and he continued all night in prayer to God.
	and called to himself those whom he wanted, and they went to him.	
10:1 He called to himself his twelve disciples,	3:14 He appointed twelve,	6:13 When it was day, he called his disciples, and from them he chose twelve, whom he also named apostles:
and gave them authority over unclean spirits, to cast them out, and to heal every disease and every sickness.	that they might be with him, and that he might send them out to preach, 3:15 and to have authority to heal sicknesses and to cast out demons:	
10:2 Now the names of the twelve apostles are these.		
The first, Simon, who is called Peter; Andrew, his brother; James the son of Zebedee; John, his brother;	3:16 Simon, to whom he gave the name Peter; 3:17 James the son of Zebedee; John, the brother of James, and he surnamed them Boanerges, which means, Sons of Thunder;	6:14 Simon, whom he also named Peter; Andrew, his brother; James; John;
10:3 Philip; Bartholomew; Thomas; Matthew the tax collector;	3:18 Andrew; Philip; Bartholomew; Matthew; Thomas;	Philip; Bartholomew; 6:15 Matthew; Thomas;
James the son of Alphaeus; Lebbaeus, whose surname was [NU lacks "Lebbaeus, whose surname was"] Thaddaeus; 10:4 Simon the Canaanite; and Judas Iscariot, who also betrayed him.	James, the son of Alphaeus; Thaddaeus; Simon the Zealot; 3:19 and Judas Iscariot, who also betrayed him.	James, the son of Alphaeus; Simon, who was called the Zealot; 6:16 Judas the son of James; and Judas Iscariot, who also became a traitor.

		6:17 He came down with them, and stood on a level place, with a crowd of his disciples, and a great number of the people from all Judea and Jerusalem, and the sea coast of Tyre and Sidon, who came to hear him and to be healed of their diseases; 6:18 as well as those who were troubled by unclean spirits, and they were being healed. 6:19 All the multitude sought to touch him, for power came out from him and healed them all.
10:5 Jesus sent these twelve out, and commanded them, saying,	6:6 He marveled because of their unbelief. He went around the villages teaching. 6:7 He called to himself the twelve, and began to send them out two by two;	8:1 It happened soon afterwards, that he went about through cities and villages, preaching and bringing the good news of the Kingdom of God. With him were the twelve,
		8:2 and certain women who had been healed of evil spirits and infirmities: Mary who was called Magdalene, from whom seven demons had gone out; 8:3 and Joanna, the wife of Chuzas, Herod's steward; Susanna; and many others; who served them from their possessions.
"Don't go among the Gentiles, and don't enter into any city of the Samaritans. 10:6 Rather, go to the lost sheep of the house of Israel.		
10:7 As you go, preach, saying, 'The Kingdom of Heaven is at hand!' 10:8 Heal the sick, cleanse the lepers, [TR adds "raise the dead"] and cast out demons.		9:1 He called the twelve [TR has instead of the twelve "his twelve disciples"] together, and gave them power and authority over all demons, and to cure diseases. 9:2 He sent them forth to preach the Kingdom of God, and to heal the sick.

Freely you received, so freely give. 10:9 Don't take any gold, nor silver, nor brass in your money belts. 10:10 Take no bag for your journey, neither two coats, nor shoes, nor staff: for the laborer is worthy of his food.		9:3 He said to them, "Take nothing for your journey—neither staffs, nor wallet, nor bread, nor money; neither have two coats apiece.
10:11 Into whatever city or village you enter, find out who in it is worthy; and stay there until you go on. 10:12 As you enter into the household, greet it. 10:13 If the household is worthy, let your peace come on it, but if it isn't worthy, let your peace return to you.		9:4 Into whatever house you enter, stay there, and depart from there.
10:14 Whoever doesn't receive you, nor hear your words, as you go out of that house or that city, shake off the dust from your feet.		9:5 As many as don't receive you, when you depart from that city, shake off even the dust from your feet for a testimony against them."
10:15 Most certainly I tell you, it will be more tolerable for the land of Sodom and Gomorrah in the day of judgment than for that city.		
10:16 "Behold, I send you out as sheep in the midst of wolves. Therefore be wise as serpents, and harmless as doves.		
10:17 But beware of men: for they will deliver you up to councils, and in their synagogues they will scourge you. 10:18 Yes, and you will be brought before governors and kings for my sake, for a testimony to them and to the nations.		

10:19 But when they deliver you up, don't be anxious how or what you will say, for it will be given you in that hour what you will say. 10:20 For it is not you who speak, but the Spirit of your Father who speaks in you.		
10:21 "Brother will deliver up brother to death, and the father his child. Children will rise up against parents, and cause them to be put to death. 10:22 You will be hated by all men for my name's sake, but he who endures to the end will be saved.		
10:23 But when they persecute you in this city, flee into the next, for most certainly I tell you, you will not have gone through the cities of Israel, until the Son of Man has come.		
10:24 "A disciple is not above his teacher, nor a servant above his lord. 10:25 It is enough for the disciple that he be like his teacher, and the servant like his lord. If they have called the master of the house Beelzebul, how much more those of his household!		
10:26 Therefore don't be afraid of them, for there is nothing covered that will not be revealed; and hidden that will not be known. 10:27		
What I tell you in the darkness, speak in the light; and what you hear whispered in the ear, proclaim on the housetops.		

10:28 Don't be afraid of those who kill the body, but are not able to kill the soul. Rather, fear him who is able to destroy both soul and body in Gehenna. [Hell] 10:29		
"Aren't two sparrows sold for an assarion coin? [a 1/2 hr wage of an agricultural labourer] Not one of them falls on the ground apart from your Father's will, 10:30 but the very hairs of your head are all numbered. 10:31Therefore don't be afraid. You are of more value than many sparrows.		
10:32 Everyone therefore who confesses me before men, him I will also confess before my Father who is in heaven.		
10:33 But whoever denies me before men, him I will also deny before my Father who is in heaven.		
10:34 "Don't think that I came to send peace on the earth. I didn't come to send peace, but a sword. 10:35 For I came to set a man at odds against his father, and a daughter against her mother, and a daughter-in-law against her mother-in-law. 10:36 A man's foes will be those of his own household. [Micah 7:6] 10:37 He who loves father or mother more than me is not worthy of me; and he who loves son or daughter more than me isn't worthy of me. 10:38 He who doesn't take his cross and follow after me, isn't worthy of me.		

10:39 He who seeks his life will lose it; and he who loses his life for my sake will find it.		
10:40 He who receives you receives me, and he who receives me receives him who sent me.		
10:41 He who receives a prophet in the name of a prophet will receive a prophet's reward: and he who receives a righteous man in the name of a righteous man will receive a righteous man's reward.		
10:42 Whoever gives one of these little ones just a cup of cold water to drink in the name of a disciple, most certainly I tell you he will in no way lose his reward."		
	and he gave them authority over the unclean spirits.	
	6:8 He commanded them that they should take nothing for their journey, except a staff only: no bread, no wallet, no money in their purse, 6:9 but to wear sandals, and not put on two tunics.	
	6:10 He said to them, "Wherever you enter into a house, stay there until you depart from there.	
	6:11 Whoever will not receive you nor hear you, as you depart from there, shake off the dust that is under your feet for a testimony against them.	
	Assuredly, I tell you, it will be more tolerable for Sodom and Gomorrah in the day of judgment than for that city!"	

	6:12 They went out and preached that people should repent. 6:13 They cast out many demons, and anointed many with oil who were sick, and healed them.	9:6 They departed, and went throughout the villages, preaching the Good News, and healing everywhere.
	6:14 King Herod heard this, for his name had become known, and he said, "John the Baptizer has risen from the dead, and therefore these powers are at work in him." 6:15 But others said, "He is Elijah." Others said, "He is a prophet, or like one of the prophets." 6:16 But Herod, when he heard this, said, "This is John, whom I beheaded. He has risen from the dead."	9:7 Now Herod the tetrarch heard of all that was done by him; and he was very perplexed, because it was said by some that John had risen from the dead, 9:8 and by some that Elijah had appeared, and by others that one of the old prophets had risen again. 9:9 Herod said, "John I beheaded, but who is this, about whom I hear such things?" He sought to see him.
	6:17 For Herod himself had sent out and arrested John, and bound him in prison for the sake of Herodias, his brother Philip's wife, for he had married her. 6:18 For John said to Herod, "It is not lawful for you to have your brother's wife." 6:19 Herodias set herself against him, and desired to kill him, but she couldn't, 6:20 for Herod feared John, knowing that he was a righteous and holy man, and kept him safe. When he heard him, he did many things, and he heard him gladly.	
	6:21 Then a convenient day came, that Herod on his birthday made a supper for his nobles, the high officers, and the chief men of Galilee. 6:22 When the daughter of	

	Herodias herself came in and danced, she pleased Herod and those sitting with him. The king said to the young lady, "Ask me whatever you want, and I will give it to you." 6:23 He swore to her, "Whatever you shall ask of me, I will give you, up to half of my kingdom." 6:24 She went out, and said to her mother, "What shall I ask?"	
	She said, "The head of John the Baptizer."	
	6:25 She came in immediately with haste to the king, and asked, "I want you to give me right now the head of John the Baptizer on a platter."	
	6:26 The king was exceedingly sorry, but for the sake of his oaths, and of his dinner guests, he didn't wish to refuse her. 6:27 Immediately the king sent out a soldier of his guard, and commanded to bring John's head, and he went and beheaded him in the prison, 6:28 and brought his head on a platter, and gave it to the young lady; and the young lady gave it to her mother.	
	6:29 When his disciples heard this, they came and took up his corpse, and laid it in a tomb.	
	6:30 The apostles gathered themselves together to Jesus, and they told him all things, whatever they had done, and whatever they had taught.	9:10 The apostles, when they had returned, told him what things they had done.

Event 43: Jesus delivers the Sermon on the Plain
Time: spring 31 A.D.
Place: Galilee

LUKE 6:17-49
6:17 He came down with them, and stood on a level place, with a crowd of his disciples, and a great number of the people from all Judea and Jerusalem, and the sea coast of Tyre and Sidon, who came to hear him and to be healed of their diseases; 6:18 as well as those who were troubled by unclean spirits, and they were being healed. 6:19 All the multitude sought to touch him, for power came out from him and healed them all.
6:20 He lifted up his eyes to his disciples, and said,
"Blessed are you who are poor, for yours is the Kingdom of God. 6:21 Blessed are you who hunger now, for you will be filled. Blessed are you who weep now, for you will laugh. 6:22 Blessed are you when men shall hate you, and when they shall exclude and mock you, and throw out your name as evil, for the Son of Man's sake. 6:23 Rejoice in that day, and leap for joy, for behold, your reward is great in heaven, for their fathers did the same thing to the prophets.
6:24 "But woe to you who are rich! For you have received your consolation. 6:25 Woe to you, you who are full now, for you will be hungry. Woe to you who laugh now, for you will mourn and weep. 6:26 Woe [TR adds "to you"], when men speak well of you, for their fathers did the same thing to [TR adds "all"] the false prophets.
6:27 "But I tell you who hear: love your enemies, do good to those who hate you, 6:28 bless those who curse you, and pray for those who mistreat you. 6:29 To him who strikes you on the cheek, offer also the other; and from him who takes away your cloak, don't withhold your coat also. 6:30 Give to everyone who asks you, and don't ask him who takes away your goods to give them back again.
6:31 "As you would like people to do to you, do exactly so to them,
6:32 If you love those who love you, what credit is that to you? For even sinners love those who love them. 6:33 If you do good to those who do good to you, what credit is that to you? For even sinners do the same. 6:34 If you lend to those from whom you hope to receive, what credit is that to you? Even sinners lend to sinners, to receive back as much. 6:35 But love your enemies, and do good, and lend, expecting nothing back; and your reward will be great, and you will be children of the Most High; for he is kind toward the unthankful and evil.
6:36 Therefore be merciful, even as your Father is also merciful.

6:37 Don't judge, and you won't be judged. Don't condemn, and you won't be condemned. Set free, and you will be set free.
6:38 "Give, and it will be given to you: good measure, pressed down, shaken together, and running over, will be given to you. For with the same measure you measure it will be measured back to you."
6:39 He spoke a parable to them. "Can the blind guide the blind? Won't they both fall into a pit?
6:40 A disciple is not above his teacher, but everyone when he is fully trained will be like his teacher.
6:41 Why do you see the speck of chaff that is in your brother's eye, but don't consider the beam that is in your own eye? 6:42 Or how can you tell your brother, 'Brother, let me remove the speck of chaff that is in your eye,' when you yourself don't see the beam that is in your own eye? You hypocrite! First remove the beam from your own eye, and then you can see clearly to remove the speck of chaff that is in your brother's eye.
6:43 For there is no good tree that brings forth rotten fruit; nor again a rotten tree that brings forth good fruit. 6:44 For each tree is known by its own fruit. For people don't gather figs from thorns, nor do they gather grapes from a bramble bush. 6:45 The good man out of the good treasure of his heart brings out that which is good, and the evil man out of the evil treasure of his heart brings out that which is evil, for out of the abundance of the heart, his mouth speaks.
6:46 "Why do you call me, 'Lord, Lord,' and don't do the things which I say? 6:47 Everyone who comes to me, and hears my words, and does them, I will show you who he is like. 6:48 He is like a man building a house, who dug and went deep, and laid a foundation on the rock. When a flood arose, the stream broke against that house, and could not shake it, because it was founded on the rock. 6:49 But he who hears, and doesn't do, is like a man who built a house on the earth without a foundation, against which the stream broke, and immediately it fell, and the ruin of that house was great."

Event 44: John the Baptist, through disciples, questions Jesus about his ministry
Time: spring 31 A.D.
Place: Galilee

MATTHEW 11:1-30	LUKE 7:18-35
11:1 It happened that when Jesus had finished directing his twelve disciples, he departed from there to teach and preach in their cities.	
	7:18 The disciples of John told him about all these things.

11:2 Now when John heard in the prison the works of Christ, he sent two of his disciples 11:3 and said to him, "Are you he who comes, or should we look for another?"	7:19 John, calling to himself two of his disciples, sent them to Jesus, saying, "Are you the one who is coming, or should we look for another?" 7:20 When the men had come to him, they said, "John the Baptizer has sent us to you, saying, 'Are you he who comes, or should we look for another?'"
	7:21 In that hour he cured many of diseases and plagues and evil spirits; and to many who were blind he gave sight.
11:4 Jesus answered them, "Go and tell John the things which you hear and see: 11:5 the blind receive their sight, the lame walk, the lepers are cleansed, the deaf hear, the dead are raised up, and the poor have good news preached to them. [Isaiah 35:5; 61:1-4] 11:6 Blessed is he who finds no occasion for stumbling in me."	7:22 Jesus answered them, "Go and tell John the things which you have seen and heard: that the blind receive their sight, the lame walk, the lepers are cleansed, the deaf hear, the dead are raised up, and the poor have good news preached to them. [Isaiah 35:5; 61:1-4] 7:23 Blessed is he who is not offended by me."
11:7 As these went their way, Jesus began to say to the multitudes concerning John,	7:24 When John's messengers had departed, he began to tell the multitudes about John,
"What did you go out into the wilderness to see? A reed shaken by the wind? 11:8 But what did you go out to see? A man in soft clothing? Behold, those who wear soft clothing are in king's houses. 11:9 But why did you go out? To see a prophet?	"What did you go out into the wilderness to see? A reed shaken by the wind? 7:25 But what did you go out to see? A man clothed in soft clothing? Behold, those who are gorgeously dressed, and live delicately, are in kings' courts. 7:26 But what did you go out to see? A prophet?
Yes, I tell you, and much more than a prophet. 11:10 For this is he, of whom it is written, 'Behold, I send my messenger before your face, who will prepare your way before you.' [Malachi 3:1]	Yes, I tell you, and much more than a prophet. 7:27 This is he of whom it is written, 'Behold, I send my messenger before your face, who will prepare your way before you.' [Malachi 3:1]
11:11 Most certainly I tell you, among those who are born of women there has not arisen anyone greater than John the Baptizer; yet he who is least in the Kingdom of Heaven is greater than he.	7:28 "For I tell you, among those who are born of women there is not a greater prophet than John the Baptizer, yet he who is least in the Kingdom of God is greater than he."
	7:29 When all the people and the tax collectors heard this, they declared God to be just, having been baptized with John's baptism.
	7:30 But the Pharisees and the lawyers rejected the counsel of God, not being baptized by him themselves.
11:12 From the days of John the Baptizer until now, the Kingdom of Heaven suffers violence, and the violent take it by force. 11:13 For all the prophets and the law prophesied until John.	

11:14 If you are willing to receive it, this is Elijah, who is to come. 11:15 He who has ears to hear, let him hear.	
11:16 "But to what shall I compare this generation? It is like children sitting in the marketplaces, who call to their companions 11:17 and say, 'We played the flute for you, and you didn't dance. We mourned for you, and you didn't lament.' 11:18 For John came neither eating nor drinking, and they say, 'He has a demon.' 11:19 The Son of Man came eating and drinking, and they say, 'Behold, a gluttonous man and a drunkard, a friend of tax collectors and sinners!' But wisdom is justified by her children." [NU has "actions" not children]	7:31 "[TR adds "But the Lord said"] To what then will I liken the people of this generation? What are they like? 7:32 They are like children who sit in the marketplace, and call one to another, saying, 'We piped to you, and you didn't dance. We mourned, and you didn't weep.' 7:33 For John the Baptizer came neither eating bread nor drinking wine, and you say, 'He has a demon.' 7:34 The Son of Man has come eating and drinking, and you say, 'Behold, a gluttonous man, and a drunkard; a friend of tax collectors and sinners!' 7:35 Wisdom is justified by all her children."
11:20 Then he began to denounce the cities in which most of his mighty works had been done, because they didn't repent. 11:21 "Woe to you, Chorazin! Woe to you, Bethsaida! For if the mighty works had been done in Tyre and Sidon which were done in you, they would have repented long ago in sackcloth and ashes. 11:22 But I tell you, it will be more tolerable for Tyre and Sidon on the day of judgment than for you. 11:23 You, Capernaum, who are exalted to heaven, you will go down to Hades. [Hell] For if the mighty works had been done in Sodom which were done in you, it would have remained until this day. 11:24 But I tell you that it will be more tolerable for the land of Sodom, on the day of judgment, than for you."	
11:25 At that time, Jesus answered, "I thank you, Father, Lord of heaven and earth, that you hid these things from the wise and understanding, and revealed them to infants. 11:26 Yes, Father, for so it was well-pleasing in your sight. 11:27 All things have been delivered to me by my Father.	
No one knows the Son, except the Father; neither does anyone know the Father, except the Son, and he to whom the Son desires to reveal him.	

11:28 "Come to me, all you who labor and are heavily burdened, and I will give you rest. 11:29 Take my yoke upon you, and learn from me, for I am gentle and lowly in heart; and you will find rest for your souls. 11:30 For my yoke is easy, and my burden is light."	

Event 45: Jesus dines at the house of Simon the Pharisee
Time: spring 31 A.D.
Place: Galilee

LUKE 7:36-50
7:36 One of the Pharisees invited him to eat with him. He entered into the Pharisee's house, and sat at the table.
7:37 Behold, a woman in the city who was a sinner, when she knew that he was reclining in the Pharisee's house, she brought an alabaster jar of ointment. 7:38 Standing behind at his feet weeping, she began to wet his feet with her tears, and she wiped them with the hair of her head, kissed his feet, and anointed them with the ointment.
7:39 Now when the Pharisee who had invited him saw it, he said to himself, "This man, if he were a prophet, would have perceived who and what kind of woman this is who touches him, that she is a sinner."
7:40 Jesus answered him, "Simon, I have something to tell you."
He said, "Teacher, say on."
7:41 "A certain lender had two debtors. The one owed five hundred denarii, and the other fifty. 7:42 When they couldn't pay, he forgave them both. Which of them therefore will love him most?"
7:43 Simon answered, "He, I suppose, to whom he forgave the most."
He said to him, "You have judged correctly."
7:44 Turning to the woman, he said to Simon, "Do you see this woman? I entered into your house, and you gave me no water for my feet, but she has wet my feet with her tears, and wiped them with the hair of her head. 7:45 You gave me no kiss, but she, since the time I came in, has not ceased to kiss my feet. 7:46 You didn't anoint my head with oil, but she has anointed my feet with ointment. 7:47 Therefore I tell you, her sins, which are many, are forgiven, for she loved much. But to whom little is forgiven, the same loves little." 7:48 He said to her, "Your sins are forgiven."
7:49 Those who sat at the table with him began to say to themselves, "Who is this who even forgives sins?"
7:50 He said to the woman, "Your faith has saved you. Go in peace."

Event 46: Jesus is walking by a grain field and his disciples pluck grain on the Sabbath
Time: spring 31 A.D.
Place: somewhere in Galilee

MATTHEW 12:1-8	MARK 2:23-28	LUKE 6:1-5
12:1 At that time, Jesus went on the Sabbath day through the grain fields. His disciples were hungry and began to pluck heads of grain and to eat.	2:23 It happened that he was going on the Sabbath day through the grain fields, and his disciples began, as they went, to pluck the ears of grain.	6:1 Now it happened on the second Sabbath after the first, that he was going through the grain fields. His disciples plucked the heads of grain, and ate, rubbing them in their hands.
12:2 But the Pharisees, when they saw it, said to him, "Behold, your disciples do what is not lawful to do on the Sabbath."	2:24 The Pharisees said to him, "Behold, why do they do that which is not lawful on the Sabbath day?"	6:2 But some of the Pharisees said to them, "Why do you do that which is not lawful to do on the Sabbath day?"
12:3 But he said to them, "Haven't you read what David did, when he was hungry, and those who were with him; 12:4 how he entered into the house of God, and ate the show bread, which was not lawful for him to eat, neither for those who were with him, but only for the priests? [1 Samuel 21:3-6]	2:25 He said to them, "Did you never read what David did, when he had need, and was hungry—he, and those who were with him? 2:26 How he entered into the house of God when Abiathar was high priest, and ate the show bread, which is not lawful to eat except for the priests, and gave also to those who were with him?"	6:3 Jesus, answering them, said, "Haven't you read what David did when he was hungry, he, and those who were with him; 6:4 how he entered into the house of God, and took and ate the show bread, and gave also to those who were with him, which is not lawful to eat except for the priests alone?"
12:5 Or have you not read in the law, that on the Sabbath day, the priests in the temple profane the Sabbath, and are guiltless?		
12:6 But I tell you that one greater than the temple is here.		
12:7 But if you had known what this means, 'I desire mercy, and not sacrifice,' [Hosea 6:6] you would not have condemned the guiltless.		
12:8 For the Son of Man is Lord of the Sabbath."	2:27 He said to them, "The Sabbath was made for man, not man for the Sabbath. 2:28 Therefore the Son of Man is lord even of the Sabbath."	6:5 He said to them, "The Son of Man is lord of the Sabbath."

Event 47: Jesus heals a man with a withered hand on the Sabbath
Time: late spring 31 A.D.
Place: Galilee

MATTHEW 12:9-14	MARK 3:1-6	LUKE 6:6-11
12:9 He departed there, and went into their synagogue. 12:10 And behold there was a man with a withered hand	3:1 He entered again into the synagogue, and there was a man there who had his hand withered.	6:6 It also happened on another Sabbath that he entered into the synagogue and taught. There was a man there, and his right hand was withered.
They asked him, "Is it lawful to heal on the Sabbath day?" that they might accuse him.	3:2 They watched him, whether he would heal him on the Sabbath day, that they might accuse him.	6:7 The scribes and the Pharisees watched him, to see whether he would heal on the Sabbath, that they might find an accusation against him.
	3:3 He said to the man who had his hand withered, "Stand up."	6:8 But he knew their thoughts; and he said to the man who had the withered hand, "Rise up, and stand in the middle." He arose and stood.
12:11 He said to them, "What man is there among you, who has one sheep, and if this one falls into a pit on the Sabbath day, won't he grab on to it, and lift it out? 12:12 Of how much more value then is a man than a sheep!		
Therefore it is lawful to do good on the Sabbath day."	3:4 He said to them, "Is it lawful on the Sabbath day to do good, or to do harm? To save a life, or to kill?" But they were silent.	6:9 Then Jesus said to them, "I will ask you something: Is it lawful on the Sabbath to do good, or to do harm? To save a life, or to kill?"
12:13 Then he told the man, "Stretch out your hand." He stretched it out; and it was restored whole, just like the other.	3:5 When he had looked around at them with anger, being grieved at the hardening of their hearts, he said to the man, "Stretch out your hand." He stretched it out, and his hand was restored as healthy as the other.	6:10 He looked around at them all, and said to the man, "Stretch out your hand." He did, and his hand was restored as sound as the other.

12:14 But the Pharisees went out, and conspired against him, how they might destroy him.	3:6 The Pharisees went out, and immediately conspired with the Herodians against him, how they might destroy him.	6:11 But they were filled with rage, and talked with one another about what they might do to Jesus.
12:15 Jesus, perceiving that, withdrew from there. Great multitudes followed him; and he healed them all, 12:16 and commanded them that they should not make him known:		
12:17 that it might be fulfilled which was spoken through Isaiah the prophet, saying, 12:18 "Behold, my servant whom I have chosen; my beloved in whom my soul is well pleased: I will put my Spirit on him. He will proclaim justice to the nations. 12:19 He will not strive, nor shout; neither will anyone hear his voice in the streets. 12:20 He won't break a bruised reed. He won't quench a smoking flax, until he leads justice to victory. 12:21 In his name, the nations will hope." [Isaiah 42:1-4]		

Event 48: Jesus heals a blind mute demoniac
Time: late spring 31 A.D.
Place: Galilee

MATTHEW 12:22-27	MARK 3:19-35
12:22 Then one possessed by a demon, blind and mute, was brought to him and he healed him, so that the blind and mute man both spoke and saw.	
12:23 All the multitudes were amazed, and said, "Can this be the son of David?"	
	He came into a house. 3:20 The multitude came together again, so that they could not so much as eat bread. 3:21 When his friends heard it, they went out to seize him: for they said, "He is insane."

12:24 But when the Pharisees heard it, they said, "This man does not cast out demons, except by Beelzebul, the prince of the demons."	3:22 The scribes who came down from Jerusalem said, "He has Beelzebul," and, "By the prince of the demons he casts out the demons."
12:25 Knowing their thoughts, Jesus said to them, "Every kingdom divided against itself is brought to desolation, and every city or house divided against itself will not stand. 12:26 If Satan casts out Satan, he is divided against himself. How then will his kingdom stand?	3:23 He summoned them, and said to them in parables, "How can Satan cast out Satan? 3:24 If a kingdom is divided against itself, that kingdom cannot stand. 3:25 If a house is divided against itself, that house cannot stand.
	3:26 If Satan has risen up against himself, and is divided, he can't stand, but has an end.
12:27 If I by Beelzebul cast out demons, by whom do your children cast them out? Therefore they will be your judges.	
12:28 But if I by the Spirit of God cast out demons, then the Kingdom of God has come upon you.	
12:29 Or how can one enter into the house of the strong man, and plunder his goods, unless he first bind the strong man? Then he will plunder his house.	3:27 But no one can enter into the house of the strong man to plunder, unless he first binds the strong man; and then he will plunder his house.
12:30 "He who is not with me is against me, and he who doesn't gather with me, scatters.	
12:31 Therefore I tell you, every sin and blasphemy will be forgiven men, but the blasphemy against the Spirit will not be forgiven men. 12:32 Whoever speaks a word against the Son of Man, it will be forgiven him; but whoever speaks against the Holy Spirit, it will not be forgiven him, neither in this age, nor in that which is to come.	3:28 Most certainly I tell you, all sins of the descendants of man will be forgiven, including their blasphemies with which they may blaspheme; 3:29 but whoever may blaspheme against the Holy Spirit never has forgiveness, but is guilty of an eternal sin" 3:30 —because they said, "He has an unclean spirit."
12:33 "Either make the tree good, and its fruit good, or make the tree corrupt, and its fruit corrupt; for the tree is known by its fruit. 12:34 You offspring of vipers, how can you, being evil, speak good things? For out of the abundance of the heart, the mouth speaks. 12:35 The good man out of his good treasure brings out good things [TR adds "of the heart"], and the evil man out of his evil treasure brings out evil things. 12:36 I tell you that every idle word that men speak, they will give account of it in the day of judgment. 12:37 For by your words you will be justified, and by your words you will be condemned."	

12:38 Then certain of the scribes and Pharisees answered, "Teacher, we want to see a sign from you."	
12:39 But he answered them, "An evil and adulterous generation seeks after a sign, but no sign will be given it but the sign of Jonah the prophet. 12:40 For as Jonah was three days and three nights in the belly of the whale, so will the Son of Man be three days and three nights in the heart of the earth. 12:41 The men of Nineveh will stand up in the judgment with this generation, and will condemn it, for they repented at the preaching of Jonah; and behold, someone greater than Jonah is here. 12:42 The queen of the south will rise up in the judgment with this generation, and will condemn it, for she came from the ends of the earth to hear the wisdom of Solomon; and behold, someone greater than Solomon is here.	
12:43 But the unclean spirit, when he is gone out of the man, passes through waterless places, seeking rest, and doesn't find it. 12:44 Then he says, 'I will return into my house from which I came out,' and when he has come back, he finds it empty, swept, and put in order. 12:45 Then he goes, and takes with himself seven other spirits more evil than he is, and they enter in and dwell there. The last state of that man becomes worse than the first. Even so will it be also to this evil generation."	
12:46 While he was yet speaking to the multitudes, behold, his mother and his brothers stood outside, seeking to speak to him. 12:47 One said to him, "Behold, your mother and your brothers stand outside, seeking to speak to you.	3:31 His mother and his brothers came, and standing outside, they sent to him, calling him. 3:32 A multitude was sitting around him, and they told him, "Behold, your mother, your brothers, and your sisters [TR lacks "and your sisters] are outside looking for you."
12:48 But he answered him who spoke to him, "Who is my mother? Who are my brothers?" 12:49 He stretched out his hand towards his disciples, and said, "Behold, my mother and my brothers! 12:50 For whoever does the will of my Father who is in heaven, he is my brother, and sister, and mother."	3:33 He answered them, "Who are my mother and my brothers?" 3:34 Looking around at those who sat around him, he said, "Behold, my mother and my brothers! 3:35 For whoever does the will of God, the same is my brother, and my sister, and mother."

Event 49: Jesus delivers a series of parables on the kingdom of heaven
Time: late spring 31 A.D.
Place: Galilee

MATTHEW 13:1-52	MARK 4:1-34	LUKE 8:4-18
13:1 On that day Jesus went out of the house, and sat by the seaside.	4:1 Again he began to teach by the seaside.	
13:2 Great multitudes gathered to him, so that he entered into a boat, and sat, and all the multitude stood on the beach. 13:3 He spoke to them many things in parables, saying,	A great multitude was gathered to him, so that he entered into a boat in the sea, and sat down. All the multitude were on the land by the sea. 4:2 He He taught them many things in parables, and told them in his teaching,	8:4 When a great multitude came together, and people from every city were coming to him, he spoke by a parable.
"Behold, a farmer went out to sow. 13:4 As he sowed, some seeds fell by the roadside, and the birds came and devoured them.	4:3 "Listen! Behold, the farmer went out to sow, 4:4 and it happened, as he sowed, some seed fell by the road, and the birds [TR adds "of the air"] came and devoured it.	8:5 "The farmer went out to sow his seed. As he sowed, some fell along the road, and it was trampled under foot, and the birds of the sky devoured it.
13:5 Others fell on rocky ground, where they didn't have much soil, and immediately they sprang up, because they had no depth of earth. 13:6 When the sun had risen, they were scorched. Because they had no root, they withered away.	4:5 Others fell on the rocky ground, where it had little soil, and immediately it sprang up, because it had no depth of soil. 4:6 When the sun had risen, it was scorched; and because it had no root, it withered away.	8:6 Other seed fell on the rock, and as soon as it grew, it withered away, because it had no moisture.
13:7 Others fell among thorns. The thorns grew up and choked them:	4:7 Others fell among the thorns, and the thorns grew up, and choked it, and it yielded no fruit.	8:7 Other fell amid the thorns, and the thorns grew with it, and choked it.
13:8 and others fell on good soil, and yielded fruit: some one hundred times as much, some sixty, and some thirty.	4:8 Others fell into the good ground, and yielded fruit, growing up and increasing. Some brought forth thirty times, some sixty times, and some one hundred times as much."	8:8 Other fell into the good ground, and grew, and brought forth fruit one hundred times."
13:9 He who has ears to hear, let him hear."	4:9 He said, "Whoever has ears to hear, let him hear."	As he said these things, he called out, "He who has ears to hear, let him hear!"

13:10 The disciples came, and said to him, "Why do you speak to them in parables?"	4:10 When he was alone, those who were around him with the twelve asked him about the parables.	8:9 Then his disciples asked him, "What does this parable mean?"
13:11 He answered them, "To you it is given to know the mysteries of the Kingdom of Heaven, but it is not given to them.	4:11 He said to them, "To you is given the mystery of the Kingdom of God, but to those who are outside, all things are done in parables,	8:10 He said, "To you it is given to know the mysteries of the Kingdom of God, but to the rest in parables;
13:12 For whoever has, to him will be given, and he will have abundance, but whoever doesn't have, from him will be taken away even that which he has.		
13:13 Therefore I speak to them in parables, because seeing they don't see, and hearing, they don't hear, neither do they understand. 13:14 In them the prophecy of Isaiah is fulfilled, which says, 'By hearing you will hear, and will in no way understand; Seeing you will see, and will in no way perceive: 13:15 for this people's heart has grown callous, their ears are dull of hearing, they have closed their eyes; or else perhaps they might perceive with their eyes, hear with their ears, understand with their heart, and should turn again; and I would heal them.' [Isaiah 6:9-10]	4:12 that 'seeing they may see, and not perceive; and hearing they may hear, and not understand; lest perhaps they should turn again, and their sins should be forgiven them.'" [Isaiah 6:9-10]	that 'seeing they may not see, and hearing they may not understand.' [Isaiah 6:9]
13:16 "But blessed are your eyes, for they see; and your ears, for they hear. 13:17 For most certainly I tell you that many prophets and righteous men desired to see the things which you see, and didn't see them; and to hear the things which you hear, and didn't hear them.		

	4:13 He said to them, "Don't you understand this parable? How will you understand all of the parables?	
13:18 "Hear, then, the parable of the farmer.	4:14 The farmer sows the word.	8:11 Now the parable is this: The seed is the word of God.
13:19 When anyone hears the word of the Kingdom, and doesn't understand it, the evil one comes, and snatches away that which has been sown in his heart. This is what was sown by the roadside.	4:15 The ones by the road are the ones where the word is sown; and when they have heard, immediately Satan comes, and takes away the word which has been sown in them.	8:12 Those along the road are those who hear, then the devil comes, and takes away the word from their heart, that they may not believe and be saved.
13:20 What was sown on the rocky places, this is he who hears the word, and immediately with joy receives it; 13:21 yet he has no root in himself, but endures for a while. When oppression or persecution arises because of the word, immediately he stumbles.	4:16 These in like manner are those who are sown on the rocky places, who, when they have heard the word, immediately receive it with joy. 4:17 They have no root in themselves, but are short-lived. When oppression or persecution arises because of the word, immediately they stumble.	8:13 Those on the rock are they who, when they hear, receive the word with joy; but these have no root, who believe for a while, then fall away in time of temptation.
13:22 What was sown among the thorns, this is he who hears the word, but the cares of this age and the deceitfulness of riches choke the word, and he becomes unfruitful.	4:18 Others are those who are sown among the thorns. These are those who have heard the word, 4:19 and the cares of this age, and the deceitfulness of riches, and the lusts of other things entering in choke the word, and it becomes unfruitful.	8:14 That which fell among the thorns, these are those who have heard, and as they go on their way they are choked with cares, riches, and pleasures of life, and bring no fruit to maturity.
13:23 What was sown on the good ground, this is he who hears the word, and understands it, who most certainly bears fruit, and brings forth, some one hundred times as much, some sixty, and some thirty."	4:20 Those which were sown on the good ground are those who hear the word, and accept it, and bear fruit, some thirty times, some sixty times, and some one hundred times."	8:15 That in the good ground, these are such as in an honest and good heart, having heard the word, hold it tightly, and bring forth fruit with patience.
	4:21 He said to them, "Is the lamp brought to be put under a basket [a dry measure basket of about 9 litres or 1 peck]	8:16 "No one, when he has lit a lamp, covers it with a container, or puts it under a bed; but puts it on a stand,

	or under a bed? Isn't it put on a stand? 4:22 For there is nothing hidden, except that it should be made known; neither was anything made secret, but that it should come to light.	that those who enter in may see the light. 8:17 For nothing is hidden, that will not be revealed; nor anything secret, that will not be known and come to light.
	4:23 If any man has ears to hear, let him hear."	
	4:24 He said to them, "Take heed what you hear. With whatever measure you measure, it will be measured to you, and more will be given to you who hear. 4:25 For whoever has, to him will more be given, and he who doesn't have, even that which he has will be taken away from him."	8:18 Be careful therefore how you hear. For whoever has, to him will be given; and whoever doesn't have, from him will be taken away even that which he thinks he has."
	4:26 He said, "The Kingdom of God is as if a man should cast seed on the earth, 4:27 and should sleep and rise night and day, and the seed should spring up and grow, he doesn't know how. 4:28 For the earth bears fruit: first the blade, then the ear, then the full grain in the ear. 4:29 But when the fruit is ripe, immediately he puts forth the sickle, because the harvest has come."	
13:24 He set another parable before them, saying,		
"The Kingdom of Heaven is like a man who sowed good seed in his field, 13:25 but while people slept, his enemy came and sowed darnel weeds also among the wheat, and went way. 13:26 But when the blade sprang up and brought forth fruit, then the darnel weeds appeared also.		

13:27 The servants of the householder came and said to him, 'Sir, didn't you sow good seed in your field? Where did this darnel come from?		
13:28 "He said to them, 'An enemy has done this.'		
"The servants asked him, 'Do you want us to go and gather them up?'		
13:29 "But he said, 'No, lest perhaps while you gather up the darnel weeds, you root up the wheat with them. 13:30 Let both grow together until the harvest, and in the harvest time I will tell the reapers, "First, gather up the darnel weeds, and bind them in bundles to burn them; but gather the wheat into my barn."'"		
13:31 He set another parable before them, saying,		
"The Kingdom of Heaven is like a grain of mustard seed, which a man took, and sowed in his field; 13:32 which indeed is smaller than all seeds. But when it is grown, it is greater than the herbs, and becomes a tree, so that the birds of the air come and lodge in its branches."	4:30 He said, "How will we liken the Kingdom of God? Or with what parable will we illustrate it? 4:31 It's like a grain of mustard seed, which, when it is sown in the earth, though it is less than all the seeds that are on the earth, 4:32 yet when it is sown, grows up, and becomes greater than all the herbs, and puts out great branches, so that the birds of the sky can lodge under its shadow."	
13:33 He spoke another parable to them.		
"The Kingdom of Heaven is like yeast, which a woman took, and hid in three measures of meal [39 litres or a bushel], until it was all leavened."		

13:34 Jesus spoke all these things in parables to the multitudes; and without a parable, he didn't speak to them,	4:33 With many such parables he spoke the word to them, as they were able to hear it. 4:34 Without a parable he didn't speak to them; but privately to his own disciples he explained everything.	
13:35 that it might be fulfilled which was spoken through the prophet, saying, "I will open my mouth in parables; I will utter things hidden from the foundation of the world." [Psalm 78:2]		
13:36 Then Jesus sent the multitudes away, and went into the house.		
His disciples came to him, saying, "Explain to us the parable of the darnel weeds of the field."		
13:37 He answered them, "He who sows the good seed is the Son of Man, 13:38 the field is the world; and the good seed, these are the children of the Kingdom; and the darnel weeds are the children of the evil one. 13:39 The enemy who sowed them is the devil. The harvest is the end of the age, and the reapers are angels. 13:40 As therefore the darnel weeds are gathered up and burned with fire; so will it be at the end of this age. 13:41 The Son of Man will send out his angels, and they will gather out of his Kingdom all things that cause stumbling, and those who do iniquity, 13:42 and will cast them into the furnace of fire. There will be weeping and the gnashing of teeth. 13:43 Then the righteous will shine forth		

like the sun in the Kingdom of their Father. He who has ears to hear, let him hear.		
13:44 "Again, the Kingdom of Heaven is like a treasure hidden in the field, which a man found, and hid. In his joy, he goes and sells all that he has, and buys that field.		
13:45 "Again, the Kingdom of Heaven is like a man who is a merchant seeking fine pearls, 13:46 who having found one pearl of great price, he went and sold all that he had, and bought it.		
13:47 "Again, the Kingdom of Heaven is like a dragnet, that was cast into the sea, and gathered some fish of every kind, 13:48 which, when it was filled, they drew up on the beach. They sat down, and gathered the good into containers, but the bad they threw away. 13:49 So will it be in the end of the world. The angels will come forth, and separate the wicked from among the righteous, 13:50 and will cast them into the furnace of fire. There will be the weeping and the gnashing of teeth."		
13:51 Jesus said to them, "Have you understood all these things?"		
They answered him, "Yes, Lord."		
13:52 He said to them, "Therefore, every scribe who has been made a disciple in the Kingdom of Heaven is like a man who is a householder, who brings out of his treasure new and old things."		

Event 50: Jesus heals an invalid at the pool of Bethesda on the Sabbath
Time: fall 31 A.D., 8th day Tabernacles, Shimini Atzaret October 27, 31 A.D. (Saturday)
Place: Jerusalem, Judea

JOHN 5:1-46
5:1 After these things, there was a feast of the Jews, and Jesus went up to Jerusalem.
5:2 Now in Jerusalem by the sheep gate, there is a pool, which is called in Hebrew, "Bethesda," having five porches. 5:3 In these lay a great multitude of those who were sick, blind, lame, or paralyzed, waiting for the moving of the water; 5:4 for an angel of the Lord went down at certain times into the pool, and stirred up the water. Whoever stepped in first after the stirring of the water was made whole of whatever disease he had.
5:5 A certain man was there, who had been sick for thirty-eight years.
5:6 When Jesus saw him lying there, and knew that he had been sick for a long time, he asked him, "Do you want to be made well?"
5:7 The sick man answered him, "Sir, I have no one to put me into the pool when the water is stirred up, but while I'm coming, another steps down before me."
5:8 Jesus said to him, "Arise, take up your mat, and walk."
5:9 Immediately, the man was made well, and took up his mat and walked.
Now it was the Sabbath on that day.
5:10 So the Jews said to him who was cured, "It is the Sabbath. It is not lawful for you to carry the mat."
5:11 He answered them, "He who made me well, the same said to me, 'Take up your mat, and walk.'"
5:12 Then they asked him, "Who is the man who said to you, 'Take up your mat, and walk'?"
5:13 But he who was healed didn't know who it was, for Jesus had withdrawn, a crowd being in the place.
5:14 Afterward Jesus found him in the temple, and said to him, "Behold, you are made well. Sin no more, so that nothing worse happens to you."
5:15 The man went away, and told the Jews that it was Jesus who had made him well.
5:16 For this cause the Jews persecuted Jesus, and sought to kill him, because he did these things on the Sabbath.
5:17 But Jesus answered them, "My Father is still working, so I am working, too." 5:18 For this cause therefore the Jews sought all the more to kill him, because he not only broke the Sabbath, but also called God his own Father, making himself equal with God.
5:19 Jesus therefore answered them, "Most certainly, I tell you, the Son can do nothing of himself, but what he sees the Father doing. For whatever things he does, these the Son also does likewise. 5:20 For the Father has affection for the Son, and shows him all things that he himself does. He will show him greater works than these, that you may marvel. 5:21 For as the Father raises the dead and gives them life, even so the Son also gives life to whom he desires. 5:22 For the Father judges no one, but he has given all judgment to the Son, 5:23 that all may honor the Son, even as they honor the Father. He who doesn't honor the Son doesn't honor the Father who sent him.

5:24 "Most certainly I tell you, he who hears my word, and believes him who sent me, has eternal life, and doesn't come into judgment, but has passed out of death into life. 5:25 Most certainly, I tell you, the hour comes, and now is, when the dead will hear the Son of God's voice; and those who hear will live. 5:26 For as the Father has life in himself, even so he gave to the Son also to have life in himself. 5:27 He also gave him authority to execute judgment, because he is a son of man. 5:28 Don't marvel at this, for the hour comes, in which all that are in the tombs will hear his voice, 5:29 and will come out; those who have done good, to the resurrection of life; and those who have done evil, to the resurrection of judgment. 5:30 I can of myself do nothing. As I hear, I judge, and my judgment is righteous; because I don't seek my own will, but the will of my Father who sent me.
5:31 "If I testify about myself, my witness is not valid. 5:32 It is another who testifies about me. I know that the testimony which he testifies about me is true. 5:33 You have sent to John, and he has testified to the truth. 5:34 But the testimony which I receive is not from man. However, I say these things that you may be saved. 5:35 He was the burning and shining lamp, and you were willing to rejoice for a while in his light. 5:36 But the testimony which I have is greater than that of John, for the works which the Father gave me to accomplish, the very works that I do, testify about me, that the Father has sent me. 5:37 The Father himself, who sent me, has testified about me. You have neither heard his voice at any time, nor seen his form. 5:38 You don't have his word living in you; because you don't believe him whom he sent.
5:39 "You search the Scriptures, because you think that in them you have eternal life; and these are they which testify about me. 5:40 Yet you will not come to me, that you may have life. 5:41 I don't receive glory from men. 5:42 But I know you, that you don't have God's love in yourselves. 5:43 I have come in my Father's name, and you don't receive me. If another comes in his own name, you will receive him. 5:44 How can you believe, who receive glory from one another, and you don't seek the glory that comes from the only God?
5:45 "Don't think that I will accuse you to the Father. There is one who accuses you, even Moses, on whom you have set your hope. 5:46 For if you believed Moses, you would believe me; for he wrote about me. 5:47 But if you don't believe his writings, how will you believe my words?"

Event 51: Jesus delivers a sermon in Nazareth
Time: late 31 A.D.
Place: Galilee

MATTHEW 13:53-58	MARK 6:1-6	LUKE 4:16-30
13:53 It happened that when Jesus had finished these parables, he departed from there. 13:54 Coming into his own country, he taught them in their synagogue,	6:1 He went out from there. He came into his own country, and his disciples followed him. 6:2 When the Sabbath had come, he began to teach in the synagogue,	4:16 He came to Nazareth, where he had been brought up. He entered, as was his custom, into the synagogue on the Sabbath day, and stood up to read.
		4:17 The book of the prophet Isaiah was handed to him. He opened the book, and found the place where it was written, 4:18 "The Spirit of the

		Lord is on me, because he has anointed me to preach good news to the poor. He has sent me to heal the brokenhearted, [NU lacks "to heal the brokenhearted] to proclaim release to the captives, recovering of sight to the blind, to deliver those who are crushed, 4:19 and to proclaim the acceptable year of the Lord." [Isaiah 61:1-2]
		4:20 He closed the book, gave it back to the attendant, and sat down. The eyes of all in the synagogue were fastened on him.
		4:21 He began to tell them, "Today, this Scripture has been fulfilled in your hearing."
so that they were astonished, and said, "Where did this man get this wisdom, and these mighty works? 13:55 Isn't this the carpenter's son? Isn't his mother called Mary, and his brothers, James, Joses, Simon, and Judas? 13:56 Aren't all of his sisters with us? Where then did this man get all of these things?"	and many hearing him were astonished, saying, "Where did this man get these things?" and, "What is the wisdom that is given to this man, that such mighty works come about by his hands? 6:3 Isn't this the carpenter, the son of Mary, and brother of James, Joses, Judah, and Simon? Aren't his sisters here with us?"	4:22 All testified about him, and wondered at the gracious words which proceeded out of his mouth, and they said, "Isn't this Joseph's son?"
13:57 They were offended by him.	They were offended at him.	4:23 He said to them, "Doubtless you will tell me this parable, 'Physician, heal yourself! Whatever we have heard done at Capernaum, do also here in your hometown.'"
But Jesus said to them, "A prophet is not without honor, except in his own country, and in his own house."	6:4 Jesus said to them, "A prophet is not without honor, except in his own country, and among his own relatives, and in his own house."	4:24 He said, "Most certainly I tell you, no prophet is acceptable in his hometown.

		4:25 But truly I tell you, there were many widows in Israel in the days of Elijah, when the sky was shut up three years and six months, when a great famine came over all the land. 4:26 Elijah was sent to none of them, except to Zarephath, in the land of Sidon, to a woman who was a widow. 4:27 There were many lepers in Israel in the time of Elisha the prophet, yet not one of them was cleansed, except Naaman, the Syrian."
		4:28 They were all filled with wrath in the synagogue, as they heard these things. 4:29 They rose up, threw him out of the city, and led him to the brow of the hill that their city was built on, that they might throw him off the cliff. 4:30 But he, passing through the midst of them, went his way.
13:58 He didn't do many mighty works there because of their unbelief.	6:5 He could do no mighty work there, except that he laid his hands on a few sick people, and healed them. 6:6 He marveled because of their unbelief. He went around the villages teaching.	

Event 52: Herod Antipas' interest in Jesus as John the Baptist returned from the dead
Time: early 32 A.D.
Place: Galilee

MATTHEW 14:1-12	MARK 6:14-29	LUKE 9:7-9
14:1 At that time, Herod the tetrarch heard the report concerning Jesus,	6:14 King Herod heard this, for his name had become known,	9:7 Now Herod the tetrarch heard of all that was done by him;
		and he was very perplexed,
14:2 and said to his servants, "This is John the	and he said, "John the Baptizer has risen from the	because it was said by some that John had

Baptizer. He is risen from the dead. That is why these powers work in him."	dead, and therefore these powers are at work in him."	risen from the dead,
	6:15 But others said, "He is Elijah."	6:15 But others said, "He is Elijah."
	Others said, "He is a prophet, or like one of the prophets."	and by others that one of the old prophets had risen again.
	6:16 But Herod, when he heard this, said, "This is John, whom I beheaded. He has risen from the dead."	Herod said, "John I beheaded, but who is this, about whom I hear such things?"
14:3 For Herod had laid hold of John, and bound him, and put him in prison for the sake of Herodias, his brother Philip's wife. 14:4 For John said to him, "It is not lawful for you to have her."	6:17 For Herod himself had sent out and arrested John, and bound him in prison for the sake of Herodias, his brother Philip's wife, for he had married her. 6:18 For John said to Herod, "It is not lawful for you to have your brother's wife."	
		He sought to see him.
	6:19 Herodias set herself against him, and desired to kill him, but she couldn't,	
14:5 When he would have put him to death, he feared the multitude, because they counted him as a prophet.	6:20 for Herod feared John, knowing that he was a righteous and holy man, and kept him safe.	
	When he heard him, he did many things, and he heard him gladly.	
14:6 But when Herod's birthday came, the daughter of Herodias danced among them and pleased Herod. 14:7 Whereupon he promised with an oath to give her whatever she should ask.	6:21 Then a convenient day came, that Herod on his birthday made a supper for his nobles, the high officers, and the chief men of Galilee. 6:22 When the daughter of Herodias herself came in and danced, she pleased Herod and those sitting with him. The king said to the young lady, "Ask me whatever you want, and I will give it to you." 6:23 He swore to her, "Whatever you shall ask of me, I will give you, up to half of my kingdom."	

14:8 She, being prompted by her mother, said, "Give me here on a platter the head of John the Baptizer."	6:24 She went out, and said to her mother, "What shall I ask?" She said, "The head of John the Baptizer." 6:25 She came in immediately with haste to the king, and asked, "I want you to give me right now the head of John the Baptizer on a platter."	
14:9 The king was grieved, but for the sake of his oaths, and of those who sat at the table with him, he commanded it to be given, 14:10 and he sent and beheaded John in the prison. 14:11 His head was brought on a platter, and given to the young lady: and she brought it to her mother.	6:26 The king was exceedingly sorry, but for the sake of his oaths, and of his dinner guests, he didn't wish to refuse her. 6:27 Immediately the king sent out a soldier of his guard, and commanded to bring John's head, and he went and beheaded him in the prison, 6:28 and brought his head on a platter, and gave it to the young lady; and the young lady gave it to her mother.	
14:12 His disciples came, and took the body, and buried it; and they went and told Jesus.	6:29 When his disciples heard this, they came and took up his corpse, and laid it in a tomb.	

Event 53: Jesus feeds 5000 and the crowds attempt to make him king
Time: spring 32 A.D.
Place: Bethsaida, Galilee

MATTHEW 14:13-21	MARK 6:30-44	LUKE 9:10-17	JOHN 6:1-15
	6:30 The apostles gathered themselves together to Jesus, and they told him all things, whatever they had done, and whatever they had taught.		

14:13 Now when Jesus heard this, he withdrew from there in a boat, to a deserted place apart.	6:31 He said to them, "You come apart into a deserted place, and rest awhile." For there were many coming and going, and they had no leisure so much as to eat. 6:32 They went away in the boat to a deserted place by themselves.	He took them, and withdrew apart to a deserted place of a city called Bethsaida.	6:1 After these things, Jesus went away to the other side of the sea of Galilee, which is also called the Sea of Tiberias.
When the multitudes heard it, they followed him on foot from the cities.	6:33 They saw them going, and many recognized him and ran there on foot from all the cities. They arrived before them and came together to him.	9:11 But the multitudes, perceiving it, followed him. He welcomed them,	6:2 A great multitude followed him, because they saw his signs which he did on those who were sick.
14:14 Jesus went out, and he saw a great multitude. He had compassion on them, and healed their sick.	6:34 Jesus came out, saw a great multitude, and he had compassion on them, because they [TR has "the multitudes" instead of they] were like sheep without a shepherd, and he began to teach them many things.	and spoke to them of the Kingdom of God, and he cured those who needed healing.	
			6:3 Jesus went up into the mountain, and he sat there with his disciples.
14:15 When evening had come,	6:35 When it was late in the day,	9:12 The day began to wear away;	6:4 Now the Passover, the feast of the Jews, was at hand.
			6:5 Jesus therefore lifting up his eyes, and seeing that a great multitude was coming to him, said to Philip, "Where are we to buy bread, that these may eat?"

his disciples came to him, saying, "This place is deserted, and the hour is already late. Send the multitudes away, that they may go into the villages, and buy themselves food."	his disciples came to him, and said, "This place is deserted, and it is late in the day. 6:36 Send them away, that they may go into the surrounding country and villages, and buy themselves bread, for they have nothing to eat."	and the twelve came, and said to him, "Send the multitude away, that they may go into the surrounding villages and farms, and lodge, and get food, for we are here in a deserted place."	
			6:6 This he said to test him, for he himself knew what he would do.
			6:7 Philip answered him, "Two hundred denarii worth of bread is not sufficient for them, that everyone of them may receive a little."
			6:8 One of his disciples, Andrew, Simon Peter's brother, said to him, 6:9 "There is a boy here who has five barley loaves and two fish, but what are these among so many?"
14:16 But Jesus said to them, "They don't need to go away. You give them something to eat."	6:37 But he answered them, "You give them something to eat."	9:13 But he said to them, "You give them something to eat."	
	They asked him, "Shall we go and buy two hundred denarii [about 7-8 months wages for an agricultural work] worth of bread, and give them something to eat?"		

	6:38 He said to them, "How many loaves do you have? Go see."		
14:17 They told him, "We only have here five loaves and two fish."	When they knew, they said, "Five, and two fish."	They said, "We have no more than five loaves and two fish, unless we should go and buy food for all these people."	
		9:14 For they were about five thousand men.	
14:18 He said, "Bring them here to me."			
14:19 He commanded the multitudes to sit down on the grass;	6:39 He commanded them that everyone should sit down in groups on the green grass. 6:40 They sat down in ranks, by hundreds and by fifties.	He said to his disciples, "Make them sit down in groups of about fifty each." 9:15 They did so, and made them all sit down.	6:10 Jesus said, "Have the people sit down." Now there was much grass in that place.
			So the men sat down, in number about five thousand.
and he took the five loaves and the two fish, and looking up to heaven, he blessed, broke and gave the loaves to the disciples, and the disciples gave to the multitudes.	6:41 He took the five loaves and the two fish, and looking up to heaven, he blessed and broke the loaves, and he gave to his disciples to set before them, and he divided the two fish among them all.	9:16 He took the five loaves and the two fish, and looking up to the sky, he blessed them, and broke them, and gave them to the disciples to set before the multitude.	6:11 Jesus took the loaves; and having given thanks, he distributed to the disciples, and the disciples to those who were sitting down; likewise also of the fish as much as they desired.
			6:12 When they were filled, he said to his disciples, "Gather up the broken pieces which are left over, that nothing be lost."
14:20 They all ate, and were filled. They took up twelve baskets full of that which remained left over from the broken pieces.	6:42 They all ate, and were filled. 6:43 They took up twelve baskets full of broken pieces and also of the fish.	9:17 They ate, and were all filled. They gathered up twelve baskets of broken pieces that were left over.	6:13 So they gathered them up, and filled twelve baskets with broken pieces from the five barley loaves, which were left over by those who had eaten.

14:21 Those who ate were about five thousand men, besides women and children.	6:44 Those who ate the loaves were [TR adds "about"] five thousand men.		
			6:14 When therefore the people saw the sign which Jesus did, they said, "This is truly the prophet who comes into the world."
			6:15 Jesus therefore, perceiving that they were about to come and take him by force, to make him king, withdrew again to the mountain by himself.

Event 54: Jesus walks on the water of the Sea of Galilee
Time: spring 32 A.D.
Place: Sea of Galilee

MATTHEW 14:24-33	MARK 6:47-52	JOHN 6:16-21
14:22 Immediately Jesus made the disciples get into the boat, and to go ahead of him to the other side, while he sent the multitudes away.	6:45 Immediately he made his disciples get into the boat, and to go ahead to the other side, to Bethsaida, while he himself sent the multitude away.	6:16 When evening came, his disciples went down to the sea, 6:17 and they entered into the boat, and were going over the sea to Capernaum.
14:23 After he had sent the multitudes away, he went up into the mountain by himself to pray. When evening had come, he was there alone.	6:46 After he had taken leave of them, he went up the mountain to pray.	
14:24 But the boat was now in the middle of the sea, distressed by the waves, for the wind was contrary.	6:47 When evening had come, the boat was in the midst of the sea, and he was alone on the land. 6:48 Seeing them distressed in rowing, for the wind was contrary to them,	It was now dark, and Jesus had not come to them. 6:18 The sea was tossed by a great wind blowing. 6:19 When therefore they had rowed about twenty-five or thirty stadia. [5-6 kilometers or 3-4 miles]
14:25 In fourth watch of the night [3:00 am to sunrise], Jesus came to them, walking on the sea. [Job 9:8]	about the fourth watch of the night he came to them, walking on the sea [Job 9:8], and he would have passed by them,	they saw Jesus walking on the sea [Job 9:8], and drawing near to the boat;

14:26 When the disciples saw him walking on the sea, they were troubled, saying, "It's a ghost!" and they cried out for fear.	6:49 but they, when they saw him walking on the sea, supposed that it was a ghost, and cried out; 6:50 for they all saw him, and were troubled.	and they were afraid.
14:27 But immediately Jesus spoke to them, saying "Cheer up! It is I! [literally "I am" or "I AM" from Exodus 3:14] Don't be afraid."	But he immediately spoke with them, and said to them, "Cheer up! It is I! [literally "I am" or "I AM" from Exodus 3:14] Don't be afraid."	6:20 But he said to them, "It is I! [lliterally "I am" or "I AM" from Exodus 3:14] Don't be afraid."
14:28 Peter answered him and said, "Lord, if it is you, command me to come to you on the waters."		
14:29 He said, "Come!"		
Peter stepped down from the boat, and walked on the waters to come to Jesus. 14:30 But when he saw that the wind was strong, he was afraid, and beginning to sink, he cried out, saying, "Lord, save me!"		
14:31 Immediately Jesus stretched out his hand, took hold of him, and said to him, "You of little faith, why did you doubt?"		
14:32 When they got up into the boat, the wind ceased.	6:51 He got into the boat with them; and the wind ceased,	6:21 They were willing therefore to receive him into the boat.
14:33 Those who were in the boat came and worshiped him, saying, "You are truly the Son of God!"	and they were very amazed among themselves, and marveled; 6:52 for they hadn't understood about the loaves, but their hearts were hardened.	
	6:53 When they had crossed over, they came to land at Gennesaret, and moored to the shore.	Immediately the boat was at the land where they were going.

Event 55: Jesus heals the sick in Gennesaret
Time: spring 32 A.D.
Place: Gennesaret, Galilee

MATTHEW 14:34-36	MARK 6:53-56
14:34 When they had crossed over, they came to the land of Gennesaret.	6:53 When they had crossed over, they came to land at Gennesaret, and moored to the shore.
14:35 When the people of that place recognized him, they sent into all that surrounding region, and brought to him all who were sick,	6:54 When they had come out of the boat, immediately the people recognized him, 6:55 and ran around that whole region, and began to bring those who were sick, on their mats, to where they heard he was. 6:56 Wherever he entered, into villages, or into cities, or into the country, they laid the sick in the marketplaces,
14:36 and they begged him that they might just touch the fringe of his garment.	and begged him that they might touch just the fringe of his garment;
As many as touched it were made whole.	and as many as touched him were made well.

Event 56: Jesus delivers the Bread of Life sermon in Capernaum
Time: spring 32 A.D.
Place: Capernaum, Galilee

JOHN 6:22-7:1
6:22 On the next day, the multitude that stood on the other side of the sea saw that there was no other boat there, except the one in which his disciples had embarked, and that Jesus hadn't entered with his disciples into the boat, but his disciples had gone away alone.
6:23 However boats from Tiberias came near to the place where they ate the bread after the Lord had given thanks. 6:24 When the multitude therefore saw that Jesus wasn't there, nor his disciples, they themselves got into the boats, and came to Capernaum, seeking Jesus.
6:25 When they found him on the other side of the sea, they asked him, "Rabbi, when did you come here?"
6:26 Jesus answered them, "Most certainly I tell you, you seek me, not because you saw signs, but because you ate of the loaves, and were filled. 6:27 Don't work for the food which perishes, but for the food which remains to eternal life, which the Son of Man will give to you. For God the Father has sealed him."
6:28 They said therefore to him, "What must we do, that we may work the works of God?"
6:29 Jesus answered them, "This is the work of God, that you believe in him whom he has sent."
6:30 They said therefore to him, "What then do you do for a sign, that we may see, and believe you? What work do you do? 6:31 Our fathers ate the manna in the wilderness. As it is written, 'He gave them bread out of heaven [Greek and Hebrew use the same word for "heaven", the heavens", "the sky", and the "air"] to eat.'" [Exodus 16:4; Nehemiah 9:15; Psalm 78:24-25]

6:32 Jesus therefore said to them, "Most certainly, I tell you, it wasn't Moses who gave you the bread out of heaven, but my Father gives you the true bread out of heaven. 6:33 For the bread of God is that which comes down out of heaven, and gives life to the world."

6:34 They said therefore to him, "Lord, always give us this bread."

6:35 Jesus said to them, "I am the bread of life. He who comes to me will not be hungry, and he who believes in me will never be thirsty. 6:36 But I told you that you have seen me, and yet you don't believe. 6:37 All those who the Father gives me will come to me. Him who comes to me I will in no way throw out. 6:38 For I have come down from heaven, not to do my own will, but the will of him who sent me. 6:39 This is the will of my Father who sent me, that of all he has given to me I should lose nothing, but should raise him up at the last day.

6:40 This is the will of the one who sent me, that everyone who sees the Son, and believes in him, should have eternal life; and I will raise him up at the last day."

6:41 The Jews therefore murmured concerning him, because he said, "I am the bread which came down out of heaven." 6:42 They said, "Isn't this Jesus, the son of Joseph, whose father and mother we know? How then does he say, 'I have come down out of heaven?'"

6:43 Therefore Jesus answered them, "Don't murmur among yourselves. 6:44 No one can come to me unless the Father who sent me draws him, and I will raise him up in the last day. 6:45 It is written in the prophets, 'They will all be taught by God.' [Isaiah 54:13] Therefore everyone who hears from the Father, and has learned, comes to me. 6:46 Not that anyone has seen the Father, except he who is from God. He has seen the Father. 6:47 Most certainly, I tell you, he who believes in me has eternal life. 6:48 I am the bread of life. 6:49 Your fathers ate the manna in the wilderness, and they died. 6:50 This is the bread which comes down out of heaven, that anyone may eat of it and not die. 6:51 I am the living bread which came down out of heaven. If anyone eats of this bread, he will live forever. Yes, the bread which I will give for the life of the world is my flesh."

6:52 The Jews therefore contended with one another, saying, "How can this man give us his flesh to eat?"

6:53 Jesus therefore said to them, "Most certainly I tell you, unless you eat the flesh of the Son of Man and drink his blood, you don't have life in yourselves. 6:54 He who eats my flesh and drinks my blood has eternal life, and I will raise him up at the last day. 6:55 For my flesh is food indeed, and my blood is drink indeed. 6:56 He who eats my flesh and drinks my blood lives in me, and I in him. 6:57 As the living Father sent me, and I live because of the Father; so he who feeds on me, he will also live because of me. 6:58 This is the bread which came down out of heaven—not as our fathers ate the manna, and died. He who eats this bread will live forever."

6:59 These things he said in the synagogue, as he taught in Capernaum.

6:60 Therefore many of his disciples, when they heard this, said, "This is a hard saying! Who can listen to it?"

6:61 But Jesus knowing in himself that his disciples murmured at this, said to them, "Does this cause you to stumble? 6:62 Then what if you would see the Son of Man ascending to where he was before? 6:63 It is the spirit who gives life. The flesh profits nothing. The words that I speak to you are spirit, and are life. 6:64 But there are some of you who don't believe." For Jesus knew from the beginning who they were who didn't believe, and who it was who would betray him. 6:65 He said, "For this cause have I said to you that no one can come to me, unless it is given to him by my Father."

6:66 At this, many of his disciples went back, and walked no more with him. 6:67 Jesus said therefore to the twelve, "You don't also want to go away, do you?"
6:68 Simon Peter answered him, "Lord, to whom would we go? You have the words of eternal life. 6:69 We have come to believe and know that you are the Christ, the Son of the living God."
6:70 Jesus answered them, "Didn't I choose you, the twelve, and one of you is a devil?" 6:71 Now he spoke of Judas, the son of Simon Iscariot, for it was he who would betray him, being one of the twelve.
7:1 After these things, Jesus was walking in Galilee, for he wouldn't walk in Judea, because the Jews sought to kill him.

Event 57: Jesus declares the oral and ceremonial law obsolete
Time: spring 32 A.D.
Place: Galilee

MATTHEW 15:1-20	MARK 7:1-23
15:1 Then Pharisees and scribes came to Jesus from Jerusalem,	7:1 Then the Pharisees, and some of the scribes gathered together to him, having come from Jerusalem.
	7:2 Now when they saw some of his disciples eating bread with defiled, that is, unwashed, hands, they found fault. 7:3 (For the Pharisees, and all the Jews, don't eat unless they wash their hands and forearms, holding to the tradition of the elders. 7:4 They don't eat when they come from the marketplace, unless they bathe themselves, and there are many other things, which they have received to hold to: washings of cups, pitchers, bronze vessels, and couches.)
saying, 15:2 "Why do your disciples disobey the tradition of the elders? For they don't wash their hands when they eat bread."	7:5 The Pharisees and the scribes asked him, "Why don't your disciples walk according to the tradition of the elders, but eat their bread with unwashed hands?"
	7:6 He answered them, "Well did Isaiah prophesy of you hypocrites, as it is written, 'This people honors me with their lips, but their heart is far from me. 7:7 But in vain do they worship me, teaching as doctrines the commandments of men.' [Isaiah 29:13]

15:3 He answered them, "Why do you also disobey the commandment of God because of your tradition? 15:4 For God commanded, 'Honor your father and your mother,' [Exodus 20:12; Deuteronomy 5:16] and, 'He who speaks evil of father or mother, let him be put to death.' [Exodus 21:27; Leviticus 20:9] 15:5 But you say, 'Whoever may tell his father or his mother, "Whatever help you might otherwise have gotten from me is a gift devoted to God," 15:6 he shall not honor his father or mother.' You have made the commandment of God void because of your tradition.	7:8 "For you set aside the commandment of God, and hold tightly to the tradition of men—the washing of pitchers and cups, and you do many other such things." 7:9 He said to them, "Full well do you reject the commandment of God, that you may keep your tradition. 7:10 For Moses said, 'Honor your father and your mother;' [Exodus 20:12; Deuteronomy 5:16] and, 'He who speaks evil of father or mother, let him be put to death.' [Exodus 20:17; Leviticus 20:9] 7:11 But you say, 'If a man tells his father or his mother, "Whatever profit you might have received from me is Corban [a Hebrew word for an offering devoted to God], that is to say, given to God;"' 7:12 then you no longer allow him to do anything for his father or his mother, 7:13 making void the word of God by your tradition, which you have handed down. You do many things like this."
15:7 You hypocrites! Well did Isaiah prophesy of you, saying, 15:8 'These people draw near to me with their mouth, and honor me with their lips; but their heart is far from me. 15:9 And in vain do they worship me, teaching as doctrine rules made by men."' [Isaiah 29:13]	
15:10 He summoned the multitude, and said to them, "Hear, and understand.	7:14 He called all the multitude to himself, and said to them, "Hear me, all of you, and understand.
15:11 That which enters into the mouth doesn't defile the man; but that which proceeds out of the mouth, this defiles the man."	7:15 There is nothing from outside of the man, that going into him can defile him; but the things which proceed out of the man are those that defile the man. 7:16 If anyone has ears to hear, let him hear!"
15:12 Then the disciples came, and said to him, "Do you know that the Pharisees were offended, when they heard this saying?"	
15:13 But he answered, "Every plant which my heavenly Father didn't plant will be uprooted. 15:14 Leave them alone. They are blind guides of the blind. If the blind guide the blind, both will fall into a pit."	
15:15 Peter answered him, "Explain the parable to us."	7:17 When he had entered into a house away from the multitude, his disciples asked him about the parable.

15:16 So Jesus said, "Do you also still not understand? 15:17 Don't you understand that whatever goes into the mouth passes into the belly, and then out of the body? 15:18 But the things which proceed out of the mouth come out of the heart, and they defile the man. 15:19 For out of the heart come forth evil thoughts, murders, adulteries, sexual sins, thefts, false testimony, and blasphemies. 15:20 These are the things which defile the man; but to eat with unwashed hands doesn't defile the man."	7:18 He said to them, "Are you thus without understanding also? Don't you perceive that whatever goes into the man from outside can't defile him, 7:19 because it doesn't go into his heart, but into his stomach, then into the latrine, thus making all foods clean?" 7:20 He said, "That which proceeds out of the man, that defiles the man. 7:21 For from within, out of the hearts of men, proceed evil thoughts, adulteries, sexual sins, murders, thefts, 7:22 covetings, wickedness, deceit, lustful desires, an evil eye, blasphemy, pride, and foolishness. 7:23 All these evil things come from within, and defile the man."

Event 58: Jesus heals the demoniac child of a Syrophoenician woman
Time: spring 32 A.D.
Place: the area of Tyre, north west of Galilee

MATTHEW 15:21-28	MARK 7:24-30
15:21 Jesus went out from there, and withdrew into the region of Tyre and Sidon.	7:24 From there he arose, and went away into the borders of Tyre and Sidon.
	He entered into a house, and didn't want anyone to know it, but he couldn't escape notice.
15:22 Behold, a Canaanite woman came out from those borders, and cried, saying, "Have mercy on me, Lord, you son of David! My daughter is severely demonized!"	7:25 For a woman, whose little daughter had an unclean spirit, having heard of him, came and fell down at his feet. 7:26 Now the woman was a Greek, a Syrophoenician by race. She begged him that he would cast the demon out of her daughter.
15:23 But he answered her not a word.	
His disciples came and begged him, saying, "Send her away; for she cries after us."	
15:24 But he answered, "I wasn't sent to anyone but the lost sheep of the house of Israel."	
15:25 But she came and worshiped him, saying, "Lord, help me."	
15:26 But he answered, "It is not appropriate to take the children's bread and throw it to the dogs."	7:27 But Jesus said to her, "Let the children be filled first, for it is not appropriate to take the children's bread and throw it to the dogs."

15:27 But she said, "Yes, Lord, but even the dogs eat the crumbs which fall from their masters' table."	7:28 But she answered him, "Yes, Lord. Yet even the dogs under the table eat the children's crumbs."
15:28 Then Jesus answered her, "Woman, great is your faith! Be it done to you even as you desire."	7:29 He said to her, "For this saying, go your way. The demon has gone out of your daughter."
And her daughter was healed from that hour.	7:30 She went away to her house, and found the child having been laid on the bed, with the demon gone out.

Event 59: Jesus heals the mute, deaf, lame and blind in Decapolis
Time: spring 32 A.D.
Place: Decapolis, east of Galilee

MATTHEW 15:29-31	MARK 7:31-37
15:29 Jesus departed there, and came near to the sea of Galilee; and he went up into the mountain, and sat there.	7:31 Again he departed from the borders of Tyre and Sidon, and came to the sea of Galilee, through the midst of the region of Decapolis.
15:30 Great multitudes came to him, having with them the lame, blind, mute, maimed, and many others, and they put them down at his feet.	
	7:32 They brought to him one who was deaf and had an impediment in his speech. They begged him to lay his hand on him. 7:33 He took him aside from the multitude, privately, and put his fingers into his ears, and he spat, and touched his tongue. 7:34 Looking up to heaven, he sighed, and said to him, "Ephphatha!" that is, "Be opened!" 7:35 Immediately his ears were opened, and the impediment of his tongue was released, and he spoke clearly. 7:36 He commanded them that they should tell no one, but the more he commanded them, so much the more widely they proclaimed it. 7:37 They were astonished beyond measure, saying, "He has done all things well. He makes even the deaf hear, and the mute speak!"
He healed them, 15:31 so that the multitude wondered when they saw the mute speaking, injured whole, lame walking, and blind seeing—and they glorified the God of Israel.	

Event 60: Jesus feeds 4000
Time: spring 32 A.D.
Place: Decapolis, east of Galilee

MATTHEW 15:32-38	MARK 8:1-9
15:32 Jesus summoned his disciples and said, "I have compassion on the multitude, because they continue with me now three days and have nothing to eat. I don't want to send them away fasting, or they might faint on the way."	8:1 In those days, when there was a very great multitude, and they had nothing to eat, Jesus called his disciples to himself, and said to them, 8:2 "I have compassion on the multitude, because they have stayed with me now three days, and have nothing to eat. 8:3 If I send them away fasting to their home, they will faint on the way, for some of them have come a long way."
15:33 The disciples said to him, "Where should we get so many loaves in a deserted place as to satisfy so great a multitude?"	8:4 His disciples answered him, "From where could one satisfy these people with bread here in a deserted place?"
15:34 Jesus said to them, "How many loaves do you have?"	8:5 He asked them, "How many loaves do you have?"
They said, "Seven, and a few small fish."	They said, "Seven."
15:35 He commanded the multitude to sit down on the ground; 15:36 and he took the seven loaves and the fish. He gave thanks and broke them, and gave to the disciples, and the disciples to the multitudes. 15:37 They all ate, and were filled.	8:6 He commanded the multitude to sit down on the ground, and he took the seven loaves. Having given thanks, he broke them, and gave them to his disciples to serve, and they served the multitude. 8:7 They had a few small fish. Having blessed them, he said to serve these also.
They took up seven baskets full of the broken pieces that were left over. 15:38 Those who ate were four thousand men, besides women and children.	8:8 They ate, and were filled. They took up seven baskets of broken pieces that were left over. 8:9 Those who had eaten were about four thousand. Then he sent them away.

Event 61: Jesus talks about the sign of Jonah and the leaven of the Pharisees
Time: spring 32 A.D.
Place: Decapolis, east of Galilee

MATTHEW 15:39- 16:12	MARK 8:10-21	JOHN 7:1
15:39 Then he sent away the multitudes, got into the boat, and came into the borders of Magdala.	8:10 Immediately he entered into the boat with his disciples, and came into the region of Dalmanutha.	7:1 After these things, Jesus was walking in Galilee, for he wouldn't walk in Judea, because the Jews sought to kill him.

16:1 The Pharisees and Sadducees came, and testing him, asked him to show them a sign from heaven.	8:11 The Pharisees came out and began to question him, seeking from him a sign from heaven, and testing him.	
16:2 But he answered them, "When it is evening, you say, 'It will be fair weather, for the sky is red.' 16:3 In the morning, 'It will be foul weather today, for the sky is red and threatening.' Hypocrites! You know how to discern the appearance of the sky, but you can't discern the signs of the times!		
16:4 An evil and adulterous generation seeks after a sign, and there will be no sign given to it, except the sign of the prophet Jonah."	8:12 He sighed deeply in his spirit, and said, "Why does this generation seek a sign? Most certainly I tell you, no sign will be given to this generation."	
He left them, and departed. 16:5 The disciples came to the other side and had forgotten to take bread.	8:13 He left them, and again entering into the boat, departed to the other side. 8:14 They forgot to take bread; and they didn't have more than one loaf in the boat with them.	
16:6 Jesus said to them, "Take heed and beware of the yeast of the Pharisees and Sadducees."	8:15 He warned them, saying, "Take heed: beware of the yeast of the Pharisees and the yeast of Herod."	
16:7 They reasoned among themselves, saying, "We brought no bread."	8:16 They reasoned with one another, saying, "It's because we have no bread."	
"Why do you reason among yourselves, you of little faith, 'because you have brought no bread?' 16:8 Jesus, perceiving it, said, 16:9 Don't you yet perceive, neither remember the five loaves for the five thousand, and how many baskets you took up? 16:10 Nor the seven loaves for the four thousand, and how many baskets you took up? 16:11	8:17 Jesus, perceiving it, said to them, "Why do you reason that it's because you have no bread? Don't you perceive yet, neither understand? Is your heart still hardened? 8:18 Having eyes, don't you see? Having ears, don't you hear? Don't you remember? 8:19 When I broke the five loaves among the five thousand, how many baskets full of broken	

How is it that you don't perceive that I didn't speak to you concerning bread?	pieces did you take up?" They told him, "Twelve." 8:20 "When the seven loaves fed the four thousand, how many baskets full of broken pieces did you take up?" They told him, "Seven." 8:21 He asked them, "Don't you understand, yet?"	
But beware of the yeast of the Pharisees and Sadducees."		
16:12 Then they understood that he didn't tell them to beware of the yeast of bread, but of the teaching of the Pharisees and Sadducees.		

Event: 62 Jesus heals a blind man
Time: spring 32 A.D.
Place: Bethsaida, Galilee

MARK 8:22-26
8:22 He came to Bethsaida. They brought a blind man to him, and begged him to touch him.
8:23 He took hold of the blind man by the hand, and brought him out of the village.
When he had spit on his eyes, and laid his hands on him, he asked him if he saw anything.
8:24 He looked up, and said, "I see men; for I see them like trees walking."
8:25 Then again he laid his hands on his eyes.
He looked intently, and was restored, and saw everyone clearly.
8:26 He sent him away to his house, saying, "Don't enter into the village, nor tell anyone in the village."

Event 63: Peter confesses Jesus to be the Messiah
Time: spring 32 A.D.
Place: Caesarea Philippi

MATTHEW 16:13-20	MARK 8:27-30	LUKE 9:18-21
16:13 Now when Jesus came into the parts of Caesarea Philippi,	8:27 Jesus went out, with his disciples, into the villages of Caesarea Philippi.	
		9:18 It happened, as he was praying alone,

he asked his disciples, saying, "Who do men say that I, the Son of Man, am?"	On the way he asked his disciples, "Who do men say that I am?"	that the disciples were with him, and he asked them, "Who do the multitudes say that I am?"
16:14 They said, "Some say John the Baptizer, some, Elijah, and others, Jeremiah, or one of the prophets."	8:28 They told him, "John the Baptizer, and others say Elijah, but others: one of the prophets."	9:19 They answered, "'John the Baptizer,' but others say, 'Elijah,' and others, that one of the old prophets is risen again."
16:15 He said to them, "But who do you say that I am?"	8:29 He said to them, "But who do you say that I am?"	9:20 He said to them, "But who do you say that I am?"
16:16 Simon Peter answered, "You are the Christ, the Son of the living God."	Peter answered, "You are the Christ."	Peter answered, "The Christ of God."
16:17 Jesus answered him, "Blessed are you, Simon Bar Jonah, for flesh and blood has not revealed this to you, but my Father who is in heaven.		
16:18 I also tell you that you are Peter [Greek word play: "Petros means single rock] and on this rock [Greek word play: "petra" means rock mass or bedrock] I will build my assembly, and the gates of Hades [Hell] will not prevail against it. 16:19 I will give to you the keys of the Kingdom of Heaven, and whatever you bind on earth will have been bound in heaven; and whatever you release on earth will have been released in heaven."		
16:20 Then he commanded the disciples that they should tell no one that he is Jesus the Christ.	8:30 He commanded them that they should tell no one about him.	9:21 But he warned them, and commanded them to tell this to no one,

Event 64: Jesus predicts his death in Jerusalem for the first time
Time: spring 32 A.D.
Place: Caesarea Philippi

MATTHEW 16:21-28	MARK 8:30-38	LUKE 9:22-27
16:21 From that time, Jesus began to show his disciples that he must go to Jerusalem and suffer many things from the elders, chief priests, and scribes, and be killed, and the third day be raised up.	8:31 He began to teach them that the Son of Man must suffer many things, and be rejected by the elders, the chief priests, and the scribes, and be killed, and after three days rise again. 8:32 He spoke to them openly.	9:22 saying, "The Son of Man must suffer many things, and be rejected by the elders, chief priests, and scribes, and be killed, and the third day be raised up."
16:22 Peter took him aside, and began to rebuke him, saying, "Far be it from you, Lord! This will never be done to you."	Peter took him, and began to rebuke him.	
16:23 But he turned, and said to Peter, "Get behind me, Satan! You are a stumbling block to me, for you are not setting your mind on the things of God, but on the things of men."	8:33 But he, turning around, and seeing his disciples, rebuked Peter, and said, "Get behind me, Satan! For you have in mind not the things of God, but the things of men."	
16:24 Then Jesus said to his disciples,	8:34 He called the multitude to himself with his disciples, and said to them,	9:23 He said to all,
"If anyone desires to come after me, let him deny himself, and take up his cross, and follow me.	"Whoever wants to come after me, let him deny himself, and take up his cross, and follow me.	"If anyone desires to come after me, let him deny himself, take up his cross [TR and NU add "daily"], and follow me.
16:25 For whoever desires to save his life will lose it, and whoever will lose his life for my sake will find it.	8:35 For whoever wants to save his life will lose it; and whoever will lose his life for my sake and the sake of the Good News will save it.	9:24 For whoever desires to save his life will lose it, but whoever will lose his life for my sake, the same will save it.
16:26 For what will it profit a man, if he gains the whole world, and forfeits his life? Or what will a man give in exchange for his life?	8:36 For what does it profit a man, to gain the whole world, and forfeit his life? 8:37 For what will a man give in exchange for his life?	9:25 For what does it profit a man if he gains the whole world, and loses or forfeits his own self?

16:27 For the Son of Man will come in the glory of his Father with his angels, and then he will render to everyone according to his deeds.	8:38 For whoever will be ashamed of me and of my words in this adulterous and sinful generation, the Son of Man also will be ashamed of him, when he comes in the glory of his Father with the holy angels."	9:26 For whoever will be ashamed of me and of my words, of him will the Son of Man be ashamed, when he comes in his glory, and the glory of the Father, and of the holy angels.
16:28 Most certainly I tell you, there are some standing here who will in no way taste of death, until they see the Son of Man coming in his Kingdom."	9:1 He said to them, "Most certainly I tell you, there are some standing here who will in no way taste death until they see the Kingdom of God come with power."	9:27 But I tell you the truth: There are some of those who stand here, who will in no way taste of death, until they see the Kingdom of God."

Event 65: Jesus is transfigured
Time: spring 32 A.D.
Place: Mount Harmon

MATTHEW 17:1-13	MARK 9:2-13	LUKE 9:28-36
17:1 After six days, Jesus took with him Peter, James, and John his brother, and brought them up into a high mountain by themselves.	9:2 After six days Jesus took with him Peter, James, and John, and brought them up onto a high mountain privately by themselves,	9:28 It happened about eight days after these sayings, that he took with him Peter, John, and James, and went up onto the mountain to pray.
17:2 He was transfigured before them. His face shone like the sun, and his garments became as white as the light.	And he was changed into another form in front of them. 9:3 His clothing became glistening, exceedingly white, like snow, such as no launderer on earth can whiten them.	9:29 As he was praying, the appearance of his face was altered, and his clothing became white and dazzling.
17:3 Behold, Moses and Elijah appeared to them talking with him.	9:4 Elijah and Moses appeared to them, and they were talking with Jesus.	9:30 Behold, two men were talking with him, who were Moses and Elijah, 9:31 who appeared in glory, and spoke of his departure which he was about to accomplish at Jerusalem.
17:4 Peter answered, and said to Jesus, "Lord, it is good for us to be here. If you want, let's make three tents here: one for you, one for Moses, and one for Elijah."	9:5 Peter answered Jesus, "Rabbi, it is good for us to be here. Let's make three tents: one for you, one for Moses, and one for Elijah." 9:6 For he didn't know what to say, for they were very afraid.	9:32 Now Peter and those who were with him were heavy with sleep, but when they were fully awake, they saw his glory, and the two men who stood with him. 9:33 It happened, as they were parting

		from him, that Peter said to Jesus, "Master, it is good for us to be here. Let's make three tents: one for you, and one for Moses, and one for Elijah," not knowing what he said.
17:5 While he was still speaking, behold, a bright cloud overshadowed them. Behold, a voice came out of the cloud, saying, "This is my beloved Son, in whom I am well pleased. Listen to him."	9:7 A cloud came, overshadowing them, and a voice came out of the cloud, "This is my beloved Son. Listen to him."	9:34 While he said these things, a cloud came and overshadowed them, and they were afraid as they entered into the cloud. 9:35 A voice came out of the cloud, saying, "This is my beloved Son. Listen to him!"
17:6 When the disciples heard it, they fell on their faces, and were very afraid. 17:7 Jesus came and touched them and said, "Get up, and don't be afraid." 17:8 Lifting up their eyes, they saw no one, except Jesus alone.	9:8 Suddenly looking around, they saw no one with them any more, except Jesus only.	
17:9 As they were coming down from the mountain, Jesus commanded them, saying, "Don't tell anyone what you saw, until the Son of Man has risen from the dead."	9:9 As they were coming down from the mountain, he commanded them that they should tell no one what things they had seen, until after the Son of Man had risen from the dead.	9:36 When the voice came, Jesus was found alone. They were silent, and told no one in those days any of the things which they had seen.
	9:10 They kept this saying to themselves, questioning what the "rising from the dead" meant.	
17:10 His disciples asked him, saying, "Then why do the scribes say that Elijah must come first?"	9:11 They asked him, saying, "Why do the scribes say that Elijah must come first?"	
17:11 Jesus answered them, "Elijah indeed comes first, and will restore all things, 17:12 but I tell you that Elijah has come already, and they didn't recognize him, but did to him whatever they wanted to. Even so the Son of Man will also suffer by them." 17:13 Then the disciples understood that he spoke to them of John the Baptizer.	9:12 He said to them, "Elijah indeed comes first, and restores all things. How is it written about the Son of Man, that he should suffer many things and be despised? 9:13 But I tell you that Elijah has come, and they have also done to him whatever they wanted to, even as it is written about him."	

Event 66: Jesus heals an epileptic demoniac child
Time: spring 32 A.D.
Place: Mount Harmon area

MATTHEW 17:14-21	MARK 9:14-29	LUKE 9:37-43
17:14 When they came to the multitude,	9:14 Coming to the disciples, he saw a great multitude around them, and scribes questioning them.	9:37 It happened on the next day, when they had come down from the mountain, that a great multitude met him.
	9:15 Immediately all the multitude, when they saw him, were greatly amazed, and running to him greeted him.	
	9:16 He asked the scribes, "What are you asking them?"	
A man came to him, kneeling down to him, saying, 17:15 "Lord, have mercy on my son, for he is epileptic, and suffers grievously; for he often falls into the fire, and often into the water. 17:16 So I brought him to your disciples, and they could not cure him."	9:17 One of the multitude answered, "Teacher, I brought to you my son, who has a mute spirit; 9:18 and wherever it seizes him, it throws him down, and he foams at the mouth, and grinds his teeth, and wastes away. I asked your disciples to cast it out, and they weren't able."	9:38 Behold, a man from the crowd called out, saying, "Teacher, I beg you to look at my son, for he is my only child. 9:39 Behold, a spirit takes him, he suddenly cries out, and it convulses him so that he foams, and it hardly departs from him, bruising him severely. 9:40 I begged your disciples to cast it out, and they couldn't."
17:17 Jesus answered, "Faithless and perverse generation! How long will I be with you? How long will I bear with you?	9:19 He answered him, "Unbelieving generation, how long shall I be with you? How long shall I bear with you?	9:41 Jesus answered, "Faithless and perverse generation, how long shall I be with you and bear with you?
Bring him here to me."	Bring him to me."	Bring your son here."
	9:20 They brought him to him, and when he saw him, immediately the spirit convulsed him, and he fell on the ground, wallowing and foaming at the mouth.	9:42 While he was still coming, the demon threw him down and convulsed him violently.
	9:21 He asked his father, "How long has it been since this has come to him?"	

	He said, "From childhood. 9:22 Often it has cast him both into the fire and into the water, to destroy him. But if you can do anything, have compassion on us, and help us."	
	9:23 Jesus said to him, "If you can believe, all things are possible to him who believes."	
	9:24 Immediately the father of the child cried out with tears, "I believe. Help my unbelief!"	
17:18 Jesus rebuked him, the demon went out of him, and the boy was cured from that hour.	9:26 Having cried out, and convulsed greatly, it came out of him. The boy became like one dead; so much that most of them said, "He is dead." 9:27 But Jesus took him by the hand, and raised him up; and he arose.	But Jesus rebuked the unclean spirit, and healed the boy, and gave him back to his father.
		9:43 They were all astonished at the majesty of God.
17:19 Then the disciples came to Jesus privately, and said, "Why weren't we able to cast it out?"	9:28 When he had come into the house, his disciples asked him privately, "Why couldn't we cast it out?"	
17:20 He said to them, "Because of your unbelief. For most certainly I tell you, if you have faith as a grain of mustard seed, you will tell this mountain, 'Move from here to there,' and it will move; and nothing will be impossible for you.		
17:21 But this kind doesn't go out except by prayer and fasting."	9:29 He said to them, "This kind can come out by nothing, except by prayer and fasting."	

Event 67: Jesus predicts his death in Jerusalem a second time
Time: spring 32 A.D.
Place: Galilee

MATTHEW 17:22-23	MARK 9:30-32	LUKE 9:43-45
17:22 While they were staying in Galilee,	9:30 They went out from there, and passed through Galilee. He didn't want anyone to know it.	But while all were marveling at all the things which Jesus did, he said to his disciples,
Jesus said to them, "The Son of Man is about to be delivered up into the hands of men, 17:23 and they will kill him, and the third day he will be raised up."	9:31 For he was teaching his disciples, and said to them, "The Son of Man is being handed over to the hands of men, and they will kill him; and when he is killed, on the third day he will rise again."	9:44 "Let these words sink into your ears, for the Son of Man will be delivered up into the hands of men."
They were exceedingly sorry.	9:32 But they didn't understand the saying, and were afraid to ask him.	9:45 But they didn't understand this saying. It was concealed from them, that they should not perceive it, and they were afraid to ask him about this saying.

Event 68: Jesus pays the temple tax
Time: spring 32 A.D.
Place: Capernaum, Galilee

MATTHEW 17:24-27
17:24 When they had come to Capernaum, those who collected the didrachma coins [2 days wages] came to Peter, and said, "Doesn't your teacher pay the didrachma?" [2 days wages]
17:25 He said, "Yes."
When he came into the house, Jesus anticipated him, saying, "What do you think, Simon? From whom do the kings of the earth receive toll or tribute? From their children, or from strangers?"
17:26 Peter said to him, "From strangers."
Jesus said to him, "Therefore the children are exempt. 17:27 But, lest we cause them to stumble, go to the sea, cast a hook, and take up the first fish that comes up. When you have opened its mouth, you will find a stater coin. [4 days wages] Take that, and give it to them for me and you."

Event 69: The disciples dispute over who is the greatest in the kingdom of heaven
Time: spring 32 A.D.
Place: Capernaum, Galilee

MATTHEW 18:1-9:1	MARK 9:33-50	LUKE 9:46-50
	9:33 He came to Capernaum, and when he was in the house he asked them, "What were you arguing among yourselves on the way?"	9:46 There arose an argument among them about which of them was the greatest.
	9:34 But they were silent, for they had disputed one with another on the way about who was the greatest.	
18:1 In that hour the disciples came to Jesus, saying, "Who then is greatest in the Kingdom of Heaven?"		
	9:35 He sat down, and called the twelve; and he said to them, "If any man wants to be first, he shall be last of all, and servant of all."	
18:2 Jesus called a little child to himself, and set him in the midst of them,	9:36 He took a little child, and set him in the midst of them. Taking him in his arms, he said to them,	9:47 Jesus, perceiving the reasoning of their hearts, took a little child, and set him by his side, 9:48 and said to them,
18:3 and said, "Most certainly I tell you, unless you turn, and become as little children, you will in no way enter into the Kingdom of Heaven.		
18:4 Whoever therefore humbles himself as this little child, the same is the greatest in the Kingdom of Heaven.		
18:5 Whoever receives one such little child in my name receives me,	9:37 "Whoever receives one such little child in my name, receives me,	"Whoever receives this little child in my name receives me.
	and whoever receives me, doesn't receive me, but him who sent me."	Whoever receives me receives him who sent me.
		For whoever is least among you all, this one will be great."

	9:38 John said to him, "Teacher, we saw someone who doesn't follow us casting out demons in your name; and we forbade him, because he doesn't follow us."	9:49 John answered, "Master, we saw someone casting out demons in your name, and we forbade him, because he doesn't follow with us."
	9:39 But Jesus said, "Don't forbid him,	9:50 Jesus said to him, "Don't forbid him,
	for there is no one who will do a mighty work in my name, and be able quickly to speak evil of me.	
	9:40 For whoever is not against us is on our side.	for he who is not against us is for us."
	9:41 For whoever will give you a cup of water to drink in my name, because you are Christ's, most certainly I tell you, he will in no way lose his reward.	
18:6 but whoever causes one of these little ones who believe in me to stumble, it would be better for him that a huge millstone should be hung around his neck, and that he should be sunk in the depths of the sea.	9:42 Whoever will cause one of these little ones who believe in me to stumble, it would be better for him if he was thrown into the sea with a millstone hung around his neck.	
18:7 "Woe to the world because of occasions of stumbling! For it must be that the occasions come, but woe to that person through whom the occasion comes!		
18:8 If your hand or your foot causes you to stumble, cut it off, and cast it from you. It is better for you to enter into life maimed or crippled, rather than having two hands or two feet to be cast into the eternal fire.	9:43 If your hand causes you to stumble, cut it off. It is better for you to enter into life maimed, rather than having your two hands to go into Gehenna [Hell], into the unquenchable fire, 9:44 'where their worm doesn't die, and the fire is not quenched. 9:45 If your foot causes you to stumble, cut it off. It is better for you to enter into life lame,	

	rather than having your two feet cast into Gehenna [Hell], into the fire that will never be quenched—9:46 "where their worm doesn't die, and their fire is not quenched".	
18:9 If your eye causes you to stumble, pluck it out, and cast it from you. It is better for you to enter into life with one eye, rather than having two eyes to be cast into the Gehenna of fire.	9:47 If your eye causes you to stumble, cast it out. It is better for you to enter into the Kingdom of God with one eye, rather than having two eyes to be cast into the Gehenna [Hell] of fire, 9:48 'where their worm doesn't die, and the fire is not quenched.' [Isaiah 66:24]	
	9:49 For everyone will be salted with fire, and every sacrifice will be seasoned with salt. 9:50 Salt is good, but if the salt has lost its saltiness, with what will you season it? Have salt in yourselves, and be at peace with one another."	
18:10 See that you don't despise one of these little ones, for I tell you that in heaven their angels always see the face of my Father who is in heaven. 18:11 For the Son of Man came to save that which was lost.		
18:12 "What do you think? If a man has one hundred sheep, and one of them goes astray, doesn't he leave the ninety-nine, go to the mountains, and seek that which has gone astray? 18:13 If he finds it, most certainly I tell you, he rejoices over it more than over the ninety-nine which have not gone astray. 18:14 Even so it is not the will of your Father who is in heaven that one of these little ones should perish.		

18:15 "If your brother sins against you, go, show him his fault between you and him alone. If he listens to you, you have gained back your brother. 18:16 But if he doesn't listen, take one or two more with you, that at the mouth of two or three witnesses every word may be established. [Deuteronomy 19:15] 18:17 If he refuses to listen to them, tell it to the assembly. If he refuses to hear the assembly also, let him be to you as a Gentile or a tax collector. 18:18 Most certainly I tell you, whatever things you bind on earth will have been bound in heaven, and whatever things you release on earth will have been released in heaven. 18:19 Again, assuredly I tell you, that if two of you will agree on earth concerning anything that they will ask, it will be done for them by my Father who is in heaven. 18:20 For where two or three are gathered together in my name, there I am in the midst of them."		
18:21 Then Peter came and said to him, "Lord, how often shall my brother sin against me, and I forgive him? Until seven times?"		
18:22 Jesus said to him, "I don't tell you until seven times, but, until seventy times seven.		
18:23 Therefore the Kingdom of Heaven is like a certain king, who wanted to reconcile accounts with his servants. 18:24 When he had begun to reconcile, one was brought to him who owed him ten		

thousand talents. [wage of an agricultural worker for 60 million days] 18:25 But because he couldn't pay, his lord commanded him to be sold, with his wife, his children, and all that he had, and payment to be made.		
18:26 The servant therefore fell down and kneeled before him, saying, 'Lord, have patience with me, and I will repay you all!' 18:27 The lord of that servant, being moved with compassion, released him, and forgave him the debt.		
18:28 "But that servant went out, and found one of his fellow servants, who owed him one hundred denarii, [1/16 of talent, or 100 days labour of an agricultural worker] and he grabbed him, and took him by the throat, saying, 'Pay me what you owe!' 18:29 "So his fellow servant fell down at his feet and begged him, saying, 'Have patience with me, and I will repay you!' 18:30 He would not, but went and cast him into prison, until he should pay back that which was due.		
18:31 So when his fellow servants saw what was done, they were exceedingly sorry, and came and told to their lord all that was done.		
18:32 Then his lord called him in, and said to him, 'You wicked servant! I forgave you all that debt, because you begged me. 18:33 Shouldn't you also have had mercy on		

your fellow servant, even as I had mercy on you?' 18:34 His lord was angry, and delivered him to the tormentors, until he should pay all that was due to him.		
18:35 So my heavenly Father will also do to you, if you don't each forgive your brother from your hearts for his misdeeds."		
19:1 It happened when Jesus had finished these words, he departed from Galilee, and came into the borders of Judea beyond the Jordan. 19:2 Great multitudes followed him, and he healed them there.		

Event 70: Jesus contemplates going to Jerusalem for the Tabernacles, leaves Galilee
Time: spring through fall 32 A.D.
Place: Galilee and Perea

JOHN 7:1-13
7:1 After these things, Jesus was walking in Galilee, for he wouldn't walk in Judea, because the Jews sought to kill him.
7:2 Now the feast of the Jews, the Feast of Booths, was at hand. 7:3 His brothers therefore said to him, "Depart from here, and go into Judea, that your disciples also may see your works which you do. 7:4 For no one does anything in secret, and himself seeks to be known openly. If you do these things, reveal yourself to the world." 7:5 For even his brothers didn't believe in him.
7:6 Jesus therefore said to them, "My time has not yet come, but your time is always ready. 7:7 The world can't hate you, but it hates me, because I testify about it, that its works are evil. 7:8 You go up to the feast.
I am not yet going up to this feast, because my time is not yet fulfilled."
7:9 Having said these things to them, he stayed in Galilee.
7:10 But when his brothers had gone up to the feast, then he also went up, not publicly, but as it were in secret.
7:11 The Jews therefore sought him at the feast, and said, "Where is he?"
7:12 There was much murmuring among the multitudes concerning him. Some said, "He is a good man." Others said, "Not so, but he leads the multitude astray." 7:13 Yet no one spoke openly of him for fear of the Jews.

Event 71: Jesus at the Feast of Tabernacles: the political controversy
Time: possibly October 12, 32 A.D.
Place: Jerusalem

JOHN 7:14-36
7:14 But when it was now the midst of the feast, Jesus went up into the temple and taught.
7:15 The Jews therefore marveled, saying, "How does this man know letters, having never been educated?"
7:16 Jesus therefore answered them, "My teaching is not mine, but his who sent me. 7:17 If anyone desires to do his will, he will know about the teaching, whether it is from God, or if I am speaking from myself. 7:18 He who speaks from himself seeks his own glory, but he who seeks the glory of him who sent him is true, and no unrighteousness is in him. 7:19 Didn't Moses give you the law, and yet none of you keeps the law? Why do you seek to kill me?"
7:20 The multitude answered, "You have a demon! Who seeks to kill you?"
7:21 Jesus answered them, "I did one work, and you all marvel because of it. 7:22 Moses has given you circumcision (not that it is of Moses, but of the fathers), and on the Sabbath you circumcise a boy. 7:23 If a boy receives circumcision on the Sabbath, that the law of Moses may not be broken, are you angry with me, because I made a man completely healthy on the Sabbath? 7:24 Don't judge according to appearance, but judge righteous judgment."
7:25 Therefore some of them of Jerusalem said, "Isn't this he whom they seek to kill? 7:26 Behold, he speaks openly, and they say nothing to him. Can it be that the rulers indeed know that this is truly the Christ? 7:27 However we know where this man comes from, but when the Christ comes, no one will know where he comes from."
7:28 Jesus therefore cried out in the temple, teaching and saying, "You both know me, and know where I am from. I have not come of myself, but he who sent me is true, whom you don't know. 7:29 I know him, because I am from him, and he sent me."
7:30 They sought therefore to take him; but no one laid a hand on him, because his hour had not yet come.
7:31 But of the multitude, many believed in him. They said, "When the Christ comes, he won't do more signs than those which this man has done, will he?"
7:32 The Pharisees heard the multitude murmuring these things concerning him, and the chief priests and the Pharisees sent officers to arrest him.
7:33 Then Jesus said, "I will be with you a little while longer, then I go to him who sent me. 7:34 You will seek me, and won't find me; and where I am, you can't come."
7:35 The Jews therefore said among themselves, "Where will this man go that we won't find him? Will he go to the Dispersion among the Greeks, and teach the Greeks? 7:36 What is this word that he said, 'You will seek me, and won't find me; and where I am, you can't come'?"

Event 72: Jesus at the Feast of Tabernacles: the water controversy
Time: October 16, 32 A.D. (Thursday)
Place: Jerusalem Temple

JOHN 7:37-8:1
7:37 Now on the last and greatest day of the feast, Jesus stood and cried out,
"If anyone is thirsty, let him come to me and drink! 7:37 He who believes in me, as the Scripture has said, from within him will flow rivers of living water."
7:37 But he said this about the Spirit, which those believing in him were to receive. For the Holy Spirit was not yet given, because Jesus wasn't yet glorified.
7:40 Many of the multitude therefore, when they heard these words, said, "This is truly the prophet." 7:41 Others said, "This is the Christ." But some said, "What, does the Christ come out of Galilee? 7:42 Hasn't the Scripture said that the Christ comes of the seed of David, [2 Samuel 7:12] and from Bethlehem, the village where David was?" [Micah 5:2] 7:43 So there arose a division in the multitude because of him.
7:44 Some of them would have arrested him, but no one laid hands on him.
7:45 The officers therefore came to the chief priests and Pharisees, and they said to them, "Why didn't you bring him?"
7:46 The officers answered, "No man ever spoke like this man!"
7:47 The Pharisees therefore answered them, "You aren't also led astray, are you? 7:48 Have any of the rulers believed in him, or of the Pharisees? 7:49 But this multitude that doesn't know the law is accursed."
7:50 Nicodemus (he who came to him by night, being one of them) said to them, 7:51 "Does our law judge a man, unless it first hears from him personally and knows what he does?" 7:52 They answered him, "Are you also from Galilee? Search, and see that no prophet has arisen out of Galilee."
7:52 They answered him, "Are you also from Galilee? Search, and see that no prophet has arisen out of Galilee."
7:53 Everyone went to his own house, 8:1 but Jesus went to the Mount of Olives.

Event 73: Jesus at the Feast of Tabernacles: the woman caught in adultery
Time: October 17, 32 A.D. (Friday)
Place: Jerusalem

JOHN 7:53-8:11
7:53 Everyone went to his own house, 8:1 but Jesus went to the Mount of Olives.
8:2 Now very early in the morning, he came again into the temple, and all the people came to him. He sat down, and taught them.
8:3 The scribes and the Pharisees brought a woman taken in adultery.
Having set her in the midst, 8:4 they told him, "Teacher, we found this woman in adultery, in the very act. 8:5 Now in our law, Moses commanded us to stone such. [Leviticus 20:10; Deuteronomy 22:22] What then do you say about her?"

8:6 They said this testing him, that they might have something to accuse him of.
But Jesus stooped down, and wrote on the ground with his finger.
8:7 But when they continued asking him, he looked up and said to them, "He who is without sin among you, let him throw the first stone at her."
8:8 Again he stooped down, and with his finger wrote on the ground.
8:9 They, when they heard it, being convicted by their conscience, went out one by one, beginning from the oldest, even to the last.
Jesus was left alone with the woman where she was, in the middle.
8:10 Jesus, standing up, saw her and said, "Woman, where are your accusers? Did no one condemn you?"
8:11 She said, "No one, Lord."
Jesus said, "Neither do I condemn you. Go your way. From now on, sin no more."

Event 74: Jesus at the Feast of Tabernacles: the light of the world controversy
Time: October 18, 32 A.D. (Saturday)
Place: Jerusalem

JOHN 8:12-8:59
8:12 Again, therefore, Jesus spoke to them, saying, "I am the light of the world. He who follows me will not walk in the darkness, but will have the light of life."
8:13 The Pharisees therefore said to him, "You testify about yourself. Your testimony is not valid."
8:14 Jesus answered them, "Even if I testify about myself, my testimony is true, for I know where I came from, and where I am going; but you don't know where I came from, or where I am going. 8:15 You judge according to the flesh. I judge no one. 8:16 Even if I do judge, my judgment is true, for I am not alone, but I am with the Father who sent me. 8:17 It's also written in your law that the testimony of two people is valid. [Deuteronomy 17:6; 19:15] 8:18 I am one who testifies about myself, and the Father who sent me testifies about me."
8:19 They said therefore to him, "Where is your Father?"
Jesus answered, "You know neither me, nor my Father. If you knew me, you would know my Father also." 8:20 Jesus spoke these words in the treasury, as he taught in the temple. Yet no one arrested him, because his hour had not yet come. 8:21 Jesus said therefore again to them, "I am going away, and you will seek me, and you will die in your sins. Where I go, you can't come."
8:22 The Jews therefore said, "Will he kill himself, that he says, 'Where I am going, you can't come?'"
8:23 He said to them, "You are from beneath. I am from above. You are of this world. I am not of this world. 8:24 I said therefore to you that you will die in your sins; for unless you believe that I am he, [literally "I am" or "I AM" from Exodus 3:14] you will die in your sins."
8:25 They said therefore to him, "Who are you?"
Jesus said to them, "Just what I have been saying to you from the beginning. 8:26 I have many things to speak and to judge concerning you. However he who sent me is true; and the things which I heard from him, these I say to the world."
8:27 They didn't understand that he spoke to them about the Father.

8:28 Jesus therefore said to them, "When you have lifted up the Son of Man, then you will know that I am he, and I do nothing of myself, but as my Father taught me, I say these things. 8:29 He who sent me is with me. The Father hasn't left me alone, for I always do the things that are pleasing to him."
8:30 As he spoke these things, many believed in him. 8:31 Jesus therefore said to those Jews who had believed him, "If you remain in my word, then you are truly my disciples. 8:32 You will know the truth, and the truth will make you free." "
8:33 They answered him, "We are Abraham's seed, and have never been in bondage to anyone. How do you say, 'You will be made free?'"
8:34 Jesus answered them, "Most certainly I tell you, everyone who commits sin is the bondservant of sin. 8:35 A bondservant doesn't live in the house forever. A son remains forever. 8:36 If therefore the Son makes you free, you will be free indeed.
8:37 I know that you are Abraham's seed, yet you seek to kill me, because my word finds no place in you. 8:38 I say the things which I have seen with my Father; and you also do the things which you have seen with your father."
8:39 They answered him, "Our father is Abraham."
Jesus said to them, "If you were Abraham's children, you would do the works of Abraham. 8:40 But now you seek to kill me, a man who has told you the truth, which I heard from God. Abraham didn't do this. 8:41 You do the works of your father."
They said to him, "We were not born of sexual immorality. We have one Father, God."
8:42 Therefore Jesus said to them, "If God were your father, you would love me, for I came out and have come from God. For I haven't come of myself, but he sent me. 8:43 Why don't you understand my speech? Because you can't hear my word. 8:44 You are of your father, the devil, and you want to do the desires of your father. He was a murderer from the beginning, and doesn't stand in the truth, because there is no truth in him. When he speaks a lie, he speaks on his own; for he is a liar, and its father. 8:45 But because I tell the truth, you don't believe me. 8:46 Which of you convicts me of sin? If I tell the truth, why do you not believe me? 8:47 He who is of God hears the words of God. For this cause you don't hear, because you are not of God."
8:48 Then the Jews answered him, "Don't we say well that you are a Samaritan, and have a demon?"
8:49 Jesus answered, "I don't have a demon, but I honor my Father, and you dishonor me. 8:50 But I don't seek my own glory. There is one who seeks and judges. 8:51 Most certainly, I tell you, if a person keeps my word, he will never see death."
8:52 Then the Jews said to him, "Now we know that you have a demon. Abraham died, and the prophets; and you say, 'If a man keeps my word, he will never taste of death.' 8:53 Are you greater than our father, Abraham, who died? The prophets died. Who do you make yourself out to be?"
8:54 Jesus answered, "If I glorify myself, my glory is nothing. It is my Father who glorifies me, of whom you say that he is our God. 8:55 You have not known him, but I know him. If I said, 'I don't know him,' I would be like you, a liar. But I know him, and keep his word. 8:56 Your father Abraham rejoiced to see my day. He saw it, and was glad."
8:57 The Jews therefore said to him, "You are not yet fifty years old, and have you seen Abraham?"
8:58 Jesus said to them, "Most certainly, I tell you, before Abraham came into existence, I am [literally "I am" or I AM from Exodus 3:14]."

8:59 Therefore they took up stones to throw at him, but Jesus was hidden, and went out of the temple, having gone through the midst of them, and so passed by.

Event 75: Jesus at the Feast of Tabernacles: the man born blind controversy
Time: October 18, 32 A.D. (Saturday)
Place: Jerusalem

JOHN 9:1-10:6
9:1 As he passed by, he saw a man blind from birth.
9:2 His disciples asked him, "Rabbi, who sinned, this man or his parents, that he was born blind?"
9:3 Jesus answered, "Neither did this man sin, nor his parents; but, that the works of God might be revealed in him.
9:4 I must work the works of him who sent me, while it is day. The night is coming, when no one can work. 9:5 While I am in the world, I am the light of the world."
9:6 When he had said this, he spat on the ground, made mud with the saliva, anointed the blind man's eyes with the mud,
9:7 and said to him, "Go, wash in the pool of Siloam" (which means "Sent").
So he went away, washed, and came back seeing.
9:8 The neighbors therefore, and those who saw that he was blind before, said, "Isn't this he who sat and begged?" 9:9 Others were saying, "It is he." Still others were saying, "He looks like him."
He said, "I am he." 9:10 They therefore were asking him, "How were your eyes opened?"
9:11 He answered, "A man called Jesus made mud, anointed my eyes, and said to me, 'Go to the pool of Siloam, and wash.' So I went away and washed, and I received sight."
9:12 Then they asked him, "Where is he?"
He said, "I don't know."
9:13 They brought him who had been blind to the Pharisees. 9:14 It was a Sabbath when Jesus made the mud and opened his eyes.
9:15 Again therefore the Pharisees also asked him how he received his sight.
He said to them, "He put mud on my eyes, I washed, and I see."
9:16 Some therefore of the Pharisees said, "This man is not from God, because he doesn't keep the Sabbath." Others said, "How can a man who is a sinner do such signs?" There was division among them.
9:17 Therefore they asked the blind man again, "What do you say about him, because he opened your eyes?"
He said, "He is a prophet."
9:18 The Jews therefore did not believe concerning him, that he had been blind, and had received his sight, until they called the parents of him who had received his sight, 9:19 and asked them, "Is this your son, who you say was born blind? How then does he now see?"
9:20 His parents answered them, "We know that this is our son, and that he was born blind; 9:21 but how he now sees, we don't know; or who opened his eyes, we don't know. He is of age. Ask him. He will speak for himself."

9:22 His parents said these things because they feared the Jews; for the Jews had already agreed that if any man would confess him as Christ, he would be put out of the synagogue. 9:23 Therefore his parents said, "He is of age. Ask him."
9:24 So they called the man who was blind a second time, and said to him, "Give glory to God. We know that this man is a sinner."
9:25 He therefore answered, "I don't know if he is a sinner. One thing I do know: that though I was blind, now I see."
9:26 They said to him again, "What did he do to you? How did he open your eyes?"
9:27 He answered them, "I told you already, and you didn't listen. Why do you want to hear it again? You don't also want to become his disciples, do you?"
9:28 They insulted him and said, "You are his disciple, but we are disciples of Moses. 9:29 We know that God has spoken to Moses. But as for this man, we don't know where he comes from."
9:30 The man answered them, "How amazing! You don't know where he comes from, yet he opened my eyes. 9:31 We know that God doesn't listen to sinners, but if anyone is a worshipper of God, and does his will, he listens to him. [Psalm 66:18; Proverbs 15:29; 28:9] 9:32 Since the world began it has never been heard of that anyone opened the eyes of someone born blind. 9:33 If this man were not from God, he could do nothing."
9:34 They answered him, "You were altogether born in sins, and do you teach us?" They threw him out.
9:35 Jesus heard that they had thrown him out, and finding him, he said, "Do you believe in the Son of God?"
9:36 He answered, "Who is he, Lord, that I may believe in him?"
9:37 Jesus said to him, "You have both seen him, and it is he who speaks with you."
9:38 He said, "Lord, I believe!" and he worshiped him.
9:39 Jesus said, "I came into this world for judgment, that those who don't see may see; and that those who see may become blind."
9:40 Those of the Pharisees who were with him heard these things, and said to him, "Are we also blind?"
9:41 Jesus said to them, "If you were blind, you would have no sin; but now you say, 'We see.' Therefore your sin remains.
10:1 "Most certainly, I tell you, one who doesn't enter by the door into the sheep fold, but climbs up some other way, the same is a thief and a robber. 10:2 But one who enters in by the door is the shepherd of the sheep. 10:3 The gatekeeper opens the gate for him, and the sheep listen to his voice. He calls his own sheep by name, and leads them out. 10:4 Whenever he brings out his own sheep, he goes before them, and the sheep follow him, for they know his voice. 10:5 They will by no means follow a stranger, but will flee from him; for they don't know the voice of strangers." 10:6 Jesus spoke this parable to them, but they didn't understand what he was telling them.

10:7 Jesus therefore said to them again, "Most certainly, I tell you, I am the sheep's door. 10:8 All who came before me are thieves and robbers, but the sheep didn't listen to them. 10:9 I am the door. If anyone enters in by me, he will be saved, and will go in and go out, and will find pasture. 10:10 The thief only comes to steal, kill, and destroy. I came that they may have life, and may have it abundantly. 10:11 I am the good shepherd. [Isaiah 40:11; Ezekiel 34:11-12,15,22] The good shepherd lays down his life for the sheep. 10:12 He who is a hired hand, and not a shepherd, who doesn't own the sheep, sees the wolf coming, leaves the sheep, and flees. The wolf snatches the sheep, and scatters them. 10:13 The hired hand flees because he is a hired hand, and doesn't care for the sheep. 10:14 I am the good shepherd. I know my own, and I'm known by my own; 10:15 even as the Father knows me, and I know the Father. I lay down my life for the sheep. 10:16 I have other sheep, which are not of this fold. [Isaiah 56:8] I must bring them also, and they will hear my voice. They will become one flock with one shepherd. 10:17 Therefore the Father loves me, because I lay down my life [Isaiah 53:7-8], that I may take it again. 10:18 No one takes it away from me, but I lay it down by myself. I have power to lay it down, and I have power to take it again. I received this commandment from my Father."
10:19 Therefore a division arose again among the Jews because of these words. 10:20 Many of them said, "He has a demon, and is insane! Why do you listen to him?" 10:21 Others said, "These are not the sayings of one possessed by a demon. It isn't possible for a demon to open the eyes of the blind, is it?" [Exodus 4:11]

Event 76: Jesus goes to Jerusalem for the Feast of Dedication
Time: between December 29, 32 A.D and January 5, 33 A.D.
Place: Jerusalem, Judea

JOHN 10:22-39
10:22 It was the Feast of the Dedication [The "Feast of Dedication" is the Greek name for "Hanukkah", a celebration of the rededication of the Temple.] at Jerusalem. 10:23 It was winter, and Jesus was walking in the temple, in Solomon's porch.
10:24 The Jews therefore came around him and said to him, "How long will you hold us in suspense? If you are the Christ, tell us plainly."
10:25 Jesus answered them, "I told you, and you don't believe. The works that I do in my Father's name, these testify about me. 10:26 But you don't believe, because you are not of my sheep, as I told you. 10:27 My sheep hear my voice, and I know them, and they follow me. 10:28 I give eternal life to them. They will never perish, and no one will snatch them out of my hand. 10:29 My Father, who has given them to me, is greater than all. No one is able to snatch them out of my Father's hand. 10:30 I and the Father are one."
10:31 Therefore Jews took up stones again to stone him.
10:32 Jesus answered them, "I have shown you many good works from my Father. For which of those works do you stone me?"
10:33 The Jews answered him, "We don't stone you for a good work, but for blasphemy: because you, being a man, make yourself God."

10:34 Jesus answered them, "Isn't it written in your law, 'I said, you are gods?' [Psalm 82:6] 10:35 If he called them gods, to whom the word of God came (and the Scripture can't be broken), 10:36 do you say of him whom the Father sanctified and sent into the world, 'You blaspheme,' because I said, 'I am the Son of God?' 10:37 If I don't do the works of my Father, don't believe me.10:38 But if I do them, though you don't believe me, believe the works; that you may know and believe that the Father is in me, and I in the Father."
10:39 They sought again to seize him, and he went out of their hand.
10:40 He went away again beyond the Jordan into the place where John was baptizing at first, and there he stayed.
10:41 Many came to him. They said, "John indeed did no sign, but everything that John said about this man is true." 10:42 Many believed in him there.

Event 77: Jesus' begins his final journey to Jerusalem
Time: early 33 A.D.
Place: Perea

MATTHEW 19:1	MARK 10:1	LUKE 9:51-52
19:1 It happened when Jesus had finished these words, he departed from Galilee, and came into the borders of Judea beyond the Jordan.	10:1 He arose from there and came into the borders of Judea and beyond the Jordan.	9:51 It came to pass, when the days were near that he should be taken up, he intently set his face to go to Jerusalem, 9:52 and sent messengers before his face.

Event 78: Jesus in Samaria: Jesus reprimands James and John, the sons of thunder
Time: early 33 A.D.
Place: Samaria

LUKE 9:51-62
9:51 It came to pass, when the days were near that he should be taken up, he intently set his face to go to Jerusalem, 9:52 and sent messengers before his face. They went, and entered into a village of the Samaritans, so as to prepare for him.
9:53 They didn't receive him, because he was traveling with his face set towards Jerusalem.
9:54 When his disciples, James and John, saw this, they said, "Lord, do you want us to command fire to come down from the sky, and destroy them, just as Elijah did?"
9:55 But he turned and rebuked them, "You don't know of what kind of spirit you are. 9:56 For the Son of Man didn't come to destroy men's lives, but to save them."
They went to another village. 9:57 As they went on the way, a certain man said to him, "I want to follow you wherever you go, Lord."
9:58 Jesus said to him, "The foxes have holes, and the birds of the sky have nests, but the Son of Man has no place to lay his head."
9:59 He said to another, "Follow me!"
But he said, "Lord, allow me first to go and bury my father."

9:60 But Jesus said to him, "Leave the dead to bury their own dead, but you go and announce the Kingdom of God."
9:61 Another also said, "I want to follow you, Lord, but first allow me to bid farewell to those who are at my house."
9:62 But Jesus said to him, "No one, having put his hand to the plow, and looking back, is fit for the Kingdom of God."

Event 79: Jesus chooses 70 disciples for a Samaritan ministry
Time: early 33 A.D.
Place: Samaria

LUKE 10:1-24
10:1 Now after these things, the Lord also appointed seventy others, and sent them two by two ahead of him into every city and place, where he was about to come.
10:2 Then he said to them, "The harvest is indeed plentiful, but the laborers are few. Pray therefore to the Lord of the harvest, that he may send out laborers into his harvest. 10:3 Go your ways. Behold, I send you out as lambs among wolves. 10:4 Carry no purse, nor wallet, nor sandals. Greet no one on the way. 10:5 Into whatever house you enter, first say, 'Peace be to this house.' 10:6 If a son of peace is there, your peace will rest on him; but if not, it will return to you. 10:7 Remain in that same house, eating and drinking the things they give, for the laborer is worthy of his wages. Don't go from house to house. 10:8 Into whatever city you enter, and they receive you, eat the things that are set before you. 10:9 Heal the sick who are therein, and tell them, 'The Kingdom of God has come near to you.' 10:10 But into whatever city you enter, and they don't receive you, go out into its streets and say, 10:11 'Even the dust from your city that clings to us, we wipe off against you. Nevertheless know this, that the Kingdom of God has come near to you.' 10:12 I tell you, it will be more tolerable in that day for Sodom than for that city.
10:13 "Woe to you, Chorazin! Woe to you, Bethsaida! For if the mighty works had been done in Tyre and Sidon which were done in you, they would have repented long ago, sitting in sackcloth and ashes. 10:14 But it will be more tolerable for Tyre and Sidon in the judgment than for you. 10:15 You, Capernaum, who are exalted to heaven, will be brought down to Hades. [Hell]
10:16 Whoever listens to you listens to me, and whoever rejects you rejects me. Whoever rejects me rejects him who sent me."
10:17 The seventy returned with joy, saying, "Lord, even the demons are subject to us in your name!"
10:18 He said to them, "I saw Satan having fallen like lightning from heaven. 10:19 Behold, I give you authority to tread on serpents and scorpions, and over all the power of the enemy. Nothing will in any way hurt you. 10:20 Nevertheless, don't rejoice in this, that the spirits are subject to you, but rejoice that your names are written in heaven."
10:21 In that same hour Jesus rejoiced in the Holy Spirit, and said, "I thank you, O Father, Lord of heaven and earth, that you have hidden these things from the wise and understanding, and revealed them to little children. Yes, Father, for so it was well-pleasing in your sight."
10:22 Turning to the disciples, he said, "All things have been delivered to me by my Father. No one knows who the Son is, except the Father, and who the Father is, except the Son, and he to whomever the Son desires to reveal him."

10:23 Turning to the disciples, he said privately, "Blessed are the eyes which see the things that you see, 10:24 for I tell you that many prophets and kings desired to see the things which you see, and didn't see them, and to hear the things which you hear, and didn't hear them."

Event 80: Jesus delivers the parable of the Good Samaritan
Time: early 33 A.D.
Place: Judea

LUKE 10:25-37
10:25 Behold, a certain lawyer stood up and tested him, saying, "Teacher, what shall I do to inherit eternal life?"
10:26 He said to him, "What is written in the law? How do you read it?"
10:27 He answered, "You shall love the Lord your God with all your heart, with all your soul, with all your strength, and with all your mind; [Deuteronomy 6:5] and your neighbor as yourself." [Leviticus 19:18]
10:28 He said to him, "You have answered correctly. Do this, and you will live."
10:29 But he, desiring to justify himself, asked Jesus, "Who is my neighbor?"
10:30 Jesus answered, "A certain man was going down from Jerusalem to Jericho, and he fell among robbers, who both stripped him and beat him, and departed, leaving him half dead.10:31 By chance a certain priest was going down that way. When he saw him, he passed by on the other side. 10:32 In the same way a Levite also, when he came to the place, and saw him, passed by on the other side. 10:33 But a certain Samaritan, as he traveled, came where he was. When he saw him, he was moved with compassion, 10:34 came to him, and bound up his wounds, pouring on oil and wine. He set him on his own animal, and brought him to an inn, and took care of him. 10:35 On the next day, when he departed, he took out two denarii, and gave them to the host, and said to him, 'Take care of him. Whatever you spend beyond that, I will repay you when I return.'
10:36 Now which of these three do you think seemed to be a neighbor to him who fell among the robbers?"
10:37 He said, "He who showed mercy on him."
Then Jesus said to him, "Go and do likewise."

Event 81: Jesus visits with Mary and Martha
Time: early 33 A.D.
Place: Bethany, Judea

LUKE 10:38-42
10:38 It happened as they went on their way, he entered into a certain village, and a certain woman named Martha received him into her house. 10:39 She had a sister called Mary, who also sat at Jesus' feet, and heard his word.
10:40 But Martha was distracted with much serving, and she came up to him, and said, "Lord, don't you care that my sister left me to serve alone? Ask her therefore to help me."

10:41 Jesus answered her, "Martha, Martha, you are anxious and troubled about many things, 10:42 but one thing is needed. Mary has chosen the good part, which will not be taken away from her."

Event 82: Jesus teaches on the power of prayer
Time: early 33 A.D.
Place: Judea

LUKE 11:1-13
11:1 It happened, that when he finished praying in a certain place, one of his disciples said to him, "Lord, teach us to pray, just as John also taught his disciples."
11:2 He said to them, "When you pray, say, 'Our Father in heaven, may your name be kept holy. May your Kingdom come. May your will be done on Earth, as it is in heaven. 11:3 Give us day by day our daily bread. 11:4 Forgive us our sins, for we ourselves also forgive everyone who is indebted to us. Bring us not into temptation, but deliver us from the evil one.'"
11:5 He said to them, "Which of you, if you go to a friend at midnight, and tell him, 'Friend, lend me three loaves of bread, 11:6 for a friend of mine has come to me from a journey, and I have nothing to set before him,' 11:7 and he from within will answer and say, 'Don't bother me. The door is now shut, and my children are with me in bed. I can't get up and give it to you'? 11:8 I tell you, although he will not rise and give it to him because he is his friend, yet because of his persistence, he will get up and give him as many as he needs.
11:9 "I tell you, keep asking, and it will be given you. Keep seeking, and you will find. Keep knocking, and it will be opened to you. 11:10 For everyone who asks receives. He who seeks finds. To him who knocks it will be opened.
11:11 "Which of you fathers, if your son asks for bread, will give him a stone? Or if he asks for a fish, he won't give him a snake instead of a fish, will he? 11:12 Or if he asks for an egg, he won't give him a scorpion, will he? 11:13 If you then, being evil, know how to give good gifts to your children, how much more will your heavenly Father give the Holy Spirit to those who ask him?"

Event 83: Jesus exorcises a demoniac and is challenged
Time: early 33 A.D.
Place: Judea

LUKE 11:14-36
11:14 He was casting out a demon, and it was mute. It happened, when the demon had gone out, the mute man spoke; and the multitudes marveled.
11:15 But some of them said, "He casts out demons by Beelzebul, the prince of the demons."
11:16 Others, testing him, sought from him a sign from heaven.

11:17 But he, knowing their thoughts, said to them, "Every kingdom divided against itself is brought to desolation. A house divided against itself falls. 11:18 If Satan also is divided against himself, how will his kingdom stand? For you say that I cast out demons by Beelzebul. 11:19 But if I cast out demons by Beelzebul, by whom do your children cast them out? Therefore will they be your judges. 11:20 But if I by the finger of God cast out demons, then the Kingdom of God has come to you.
11:21 "When the strong man, fully armed, guards his own dwelling, his goods are safe. 11:22 But when someone stronger attacks him and overcomes him, he takes from him his whole armor in which he trusted, and divides his spoils.
11:23 "He that is not with me is against me. He who doesn't gather with me scatters. 11:24 The unclean spirit, when he has gone out of the man, passes through dry places, seeking rest, and finding none, he says, 'I will turn back to my house from which I came out.' 11:25 When he returns, he finds it swept and put in order. 11:26 Then he goes, and takes seven other spirits more evil than himself, and they enter in and dwell there. The last state of that man becomes worse than the first."
11:27 It came to pass, as he said these things, a certain woman out of the multitude lifted up her voice, and said to him, "Blessed is the womb that bore you, and the breasts which nursed you!"
11:28 But he said, "On the contrary, blessed are those who hear the word of God, and keep it."
11:29 When the multitudes were gathering together to him, he began to say, "This is an evil generation. It seeks after a sign. No sign will be given to it but the sign of Jonah, the prophet. 11:30 For even as Jonah became a sign to the Ninevites, so will also the Son of Man be to this generation. 11:31 The Queen of the South will rise up in the judgment with the men of this generation, and will condemn them: for she came from the ends of the earth to hear the wisdom of Solomon; and behold, one greater than Solomon is here. 11:32 The men of Nineveh will stand up in the judgment with this generation, and will condemn it: for they repented at the preaching of Jonah, and behold, one greater than Jonah is here.
11:33 "No one, when he has lit a lamp, puts it in a cellar or under a basket, but on a stand, that those who come in may see the light. 11:34 The lamp of the body is the eye. Therefore when your eye is good, your whole body is also full of light; but when it is evil, your body also is full of darkness. 11:35 Therefore see whether the light that is in you isn't darkness. 11:36 If therefore your whole body is full of light, having no part dark, it will be wholly full of light, as when the lamp with its bright shining gives you light."

Event 84: Jesus dines with a Pharisee
Time: early 33 A.D.
Place: Judea

LUKE 11:37-54
11:37 Now as he spoke, a certain Pharisee asked him to dine with him. He went in, and sat at the table.
11:38 When the Pharisee saw it, he marveled that he had not first washed himself before dinner.

11:39 The Lord said to him, "Now you Pharisees cleanse the outside of the cup and of the platter, but your inward part is full of extortion and wickedness. 11:40 You foolish ones, didn't he who made the outside make the inside also? 11:41 But give for gifts to the needy those things which are within, and behold, all things will be clean to you. 11:42 But woe to you Pharisees! For you tithe mint and rue and every herb, but you bypass justice and the love of God. You ought to have done these, and not to have left the other undone. 11:43 Woe to you Pharisees! For you love the best seats in the synagogues, and the greetings in the marketplaces. 11:44 Woe to you, scribes and Pharisees, hypocrites! For you are like hidden graves, and the men who walk over them don't know it."
11:45 One of the lawyers answered him, "Teacher, in saying this you insult us also."
11:46 He said, "Woe to you lawyers also! For you load men with burdens that are difficult to carry, and you yourselves won't even lift one finger to help carry those burdens. 11:47 Woe to you! For you build the tombs of the prophets, and your fathers killed them. 11:48 So you testify and consent to the works of your fathers. For they killed them, and you build their tombs. 11:49 Therefore also the wisdom of God said, 'I will send to them prophets and apostles; and some of them they will kill and persecute, 11:50 that the blood of all the prophets, which was shed from the foundation of the world, may be required of this generation; 11:51 from the blood of Abel to the blood of Zachariah, who perished between the altar and the sanctuary.' Yes, I tell you, it will be required of this generation. 11:52 Woe to you lawyers! For you took away the key of knowledge. You didn't enter in yourselves, and those who were entering in, you hindered."
11:53 As he said these things to them, the scribes and the Pharisees began to be terribly angry, and to draw many things out of him; 11:54 lying in wait for him, and seeking to catch him in something he might say, that they might accuse him.

Event 85: Jesus teaches about blasphemy against the Spirit
Time: early 33 A.D.
Place: Judea

LUKE 12:1-12
12:1 Meanwhile, when a multitude of many thousands had gathered together, so much so that they trampled on each other, he began to tell his disciples first of all, "Beware of the yeast of the Pharisees, which is hypocrisy. 12:2 But there is nothing covered up, that will not be revealed, nor hidden, that will not be known. 12:3 Therefore whatever you have said in the darkness will be heard in the light. What you have spoken in the ear in the inner chambers will be proclaimed on the housetops.
12:4 "I tell you, my friends, don't be afraid of those who kill the body, and after that have no more that they can do. 12:5 But I will warn you whom you should fear. Fear him, who after he has killed, has power to cast into Gehenna. Yes, I tell you, fear him.
12:6 "Aren't five sparrows sold for two assaria coins? [about an hour's wages for an agricultural worker] Not one of them is forgotten by God. 12:7 But the very hairs of your head are all numbered. Therefore don't be afraid. You are of more value than many sparrows.
12:8 "I tell you, everyone who confesses me before men, him will the Son of Man also confess before the angels of God; 12:9 but he who denies me in the presence of men will be denied in the presence of the angels of God. 12:10 Everyone who speaks a word against the Son of Man will be forgiven, but those who blaspheme against the Holy Spirit will not be forgiven.

12:11 When they bring you before the synagogues, the rulers, and the authorities, don't be anxious how or what you will answer, or what you will say; 12:12 for the Holy Spirit will teach you in that same hour what you must say."

Event 86: Jesus delivers a series of parables
Time: early 33 A.D.
Place: Judea

LUKE 12:13-13:9
12:13 One of the multitude said to him, "Teacher, tell my brother to divide the inheritance with me."
12:14 But he said to him, "Man, who made me a judge or an arbitrator over you?" 12:15 He said to them, "Beware! Keep yourselves from covetousness, for a man's life doesn't consist of the abundance of the things which he possesses."
12:16 He spoke a parable to them, saying, "The ground of a certain rich man brought forth abundantly. 12:17 He reasoned within himself, saying, 'What will I do, because I don't have room to store my crops?' 12:18 He said, 'This is what I will do. I will pull down my barns, and build bigger ones, and there I will store all my grain and my goods. 12:19 I will tell my soul, "Soul, you have many goods laid up for many years. Take your ease, eat, drink, be merry."'
12:20 "But God said to him, 'You foolish one, tonight your soul is required of you. The things which you have prepared—whose will they be?' 12:21 So is he who lays up treasure for himself, and is not rich toward God."
12:22 He said to his disciples, "Therefore I tell you, don't be anxious for your life, what you will eat, nor yet for your body, what you will wear. 12:23 Life is more than food, and the body is more than clothing. 12:24 Consider the ravens: they don't sow, they don't reap, they have no warehouse or barn, and God feeds them. How much more valuable are you than birds! 12:25 Which of you by being anxious can add a cubit to his height? 12:26 If then you aren't able to do even the least things, why are you anxious about the rest? 12:27 Consider the lilies, how they grow. They don't toil, neither do they spin; yet I tell you, even Solomon in all his glory was not arrayed like one of these. 12:28 But if this is how God clothes the grass in the field, which today exists, and tomorrow is cast into the oven, how much more will he clothe you, O you of little faith? 12:29 Don't seek what you will eat or what you will drink; neither be anxious.12:30 For the nations of the world seek after all of these things, but your Father knows that you need these things. 12:31 But seek God's Kingdom, and all these things will be added to you.12:32 Don't be afraid, little flock, for it is your Father's good pleasure to give you the Kingdom. 12:33 Sell that which you have, and give gifts to the needy. Make for yourselves purses which don't grow old, a treasure in the heavens that doesn't fail, where no thief approaches, neither moth destroys. 12:34 For where your treasure is, there will your heart be also.

12:35 "Let your waist be girded and your lamps burning. 12:36 Be like men watching for their lord, when he returns from the marriage feast; that, when he comes and knocks, they may immediately open to him. 12:37 Blessed are those servants, whom the lord will find watching when he comes. Most certainly I tell you, that he will dress himself, and make them recline, and will come and serve them. 12:38 They will be blessed if he comes in the second or third watch, and finds them so. 12:39 But know this, that if the master of the house had known in what hour the thief was coming, he would have watched, and not allowed his house to be broken into. 12:40 Therefore be ready also, for the Son of Man is coming in an hour that you don't expect him."

12:41 Peter said to him, "Lord, are you telling this parable to us, or to everybody?"

12:42 The Lord said, "Who then is the faithful and wise steward, whom his lord will set over his household, to give them their portion of food at the right times? 12:43 Blessed is that servant whom his lord will find doing so when he comes. 12:44 Truly I tell you, that he will set him over all that he has. 12:45 But if that servant says in his heart, 'My lord delays his coming,' and begins to beat the menservants and the maidservants, and to eat and drink, and to be drunken, 12:46 then the lord of that servant will come in a day when he isn't expecting him, and in an hour that he doesn't know, and will cut him in two, and place his portion with the unfaithful. 12:47 That servant, who knew his lord's will, and didn't prepare, nor do what he wanted, will be beaten with many stripes, 12:48 but he who didn't know, and did things worthy of stripes, will be beaten with few stripes. To whoever much is given, of him will much be required; and to whom much was entrusted, of him more will be asked.

12:49 "I came to throw fire on the earth. I wish it were already kindled. 12:50 But I have a baptism to be baptized with, and how distressed I am until it is accomplished! 12:51 Do you think that I have come to give peace in the earth? I tell you, no, but rather division. 12:52 For from now on, there will be five in one house divided, three against two, and two against three. 12:53 They will be divided, father against son, and son against father; mother against daughter, and daughter against her mother; mother-in-law against her daughter-in-law, and daughter-in-law against her mother-in-law."

12:54 He said to the multitudes also, "When you see a cloud rising from the west, immediately you say, 'A shower is coming,' and so it happens. 12:55 When a south wind blows, you say, 'There will be a scorching heat,' and it happens. 12:56 You hypocrites! You know how to interpret the appearance of the earth and the sky, but how is it that you don't interpret this time? 12:57 Why don't you judge for yourselves what is right? 12:58 For when you are going with your adversary before the magistrate, try diligently on the way to be released from him, lest perhaps he drag you to the judge, and the judge deliver you to the officer, and the officer throw you into prison. 12:59 I tell you, you will by no means get out of there, until you have paid the very last penny."

13:1 Now there were some present at the same time who told him about the Galileans, whose blood Pilate had mixed with their sacrifices. 13:2 Jesus answered them, "Do you think that these Galileans were worse sinners than all the other Galileans, because they suffered such things?

13:3 I tell you, no, but, unless you repent, you will all perish in the same way. 13:4 Or those eighteen, on whom the tower in Siloam fell, and killed them; do you think that they were worse offenders than all the men who dwell in Jerusalem? 13:5 I tell you, no, but, unless you repent, you will all perish in the same way."

13:6 He spoke this parable. "A certain man had a fig tree planted in his vineyard, and he came seeking fruit on it, and found none. 13:7 He said to the vine dresser, 'Behold, these three years I have come looking for fruit on this fig tree, and found none. Cut it down. Why does it waste the soil?' 13:8 He answered, 'Lord, leave it alone this year also, until I dig around it, and fertilize it. 13:9 If it bears fruit, fine; but if not, after that, you can cut it down.'"

Event 87: Jesus heals a crippled woman on the Sabbath
Time: early 33 A.D.
Place: Judea or Perea

LUKE 13:10-17
13:10 He was teaching in one of the synagogues on the Sabbath day.
13:11 Behold, there was a woman who had a spirit of infirmity eighteen years, and she was bent over, and could in no way straighten herself up.
13:12 When Jesus saw her, he called her, and said to her, "Woman, you are freed from your infirmity." 13:13 He laid his hands on her, and immediately she stood up straight, and glorified God.
13:14 The ruler of the synagogue, being indignant because Jesus had healed on the Sabbath, said to the multitude, "There are six days in which men ought to work. Therefore come on those days and be healed, and not on the Sabbath day!"
13:15 Therefore the Lord answered him, "You hypocrites! Doesn't each one of you free his ox or his donkey from the stall on the Sabbath, and lead him away to water? 13:16 Ought not this woman, being a daughter of Abraham, whom Satan had bound eighteen long years, be freed from this bondage on the Sabbath day?"
13:17 As he said these things, all his adversaries were disappointed, and all the multitude rejoiced for all the glorious things that were done by him.

Event 88: Jesus delivers a further series of parables
Time: early 33 A.D.
Place: Judea or Perea

LUKE 13:18-21
13:18 He said, "What is the Kingdom of God like? To what shall I compare it? 13:19 It is like a grain of mustard seed, which a man took, and put in his own garden. It grew, and became a large tree, and the birds of the sky lodged in its branches."
13:20 Again he said, "To what shall I compare the Kingdom of God? 13:21 It is like yeast, which a woman took and hid in three measures [about 39 litres or a bushel] of flour, until it was all leavened."

Event 89: Jesus speaks of the narrow gate
Time: early 33 A.D.
Place: Judea or Perea

LUKE 13:22-30

13:22 He went on his way through cities and villages, teaching, and traveling on to Jerusalem.
13:23 One said to him, "Lord, are they few who are saved?"
He said to them, 13:24 "Strive to enter in by the narrow door, for many, I tell you, will seek to enter in, and will not be able. 13:25 When once the master of the house has risen up, and has shut the door, and you begin to stand outside, and to knock at the door, saying, 'Lord, Lord, open to us!' then he will answer and tell you, 'I don't know you or where you come from.'
13:26 Then you will begin to say, 'We ate and drank in your presence, and you taught in our streets.'
13:27 He will say, 'I tell you, I don't know where you come from. Depart from me, all you workers of iniquity.' 13:28 There will be weeping and gnashing of teeth, when you see Abraham, Isaac, Jacob, and all the prophets, in the Kingdom of God, and yourselves being thrown outside. 13:29 They will come from the east, west, north, and south, and will sit down in the Kingdom of God. 13:30 Behold, there are some who are last who will be first, and there are some who are first who will be last."

Event 90: Jesus is warned about Herod Antipas and laments over Jerusalem
Time: early 33 A.D.
Place: Judea or Perea

LUKE 13:31-35
13:31 On that same day, some Pharisees came, saying to him, "Get out of here, and go away, for Herod wants to kill you."
13:32 He said to them, "Go and tell that fox, 'Behold, I cast out demons and perform cures today and tomorrow, and the third day I complete my mission. 13:33 Nevertheless I must go on my way today and tomorrow and the next day, for it can't be that a prophet perish outside of Jerusalem.'
13:34 "Jerusalem, Jerusalem, that kills the prophets, and stones those who are sent to her! How often I wanted to gather your children together, like a hen gathers her own brood under her wings, and you refused! 13:35 Behold, your house is left to you desolate. I tell you, you will not see me, until you say, 'Blessed is he who comes in the name of the Lord!'"

Event 91: Jesus heals a man with dropsy on the Sabbath
Time: early 33 A.D.
Place: Judea or Perea

LUKE 14:1-6
14:1 It happened, when he went into the house of one of the rulers of the Pharisees on a Sabbath to eat bread, that they were watching him. 14:2 Behold, a certain man who had dropsy was in front of him.
14:3 Jesus, answering, spoke to the lawyers and Pharisees, saying, "Is it lawful to heal on the Sabbath?"
14:4 But they were silent.

He took him, and healed him, and let him go. 14:5 He answered them, "Which of you, if your son or an ox fell into a well, wouldn't immediately pull him out on a Sabbath day?"
14:6 They couldn't answer him regarding these things.

Event 92: Jesus delivers a further series of parables
Time: early 33 A.D.
Place: Perea

LUKE 14:7-17:10
14:7 He spoke a parable to those who were invited, when he noticed how they chose the best seats, and said to them, 14:8 "When you are invited by anyone to a marriage feast, don't sit in the best seat, since perhaps someone more honorable than you might be invited by him, 14:9 and he who invited both of you would come and tell you, 'Make room for this person.' Then you would begin, with shame, to take the lowest place. 14:10 But when you are invited, go and sit in the lowest place, so that when he who invited you comes, he may tell you, 'Friend, move up higher.' Then you will be honored in the presence of all who sit at the table with you. 14:11 For everyone who exalts himself will be humbled, and whoever humbles himself will be exalted."
14:12 He also said to the one who had invited him, "When you make a dinner or a supper, don't call your friends, nor your brothers, nor your kinsmen, nor rich neighbors, or perhaps they might also return the favor, and pay you back. 14:13 But when you make a feast, ask the poor, the maimed, the lame, or the blind; 14:14 and you will be blessed, because they don't have the resources to repay you. For you will be repaid in the resurrection of the righteous."
14:15 When one of those who sat at the table with him heard these things, he said to him, "Blessed is he who will feast in the Kingdom of God!"
14:16 But he said to him, "A certain man made a great supper, and he invited many people. 14:17 He sent out his servant at supper time to tell those who were invited, 'Come, for everything is ready now.' 14:18 They all as one began to make excuses.
"The first said to him, 'I have bought a field, and I must go and see it. Please have me excused.'
14:19 "Another said, 'I have bought five yoke of oxen, and I must go try them out. Please have me excused.'
14:20 "Another said, 'I have married a wife, and therefore I can't come.'
14:21 "That servant came, and told his lord these things.
Then the master of the house, being angry, said to his servant, 'Go out quickly into the streets and lanes of the city, and bring in the poor, maimed, blind, and lame.'
14:22 "The servant said, 'Lord, it is done as you commanded, and there is still room.'
14:23 "The lord said to the servant, 'Go out into the highways and hedges, and compel them to come in, that my house may be filled. 14:24 For I tell you that none of those men who were invited will taste of my supper.'"
14:25 Now great multitudes were going with him.

He turned and said to them, 14:26 "If anyone comes to me, and doesn't hate his own father, mother, wife, children, brothers, and sisters, yes, and his own life also, he can't be my disciple. 14:27 Whoever doesn't bear his own cross, and come after me, can't be my disciple. 14:28 For which of you, desiring to build a tower, doesn't first sit down and count the cost, to see if he has enough to complete it? 14:29 Or perhaps, when he has laid a foundation, and is not able to finish, everyone who sees begins to mock him, 14:30 saying, 'This man began to build, and wasn't able to finish.' 14:31 Or what king, as he goes to encounter another king in war, will not sit down first and consider whether he is able with ten thousand to meet him who comes against him with twenty thousand? 14:32 Or else, while the other is yet a great way off, he sends an envoy, and asks for conditions of peace.14:33 So therefore whoever of you who doesn't renounce all that he has, he can't be my disciple. 14:34 Salt is good, but if the salt becomes flat and tasteless, with what do you season it?14:35 It is fit neither for the soil nor for the manure pile. It is thrown out. He who has ears to hear, let him hear."

15:1 Now all the tax collectors and sinners were coming close to him to hear him. 15:2 The Pharisees and the scribes murmured, saying, "This man welcomes sinners, and eats with them."

15:3 He told them this parable. 15:4 "Which of you men, if you had one hundred sheep, and lost one of them, wouldn't leave the ninety-nine in the wilderness, and go after the one that was lost, until he found it? 15:5 When he has found it, he carries it on his shoulders, rejoicing. 15:6 When he comes home, he calls together his friends and his neighbors, saying to them, 'Rejoice with me, for I have found my sheep which was lost!' 15:7 I tell you that even so there will be more joy in heaven over one sinner who repents, than over ninety-nine righteous people who need no repentance.

15:8 Or what woman, if she had ten drachma coins, if she lost one drachma coin [about 2 days wages for an agricultural worker], wouldn't light a lamp, sweep the house, and seek diligently until she found it? 15:9 When she has found it, she calls together her friends and neighbors, saying, 'Rejoice with me, for I have found the drachma which I had lost.'

15:10 Even so, I tell you, there is joy in the presence of the angels of God over one sinner repenting."

15:11 He said, "A certain man had two sons. 15:12 The younger of them said to his father, 'Father, give me my share of your property.' He divided his livelihood between them. 15:13 Not many days after, the younger son gathered all of this together and traveled into a far country. There he wasted his property with riotous living.

15:14 When he had spent all of it, there arose a severe famine in that country, and he began to be in need.

15:15 He went and joined himself to one of the citizens of that country, and he sent him into his fields to feed pigs. 15:16 He wanted to fill his belly with the husks that the pigs ate, but no one gave him any. 15:17 But when he came to himself he said, 'How many hired servants of my father's have bread enough to spare, and I'm dying with hunger! 15:18 I will get up and go to my father, and will tell him, "Father, I have sinned against heaven, and in your sight. 15:19 I am no more worthy to be called your son. Make me as one of your hired servants."'

15:20 "He arose, and came to his father.

But while he was still far off, his father saw him, and was moved with compassion, and ran, and fell on his neck, and kissed him.

15:21 The son said to him, 'Father, I have sinned against heaven, and in your sight. I am no longer worthy to be called your son.'

15:22 "But the father said to his servants, 'Bring out the best robe, and put it on him. Put a ring on his hand, and shoes on his feet. 15:23 Bring the fattened calf, kill it, and let us eat, and celebrate; 15:24 for this, my son, was dead, and is alive again. He was lost, and is found.'

They began to celebrate.

15:25 "Now his elder son was in the field. As he came near to the house, he heard music and dancing. 15:26 He called one of the servants to him, and asked what was going on.

15:27 He said to him, 'Your brother has come, and your father has killed the fattened calf, because he has received him back safe and healthy.'

15:28 But he was angry, and would not go in.

Therefore his father came out, and begged him.

15:29 But he answered his father, 'Behold, these many years I have served you, and I never disobeyed a commandment of yours, but you never gave me a goat, that I might celebrate with my friends. 15:30 But when this, your son, came, who has devoured your living with prostitutes, you killed the fattened calf for him.'

15:31 "He said to him, 'Son, you are always with me, and all that is mine is yours. 15:32 But it was appropriate to celebrate and be glad, for this, your brother, was dead, and is alive again. He was lost, and is found.'"

16:1 He also said to his disciples, "There was a certain rich man who had a manager. An accusation was made to him that this man was wasting his possessions. 16:2 He called him, and said to him, 'What is this that I hear about you? Give an accounting of your management, for you can no longer be manager.'

16:3 "The manager said within himself, 'What will I do, seeing that my lord is taking away the management position from me? I don't have strength to dig. I am ashamed to beg. 16:4 I know what I will do, so that when I am removed from management, they may receive me into their houses.' 16:5 Calling each one of his lord's debtors to him, he said to the first, 'How much do you owe to my lord?' 16:6 He said, 'A hundred batos [about 395 litres, 104 US gallons, 87 imperial gallons] of oil.' He said to him, 'Take your bill, and sit down quickly and write fifty.' 16:7 Then said he to another, 'How much do you owe?' He said, 'A hundred cors [about 3910 litres, 600 bushels] of wheat.' He said to him, 'Take your bill, and write eighty.'

16:8 "His lord commended the dishonest manager because he had done wisely, for the children of this world are, in their own generation, wiser than the children of the light. 16:9 I tell you, make for yourselves friends by means of unrighteous mammon, so that when you fail, they may receive you into the eternal tents. 16:10 He who is faithful in a very little is faithful also in much. He who is dishonest in a very little is also dishonest in much. 16:11 If therefore you have not been faithful in the unrighteous mammon, who will commit to your trust the true riches? 16:12 If you have not been faithful in that which is another's, who will give you that which is your own? 16:13 No servant can serve two masters, for either he will hate the one, and love the other; or else he will hold to one, and despise the other. You aren't able to serve God and mammon. [Mammon refers to riches or a false god of wealth]"

16:14 The Pharisees, who were lovers of money, also heard all these things, and they scoffed at him.

16:15 He said to them, "You are those who justify yourselves in the sight of men, but God knows your hearts. For that which is exalted among men is an abomination in the sight of God. 16:16 The law and the prophets were until John. From that time the Good News of the Kingdom of God is preached, and everyone is forcing his way into it. 16:17 But it is easier for heaven and earth to pass away, than for one tiny stroke of a pen in the law to fall. 16:18 Everyone who divorces his wife, and marries another, commits adultery. He who marries one who is divorced from a husband commits adultery.

16:19 "Now there was a certain rich man, and he was clothed in purple and fine linen, living in luxury every day. 16:20 A certain beggar, named Lazarus, was laid at his gate, full of sores, 16:21 and desiring to be fed with the crumbs that fell from the rich man's table. Yes, even the dogs came and licked his sores. 16:22 It happened that the beggar died, and that he was carried away by the angels to Abraham's bosom. The rich man also died, and was buried. 16:23 In Hades [Hell], he lifted up his eyes, being in torment, and saw Abraham far off, and Lazarus at his bosom. 16:24 He cried and said, 'Father Abraham, have mercy on me, and send Lazarus, that he may dip the tip of his finger in water, and cool my tongue! For I am in anguish in this flame.'

16:25 "But Abraham said, 'Son, remember that you, in your lifetime, received your good things, and Lazarus, in like manner, bad things. But now here he is comforted and you are in anguish. 16:26 Besides all this, between us and you there is a great gulf fixed, that those who want to pass from here to you are not able, and that none may cross over from there to us.'

16:27 "He said, 'I ask you therefore, father, that you would send him to my father's house; 16:28 for I have five brothers, that he may testify to them, so they won't also come into this place of torment.'

16:29 "But Abraham said to him, 'They have Moses and the prophets. Let them listen to them.'

16:30 "He said, 'No, father Abraham, but if one goes to them from the dead, they will repent.'

16:31 "He said to him, 'If they don't listen to Moses and the prophets, neither will they be persuaded if one rises from the dead.'"

17:1 He said to the disciples, "It is impossible that no occasions of stumbling should come, but woe to him through whom they come! 17:2 It would be better for him if a millstone were hung around his neck, and he were thrown into the sea, rather than that he should cause one of these little ones to stumble.

17:3 Be careful. If your brother sins against you, rebuke him. If he repents, forgive him. 17:4 If he sins against you seven times in the day, and seven times returns, saying, 'I repent,' you shall forgive him."

17:5 The apostles said to the Lord, "Increase our faith."

17:6 The Lord said, "If you had faith like a grain of mustard seed, you would tell this sycamore tree, 'Be uprooted, and be planted in the sea,' and it would obey you.

17:7 But who is there among you, having a servant plowing or keeping sheep, that will say, when he comes in from the field, 'Come immediately and sit down at the table,' 17:8 and will not rather tell him, 'Prepare my supper, clothe yourself properly, and serve me, while I eat and drink. Afterward you shall eat and drink'? 17:9 Does he thank that servant because he did the things that were commanded? I think not.

17:10 Even so you also, when you have done all the things that are commanded you, say, 'We are unworthy servants. We have done our duty.'"

Event 93: Jesus heals 10 lepers
Time: early 33 A.D.
Place: border of Samaria and Galilee

LUKE 17:11-19
17:11 It happened as he was on his way to Jerusalem, that he was passing along the borders of Samaria and Galilee.
17:12 As he entered into a certain village, ten men who were lepers met him, who stood at a distance. They lifted up their voices, saying, "Jesus, Master, have mercy on us!"
17:14 When he saw them, he said to them, "Go and show yourselves to the priests." It happened that as they went, they were cleansed.
17:15 One of them, when he saw that he was healed, turned back, glorifying God with a loud voice.
17:16 He fell on his face at Jesus' feet, giving him thanks; and he was a Samaritan.
17:17 Jesus answered, "Weren't the ten cleansed? But where are the nine? 17:18 Were there none found who returned to give glory to God, except this stranger?"
17:19 Then he said to him, "Get up, and go your way. Your faith has healed you."

Event 94: Jesus speaks of the coming of the Son of Man
Time: early 33 A.D.
Place: Judea

LUKE 17:20-37
17:20 Being asked by the Pharisees when the Kingdom of God would come, he answered them,
"The Kingdom of God doesn't come with observation; 17:21 neither will they say, 'Look, here!' or, 'Look, there!' for behold, the Kingdom of God is within you."
17:22 He said to the disciples, "The days will come, when you will desire to see one of the days of the Son of Man, and you will not see it. 17:23 They will tell you, 'Look, here!' or 'Look, there!' Don't go away, nor follow after them, 17:24 for as the lightning, when it flashes out of the one part under the sky, shines to the other part under the sky; so will the Son of Man be in his day. 17:25 But first, he must suffer many things and be rejected by this generation. 17:26 As it happened in the days of Noah, even so will it be also in the days of the Son of Man. 17:27They ate, they drank, they married, they were given in marriage, until the day that Noah entered into the ship, and the flood came, and destroyed them all. 17:28 Likewise, even as it happened in the days of Lot: they ate, they drank, they bought, they sold, they planted, they built; 17:29 but in the day that Lot went out from Sodom, it rained fire and sulfur from the sky, and destroyed them all. 17:30 It will be the same way in the day that the Son of Man is revealed. 17:31 In that day, he who will be on the housetop, and his goods in the house, let him not go down to take them away. Let him who is in the field likewise not turn back. 17:32 Remember Lot's wife! 17:33 Whoever seeks to save his life loses it, but whoever loses his life preserves it.17:34 I tell you, in that night there will be two people in one bed. The one will be taken, and the other will be left. 17:35 There will be two grinding grain together. One will be taken, and the other will be left." 17:36 Two will be in the field: the one taken, and the other left.
17:37 They, answering, asked him, "Where, Lord?"

He said to them, "Where the body is, there will the vultures also be gathered together."

Event 95: Jesus delivers a further series of parables
Time: early 33 A.D.
Place: Judea

LUKE 18:1-14
18:1 He also spoke a parable to them that they must always pray, and not give up, 18:2 saying, "There was a judge in a certain city who didn't fear God, and didn't respect man. 18:3 A widow was in that city, and she often came to him, saying, 'Defend me from my adversary!' 18:4 He wouldn't for a while, but afterward he said to himself, 'Though I neither fear God, nor respect man, 18:5 yet because this widow bothers me, I will defend her, or else she will wear me out by her continual coming.'"
18:6 The Lord said, "Listen to what the unrighteous judge says. 18:7 Won't God avenge his chosen ones, who are crying out to him day and night, and yet he exercises patience with them? 18:8 I tell you that he will avenge them quickly. Nevertheless, when the Son of Man comes, will he find faith on the earth?"
18:9 He spoke also this parable to certain people who were convinced of their own righteousness, and who despised all others. 18:10 "Two men went up into the temple to pray; one was a Pharisee, and the other was a tax collector. 18:11 The Pharisee stood and prayed to himself like this: 'God, I thank you, that I am not like the rest of men, extortioners, unrighteous, adulterers, or even like this tax collector. 18:12 I fast twice a week. I give tithes of all that I get.' 18:13 But the tax collector, standing far away, wouldn't even lift up his eyes to heaven, but beat his breast, saying, 'God, be merciful to me, a sinner!' 18:14 I tell you, this man went down to his house justified rather than the other; for everyone who exalts himself will be humbled, but he who humbles himself will be exalted."

Event 96: Jesus speaks on marriage, divorce, celibacy and blesses children
Time: early 33 A.D.
Place: Judea

MATTHEW 19:3-15	MARK 10:2-16	LUKE 18:15-17
19:3 Pharisees came to him, testing him, and saying, "Is it lawful for a man to divorce his wife for any reason?"	10:2 Pharisees came to him testing him, and asked him, "Is it lawful for a man to divorce his wife?"	
	10:3 He answered, "What did Moses command you?"	
	10:4 They said, "Moses allowed a certificate of divorce to be written, and to divorce her."	

19:4 He answered, "Haven't you read that he who made them from the beginning made them male and female, [Genesis 1:27] 19:5 and said, 'For this cause a man shall leave his father and mother, and shall join to his wife; and the two shall become one flesh?' [Genesis 2:24] 19:6 So that they are no more two, but one flesh. What therefore God has joined together, don't let man tear apart."	10:5 But Jesus said to them, "For your hardness of heart, he wrote you this commandment. 10:6 But from the beginning of the creation, God made them male and female. [Genesis 1:27] 10:7 For this cause a man will leave his father and mother, and will join to his wife, 10:8 and the two will become one flesh, so that they are no longer two, but one flesh. [Genesis 2:24] 10:9 What therefore God has joined together, let no man separate."		
19:7 They asked him, "Why then did Moses command us to give her a bill of divorce, and divorce her?"			
19:8 He said to them, "Moses, because of the hardness of your hearts, allowed you to divorce your wives, but from the beginning it has not been so. 19:9 I tell you that whoever divorces his wife, except for sexual immorality, and marries another, commits adultery; and he who marries her when she is divorced commits adultery."			
19:10 His disciples said to him, "If this is the case of the man with his wife, it is not expedient to marry."	10:10 In the house, his disciples asked him again about the same matter.		
	10:11 He said to them, "Whoever divorces his wife, and marries another, commits adultery against her. 10:12 If a woman herself divorces her husband, and marries another, she commits adultery."		

19:11 But he said to them, "Not all men can receive this saying, but those to whom it is given. 19:12 For there are eunuchs who were born that way from their mother's womb, and there are eunuchs who were made eunuchs by men; and there are eunuchs who made themselves eunuchs for the Kingdom of Heaven's sake. He who is able to receive it, let him receive it."		
19:13 Then little children were brought to him, that he should lay his hands on them and pray; and the disciples rebuked them.	10:13 They were bringing to him little children, that he should touch them, but the disciples rebuked those who were bringing them.	18:15 They were also bringing their babies to him, that he might touch them. But when the disciples saw it, they rebuked them.
19:14 But Jesus said, "Allow the little children, and don't forbid them to come to me; for the Kingdom of Heaven belongs to ones like these." 19:15 He laid his hands on them, and departed from there.	10:14 But when Jesus saw it, he was moved with indignation, and said to them, "Allow the little children to come to me! Don't forbid them, for the Kingdom of God belongs to such as these.	18:16 Jesus summoned them, saying, "Allow the little children to come to me, and don't hinder them, for the Kingdom of God belongs to such as these.
	10:15 Most certainly I tell you, whoever will not receive the Kingdom of God like a little child, he will in no way enter into it." 10:16 He took them in his arms, and blessed them, laying his hands on them.	18:17 Most certainly, I tell you, whoever doesn't receive the Kingdom of God like a little child, he will in no way enter into it."

Event 97: Jesus encounters a rich ruler
Time: early 33 A.D.
Place:

MATTHEW 19:16-30	MARK 10:17-31	LUKE 18:18-30
19:16 Behold, one came to him and said, "Good teacher, what good thing shall I do, that I may have eternal life?"	10:17 As he was going out into the way, one ran to him, knelt before him, and asked him, "Good Teacher, what shall I do that I may inherit eternal life?"	18:18 A certain ruler asked him, saying, "Good Teacher, what shall I do to inherit eternal life?"

19:17 He said to him, "Why do you call me good? No one is good but one, that is, God.	10:18 Jesus said to him, "Why do you call me good? No one is good except one—God.	18:19 Jesus asked him, "Why do you call me good? No one is good, except one—God.
But if you want to enter into life, keep the commandments."		
19:18 He said to him, "Which ones?"		
Jesus said, "'You shall not murder.' 'You shall not commit adultery.' 'You shall not steal.' 'You shall not offer false testimony.' 19:19 'Honor your father and mother.' [Exodus 20:12-16; Deuteronomy 5:16-20]	10:19 You know the commandments: 'Do not murder,' 'Do not commit adultery,' 'Do not steal,' 'Do not give false testimony,' 'Do not defraud,' 'Honor your father and mother.'" [Exodus 20:12-16; Deuteronomy 5:16-20]	18:20 You know the commandments: 'Don't commit adultery,' 'Don't murder,' 'Don't steal,' 'Don't give false testimony,' 'Honor your father and your mother.'" [Exodus 20:12-16; Deuteronomy 5:16-20]
And, 'You shall love your neighbor as yourself.'" [Leviticus 19:18]		
19:20 The young man said to him, "All these things I have observed from my youth. What do I still lack?"	10:20 He said to him, "Teacher, I have observed all these things from my youth."	18:21 He said, "I have observed all these things from my youth up."
19:21 Jesus said to him, "If you want to be perfect, go, sell what you have, and give to the poor, and you will have treasure in heaven; and come, follow me."	10:21 Jesus looking at him loved him, and said to him, "One thing you lack. Go, sell whatever you have, and give to the poor, and you will have treasure in heaven; and come, follow me, taking up the cross."	18:22 When Jesus heard these things, he said to him, "You still lack one thing. Sell all that you have, and distribute it to the poor. You will have treasure in heaven. Come, follow me."
19:22 But when the young man heard the saying, he went away sad, for he was one who had great possessions.	10:22 But his face fell at that saying, and he went away sorrowful, for he was one who had great possessions.	18:23 But when he heard these things, he became very sad, for he was very rich.
19:23 Jesus said to his disciples, "Most certainly I say to you.	10:23 Jesus looked around, and said to his disciples,	18:24 Jesus, seeing that he became very sad, said,
"Most certainly I say to you, a rich man will enter into the Kingdom of Heaven with difficulty.	"How difficult it is for those who have riches to enter into the Kingdom of God!"	"How hard it is for those who have riches to enter into the Kingdom of God!
	10:24 The disciples were amazed at his words.	

	But Jesus answered again, "Children, how hard is it for those who trust in riches to enter into the Kingdom of God!	
19:24 Again I tell you, it is easier for a camel to go through a needle's eye, than for a rich man to enter into the Kingdom of God."	10:25 It is easier for a camel to go through a needle's eye than for a rich man to enter into the Kingdom of God."	18:25 For it is easier for a camel to enter in through a needle's eye, than for a rich man to enter into the Kingdom of God."
19:25 When the disciples heard it, they were exceedingly astonished, saying, "Who then can be saved?"	10:26 They were exceedingly astonished, saying to him, "Then who can be saved?"	18:26 Those who heard it said, "Then who can be saved?"
19:26 Looking at them, Jesus said, "With men this is impossible, but with God all things are possible."	10:27 Jesus, looking at them, said, "With men it is impossible, but not with God, for all things are possible with God."	18:27 But he said, "The things which are impossible with men are possible with God."
19:27 Then Peter answered, "Behold, we have left everything, and followed you. What then will we have?"	10:28 Peter began to tell him, "Behold, we have left all, and have followed you."	18:28 Peter said, "Look, we have left everything, and followed you."
19:28 Jesus said to them, "Most certainly I tell you that you who have followed me, in the regeneration when the Son of Man will sit on the throne of his glory, you also will sit on twelve thrones, judging the twelve tribes of Israel.		
19:29 Everyone who has left houses, or brothers, or sisters, or father, or mother, or wife, or children, or lands, for my name's sake, will	10:29 Jesus said, "Most certainly I tell you, there is no one who has left house, or brothers, or sisters, or father, or mother, or wife, or children,	18:29 He said to them, "Most certainly I tell you, there is no one who has left house, or wife, or brothers, or parents, or children, for the Kingdom
receive one hundred times, and will inherit eternal life.	or land, for my sake, and for the sake of the Good News, 10:30 but he will receive one hundred times more now in this time, houses, brothers, sisters, mothers, children, and land, with persecutions; and in the age to come eternal life.	of God's sake, 18:30 who will not receive many times more in this time, and in the world to come, eternal life."

19:30 But many will be last who are first; and first who are last.	10:31 But many who are first will be last; and the last first."	

Event 98: Jesus delivers the parable of labourers in the vineyard
Time: early 33 A.D.
Place:

MATTHEW 20:1-16
20:1 "For the Kingdom of Heaven is like a man who was the master of a household, who went out early in the morning to hire laborers for his vineyard. 20:2 When he had agreed with the laborers for a denarius a day [common wage for a day of farm labour], he sent them into his vineyard. 20:3 He went out about the third hour [about 9:00 am] and saw others standing idle in the marketplace. 20:4 To them he said, 'You also go into the vineyard, and whatever is right I will give you.' So they went their way. 20:5 Again he went out about the sixth [12:00 pm] and ninth hour [3:00 pm] and did likewise. 20:6 About the eleventh [5:00 pm] he went out, and found others standing idle. He said to them, 'Why do you stand here all day idle?'
20:7 "They said to him, 'Because no one has hired us.'
"He said to them, 'You also go into the vineyard, and you will receive whatever is right.' 20:8
When evening had come, the lord of the vineyard said to his manager, 'Call the laborers and pay them their wages, beginning from the last to the first.'
20:9 "When those who were hired at about the eleventh hour came, they each received a denarius. 20:10 When the first came, they supposed that they would receive more; and they likewise each received a denarius. 20:11 When they received it, they murmured against the master of the household, 20:12 saying, 'These last have spent one hour, and you have made them equal to us, who have borne the burden of the day and the scorching heat!'
20:13 "But he answered one of them, 'Friend, I am doing you no wrong. Didn't you agree with me for a denarius? 20:14 Take that which is yours, and go your way. It is my desire to give to this last just as much as to you. 20:15 Isn't it lawful for me to do what I want to with what I own? Or is your eye evil, because I am good?'
20:16 So the last will be first, and the first last. For many are called, but few are chosen."

Event 99: Jesus raises Lazarus from the dead
Time: March 15, 33 A.D. (Sunday, 19 days before Passover April 3)
Place: Bethany, Judea

JOHN 11:1-54
11:1 Now a certain man was sick, Lazarus from Bethany, of the village of Mary and her sister, Martha. 11:2 It was that Mary who had anointed the Lord with ointment, and wiped his feet with her hair, whose brother, Lazarus, was sick.
11:3 The sisters therefore sent to him, saying, "Lord, behold, he for whom you have great affection is sick." 11:4 But when Jesus heard it, he said, "This sickness is not to death, but for the glory of God, that God's Son may be glorified by it."

11:5 Now Jesus loved Martha, and her sister, and Lazarus.
11:6 When therefore he heard that he was sick, he stayed two days in the place where he was. 11:7 Then after this he said to the disciples, "Let's go into Judea again."
11:8 The disciples told him, "Rabbi, the Jews were just trying to stone you, and are you going there again?"
11:9 Jesus answered, "Aren't there twelve hours of daylight? If a man walks in the day, he doesn't stumble, because he sees the light of this world. 11:10 But if a man walks in the night, he stumbles, because the light isn't in him." 11:11 He said these things, and after that, he said to them, "Our friend, Lazarus, has fallen asleep, but I am going so that I may awake him out of sleep."
11:12 The disciples therefore said, "Lord, if he has fallen asleep, he will recover."
11:13 Now Jesus had spoken of his death, but they thought that he spoke of taking rest in sleep. 11:14 So Jesus said to them plainly then, "Lazarus is dead. 11:15 I am glad for your sakes that I was not there, so that you may believe. Nevertheless, let's go to him."
11:16 Thomas therefore, who is called Didymus ["Didymus" means "Twin"] said to his fellow disciples, "Let's go also, that we may die with him."
11:17 So when Jesus came, he found that he had been in the tomb four days already.
11:18 Now Bethany was near Jerusalem, about fifteen stadia away. [about 2.8 kilometers or 1.7 miles]
11:19 Many of the Jews had joined the women around Martha and Mary, to console them concerning their brother.
11:20 Then when Martha heard that Jesus was coming, she went and met him, but Mary stayed in the house.
11:21 Therefore Martha said to Jesus, "Lord, if you would have been here, my brother wouldn't have died. 11:22 Even now I know that, whatever you ask of God, God will give you."
11:23 Jesus said to her, "Your brother will rise again."
11:24 Martha said to him, "I know that he will rise again in the resurrection at the last day."
11:25 Jesus said to her, "I am the resurrection and the life. He who believes in me will still live, even if he dies. 11:26 Whoever lives and believes in me will never die. Do you believe this?"
11:27 She said to him, "Yes, Lord. I have come to believe that you are the Christ, God's Son, he who comes into the world."
11:28 When she had said this, she went away, and called Mary, her sister, secretly, saying, "The Teacher is here, and is calling you." 11:29 When she heard this, she arose quickly, and went to him. 11:30 Now Jesus had not yet come into the village, but was in the place where Martha met him. 11:31 Then the Jews who were with her in the house, and were consoling her, when they saw Mary, that she rose up quickly and went out, followed her, saying, "She is going to the tomb to weep there."
11:32 Therefore when Mary came to where Jesus was, and saw him, she fell down at his feet, saying to him, "Lord, if you would have been here, my brother wouldn't have died."
11:33 When Jesus therefore saw her weeping, and the Jews weeping who came with her, he groaned in the spirit, and was troubled, 11:34 and said, "Where have you laid him?" They told him, "Lord, come and see." 11:35 Jesus wept.

11:36 The Jews therefore said, "See how much affection he had for him!" 11:37 Some of them said, "Couldn't this man, who opened the eyes of him who was blind, have also kept this man from dying?"
11:38 Jesus therefore, again groaning in himself, came to the tomb. Now it was a cave, and a stone lay against it. 11:39 Jesus said, "Take away the stone."
Martha, the sister of him who was dead, said to him, "Lord, by this time there is a stench, for he has been dead four days."
11:40 Jesus said to her, "Didn't I tell you that if you believed, you would see God's glory?" 11:41 So they took away the stone from the place where the dead man was lying. [NU lacks "from the place where the dead man was lying.]
Jesus lifted up his eyes, and said, "Father, I thank you that you listened to me. 11:42 I know that you always listen to me, but because of the multitude that stands around I said this, that they may believe that you sent me." 11:43 When he had said this, he cried with a loud voice, "Lazarus, come out!"
Jesus said to them, "Free him, and let him go."
11:44 He who was dead came out, bound hand and foot with wrappings, and his face was wrapped around with a cloth.
11:45 Therefore many of the Jews, who came to Mary and saw what Jesus did, believed in him.
11:46 But some of them went away to the Pharisees, and told them the things which Jesus had done. 11:47 The chief priests therefore and the Pharisees gathered a council, and said, "What are we doing? For this man does many signs. 11:48 If we leave him alone like this, everyone will believe in him, and the Romans will come and take away both our place and our nation."
11:49 But a certain one of them, Caiaphas, being high priest that year, said to them, "You know nothing at all, 11:50 nor do you consider that it is advantageous for us that one man should die for the people, and that the whole nation not perish." 11:51 Now he didn't say this of himself, but being high priest that year, he prophesied that Jesus would die for the nation, 11:52 and not for the nation only, but that he might also gather together into one the children of God who are scattered abroad. 11:53 So from that day forward they took counsel that they might put him to death.
11:54 Jesus therefore walked no more openly among the Jews, but departed from there into the country near the wilderness, to a city called Ephraim. He stayed there with his disciples.

Event 100: Jesus predicts his death in Jerusalem a third time
Time: late March 33 A.D.
Place: Jordan valley

MATTHEW 20:17-19	MARK 10:32-34	LUKE 18:31-34
20:17 As Jesus was going up to Jerusalem,	10:32 They were on the way, going up to Jerusalem; and Jesus was going in front of them, and they were amazed; and those who followed were afraid.	

he took the twelve disciples aside, and on the way he said to them,	He again took the twelve, and began to tell them the things that were going to happen to him.	18:31 He took the twelve aside, and said to them,
20:18 "Behold, we are going up to Jerusalem, and the Son of Man will be delivered to the chief priests and scribes, and they will condemn him to death, 20:19 and will hand him over to the Gentiles to mock, to scourge, and to crucify; and the third day he will be raised up."	10:33 "Behold, we are going up to Jerusalem. The Son of Man will be delivered to the chief priests and the scribes. They will condemn him to death, and will deliver him to the Gentiles. 10:34 They will mock him, spit on him, scourge him, and kill him. On the third day he will rise again."	"Behold, we are going up to Jerusalem, and all the things that are written through the prophets concerning the Son of Man will be completed. 18:32 For he will be delivered up to the Gentiles, will be mocked, treated shamefully, and spit on. 18:33 They will scourge and kill him. On the third day, he will rise again."
		18:34 They understood none of these things. This saying was hidden from them, and they didn't understand the things that were said.

Event 101: James and John vie for positions in the kingdom of heaven
Time: late March 33 A.D.
Place: Jordan valley

MATTHEW 20:20-28	MARK 10:35-45
20:20 Then the mother of the sons of Zebedee came to him with her sons, kneeling and asking a certain thing of him. 20:21 He said to her, "What do you want?"	10:35 James and John, the sons of Zebedee, came near to him, saying, "Teacher, we want you to do for us whatever we will ask." 10:36 He said to them, "What do you want me to do for you?"
She said to him, "Command that these, my two sons, may sit, one on your right hand, and one on your left hand, in your Kingdom."	10:37 They said to him, "Grant to us that we may sit, one at your right hand, and one at your left hand, in your glory."
20:22 But Jesus answered, "You don't know what you are asking. Are you able to drink the cup that I am about to drink, and be baptized with the baptism that I am baptized with?"	10:38 But Jesus said to them, "You don't know what you are asking. Are you able to drink the cup that I drink, and to be baptized with the baptism that I am baptized with?"
They said to him, "We are able."	10:39 They said to him, "We are able."
20:23 He said to them, "You will indeed drink my cup, and be baptized with the baptism that I am baptized with, but to sit on my right hand and on my left hand is not mine to give; but it is for whom it has been prepared by my Father."	Jesus said to them, "You shall indeed drink the cup that I drink, and you shall be baptized with the baptism that I am baptized with; 10:40 but to sit at my right hand and at my left hand is not mine to give, but for whom it has been prepared."

20:24 When the ten heard it, they were indignant with the two brothers.	10:41 When the ten heard it, they began to be indignant towards James and John.
20:25 But Jesus summoned them, and said, "You know that the rulers of the nations lord it over them, and their great ones exercise authority over them. 20:26 It shall not be [TR has instead "let not be"] so among you, but whoever desires to become great among you shall be your servant. 20:27 Whoever desires to be first among you shall be your bondservant, 20:28 even as the Son of Man came not to be served, but to serve, and to give his life as a ransom for man	10:42 Jesus summoned them, and said to them, "You know that they who are recognized as rulers over the nations lord it over them, and their great ones exercise authority over them. 10:43 But it shall not be so among you, but whoever wants to become great among you shall be your servant. 10:44 Whoever of you wants to become first among you, shall be bondservant of all. 10:45 For the Son of Man also came not to be served, but to serve, and to give his life as a ransom for many."

Event 102: Jesus heals a blind man Bartimaus
Time: late March 33 A.D.
Place: Jericho, Judea

MATTHEW 20:29-34	MARK 10:46-52	LUKE 18:35-43
20:29 As they went out from Jericho, a great multitude followed him.	10:46 They came to Jericho.	18:35 It happened, as he came near Jericho,
20:30 Behold, two blind men sitting by the road,	As he went out from Jericho, with his disciples and a great multitude, the son of Timaeus, Bartimaeus, a blind beggar, was sitting by the road.	a certain blind man sat by the road, begging.
when they heard that Jesus was passing by, cried out, "Lord, have mercy on us, you son of David!" 20:31 The multitude rebuked them, telling them that they should be quiet, but they cried out even more, "Lord, have mercy on us, you son of David!"	10:47 When he heard that it was Jesus the Nazarene, he began to cry out, and say, "Jesus, you son of David, have mercy on me!" 10:48 Many rebuked him, that he should be quiet, but he cried out much more, "You son of David, have mercy on me!"	8:36 Hearing a multitude going by, he asked what this meant. 18:37 They told him that Jesus of Nazareth was passing by. 18:38 He cried out, "Jesus, you son of David, have mercy on me!" 18:39 Those who led the way rebuked him, that he should be quiet; but he cried out all the more, "You son of David, have mercy on me!"
20:32 Jesus stood still, and called them,	10:49 Jesus stood still, and said, "Call him."	18:40 Standing still, Jesus commanded him to be brought to him.
	They called the blind man, saying to him, "Cheer up! Get up. He is calling you!"	

	10:50 He, casting away his cloak, sprang up, and came to Jesus.	
and asked, "What do you want me to do for you?"	10:51 Jesus asked him, "What do you want me to do for you?"	When he had come near, he asked him, 18:41 "What do you want me to do?"
20:33 They told him, "Lord, that our eyes may be opened."	The blind man said to him, "that Rhabboni [a transliteration of the Hebrew word for "great teacher"], I may see again."	He said, "Lord, that I may see again."
20:34 Jesus, being moved with compassion, touched their eyes; and immediately their eyes received their sight, and they followed him.	10:52 Jesus said to him, "Go your way. Your faith has made you well." Immediately he received his sight, and followed Jesus in the way.	18:42 Jesus said to him, "Receive your sight. Your faith has healed you." 18:43 Immediately he received his sight, and followed him, glorifying God.
		All the people, when they saw it, praised God.

Event 103: Jesus meets a future disciple Zacchaeus
Time: late March 33 A.D.
Place: Jericho, Judea

LUKE 19:1-10
19:1 He entered and was passing through Jericho.
19:2 There was a man named Zacchaeus. He was a chief tax collector, and he was rich. 19:3 He was trying to see who Jesus was, and couldn't because of the crowd, because he was short. 19:4 He ran on ahead, and climbed up into a sycamore tree to see him, for he was to pass that way.
19:5 When Jesus came to the place, he looked up and saw him, and said to him, "Zacchaeus, hurry and come down, for today I must stay at your house."
19:6 He hurried, came down, and received him joyfully. 19:7 When they saw it, they all murmured, saying, "He has gone in to lodge with a man who is a sinner."
19:8 Zacchaeus stood and said to the Lord, "Behold, Lord, half of my goods I give to the poor. If I have wrongfully exacted anything of anyone, I restore four times as much."
19:9 Jesus said to him, "Today, salvation has come to this house, because he also is a son of Abraham. 19:10 For the Son of Man came to seek and to save that which was lost."

Event 104: Jesus delivers the parable of the 10 servants
Time: late March 33 A.D.
Place: Judea

LUKE 19:11-28

19:11 As they heard these things, he went on and told a parable, because he was near Jerusalem, and they supposed that the Kingdom of God would be revealed immediately.
19:12 He said therefore, "A certain nobleman went into a far country to receive for himself a kingdom, and to return. 19:13 He called ten servants of his, and gave them ten mina coins [about 3 year's wages for an agricultural worker], and told them, 'Conduct business until I come.'
19:14 But his citizens hated him, and sent an envoy after him, saying, 'We don't want this man to reign over us.'
19:15 "It happened when he had come back again, having received the kingdom, that he commanded these servants, to whom he had given the money, to be called to him, that he might know what they had gained by conducting business.
19:16 The first came before him, saying, 'Lord, your mina has made ten more minas.' 19:17 "He said to him, 'Well done, you good servant! Because you were found faithful with very little, you shall have authority over ten cities.'
19:18 "The second came, saying, 'Your mina, Lord, has made five minas.' 19:19 "So he said to him, 'And you are to be over five cities.'
19:20 Another came, saying, 'Lord, behold, your mina, which I kept laid away in a handkerchief, 19:21 for I feared you, because you are an exacting man. You take up that which you didn't lay down, and reap that which you didn't sow.' 19:22 "He said to him, 'Out of your own mouth will I judge you, you wicked servant! You knew that I am an exacting man, taking up that which I didn't lay down, and reaping that which I didn't sow. 19:23 Then why didn't you deposit my money in the bank, and at my coming, I might have earned interest on it?' 19:24 He said to those who stood by, 'Take the mina away from him, and give it to him who has the ten minas.' 19:25 "They said to him, 'Lord, he has ten minas!"
19:26 'For I tell you that to everyone who has, will more be given; but from him who doesn't have, even that which he has will be taken away from him. 19:27 But bring those enemies of mine who didn't want me to reign over them here, and kill them before me.'"
19:28 Having said these things, he went on ahead, going up to Jerusalem.

Event 105: Jesus is anointed the first time
Time: March 28, 33 A.D. (Saturday)
Place: Bethany, Judea

JOHN 12:1-11
12:1 Then six days before the Passover, Jesus came to Bethany, where Lazarus was, who had been dead, whom he raised from the dead.
12:2 So they made him a supper there. Martha served, but Lazarus was one of those who sat at the table with him.
12:3 Mary, therefore, took a pound [a Roman pound of 12 ounces or about 340 grams] of ointment of pure nard, very precious, and anointed the feet of Jesus, and wiped his feet with her hair. The house was filled with the fragrance of the ointment.
12:4 Then Judas Iscariot, Simon's son, one of his disciples, who would betray him, said, 12:5 "Why wasn't this ointment sold for three hundred denarii [about a year's wages for an agricultural labourer] and given to the poor?"

12:6 Now he said this, not because he cared for the poor, but because he was a thief, and having the money box, used to steal what was put into it.
12:7 But Jesus said, "Leave her alone. She has kept this for the day of my burial. 12:8 For you always have the poor with you, but you don't always have me."
12:9 A large crowd therefore of the Jews learned that he was there, and they came, not for Jesus' sake only, but that they might see Lazarus also, whom he had raised from the dead.
12:10 But the chief priests conspired to put Lazarus to death also, 12:11 because on account of him many of the Jews went away and believed in Jesus.

Event 106: Jesus enters Jerusalem triumphantly
Time: March 29, 33 A.D. (Sunday)
Place: Jerusalem, Judea

MATTHEW 21:1-16	MARK 11:1-11	LUKE 19:28-44	JOHN 12:12-19
21:1 When they drew near to Jerusalem, and came to Bethsphage, [TR and NU have instead of Bethsphage "Bethphage"] to the Mount of Olives, then Jesus sent two disciples, 21:2 saying to them,	11:1 When they drew near to Jerusalem, to Bethsphage [TR and NU have instead of Bethsphage "Bethphage"] and Bethany, at the Mount of Olives, he sent two of his disciples, 11:2 and said to them,	19:28 Having said these things, he went on ahead, going up to Jerusalem. 19:29 It happened, when he drew near to Bethsphage [TR and NU have instead of Bethsphage "Bethpage"] and Bethany, at the mountain that is called Olivet, he sent two of his disciples, 19:30 saying,	12:12 On the next day
"Go into the village that is opposite you, and immediately you will find a donkey tied, and a colt with her. Untie them, and bring them to me. 21:3 If anyone says anything to you, you shall say, 'The Lord needs them,' and immediately he will send them."	"Go your way into the village that is opposite you. Immediately as you enter into it, you will find a young donkey tied, on which no one has sat. Untie him, and bring him. 11:3 If anyone asks you, 'Why are you doing this?' say, 'The Lord needs him;' and immediately he will send him back here."	"Go your way into the village on the other side, in which, as you enter, you will find a colt tied, whereon no man ever yet sat. Untie it, and bring it. 19:31 If anyone asks you, 'Why are you untying it?' say to him: 'The Lord needs it.'"	

21:4 All this was done, that it might be fulfilled which was spoken through the prophet, saying, 21:5 "Tell the daughter of Zion, behold, your King comes to you, humble, and riding on a donkey, on a colt, the foal of a donkey." [Zechariah 9:9]			
21:6 The disciples went, and did just as Jesus commanded them,	11:4 They went away, and found a young donkey tied at the door outside in the open street, and they untied him.	19:32 Those who were sent went away, and found things just as he had told them.	
	11:5 Some of those who stood there asked them, "What are you doing, untying the young donkey?"	19:33 As they were untying the colt, its owners said to them, "Why are you untying the colt?"	
	11:6 They said to them just as Jesus had said, and they let them go.	19:34 They said, "The Lord needs it."	
21:7 and brought the donkey and the colt, and laid their clothes on them; and he sat on them.	11:7 They brought the young donkey to Jesus, and threw their garments on it, and Jesus sat on it.	19:35 They brought it to Jesus. They threw their cloaks on the colt, and set Jesus on them.	
		19:36 As he went, they spread their cloaks in the way.	
		19:37 As he was now getting near, at the descent of the Mount of Olives,	

		the whole multitude of the disciples began to rejoice and praise God with a loud voice for all the mighty works which they had seen, 19:38 saying, "Blessed is the King who comes in the name of the Lord! Peace in heaven, and glory in the highest!" [Psalm 118:26]	a great multitude had come to the feast. When they heard that Jesus was coming to Jerusalem,
		19:39 Some of the Pharisees from the multitude said to him, "Teacher, rebuke your disciples!"	
		19:40 He answered them, "I tell you that if these were silent, the stones would cry out."	
		19:41 When he drew near, he saw the city and wept over it, 19:42 saying, "If you, even you, had known today the things which belong to your peace! But now, they are hidden from your eyes. 19:43 For the days will come on you, when your enemies will throw up a barricade against you, surround you,	

		hem you in on every side, 19:44 and will dash you and your children within you to the ground. They will not leave in you one stone on another, because you didn't know the time of your visitation."	
21:8 A very great multitude spread their clothes on the road.	11:8 Many spread their garments on the way,		
Others cut branches from the trees, and spread them on the road.	and others were cutting down branches from the trees, and spreading them on the road.		12:13 they took the branches of the palm trees,
21:9 The multitudes who went before him, and who followed kept shouting,	11:9 Those who went in front, and those who followed, cried out,		and went out to meet him, and cried out,
"Hosanna [Hosanna means "save us", "help us"] to the son of David! Blessed is he who comes in the name of the Lord! Hosanna in the highest!" [Psalm 118:25-26]	"Hosanna! [Hosanna means "save us", "help us"] Blessed is he who comes in the name of the Lord! 11:10 Blessed is the kingdom of our father David that is coming in the name of the Lord! Hosanna in the highest!"[Psalm 118:25-26]		"Hosanna! [Hosanna means "save us", "help us"] Blessed is he who comes in the name of the Lord, the King of Israel!" [Psalm 118:25-26]
			12:14 Jesus, having found a young donkey, sat on it. As it is written, 12:15 "Don't be afraid, daughter of Zion. Behold, your King comes, sitting on a donkey's colt." [Zechariah 9:9]

			12:16 His disciples didn't understand these things at first, but when Jesus was glorified, then they remembered that these things were written about him, and that they had done these things to him.
			12:17 The multitude therefore that was with him when he called Lazarus out of the tomb, and raised him from the dead, was testifying about it.
			12:18 For this cause also the multitude went and met him, because they heard that he had done this sign.
			12:19 The Pharisees therefore said among themselves, "See how you accomplish nothing. Behold, the world has gone after him."
21:10 When he had come into Jerusalem,			
all the city was stirred up, saying, "Who is this?"			
21:11 The multitudes said, "This is the prophet, Jesus, from Nazareth of Galilee."			
	11:11 Jesus entered into the temple in Jerusalem. When he had looked around at everything, it being now evening, he went out to Bethany with the twelve.		

Event 107: Greeks come to Jesus through Phillip
Time: March 29, 33 A.D. (Sunday)
Place: Jerusalem, Judea

JOHN 12:20-50
12:20 Now there were certain Greeks among those that went up to worship at the feast. 12:21 These, therefore, came to Philip, who was from Bethsaida of Galilee, and asked him, saying, "Sir, we want to see Jesus." 12:22 Philip came and told Andrew, and in turn, Andrew came with Philip, and they told Jesus.
12:23 Jesus answered them, "The time has come for the Son of Man to be glorified. 12:24 Most certainly I tell you, unless a grain of wheat falls into the earth and dies, it remains by itself alone. But if it dies, it bears much fruit. 12:25 He who loves his life will lose it. He who hates his life in this world will keep it to eternal life. 12:26 If anyone serves me, let him follow me. Where I am, there will my servant also be. If anyone serves me, the Father will honor him.
12:27 "Now my soul is troubled. What shall I say? 'Father, save me from this time?' But for this cause I came to this time. 12:28 Father, glorify your name!" Then there came a voice out of the sky, saying, "I have both glorified it, and will glorify it again."
12:29 The multitude therefore, who stood by and heard it, said that it had thundered. Others said, "An angel has spoken to him."
12:30 Jesus answered, "This voice hasn't come for my sake, but for your sakes. 12:31 Now is the judgment of this world. Now the prince of this world will be cast out. 12:32 And I, if I am lifted up from the earth, will draw all people to myself." 12:33 But he said this, signifying by what kind of death he should die.
12:34 The multitude answered him, "We have heard out of the law that the Christ remains forever. [Isaiah 9:7; Daniel 2:44, Isaiah 53:8] How do you say, 'The Son of Man must be lifted up?' Who is this Son of Man?"
12:35 Jesus therefore said to them, "Yet a little while the light is with you. Walk while you have the light, that darkness doesn't overtake you. He who walks in the darkness doesn't know where he is going. 12:36 While you have the light, believe in the light, that you may become children of light."
Jesus said these things, and he departed and hid himself from them.
12:37 But though he had done so many signs before them, yet they didn't believe in him, 12:38 that the word of Isaiah the prophet might be fulfilled, which he spoke, "Lord, who has believed our report? To whom has the arm of the Lord been revealed?" [Isaiah 53:1]12:39 For this cause they couldn't believe, for Isaiah said again, 12:40 "He has blinded their eyes and he hardened their heart, lest they should see with their eyes, and perceive with their heart, and would turn, and I would heal them." [Isaiah 6:10] 12:41 Isaiah said these things when he saw his glory, and spoke of him. [Isaiah 6:1]
12:42 Nevertheless even of the rulers many believed in him, but because of the Pharisees they didn't confess it, so that they wouldn't be put out of the synagogue, 12:43 for they loved men's praise more than God's praise.
12:44 Jesus cried out and said, "Whoever believes in me, believes not in me, but in him who sent me. 12:45 He who sees me sees him who sent me. 12:46 I have come as a light into the world, that whoever believes in me may not remain in the darkness. 12:47 If anyone

listens to my sayings, and doesn't believe, I don't judge him. For I came not to judge the world, but to save the world. 12:48 He who rejects me, and doesn't receive my sayings, has one who judges him. The word that I spoke, the same will judge him in the last day. 12:49 For I spoke not from myself, but the Father who sent me, he gave me a commandment, what I should say, and what I should speak. 12:50 I know that his commandment is eternal life. The things therefore which I speak, even as the Father has said to me, so I speak."

Event 108: Jesus cleanses the Temple a second time
Time: March 30, 33 A.D. (Monday)
Place: Jerusalem, Judea

MATTHEW 21:12-17	MARK 11:12-19	LUKE 19:45-48
	11:12 The next day, when they had come out from Bethany, he was hungry. 11:13 Seeing a fig tree afar off having leaves, he came to see if perhaps he might find anything on it. When he came to it, he found nothing but leaves, for it was not the season for figs. 11:14 Jesus told it, "May no one ever eat fruit from you again!" and his disciples heard it.	
21:12 Jesus entered into the temple of God, and drove out all of those who sold and bought in the temple, and overthrew the money changers' tables and the seats of those who sold the doves.	11:15 They came to Jerusalem, and Jesus entered into the temple, and began to throw out those who sold and those who bought in the temple, and overthrew the tables of the money changers, and the seats of those who sold the doves. 11:16 He would not allow anyone to carry a container through the temple.	19:45 He entered into the temple, and began to drive out those who bought and sold in it,
21:13 He said to them, "It is written, 'My house shall be called a house of prayer,'[Isaiah 56:7] but you have made it a den of robbers!" [Jeremiah 7:11]	11:17 He taught, saying to them, "Isn't it written, 'My house will be called a house of prayer for all the nations?' [Isaiah 56:7] But you have made it a den of robbers!" [Jeremiah 7:11]	19:46 saying to them, "It is written, 'My house is a house of prayer,' [Isaiah 56:7] but you have made it a 'den of robbers'!" [Jeremiah 7:11]
21:14 The blind and the lame came to him in the temple, and he healed them.		

and the children who were crying in the temple and saying, "Hosanna to the son of David!"		
they were indignant, 21:16 and said to him, "Do you hear what these are saying?"		
Jesus said to them, "Yes. Did you never read, 'Out of the mouth of babes and nursing babies you have perfected praise?'" [Psalm 8:2]		
	11:18 The chief priests and the scribes heard it, and sought how they might destroy him. For they feared him, because all the multitude was astonished at his teaching.	19:47 He was teaching daily in the temple, but the chief priests and the scribes and the leading men among the people sought to destroy him. 19:48 They couldn't find what they might do, for all the people hung on to every word that he said.
21:17 He left them, and went out of the city to Bethany, and lodged there.	11:19 When evening came, he went out of the city.	

Event 109: Jesus delivers the parable of the fig tree
Time: March 31, 33 A.D. (Tuesday)
Place: Jerusalem, Judea

MATTHEW 21:18-22	MARK 11:20-26
21:18 Now in the morning, as he returned to the city, he was hungry. 21:19 Seeing a fig tree by the road, he came to it, and found nothing on it but leaves. He said to it, "Let there be no fruit from you forever!" Immediately the fig tree withered away. 21:20 When the disciples saw it, they marveled, saying, "How did the fig tree immediately wither away?"	11:20 As they passed by in the morning, they saw the fig tree withered away from the roots. 11:21 Peter, remembering, said to him, "Rabbi, look! The fig tree which you cursed has withered away."
21:21 Jesus answered them, "Most certainly I tell you, if you have faith, and don't doubt, you will not only do what was done to the fig tree, but even if you told this mountain, 'Be taken up and cast into the sea,' it would be done. 21:22	11:22 Jesus answered them, "Have faith in God. 11:23 For most certainly I tell you, whoever may tell this mountain, 'Be taken up and cast into the sea,' and doesn't doubt in his heart, but believes that what he says is happening; he shall have whatever he says.

All things, whatever you ask in prayer, believing, you will receive."	11:24 Therefore I tell you, all things whatever you pray and ask for, believe that you have received them, and you shall have them.
	11:25 Whenever you stand praying, forgive, if you have anything against anyone; so that your Father, who is in heaven, may also forgive you your transgressions. 11:26 But if you do not forgive, neither will your Father in heaven forgive your transgressions."

Event 110: Jesus comments on his authority and his relationship to John the Baptist
Time: March 31, 33 A.D. (Tuesday)
Place: Jerusalem, Judea

MATTHEW 21:23-27	MARK 11:27-33	LUKE 20:1-8
21:23 When he had come into the temple,	11:27 They came again to Jerusalem, and as he was walking in the temple,	20:1 It happened on one of those days, as he was teaching the people in the temple and preaching the Good News,
the chief priests and the elders of the people came to him as he was teaching, and said,	the chief priests, and the scribes, and the elders came to him, 11:28 and they began saying to him,	that the [TR adds "chief"] priests and scribes came to him with the elders. 20:2 They asked him,
"Tell us: by what authority do you do these things? Or who is giving you this authority?"	"By what authority do you do these things? Or who gave you this authority to do these things?"	"Tell us: by what authority do you do these things? Or who is giving you this authority?"
21:24 Jesus answered them, "I also will ask you one question, which if you tell me, I likewise will tell you by what authority I do these things. 21:25 The baptism of John, where was it from? From heaven or from men?"	11:29 Jesus said to them, "I will ask you one question. Answer me, and I will tell you by what authority I do these things. 11:30 The baptism of John-was it from heaven, or from men? Answer me."	20:3 He answered them, "I also will ask you one question. Tell me: 20:4 the baptism of John, was it from heaven, or from men?"
They reasoned with themselves, saying, "If we say, 'From heaven,' he will ask us, 'Why then did you not believe him?' 21:26 But if we say, 'From men,' we fear the multitude, for all hold	11:31 They reasoned with themselves, saying, "If we should say, 'From heaven;' he will say, 'Why then did you not believe him?' 11:32 If we should say, 'From men'"—they feared the people, for all held	20:5 They reasoned with themselves, saying, "If we say, 'From heaven,' he will say, 'Why didn't you believe him?' 20:6 But if we say, 'From men,' all the people will stone us, for they are persuaded that John

John as a prophet." 21:27 They answered Jesus, and said, "We don't know."	John to really be a prophet. 11:33 They answered Jesus, "We don't know."	was a prophet." 20:7 They answered that they didn't know where it was from.
He also said to them, "Neither will I tell you by what authority I do these things."	Jesus said to them, "Neither do I tell you by what authority I do these things."	20:8 Jesus said to them, "Neither will I tell you by what authority I do these things.

Event 111: Jesus delivers the parable of the 2 sons
Time: March 31, 33 AD (Tuesday)
Place: Jerusalem, Judea

MATTHEW 21:28-32
21:28 But what do you think? A man had two sons, and he came to the first, and said, 'Son, go work today in my vineyard.'
21:29 He answered, 'I will not,' but afterward he changed his mind, and went.
21:30 He came to the second, and said the same thing.
He answered, 'I go, sir,' but he didn't go.
21:31 Which of the two did the will of his father?"
They said to him, "The first."
Jesus said to them, "Most certainly I tell you that the tax collectors and the prostitutes are entering into the Kingdom of God before you.
21:32 For John came to you in the way of righteousness, and you didn't believe him, but the tax collectors and the prostitutes believed him. When you saw it, you didn't even repent afterward, that you might believe him."

Event 112: Jesus delivers the parable of the vineyard
Time: March 31, 33 A.D. (Tuesday)
Place: Jerusalem, Judea

MATTHEW 21:33-46	MARK 12:1-12	LUKE 20:9-19
21:33 "Hear another parable.	12:1 He began to speak to them in parables.	20:9 He began to tell the people this parable.
There was a man who was a master of a household, who planted a vineyard, set a hedge about it, dug a winepress in it, built a tower, leased it out to farmers, and went into another country.	"A man planted a vineyard, put a hedge around it, dug a pit for the winepress, built a tower, rented it out to a farmer, and went into another country.	"A [TR adds "certain" and NU brackets "certain"] man planted a vineyard, and rented it out to some farmers, and went into another country for a long time.
21:34 When the season for the fruit drew near, he sent his servants to the farmers, to receive his fruit.	12:2 When it was time, he sent a servant to the farmer to get from the farmer his share of the fruit of the vineyard.	20:10 At the proper season, he sent a servant to the farmers to collect his share of the fruit of the vineyard.

21:35 The farmers took his servants, beat one, killed another, and stoned another.	12:3 They took him, beat him, and sent him away empty.	But the farmers beat him, and sent him away empty.
21:36 Again, he sent other servants more than the first: and they treated them the same way.	12:4 Again, he sent another servant to them; and they threw stones at him, wounded him in the head, and sent him away shamefully treated.	20:11 He sent yet another servant, and they also beat him, and treated him shamefully, and sent him away empty.
	12:5 Again he sent another; and they killed him; and many others, beating some, and killing some.	20:12 He sent yet a third, and they also wounded him, and threw him out.
	12:6 Therefore still having one, his beloved son, he sent him last to them, saying, 'They will respect my son.'	20:13 The lord of the vineyard said, 'What shall I do? I will send my beloved son. It may be that seeing him, they will respect him.'
21:38 But the farmers, when they saw the son, said among themselves, 'This is the heir. Come, let's kill him, and seize his inheritance.' 21:39 So they took him, and threw him out of the vineyard, and killed him.	12:7 But those farmers said among themselves, 'This is the heir. Come, let's kill him, and the inheritance will be ours.' 12:8 They took him, killed him, and cast him out of the vineyard.	20:14 "But when the farmers saw him, they reasoned among themselves, saying, 'This is the heir. Come, let's kill him, that the inheritance may be ours.' 20:15 They threw him out of the vineyard, and killed him.
21:40 When therefore the lord of the vineyard comes, what will he do to those farmers?"	12:9 What therefore will the lord of the vineyard do?	What therefore will the lord of the vineyard do to them?
21:41 They told him, "He will miserably destroy those miserable men, and will lease out the vineyard to other farmers, who will give him the fruit in its season."	He will come and destroy the farmers, and will give the vineyard to others.	20:16 He will come and destroy these farmers, and will give the vineyard to others."
		When they heard it, they said, "May it never be!"
21:42 Jesus said to them, "Did you never read in the Scriptures, 'The stone which the builders rejected, the same was made the head of the corner.	12:10 Haven't you even read this Scripture: 'The stone which the builders rejected, the same was made the head of the corner.	20:17 But he looked at them, and said, "Then what is this that is written, 'The stone which the builders rejected, the same was made the chief cornerstone?' [Psalm 118:22]
This was from the Lord. It is marvelous in our eyes?' [Psalm 118:22-23]	12:11 This was from the Lord, it is marvelous in our eyes'?" [Psalm 118:22-23]	

21:43 "Therefore I tell you, the Kingdom of God will be taken away from you, and will be given to a nation bringing forth its fruit.		
21:44 He who falls on this stone will be broken to pieces, but on whoever it will fall, it will scatter him as dust."		but it will crush whomever it falls on to dust." 20:18 Everyone who falls on that stone will be broken to pieces, but it will crush whomever it falls on to dust."
21:45 When the chief priests and the Pharisees heard his parables, they perceived that he spoke about them.		
21:46 When they sought to seize him,	12:12 They tried to seize him, but they feared the multitude; for they perceived that he spoke the parable against them.	20:19 The chief priests and the scribes sought to lay hands on him that very hour,
they feared the multitudes, because they considered him to be a prophet		but they feared the people—for they knew he had spoken this parable against them.
	They left him, and went away.	

Event 113: Jesus delivers the parable of the banquet
Time: March 31, 33 A.D. (Tuesday)
Place: Jerusalem, Judea

MATTHEW 22:1-14
22:1 Jesus answered and spoke again in parables to them, saying, 22:2 "The Kingdom of Heaven is like a certain king, who made a marriage feast for his son, 22:3 and sent out his servants to call those who were invited to the marriage feast, but they would not come. 22:4 Again he sent out other servants, saying, 'Tell those who are invited, "Behold, I have made ready my dinner. My cattle and my fatlings are killed, and all things are ready. Come to the marriage feast!"' 22:5 But they made light of it, and went their ways, one to his own farm, another to his merchandise, 22:6 and the rest grabbed his servants, and treated them shamefully, and killed them. 22:7 When the king heard that, he was angry, and sent his armies, destroyed those murderers, and burned their city.
22:8 "Then he said to his servants, 'The wedding is ready, but those who were invited weren't worthy. 22:9 Go therefore to the intersections of the highways, and as many as you may find, invite to the marriage feast.' 22:10 Those servants went out into the highways, and gathered together as many as they found, both bad and good. The wedding was filled with guests. 22:11 But when the king came in to see the guests, he saw there a man who didn't have on wedding clothing, 22:12 and he said to him, 'Friend, how did you come in

here not wearing wedding clothing?' He was speechless. 22:13 Then the king said to the servants, 'Bind him hand and foot, take him away, and throw him into the outer darkness; there is where the weeping and grinding of teeth will be.'
22:14 For many are called, but few chosen."

Event 114: Jesus comments on payment of taxes to Caesar
Time: March 31, 33 A.D. (Tuesday)
Place: Jerusalem, Judea

MATTHEW 22:15-22	MARK 12:13-17	LUKE 20:20-26
22:15 Then the Pharisees went and took counsel how they might entrap him in his talk. 22:16 They sent their disciples to him, along with the Herodians, saying,	12:13 They sent some of the Pharisees and of the Herodians to him, that they might trap him with words. 12:14 When they had come, they asked him,	20:20 They watched him, and sent out spies, who pretended to be righteous, that they might trap him in something he said, so as to deliver him up to the power and authority of the governor.
"Teacher, we know that you are honest, and teach the way of God in truth, no matter who you teach, for you aren't partial to anyone. 22:17 Tell us therefore, what do you think? Is it lawful to pay taxes to Caesar, or not?"	"Teacher, we know that you are honest, and don't defer to anyone; for you aren't partial to anyone, but truly teach the way of God. Is it lawful to pay taxes to Caesar, or not? 12:15 Shall we give, or shall we not give?"	20:21 They asked him, "Teacher, we know that you say and teach what is right, and aren't partial to anyone, but truly teach the way of God. 20:22 Is it lawful for us to pay taxes to Caesar, or not?"
22:18 But Jesus perceived their wickedness, and said, "Why do you test me, you hypocrites?	But he, knowing their hypocrisy, said to them, "Why do you test me?	20:23 But he perceived their craftiness, and said to them, "Why do you test me?
22:19 Show me the tax money."	Bring me a denarius, that I may see it."	20:24 Show me a denarius.
They brought to him a denarius.	12:16 They brought it.	
22:20 He asked them, "Whose is this image and inscription?"	He said to them, "Whose is this image and inscription?"	Whose image and inscription are on it?
22:21 They said to him, "Caesar's."	They said to him, "Caesar's."	They answered, "Caesar's."
Then he said to them, "Give therefore to Caesar the things that are Caesar's, and to God the things that are God's."	12:17 Jesus answered them, "Render to Caesar the things that are Caesar's, and to God the things that are God's."	20:25 He said to them, "Then give to Caesar the things that are Caesar's, and to God the things that are God's."
22:22 When they heard it, they marveled, and left him, and went away.	They marveled greatly at him.	20:26 They weren't able to trap him in his words before the people. They marveled at his answer, and were silent.

Event 115: Jesus comments on the afterlife
Time: March 31, 33 A.D. (Tuesday)
Place: Jerusalem, Judea

MATTHEW 22:23-33	MARK 12:18-27	LUKE 20:27-40
22:23 On that day Sadducees (those who say that there is no resurrection) came to him.	12:18 There came to him Sadducees, who say that there is no resurrection.	
They asked him, 22:24 saying, "Teacher, Moses said, 'If a man dies, having no children, his brother shall marry his wife, and raise up seed for his brother.' 22:25 Now there were with us seven brothers. The first married and died, and having no seed left his wife to his brother. 22:26 In like manner the second also, and the third, to the seventh. 22:27 After them all, the woman died. 22:28	They asked him, saying, 12:19 "Teacher, Moses wrote to us, 'If a man's brother dies, and leaves a wife behind him, and leaves no children, that his brother should take his wife, and raise up offspring for his brother.' 12:20 There were seven brothers. The first took a wife, and dying left no offspring.12:21 The second took her, and died, leaving no children behind him. The third likewise; 12:22 and the seven took her and left no children.	20:28 They asked him, "Teacher, Moses wrote to us that if a man's brother dies having a wife, and he is childless, his brother should take the wife, and raise up children for his brother. 20:29 There were therefore seven brothers. The first took a wife, and died childless. 20:30 The second took her as wife, and he died childless. 20:31 The third took her, and likewise the seven all left no children, and died. 20:32
In the resurrection therefore, whose wife will she be of the seven? For they all had her."	Last of all the woman also died. 12:23 In the resurrection, when they rise, whose wife will she be of them? For the seven had her as a wife."	Afterward the woman also died. 20:33 Therefore in the resurrection whose wife of them will she be? For the seven had her as a wife."
22:29 But Jesus answered them, "You are mistaken, not knowing the Scriptures, nor the power of God.	12:24 Jesus answered them, "Isn't this because you are mistaken, not knowing the Scriptures, nor the power of God?	
22:30 For in the resurrection they neither marry, nor are given in marriage,	12:25 For when they will rise from the dead, they neither marry, nor are given in marriage,	20:34 Jesus said to them, "The children of this age marry, and are given in marriage. 20:35 But those who are considered worthy to attain to that age and the resurrection from the dead, neither marry, nor are given in marriage.

but are like God's angels in heaven.	but are like angels in heaven.	20:36 For they can't die any more, for they are like the angels, and are children of God, being children of the resurrection.
22:31 But concerning the resurrection of the dead, haven't you read that which was spoken to you by God, saying, 22:32 'I am the God of Abraham, and the God of Isaac, and the God of Jacob?' [Exodus 3:6]	12:26 But about the dead, that they are raised; haven't you read in the book of Moses, about the Bush, how God spoke to him, saying, 'I am the God of Abraham, the God of Isaac, and the God of Jacob'? [Exodus 3:6]	20:37 But that the dead are raised, even Moses showed at the bush, when he called the Lord 'The God of Abraham, the God of Isaac, and the God of Jacob.' [Exodus 3:6]
God is not the God of the dead, but of the living."	12:27 He is not the God of the dead, but of the living.	20:38 Now he is not the God of the dead, but of the living, for all are alive to him."
	You are therefore badly mistaken."	
22:33 When the multitudes heard it, they were astonished at his teaching.		20:39 Some of the scribes answered, "Teacher, you speak well."
		20:40 They didn't dare to ask him any more questions.

Event 116: Jesus comments on the greatest commandment
Time: March 31, 33 A.D. (Tuesday)
Place: Jerusalem, Judea

MATTHEW 22:34-40	MARK 12:28-34
22:34 But the Pharisees, when they heard that he had silenced the Sadducees, gathered themselves together.	
22:35 One of them, a lawyer, asked him a question, testing him. 22:36 "Teacher, which is the greatest commandment in the law?"	12:28 One of the scribes came, and heard them questioning together. Knowing that he had answered them well, asked him, "Which commandment is the greatest of all?"
	12:29 Jesus answered, "The greatest is, 'Hear, Israel, the Lord our God, the Lord is one:
22:37 Jesus said to him, "'You shall love the Lord your God with all your heart, with all your soul, and with all your mind.' [Deuteronomy 6:5] 22:38 This is the first and great commandment.	12:30 you shall love the Lord your God with all your heart, and with all your soul, and with all your mind, and with all your strength.' This is the first commandment. [Deuteronomy 6:4-5]

22:39 A second likewise is this, 'You shall love your neighbor as yourself.' [Leviticus 19:18]	12:31 The second is like this, 'You shall love your neighbor as yourself.' [Leviticus 19:18]
	There is no other commandment greater than these."
22:40 The whole law and the prophets depend on these two commandments."	
	12:32 The scribe said to him, "Truly, teacher, you have said well that he is one, and there is none other but he, 12:33 and to love him with all the heart, and with all the understanding, with all the soul, and with all the strength, and to love his neighbor as himself, is more important than all whole burnt offerings and sacrifices."
	12:34 When Jesus saw that he answered wisely, he said to him, "You are not far from the Kingdom of God."
	No one dared ask him any question after that.

Event 117: Jesus comments on David's son and David's lord
Time: March 31, 33 A.D. (Tuesday)
Place: Jerusalem, Judea

MATTHEW 22:41-46	MARK 12:35-37	LUKE 20:40-44
22:41 Now while the Pharisees were gathered together,		
Jesus asked them a question, 22:42 saying,	12:35 Jesus responded, as he taught in the temple,	20:41 He said to them,
"What do you think of the Christ? Whose son is he?" They said to him, "Of David."		
22:43 He said to them, "How then does David in the Spirit call him Lord, saying, 22:44 'The Lord said to my Lord, sit on my right hand, until I make your enemies a footstool for your feet?' [Psalm 110:1]	"How is it that the scribes say that the Christ is the son of David? 12:36 For David himself said in the Holy Spirit, 'The Lord said to my Lord, "Sit at my right hand, until I make your enemies the footstool of your feet."' [Psalm 110:1]	"Why do they say that the Christ is David's son? 20:42 David himself says in the book of Psalms, Lord said to my Lord, "Sit at my right hand 20:43 until I make your enemies the footstool of your feet." [Psalm 110:1]
22:45 "If then David calls him Lord, how is he his son?"	12:37 Therefore David himself calls him Lord, so how can he be his son?"	20:44 "David therefore calls him Lord, so how is he his son?"
	The common people heard him gladly.	

22:46 No one was able to answer him a word, neither did any man dare ask him any more questions from that day forth.		

Event 118: Jesus condemns the Pharisees
Time: March 31, 33 A.D. (Tuesday)
Place: Jerusalem, Judea

MATTHEW 23:1-39	MARK 12:38-40	LUKE 20:45-47
23:1 Then Jesus spoke to the multitudes and to his disciples, 23:2 saying,	12:38 In his teaching he said to them,	20:45 In the hearing of all the people, he said to his disciples,
"The scribes and the Pharisees sat on Moses' seat. 23:3 All things therefore whatever they tell you to observe, observe and do, but don't do their works; for they say, and don't do. 23:4 For they bind heavy burdens that are grievous to be borne, and lay them on men's shoulders; but they themselves will not lift a finger to help them.		
23:5 But all their works they do to be seen by men.		
They make their phylacteries [small leather pouches worn on forehead and arm in prayer following Deuteronomyu 6:8] broad, enlarge the fringes of their garments, 23:6 and love the place of honor at feasts, the best seats in the synagogues,	"Beware of the scribes, who like to walk in long robes, and to get greetings in the marketplaces, 12:39 and the best seats in the synagogues, and the best places at feasts:	20:46 "Beware of the scribes, who like to walk in long robes, and love greetings in the marketplaces, the best seats in the synagogues, and the best places at feasts;
23:7 the salutations in the marketplaces,		
and to be called 'Rabbi, Rabbi' by men.		
23:8 But don't you be called 'Rabbi,' for one is your teacher, the Christ, and all of you are brothers.		

23:9 Call no man on the earth your father, for one is your Father, he who is in heaven.		
23:10 Neither be called masters, for one is your master, the Christ. 23:11 But he who is greatest among you will be your servant.		
23:12 Whoever exalts himself will be humbled, and whoever humbles himself will be exalted.		
23:13 "Woe to you, scribes and Pharisees, hypocrites! For you devour widow's houses, and a pretense you make long prayers.	12:40 those who devour widows' houses, and for a pretense make long prayers	20:47 who devour widows' houses, and for a pretense make long prayers:
Therefore you will receive greater condemnation.	These will receive greater condemnation."	these will receive greater condemnation."
23:14 "But woe to you, scribes and Pharisees, hypocrites! Because you shut up the Kingdom of Heaven against men; for you don't enter in yourselves, neither do you allow those who are entering in to enter.		
23:15 Woe to you, scribes and Pharisees, hypocrites! For you travel around by sea and land to make one proselyte; and when he becomes one, you make him twice as much of a son of Gehenna [Hell] as yourselves.		
23:16 "Woe to you, you blind guides, who say, 'Whoever swears by the temple, it is nothing; but whoever swears by the gold of the temple, he is obligated.' 23:17 You blind fools! For which is greater, the gold, or the temple that sanctifies the gold? 23:18		

'Whoever swears by the altar, it is nothing; but whoever swears by the gift that is on it, he is obligated?' 23:19 You blind fools! For which is greater, the gift, or the altar that sanctifies the gift? 23:20 He therefore who swears by the altar, swears by it, and by everything on it. 23:21 He who swears by the temple, swears by it, and by him who was living in it. 23:22 He who swears by heaven, swears by the throne of God, and by him who sits on it.		
23:23 "Woe to you, scribes and Pharisees, hypocrites! For you tithe mint, dill, and cumin [an aromatic seed like caraway], and have left undone the weightier matters of the law: justice, mercy, and faith. But you ought to have done these, and not to have left the other undone. 23:24 You blind guides, who strain out a gnat, and swallow a camel!		
23:25 "Woe to you, scribes and Pharisees, hypocrites! For you clean the outside of the cup and of the platter, but within they are full of extortion and unrighteousness. [TR has instead "self-indulgence] 23:26 You blind Pharisee, first clean the inside of the cup and of the platter, that its outside may become clean also.		
23:27 "Woe to you, scribes and Pharisees, hypocrites! For you are like whitened tombs, which outwardly appear beautiful, but inwardly are full of dead men's bones, and of all uncleanness.		

23:28 Even so you also outwardly appear righteous to men, but inwardly you are full of hypocrisy and iniquity.		
23:29 "Woe to you, scribes and Pharisees, hypocrites! For you build the tombs of the prophets, and decorate the tombs of the righteous, 23:30 and say, 'If we had lived in the days of our fathers, we wouldn't have been partakers with them in the blood of the prophets.' 23:31 Therefore you testify to yourselves that you are children of those who killed the prophets. 23:32 Fill up, then, the measure of your fathers. 23:33 You serpents, you offspring of vipers, how will you escape the judgment of Gehenna? [Hell]		
23:34 Therefore, behold, I send to you prophets, wise men, and scribes. Some of them you will kill and crucify; and some of them you will scourge in your synagogues, and persecute from city to city; 23:35 that on you may come all the righteous blood shed on the earth, from the blood of righteous Abel to the blood of Zachariah son of Barachiah, whom you killed between the sanctuary and the altar.		
23:36 Most certainly I tell you, all these things will come upon this generation.		
23:37 "Jerusalem, Jerusalem, who kills the prophets, and stones those who are sent to her! How often I would have gathered your children together, even as a hen gathers her chicks under her wings,		

and you would not! 23:38 Behold, your house is left to you desolate.		
23:39 For I tell you, you will not see me from now on, until you say, 'Blessed is he who comes in the name of the Lord!'" [Psalm 118:26]		

Event 119: Jesus comments on the widow's mite
Time: March 31, 33 A.D. (Tuesday)
Place: Jerusalem, Judea

MARK 12:41-44	LUKE 21:1-4
12:41 Jesus sat down opposite the treasury, and saw how the multitude cast money into the treasury. Many who were rich cast in much.	21:1 He looked up, and saw the rich people who were putting their gifts into the treasury.
12:42 A poor widow came, and she cast in two small brass coins, which equal a quadrans coin. [1/64 of a day's wages for an agricultural worker]	21:2 He saw a certain poor widow casting in two small brass coins [about 1% of a day's wages for an agricultural worker].
12:43 He called his disciples to himself, and said to them, "Most certainly I tell you, this poor widow gave more than all those who are giving into the treasury, 12:44 for they all gave out of their abundance, but she, out of her poverty, gave all that she had to live on."	21:3 He said, "Truly I tell you, this poor widow put in more than all of them, 21:4 for all these put in gifts for God from their abundance, but she, out of her poverty, put in all that she had to live on."

Event 120: Jesus delivers the Olivet discourse to his disciples
Time: March 31, 33 A.D. (Tuesday)
Place: Jerusalem, Judea

MATTHEW 24:1-25:30	MARK 13:1-37	LUKE 21:5-38
24:1 Jesus went out from the temple, and was going on his way. His disciples came to him to show him the buildings of the temple.	13:1 As he went out of the temple, one of his disciples said to him, "Teacher, see what kind of stones and what kind of buildings!"	21:5 As some were talking about the temple and how it was decorated with beautiful stones and gifts,
24:2 But he answered them, "Don't you see all of these things? Most certainly I tell you, there will not be left here one stone on another, that will not be thrown down."	13:2 Jesus said to him, "Do you see these great buildings? There will not be left here one stone on another, which will not be thrown down."	he said, 21:6 "As for these things which you see, the days will come, in which there will not be left here one stone on another that will not be thrown down."

24:3 As he sat on the Mount of Olives, the disciples came to him privately, saying, "Tell us, when will these things be? What is the sign of your coming, and of the end of the age?"	13:3 As he sat on the Mount of Olives opposite the temple, Peter, James, John, and Andrew asked him privately, 13:4 "Tell us, when will these things be? What is the sign that these things are all about to be fulfilled?"	21:7 They asked him, "Teacher, so when will these things be? What is the sign that these things are about to happen?"
24:4 Jesus answered them, "Be careful that no one leads you astray. 24:5 For many will come in my name, saying, 'I am the Christ,' and will lead many astray.	13:5 Jesus, answering, began to tell them, "Be careful that no one leads you astray. 13:6 For many will come in my name, saying, 'I am he!' [literally "I am" or "I AM" from Exodus 3:14] and will lead many astray.	21:8 He said, "Watch out that you don't get led astray, for many will come in my name, saying, 'I am he,' [literally "I am" or "I AM" from Exodus 3:14] and, 'The time is at hand.' Therefore don't follow them.
24:6 You will hear of wars and rumors of wars. See that you aren't troubled, for all this must happen, but the end is not yet. 24:7 For nation will rise against nation, and kingdom against kingdom;	13:7 "When you hear of wars and rumors of wars, don't be troubled. For those must happen, but the end is not yet. 13:8 For nation will rise against nation, and kingdom against kingdom.	21:9 When you hear of wars and disturbances, don't be terrified, for these things must happen first, but the end won't come immediately." 21:10 Then he said to them, "Nation will rise against nation, and kingdom against kingdom.
and there will be famines, plagues, and earthquakes in various places. 24:8 But all these things are the beginning of birth pains.	There will be earthquakes in various places. There will be famines and troubles. These things are the beginning of birth pains.	21:11 There will be great earthquakes, famines, and plagues in various places. There will be terrors and great signs from heaven.
24:9 Then they will deliver you up to oppression, and will kill you. You will be hated by all of the nations for my name's sake. 24:10 Then many will stumble, and will deliver up one another, and will hate one another.	13:9 But watch yourselves, for they will deliver you up to councils. You will be beaten in synagogues. You will stand before rulers and kings for my sake, for a testimony to them.	21:12 But before all these things, they will lay their hands on you and will persecute you, delivering you up to synagogues and prisons, bringing you before kings and governors for my name's sake.
24:11 Many false prophets will arise, and will lead many astray. 24:12 Because iniquity will be multiplied, the love of many will grow cold. 24:13 But he who endures to the end, the same will be saved.		

24:14 This Good News of the Kingdom will be preached in the whole world for a testimony to all the nations, and then the end will come.	13:10 The Good News must first be preached to all the nations.	21:13 It will turn out as a testimony for you.
	13:11 When they lead you away and deliver you up, don't be anxious beforehand, or premeditate what you will say, but say whatever will be given you in that hour. For it is not you who speak, but the Holy Spirit.	21:14 Settle it therefore in your hearts not to meditate beforehand how to answer, 21:15 for I will give you a mouth and wisdom which all your adversaries will not be able to withstand or to contradict.
	13:12 "Brother will deliver up brother to death, and the father his child. Children will rise up against parents, and cause them to be put to death. 13:13 You will be hated by all men for my name's sake,	21:16 You will be handed over even by parents, brothers, relatives, and friends. They will cause some of you to be put to death. 21:17 You will be hated by all men for my name's sake.
		21:18 And not a hair of your head will perish.
	but he who endures to the end, the same will be saved.	21:19 "By your endurance you will win your lives.
24:15 "When, therefore, you see the abomination of desolation, which was spoken of through Daniel the prophet, standing in the holy place [Daniel 9:7; 11:31; 12:11] (let the reader understand), 24:16 then let those who are in Judea flee to the mountains.	13:14 But when you see the abomination of desolation, spoken of by Daniel the prophet, standing where it ought not), [Daniel 9:7; 11:31; 12:11] (let the reader understand) then let those who are in Judea flee to the mountains,	21:20 "But when you see Jerusalem surrounded by armies, then know that its desolation is at hand. 21:21 Then let those who are in Judea flee to the mountains.
24:17 Let him who is on the housetop not go down to take out things that are in his house.	13:15 and let him who is on the housetop not go down, nor enter in, to take anything out of his house.	Let those who are in the midst of her depart.
24:18 Let him who is in the field not return back to get his clothes.	13:16 Let him who is in the field not return back to take his cloak.	Let those who are in the country not enter therein.
		21:22 For these are days of vengeance, that all things which are written may be fulfilled.

24:19 But woe to those who are with child and to nursing mothers in those days! 24:20 Pray that your flight will not be in the winter, nor on a Sabbath,	13:17 But woe to those who are with child and to those who nurse babies in those days! 13:18 Pray that your flight won't be in the winter.	21:23 Woe to those who are pregnant and to those who nurse infants in those days! For there will be great distress in the land, and wrath to this people.
24:21 for then there will be great oppression, such as has not been from the beginning of the world until now, no, nor ever will be. 24:22 Unless those days had been shortened, no flesh would have been saved. But for the sake of the chosen ones, those days will be shortened.	13:19 For in those days there will be oppression, such as there has not been the like from the beginning of the creation which God created until now, and never will be. 13:20 Unless the Lord had shortened the days, no flesh would have been saved; but for the sake of the chosen ones, whom he picked out, he shortened the days.	
24:23 "Then if any man tells you, 'Behold, here is the Christ,' or, 'There,' don't believe it. 24:24 For there will arise false christs, and false prophets, and they will show great signs and wonders, so as to lead astray, if possible, even the chosen ones.	13:21 Then if anyone tells you, 'Look, here is the Christ!' or, 'Look, there!' don't believe it. 13:22 For there will arise false christs and false prophets, and will show signs and wonders, that they may lead astray, if possible, even the chosen ones.	
24:25 "Behold, I have told you beforehand. 24:26 If therefore they tell you, 'Behold, he is in the wilderness,' don't go out; 'Behold, he is in the inner chambers,' don't believe it.	13:23 But you watch. "Behold, I have told you all things beforehand.	
		21:24 They will fall by the edge of the sword, and will be led captive into all the nations. Jerusalem will be trampled down by the Gentiles, until the times of the Gentiles are fulfilled.
24:27 For as the lightning flashes from the east, and is seen even to the west, so will be the coming of the Son of Man. 24:28 For wherever	13:24 But in those days, after that oppression, the sun will be darkened, the moon will not give its light, 13:25 the stars will be falling from	21:25 There will be signs in the sun, moon, and stars; and on the earth anxiety of nations, in perplexity for the roaring of the sea and the waves;

the carcass is, there is where the vultures gather together. 24:29 But immediately after the oppression of those days, the sun will be darkened, the moon will not give its light, the stars will fall from the sky, and the powers of the heavens will be shaken; [Isaiah 13:10; 34:4]	the sky, and the powers that are in the heavens will be shaken. [Isaiah 13:10; 34:4]	21:26 men fainting for fear, and for expectation of the things which are coming on the world: for the powers of the heavens will be shaken. [Isaiah 13:10; 34:4]
24:30 and then the sign of the Son of Man will appear in the sky. Then all the tribes of the earth will mourn, and they will see the Son of Man coming on the clouds of the sky with power and great glory.	13:26 Then they will see the Son of Man coming in clouds with great power and glory.	21:27 Then they will see the Son of Man coming in a cloud with power and great glory.
24:31 He will send out his angels with a great sound of a trumpet, and they will gather together his chosen ones from the four winds, from one end of the sky to the other.	13:27 Then he will send out his angels, and will gather together his chosen ones from the four winds, from the ends of the earth to the ends of the sky.	
		21:28 But when these things begin to happen, look up, and lift up your heads, because your redemption is near."
24:32 "Now from the fig tree learn this parable. When its branch has now become tender, and puts forth its leaves, you know that the summer is near. 24:33 Even so you also, when you see all these things, know that it is near, even at the doors.	13:28 "Now from the fig tree, learn this parable. When the branch has now become tender, and puts forth its leaves, you know that the summer is near; 13:29 even so you also, when you see these things coming to pass, know that it is near, at the doors.	21:29 He told them a parable. "See the fig tree, and all the trees. 21:30 When they are already budding, you see it and know by your own selves that the summer is already near.
		21:31Even so you also, when you see these things happening, know that the Kingdom of God is near.
24:34 Most certainly I tell you, this generation will not pass away, until all these things are accomplished.	13:30 Most certainly I say to you, this generation will not pass away until all these things happen.	21:32 Most certainly I tell you, this generation will not pass away until all things are accomplished.

24:35 Heaven and earth will pass away, but my words will not pass away.	13:31 Heaven and earth will pass away, but my words will not pass away.	21:33 Heaven and earth will pass away, but my words will by no means pass away.
24:36 But no one knows of that day and hour, not even the angels of heaven, but my Father only.	13:32 But of that day or that hour no one knows, not even the angels in heaven, nor the Son, but only the Father.	
	13:33 Watch, keep alert, and pray; for you don't know when the time is.	21:34 "So be careful,
24:37 "As the days of Noah were, so will be the coming of the Son of Man. 24:38 For as in those days which were before the flood they were eating and drinking, marrying and giving in marriage, until the day that Noah entered into the ship, 24:39 and they didn't know until the flood came, and took them all away, so will be the coming of the Son of Man. 24:40 Then two men will be in the field: one will be taken and one will be left; 24:41 two women grinding at the mill, one will be taken and one will be left.		with carousing, drunkenness, and cares of this life, and that day will come on you suddenly. 21:35 For it will come like a snare on all those who dwell on the surface of all the earth.
		or your hearts will be loaded down.
24:42 Watch therefore, for you don't know in what hour your Lord comes.		21:36 Therefore be watchful all the time, praying that you may be counted worthy to escape all these things that will happen, and to stand before the Son of Man."
24:43 But know this, that if the master of the house had known in what watch of the night the thief was coming, he would have watched, and would not have allowed his house to be broken into.	13:34 "It is like a man, traveling to another country, having left his house, and given authority to his servants, and to each one his work, and also commanded the doorkeeper to keep watch.	

24:44 Therefore also be ready, for in an hour that you don't expect, the Son of Man will come.	13:35 Watch therefore, for you don't know when the lord of the house is coming, whether at evening, or at midnight, or when the rooster crows, or in the morning; 13:36 lest coming suddenly he might find you sleeping. 13:37 What I tell you, I tell all: Watch."	
24:45 "Who then is the faithful and wise servant, whom his lord has set over his household, to give them their food in due season?		
24:46 Blessed is that servant whom his lord finds doing so when he comes. 24:47 Most certainly I tell you that he will set him over all that he has. 24:48 But if that evil servant should say in his heart, 'My lord is delaying his coming,' 24:49 and begins to beat his fellow servants, and eat and drink with the drunkards, 24:50 the lord of that servant will come in a day when he doesn't expect it, and in an hour when he doesn't know it,24:51 and will cut him in pieces, and appoint his portion with the hypocrites. There is where the weeping and grinding of teeth will be.		
25:1 "Then the Kingdom of Heaven will be like ten virgins, who took their lamps, and went out to meet the bridegroom. 25:2 Five of them were foolish, and five were wise. 25:3 Those who were foolish, when they took their lamps, took no oil with them, 25:4 but the wise took oil in their vessels with their lamps. 25:5 Now while the		

bridegroom delayed, they all slumbered and slept. 25:6 But at midnight there was a cry, 'Behold! The bridegroom is coming! Come out to meet him!' 25:7 Then all those virgins arose, and trimmed their lamps. 25:8 The foolish said to the wise, 'Give us some of your oil, for our lamps are going out.' 25:9 But the wise answered, saying, 'What if there isn't enough for us and you? You go rather to those who sell, and buy for yourselves.' 25:10 While they went away to buy, the bridegroom came, and those who were ready went in with him to the marriage feast, and the door was shut. 25:11 Afterward the other virgins also came, saying, 'Lord, Lord, open to us.' 25:12 But he answered, 'Most certainly I tell you, I don't know you.' 25:13 Watch therefore, for you don't know the day nor the hour in which the Son of Man is coming.			
25:14 "For it is like a man, going into another country, who called his own servants, and entrusted his goods to them. 25:15 To one he gave five talents, to another two, to another one; to each according to his own ability. Then he went on his journey. 25:16 Immediately he who received the five talents went and traded with them, and made another five talents. 25:17 In like manner he also who got the two gained another two. 25:18 But he			

who received the one went away and dug in the earth, and hid his lord's money.		
25:19 "Now after a long time the lord of those servants came, and reconciled accounts with them. 25:20 He who received the five talents came and brought another five talents, saying, 'Lord, you delivered to me five talents. Behold, I have gained another five talents besides them.'		
25:21 "His lord said to him, 'Well done, good and faithful servant. You have been faithful over a few things, I will set you over many things. Enter into the joy of your lord.'		
25:22 "He also who got the two talents came and said, 'Lord, you delivered to me two talents. Behold, I have gained another two talents besides them.'		
25:23 "His lord said to him, 'Well done, good and faithful servant. You have been faithful over a few things, I will set you over many things. Enter into the joy of your lord.'		
25:24 "He also who had received the one talent came and said, 'Lord, I knew you that you are a hard man, reaping where you did not sow, and gathering where you did not scatter. 25:25 I was afraid, and went away and hid your talent in the earth. Behold, you have what is yours.'		
25:26 "But his lord answered him, 'You wicked and slothful servant. You knew that I reap		

where I didn't sow, and gather where I didn't scatter. 25:27 You ought therefore to have deposited my money with the bankers, and at my coming I should have received back my own with interest. 25:28 Take away therefore the talent from him, and give it to him who has the ten talents. 25:29 For to everyone who has will be given, and he will have abundance, but from him who doesn't have, even that which he has will be taken away. 25:30 Throw out the unprofitable servant into the outer darkness, where there will be weeping and gnashing of teeth.'		
25:31 "But when the Son of Man comes in his glory, and all the holy angels with him, then he will sit on the throne of his glory. 25:32 Before him all the nations will be gathered, and he will separate them one from another, as a shepherd separates the sheep from the goats. 25:33 He will set the sheep on his right hand, but the goats on the left.		
25:34 Then the King will tell those on his right hand, 'Come, blessed of my Father, inherit the Kingdom prepared for you from the foundation of the world; 25:35 for I was hungry, and you gave me food to eat; I was thirsty, and you gave me drink; I was a stranger, and you took me in; 25:36 naked, and you clothed me; I was sick, and you visited me; I was in prison, and you came to me.'		

25:37 "Then the righteous will answer him, saying, 'Lord, when did we see you hungry, and feed you; or thirsty, and give you a drink? 25:38 When did we see you as a stranger, and take you in; or naked, and clothe you? 25:39 When did we see you sick, or in prison, and come to you?'		
25:40 "The King will answer them, 'Most certainly I tell you, inasmuch as you did it to one of the least of these my brothers, you did it to me.'		
25:41 Then he will say also to those on the left hand, 'Depart from me, you cursed, into the eternal fire which is prepared for the devil and his angels; 25:42 for I was hungry, and you didn't give me food to eat; I was thirsty, and you gave me no drink; 25:43 I was a stranger, and you didn't take me in; naked, and you didn't clothe me; sick, and in prison, and you didn't visit me.'		
25:44 "Then they will also answer, saying, 'Lord, when did we see you hungry, or thirsty, or a stranger, or naked, or sick, or in prison, and didn't help you?'		
25:45 "Then he will answer them, saying, 'Most certainly I tell you, inasmuch as you didn't do it to one of the least of these, you didn't do it to me.' 25:46 These will go away into eternal punishment, but the righteous into eternal life."		

		21:37 Every day Jesus was teaching in the temple, and every night he would go out and spend the night on the mountain that is called Olivet. 21:38 All the people came early in the morning to him in the temple to hear him.

Event 121: Jesus' opponents finalize their plot
Time: April 1, 33 A.D. (Wednesday)
Place: Jerusalem, Judea

MATTHEW 26:1-5, 14-16	MARK 14:1-2, 10-11	LUKE 22:1-6
26:1 It happened, when Jesus had finished all these words, that he said to his disciples,		
26:2 "You know that after two days the Passover is coming, and the Son of Man will be delivered up to be crucified."	14:1 It was now two days before the feast of the Passover and the unleavened bread,	22:1 Now the feast of unleavened bread, which is called the Passover, drew near.
26:3 Then the chief priests, the scribes, and the elders of the people were gathered together in the court of the high priest, who was called Caiaphas. 26:4 They took counsel together that they might take Jesus by deceit, and kill him. 26:5 But they said, "Not during the feast, lest a riot occur among the people."	and the chief priests and the scribes sought how they might seize him by deception, and kill him. 14:2 or they said, "Not during the feast, because there might be a riot of the people."	22:2 The chief priests and the scribes sought how they might put him to death, for they feared the people.
		22:3 Satan entered into Judas, who was surnamed Iscariot, who was numbered with the twelve. 22:4 He went away, and talked with the chief priests and captains about how he might deliver him to them. 22:5 They were glad, and agreed to give him money. 22:6 He consented, and sought an opportunity to deliver him to them in the absence of the multitude.

26:14 Then one of the twelve, who was called Judas Iscariot, went to the chief priests, 26:15 and said, "What are you willing to give me, that I should deliver him to you?" They weighed out for him thirty pieces of silver. 26:16 From that time he sought opportunity to betray him.	14:10 Judas Iscariot, who was one of the twelve, went away to the chief priests, that he might deliver him to them. 14:11 They, when they heard it, were glad, and promised to give him money. He sought how he might conveniently deliver him.	

Event 122: Jesus is anointed a second time
Time: April 1, 33 A.D. (Wednesday)
Place: Jerusalem, Judea

MATTHEW 26:6-13	MARK 14:3-9
26:6 Now when Jesus was in Bethany, in the house of Simon the leper,	14:3 While he was at Bethany, in the house of Simon the leper, as he sat at the table,
26:7 a woman came to him having an alabaster jar of very expensive ointment, and she poured it on his head as he sat at the table.	a woman came having an alabaster jar of ointment of pure nard—very costly. She broke the jar, and poured it over his head.
26:8 But when his disciples saw this, they were indignant, saying, "Why this waste? 26:9 For this ointment might have been sold for much, and given to the poor."	14:4 But there were some who were indignant among themselves, saying, "Why has this ointment been wasted? 14:5 For this might have been sold for more than three hundred denarii [about a year's wage for an agricultural labourer], and given to the poor." They grumbled against her.
26:10 However, knowing this, Jesus said to them, "Why do you trouble the woman? Because she has done a good work for me. 26:11 For you always have the poor with you; but you don't always have me. 26:12 For in pouring this ointment on my body, she did it to prepare me for burial.	14:6 But Jesus said, "Leave her alone. Why do you trouble her? She has done a good work for me. 14:7 For you always have the poor with you, and whenever you want to, you can do them good; but you will not always have me. 14:8 She has done what she could. She has anointed my body beforehand for the burying.
26:13 Most certainly I tell you, wherever this Good News is preached in the whole world, what this woman has done will also be spoken of as a memorial of her."	14:9 Most certainly I tell you, wherever this Good News may be preached throughout the whole world, that which this woman has done will also be spoken of for a memorial of her."

Appendix: one or two anointings? New event or flashback?

MATTHEW 26:6-13	MARK 14:3-9	JOHN 12:1-11
26:6 Now when Jesus was in Bethany, in the house of Simon the leper,	14:3 While he was at Bethany, in the house of Simon the leper, as he sat at the table,	12:1 The six days before the Passover, Jesus came to Bethany, where Lazarus was, who had been dead, whom he raised from the dead.
		12:2 So they made him a supper there. Martha served, but Lazarus was one of those who sat at the table with him.
26:7 a woman came to him having an alabaster jar of very expensive ointment, and she poured it on his head as he sat at the table.	a woman came having an alabaster jar of ointment of pure nard—very costly. She broke the jar, and poured it over his head.	12:3 Mary, therefore, took a pound of ointment of pure nard, very precious, and anointed the feet of Jesus, and wiped his feet with her hair.
		The house was filled with the fragrance of the ointment.
26:8 But when his disciples saw this, they were indignant, saying, "Why this waste? 26:9 For this ointment might have been sold for much, and given to the poor."	14:4 But there were some who were indignant among themselves, saying, "Why has this ointment been wasted? 14:5 For this might have been sold for more than three hundred denarii [about a year's wage for an agricultural labourer], and given to the poor." They grumbled against her.	12:4 Then Judas Iscariot, Simon's son, one of his disciples, who would betray him, said, 12:5 "Why wasn't this ointment sold for three hundred denarii [about a year's wages for an agricultural labourer], and given to the poor?"
		12:6 Now he said this, not because he cared for the poor, but because he was a thief, and having the money box, used to steal what was put into it.
26:10 However, knowing this, Jesus said to them, "Why do you trouble the woman? Because she has done a good work for me. 26:11 For you always have the poor with you; but you don't always have me. 26:12 For in pouring this ointment on my body, she did it to prepare me for burial.	14:6 But Jesus said, "Leave her alone. Why do you trouble her? She has done a good work for me. 14:7 For you always have the poor with you, and whenever you want to, you can do them good; but you will not always have me. 14:8 She has done what she could. She has anointed my body beforehand for the burying.	12:7 But Jesus said, "Leave her alone. She has kept this for the day of my burial. 12:8 For you always have the poor with you, but you don't always have me."

26:13 Most certainly I tell you, wherever this Good News is preached in the whole world, what this woman has done will also be spoken of as a memorial of her."	14:9 Most certainly I tell you, wherever this Good News may be preached throughout the whole world, that which this woman has done will also be spoken of for a memorial of her."	
		12:9 A large crowd therefore of the Jews learned that he was there, and they came, not for Jesus' sake only, but that they might see Lazarus also, whom he had raised from the dead.
26:14 Then one of the twelve, who was called Judas Iscariot, went to the chief priests, 26:15 and said, "What are you willing to give me, that I should deliver him to you?" They weighed out for him thirty pieces of silver. 26:16 From that time he sought opportunity to betray him.		
		12:10 But the chief priests conspired to put Lazarus to death also, 12:11 because on account of him many of the Jews went away and believed in Jesus.

Event 123: Jesus celebrates the Last Supper
Time: April 2, 33 A.D. (Thursday)
Place: Jerusalem, Judea

MATTHEW 26:17-35	MARK 14:12-31	LUKE 22:7-38	JOHN 13:1-17:26
26:17 Now on the first day of unleavened bread, the disciples came to Jesus, saying to him, "Where do you want us to prepare for you to eat the Passover?"	14:12 On the first day of unleavened bread, when they sacrificed the Passover, his disciples asked him, "Where do you want us to go and make ready that you may eat the Passover?"	22:7 The day of unleavened bread came, on which the Passover must be sacrificed.	13:1 Now before the feast of the Passover, Jesus, knowing that his time had come that he would depart from this world to the Father, having loved his own who were in the world, he loved them to the end.

26:18 He said,	14:13 He sent two of his disciples, and said to them,	22:8 He sent Peter and John, saying,	
"Go into the city to a certain person, and tell him, 'The Teacher says, "My time is at hand. I will keep the Passover at your house with my disciples."'"	"Go into the city, and there you will meet a man carrying a pitcher of water. Follow him, 14:14 and wherever he enters in, tell the master of the house, 'The Teacher says, "Where is the guest room, where I may eat the Passover with my disciples?"' 14:15 He will himself show you a large upper room furnished and ready. Make ready for us there."	"Go and prepare the Passover for us, that we may eat." 22:9 They said to him, "Where do you want us to prepare?" 22:10 He said to them, "Behold, when you have entered into the city, a man carrying a pitcher of water will meet you. Follow him into the house which he enters. 22:11 Tell the master of the house, 'The Teacher says to you, "Where is the guest room, where I may eat the Passover with my disciples?"' 22:12 He will show you a large, furnished upper room. Make preparations there."	
26:19 The disciples did as Jesus commanded them, and they prepared the Passover.	14:16 His disciples went out, and came into the city, and found things as he had said to them, and they prepared the Passover.	22:13 They went, found things as he had told them, and they prepared the Passover.	
26:20 Now when evening had come, he was reclining at the table with the twelve disciples.	14:17 When it was evening he came with the twelve.	22:14 When the hour had come, he sat down with the twelve apostles.	
		22:15 He said to them, "I have earnestly desired to eat this Passover with you before I suffer, 22:16 for I tell you, I will no longer by any means eat of it until it is fulfilled in the Kingdom of God."	

		22:17 He received a cup, and when he had given thanks, he said, "Take this, and share it among yourselves, 22:18 for I tell you, I will not drink at all again from the fruit of the vine, until the Kingdom of God comes."	
26:21 As they were eating, he said, "Most certainly I tell you that one of you will betray me."	14:18 As they sat and were eating, Jesus said, "Most certainly I tell you, one of you will betray me—he who eats with me."		
26:22 They were exceedingly sorrowful, and each began to ask him, "It isn't me, is it, Lord?"	14:19 They began to be sorrowful, and to ask him one by one, "Surely not I?" And another said, "Surely not I?"		
26:23 He answered, "He who dipped his hand with me in the dish, the same will betray me.	14:20 He answered them, "It is one of the twelve, he who dips with me in the dish.		
26:24 The Son of Man goes, even as it is written of him, but woe to that man through whom the Son of Man is betrayed! It would be better for that man if he had not been born."	14:21 For the Son of Man goes, even as it is written about him, but woe to that man by whom the Son of Man is betrayed! It would be better for that man if he had not been born."		
26:25 Judas, who betrayed him, answered, "It isn't me, is it, Rabbi?"			
He said to him, "You said it."			

			13:2 After supper, the devil having already put into the heart of Judas Iscariot, Simon's son, to betray him,
26:26 As they were eating, Jesus took bread, gave thanks for [TR has "blessed" instead of gave thanks for] it, and broke it. He gave to the disciples, and said,	14:22 As they were eating, Jesus took bread, and when he had blessed, he broke it, and gave to them, and said,	22:19 He took bread, and when he had given thanks, he broke it, and gave to them, saying,	
"Take, eat; this is my body."	"Take, eat. This is my body."	"This is my body which is given for you.	
		Do this in memory of me."	
26:27 He took the cup, gave thanks, and gave to them, saying, "All of you drink it, 26:28 for this is my blood of the new covenant, which is poured out for many for the remission of sins.	14:23 He took the cup, and when he had given thanks, he gave to them. They all drank of it. 14:24 He said to them, "This is my blood of the new covenant, which is poured out for many.	22:20 Likewise, he took the cup after supper, saying, "This cup is the new covenant in my blood, which is poured out for you.	
26:29 But I tell you that I will not drink of this fruit of the vine from now on, until that day when I drink it anew with you in my Father's Kingdom."	14:25 Most certainly I tell you, I will no more drink of the fruit of the vine, until that day when I drink it anew in the Kingdom of God."		
		22:21 But behold, the hand of him who betrays me is with me on the table.	
		22:22 The Son of Man indeed goes, as it has been determined, but woe to that man through whom he is betrayed!"	

		22:23 They began to question among themselves, which of them it was who would do this thing.	
		22:24 There arose also a contention among them, which of them was considered to be greatest.	
		22:25 He said to them, "The kings of the nations lord it over them, and those who have authority over them are called 'benefactors.' 22:26 But not so with you. But one who is the greater among you, let him become as the younger, and one who is governing, as one who serves.	
			13:3 Jesus, knowing that the Father had given all things into his hands, and that he came forth from God, and was going to God, 13:4 arose from supper, and laid aside his outer garments. He took a towel, and wrapped a towel around his waist. 13:5 Then he poured water into the basin, and began to wash the disciples' feet, and to wipe them with the towel that was wrapped around him. 13:6 Then he came to Simon Peter. He said to him, "Lord, do you wash my feet?"

			13:7 Jesus answered him, "You don't know what I am doing now, but you will understand later."
			13:8 Peter said to him, "You will never wash my feet!"
			Jesus answered him, "If I don't wash you, you have no part with me."
			13:9 Simon Peter said to him, "Lord, not my feet only, but also my hands and my head!"
			13:10 Jesus said to him, "Someone who has bathed only needs to have his feet washed, but is completely clean.
			You are clean, but not all of you." 13:11 For he knew him who would betray him, therefore he said, "You are not all clean."
			13:12 So when he had washed their feet, put his outer garment back on, and sat down again, he said to them,
			Do you know what I have done to you? 'Teacher' and 'Lord.' You say so correctly, for so I am. 13:14 If I then, the Lord and the Teacher, have washed your feet, you

			also ought to wash one another's feet. 13:15 For I have given you an example, that you also should do as I have done to you."
			13:16 Most certainly I tell you, a servant is not greater than his lord, neither one who is sent greater than he who sent him. 13:17 If you know these things, blessed are you if you do them.
			13:18 I don't speak concerning all of you. I know whom I have chosen. But that the Scripture may be fulfilled, 'He who eats bread with me has lifted up his heel against me.' [Psalm 41:9]
			13:19 From now on, I tell you before it happens, that when it happens, you may believe that I am he.
			13:20 Most certainly I tell you, he who receives whomever I send, receives me; and he who receives me, receives him who sent me."
			13:21 When Jesus had said this, he was troubled in spirit, and testified, "Most certainly I tell you that one of you will betray me."

			3:22 The disciples looked at one another, perplexed about whom he spoke. 13:23 One of his disciples, whom Jesus loved, was at the table, leaning against Jesus' breast.
			13:23 One of his disciples, whom Jesus loved, was at the table, leaning against Jesus' breast.
			13:24 Simon Peter therefore beckoned to him, and said to him, "Tell us who it is of whom he speaks."
			13:25 He, leaning back, as he was, on Jesus' breast, asked him, "Lord, who is it?"
			13:26 Jesus therefore answered, "It is he to whom I will give this piece of bread when I have dipped it."
			So when he had dipped the piece of bread, he gave it to Judas, the son of Simon Iscariot. 13:27 After the piece of bread, then Satan entered into him.
			Then Jesus said to him, "What you do, do quickly."
			13:28 Now no man at the table knew why he said this to him. 13:29

			For some thought, because Judas had the money box, that Jesus said to him, "Buy what things we need for the feast," or that he should give something to the poor. 13:30 Therefore, having received that morsel, he went out immediately. It was night.
			13:31 When he had gone out, Jesus said, "Now the Son of Man has been glorified, and God has been glorified in him. 13:32 If God has been glorified in him, God will also glorify him in himself, and he will glorify him immediately.
			13:33 Little children, I will be with you a little while longer. You will seek me, and as I said to the Jews, 'Where I am going, you can't come,' so now I tell you.
			13:34 A new commandment I give to you, that you love one another, just like I have loved you; that you also love one another. 13:35 By this everyone will know that you are my disciples, if you have love for one another."

			13:36 Simon Peter said to him, "Lord, where are you going?"
			Jesus answered, "Where I am going, you can't follow now, but you will follow afterwards."
			13:37 Peter said to him, "Lord, why can't I follow you now? I will lay down my life for you."
			13:38 Jesus answered him, "Will you lay down your life for me? Most certainly I tell you, the rooster won't crow until you have denied me three times.
			14:1 "Don't let your heart be troubled. Believe in God. Believe also in me.
			14:2 In my Father's house are many homes. If it weren't so, I would have told you. I am going to prepare a place for you. 14:3 If I go and prepare a place for you, I will come again, and will receive you to myself; that where I am, you may be there also. 14:4 Where I go, you know, and you know the way."
			14:5 Thomas said to him, "Lord, we don't know where you are going. How can we know the way?"

			14:6 Jesus said to him, "I am the way, the truth, and the life. No one comes to the Father, except through me.
			14:7 If you had known me, you would have known my Father also. From now on, you know him, and have seen him."
			14:8 Philip said to him, "Lord, show us the Father, and that will be enough for us."
			14:9 Jesus said to him, "Have I been with you such a long time, and do you not know me, Philip? He who has seen me has seen the Father. How do you say, 'Show us the Father?'
			14:10 Don't you believe that I am in the Father, and the Father in me? The words that I tell you, I speak not from myself; but the Father who lives in me does his works. 14:11 Believe me that I am in the Father, and the Father in me; or else believe me for the very works' sake.
			14:12 Most certainly I tell you, he who believes in me, the works that I do, he

			will do also; and he will do greater works than these, because I am going to my Father.
			14:13 Whatever you will ask in my name, that will I do, that the Father may be glorified in the Son. 14:14 If you will ask anything in my name, I will do it.
			14:15 If you love me, keep my commandments.
			14:16 I will pray to the Father, and he will give you another Counselor [Greek "Parakleton" means Counselor, Helper, Advocate, Intercessor and Comfortor] that he may be with you forever,—14:17 the Spirit of truth, whom the world can't receive; for it doesn't see him, neither knows him. You know him, for he lives with you, and will be in you.
			14:18 I will not leave you orphans. I will come to you.
			14:19 Yet a little while, and the world will see me no more; but you will see me.
			Because I live, you will live also.
			14:20 In that day you will know that I am in my Father, and you in me, and I in you.

			14:21 One who has my commandments, and keeps them, that person is one who loves me. One who loves me will be loved by my Father, and I will love him, and will reveal myself to him."
			14:22 Judas (not Iscariot) said to him, "Lord, what has happened that you are about to reveal yourself to us, and not to the world?"
			14:23 Jesus answered him, "If a man loves me, he will keep my word. My Father will love him, and we will come to him, and make our home with him.
			14:24 He who doesn't love me doesn't keep my words. The word which you hear isn't mine, but the Father's who sent me. 14:25 I have said these things to you, while still living with you.
			14:26 But the Counselor, the Holy Spirit, whom the Father will send in my name, he will teach you all things, and will remind you of all that I said to you.

			14:27 Peace I leave with you. My peace I give to you; not as the world gives, give I to you. Don't let your heart be troubled, neither let it be fearful. 14:28 You heard how I told you, 'I go away, and I come to you.' If you loved me, you would have rejoiced, because I said 'I am going to my Father;' for the Father is greater than I.
			14:29 Now I have told you before it happens so that, when it happens, you may believe.
			14:30 I will no more speak much with you, for the prince of the world comes, and he has nothing in me.
			14:31 But that the world may know that I love the Father, and as the Father commanded me, even so I do. Arise, let us go from here.
			15:1 "I am the true vine, and my Father is the farmer. 15:2 Every branch in me that doesn't bear fruit, he takes away. Every branch that bears fruit, he prunes, that it may bear more fruit.15:3

			You are already pruned clean because of the word which I have spoken to you. 15:4 Remain in me, and I in you. As the branch can't bear fruit by itself, unless it remains in the vine, so neither can you, unless you remain in me. 15:5 I am the vine. You are the branches. He who remains in me, and I in him, the same bears much fruit, for apart from me you can do nothing. 15:6 If a man doesn't remain in me, he is thrown out as a branch, and is withered; and they gather them, throw them into the fire, and they are burned. 15:7 If you remain in me, and my words remain in you, you will ask whatever you desire, and it will be done for you.
			15:8 "In this is my Father glorified, that you bear much fruit; and so you will be my disciples. 15:9 Even as the Father has loved me, I also have loved you. Remain in my love.

			5:10 If you keep my commandments, you will remain in my love; even as I have kept my Father's commandments, and remain in his love.
			15:11 I have spoken these things to you, that my joy may remain in you, and that your joy may be made full.
			15:12 "This is my commandment, that you love one another, even as I have loved you.
			15:13 Greater love has no one than this, that someone lay down his life for his friends.
			15:14 You are my friends, if you do whatever I command you. 15:15 No longer do I call you servants, for the servant doesn't know what his lord does. But I have called you friends, for everything that I heard from my Father, I have made known to you.
			15:16 You didn't choose me, but I chose you, and appointed you, that you should go and bear fruit, and that your fruit should

			remain; that whatever you will ask of the Father in my name, he may give it to you.
			15:17 "I command these things to you, that you may love one another.
			15:18 If the world hates you, you know that it has hated me before it hated you. 15:19 If you were of the world, the world would love its own. But because you are not of the world, since I chose you out of the world, therefore the world hates you.
			15:20 Remember the word that I said to you: 'A servant is not greater than his lord.' [John 13:16] If they persecuted me, they will also persecute you. If they kept my word, they will keep yours also.
			15:21 But all these things will they do to you for my name's sake, because they don't know him who sent me. 15:22 If I had not come and spoken to them, they would not have had sin; but now they have no excuse for their sin. 15:23 He who hates me, hates my Father also. 15:24

			If I hadn't done among them the works which no one else did, they wouldn't have had sin. But now have they seen and also hated both me and my Father.
			15:25 But this happened so that the word may be fulfilled which was written in their law, 'They hated me without a cause.' [Psalm 35:19; 69:4]
			15:26 "When the Counselor [Greek "Paraketon" means Counselor, Helper, Advocate, Intercessor, and Comfortor] has come, whom I will send to you from the Father, the Spirit of truth, who proceeds from the Father, he will testify about me. 15:27 You will also testify, because you have been with me from the beginning.
			16:1 "These things have I spoken to you, so that you wouldn't be caused to stumble. 16:2 They will put you out of the synagogues. Yes, the time comes that whoever kills you will think that he offers service to God. 16:3 They will do these things [TR adds "to you"] because they have not known the Father, nor me.

			16:4 But I have told you these things, so that when the time comes, you may remember that I told you about them. I didn't tell you these things from the beginning, because I was with you. 16:5 But now I am going to him who sent me, and none of you asks me, 'Where are you going?' 16:6 But because I have told you these things, sorrow has filled your heart.
			16:7 Nevertheless I tell you the truth: It is to your advantage that I go away, for if I don't go away, the Counselor won't come to you. But if I go, I will send him to you.
			16:8 When he has come, he will convict the world about sin, about righteousness, and about judgment; 16:9 about sin, because they don't believe in me; 16:10 about righteousness, because I am going to my Father, and you won't see me any more; 16:11 about judgment, because the prince of this world has been judged.

			16:12 "I have yet many things to tell you, but you can't bear them now.
			16:13 However when he, the Spirit of truth, has come, he will guide you into all truth, for he will not speak from himself; but whatever he hears, he will speak. He will declare to you things that are coming.
			16:14 He will glorify me, for he will take from what is mine, and will declare it to you. 16:15 All things whatever the Father has are mine; therefore I said that he takes [TR has instead of takes "will take"] of mine, and will declare it to you.
			16:16 A little while, and you will not see me. Again a little while, and you will see me."
			16:17 Some of his disciples therefore said to one another, "What is this that he says to us, 'A little while, and you won't see me, and again a little while, and you will see me;' and, 'Because I go to the Father?'" 16:18

			They said therefore, "What is this that he says, 'A little while?' We don't know what he is saying."
			16:19 Therefore Jesus perceived that they wanted to ask him, and he said to them, "Do you inquire among yourselves concerning this, that I said, 'A little while, and you won't see me, and again a little while, and you will see me?'
			16:20 Most certainly I tell you, that you will weep and lament, but the world will rejoice. You will be sorrowful, but your sorrow will be turned into joy.
			16:21 A woman, when she gives birth, has sorrow, because her time has come. But when she has delivered the child, she doesn't remember the anguish any more, for the joy that a human being is born into the world. 16:22 Therefore you now have sorrow, but I will see you again, and your heart will rejoice, and no one will take your joy away from you.
			16:23 "In that day you will ask me no questions.

			Most certainly I tell you, whatever you may ask of the Father in my name, he will give it to you. 16:24 Until now, you have asked nothing in my name. Ask, and you will receive, that your joy may be made full.
			16:25 I have spoken these things to you in figures of speech. But the time is coming when I will no more speak to you in figures of speech, but will tell you plainly about the Father.
			16:26 In that day you will ask in my name; and I don't say to you, that I will pray to the Father for you, 16:27 for the Father himself loves you, because you have loved me, and have believed that I came forth from God. 16:28 I came out from the Father, and have come into the world. Again, I leave the world, and go to the Father."
			16:29 His disciples said to him, "Behold, now you speak plainly, and speak no figures of speech.

			16:30 Now we know that you know all things, and don't need for anyone to question you. By this we believe that you came forth from God."
			16:31 Jesus answered them, "Do you now believe? 16:32 Behold, the time is coming, yes and has now come, that you will be scattered, everyone to his own place, and you will leave me alone.
			Yet I am not alone, because the Father is with me.
			16:33 I have told you these things, that in me you may have peace. In the world you have oppression; but cheer up! I have overcome the world."
			17:1 Jesus said these things, and lifting up his eyes to heaven, he said, "Father, the time has come. Glorify your Son, that your Son may also glorify you; 17:2 even as you gave him authority over all flesh, he will give eternal life to all whom you have given him.

			17:3 This is eternal life, that they should know you, the only true God, and him whom you sent, Jesus Christ.
			17:4 I glorified you on the earth. I have accomplished the work which you have given me to do. 17:5 Now, Father, glorify me with your own self with the glory which I had with you before the world existed. 17:6 I revealed your name to the people whom you have given me out of the world. They were yours, and you have given them to me. They have kept your word.
			17:7 Now they have known that all things whatever you have given me are from you, 17:8 for the words which you have given me I have given to them, and they received them, and knew for sure that I came forth from you, and they have believed that you sent me.
			17:9 I pray for them. I don't pray for the world, but for those whom you have given me, for they are yours.

			17:10 All things that are mine are yours, and yours are mine, and I am glorified in them.
			17:11 I am no more in the world, but these are in the world, and I am coming to you. Holy Father, keep them through your name which you have given me, that they may be one, even as we are. 17:12 While I was with them in the world, I kept them in your name. Those whom you have given me I have kept. None of them is lost, except the son of destruction, that the Scripture might be fulfilled. 17:13 But now I come to you, and I say these things in the world, that they may have my joy made full in themselves.
			17:14 I have given them your word. The world hated them, because they are not of the world, even as I am not of the world.
			17:15 I pray not that you would take them from the world, but that you would keep them from the evil one.

			17:16 They are not of the world even as I am not of the world. 17:17 Sanctify them in your truth. Your word is truth. [Psalm 119:142]
			17:18 As you sent me into the world, even so I have sent them into the world. 17:19 For their sakes I sanctify myself, that they themselves also may be sanctified in truth.
			17:20 Not for these only do I pray, but for those also who believe in me through their word, 17:21 that they may all be one; even as you, Father, are in me, and I in you, that they also may be one in us; that the world may believe that you sent me.
			17:24 Father, I desire that they also whom you have given me be with me where I am, that they may see my glory, which you have given me, for you loved me before the foundation of the world.
			17:25 Righteous Father, the world hasn't known you, but I knew you; and these knew that you sent me.

			17:26 I made known to them your name, and will make it known; that the love with which you loved me may be in them, and I in them."
26:30 When they had sung a hymn, they went out to the Mount of Olives.	14:26 When they had sung a hymn, they went out to the Mount of Olives.		
		22:27 For who is greater, one who sits at the table, or one who serves? Isn't it he who sits at the table? But I am in the midst of you as one who serves.	
		22:28 But you are those who have continued with me in my trials. 22:29 I confer on you a kingdom, even as my Father conferred on me, 22:30 that you may eat and drink at my table in my Kingdom. You will sit on thrones, judging the twelve tribes of Israel."	
26:31 Then Jesus said to them, "All of you will be made to stumble because of me tonight, for it is written, 'I will strike the shepherd, and the sheep of the flock will be scattered.' [Zechariah 13:7] 26:32 But after I am raised up, I will go before you into Galilee."	14:27 Jesus said to them, "All of you will be made to stumble because of me tonight, for it is written, 'I will strike the shepherd, and the sheep will be scattered.' [Zechariah 13:7] 14:28 However, after I am raised up, I will go before you into Galilee."		

26:33 But Peter answered him, "Even if all will be made to stumble because of you, I will never be made to stumble."	14:29 But Peter said to him, "Although all will be offended, yet I will not."		
		22:31 The Lord said, "Simon, Simon, behold, Satan asked to have you, that he might sift you as wheat, 22:32 but I prayed for you, that your faith wouldn't fail. You, when once you have turned again, establish your brothers."	
		22:33 He said to him, "Lord, I am ready to go with you both to prison and to death!"	
26:34 Jesus said to him, "Most certainly I tell you that tonight, before the rooster crows, you will deny me three times."	14:30 Jesus said to him, "Most certainly I tell you, that you today, even this night, before the rooster crows twice, you will deny me three times."	22:34 He said, "I tell you, Peter, the rooster will by no means crow today until you deny that you know me three times."	
		22:35 He said to them, "When I sent you out without purse, and wallet, and shoes, did you lack anything?"	
		They said, "Nothing."	

		22:36 Then he said to them, "But now, whoever has a purse, let him take it, and likewise a wallet. Whoever has none, let him sell his cloak, and buy a sword. 22:37 For I tell you that this which is written must still be fulfilled in me: 'He was counted with the lawless.' [Isaiah 53:12] For that which concerns me has an end."	
		22:38 They said, "Lord, behold, here are two swords."	
		He said to them, "That is enough."	
26:35 Peter said to him, "Even if I must die with you, I will not deny you." All of the disciples also said likewise.	14:31 But he spoke all the more, "If I must die with you, I will not deny you." They all said the same thing.		

Event 124: Jesus is arrested in the Garden of Gethsemane
Time: April 2, 33 A.D. (Thursday)
Place: Jerusalem, Judea

MATTHEW 26:36-56	MARK 14:32-52	LUKE 22:39-53	JOHN 18:1-12
26:36 Then Jesus came with them to a place called Gethsemane, and said to his disciples, "Sit here, while I go there and pray."	14:32 They came to a place which was named Gethsemane. He said to his disciples, "Sit here, while I pray."	22:39 He came out, and went, as his custom was, to the Mount of Olives. His disciples also followed him.	18:1 When Jesus had spoken these words, he went out with his disciples over the brook Kidron, where there was a garden, into which he and his disciples entered.

26:37 He took with him Peter and the two sons of Zebedee, and began to be sorrowful and severely troubled.	14:33 He took with him Peter, James, and John, and began to be greatly troubled and distressed.		
6:38 Then he said to them, "My soul is exceedingly sorrowful, even to death. Stay here, and watch with me."	14:34 He said to them, "My soul is exceedingly sorrowful, even to death. Stay here, and watch."	22:40 When he was at the place, he said to them, "Pray that you don't enter into temptation."	
26:39 He went forward a little, fell on his face, and prayed, saying, "My Father, if it is possible, let this cup pass away from me; nevertheless, not what I desire, but what you desire."	14:35 He went forward a little, and fell on the ground, and prayed that, if it were possible, the hour might pass away from him. 14:36 He said, "Abba, Father, all things are possible to you. Please remove this cup from me. However, not what I desire, but what you desire."	22:41 He was withdrawn from them about a stone's throw, and he knelt down and prayed, 22:42 saying, "Father, if you are willing, remove this cup from me. Nevertheless, not my will, but yours, be done."	
		22:43 An angel from heaven appeared to him, strengthening him.	
		22:44 Being in agony he prayed more earnestly. His sweat became like great drops of blood falling down on the ground.	
26:40 He came to the disciples, and found them sleeping, and said to Peter, "What, couldn't you watch with me for one hour? 26:41 Watch and pray, that you don't enter into temptation. The spirit indeed is willing, but the flesh is weak."	14:37 He came and found them sleeping, and said to Peter, "Simon, are you sleeping? Couldn't you watch one hour? 14:38 Watch and pray, that you may not enter into temptation. The spirit indeed is willing, but the flesh is weak."	22:45 When he rose up from his prayer, he came to the disciples, and found them sleeping because of grief, 22:46 and said to them, "Why do you sleep? Rise and pray that you may not enter into temptation."	

26:42 Again, a second time he went away, and prayed, saying, "My Father, if this cup can't pass away from me unless I drink it, your desire be done."	14:39 Again he went away, and prayed, saying the same words.		
26:43 He came again and found them sleeping, for their eyes were heavy.	14:40 Again he returned, and found them sleeping, for their eyes were very heavy, and they didn't know what to answer him.		
26:44 He left them again, went away, and prayed a third time, saying the same words. 26:45 Then he came to his disciples, and said to them, "Sleep on now, and take your rest.	14:41 He came the third time, and said to them, "Sleep on now, and take your rest. It is enough. The hour has come.		
Behold, the hour is at hand, and the Son of Man is betrayed into the hands of sinners.	Behold, the Son of Man is betrayed into the hands of sinners.		
26:46 Arise, let's be going. Behold, he who betrays me is at hand."	14:42 Arise, let us be going. Behold, he who betrays me is at hand."		
26:47 While he was still speaking, behold, Judas, one of the twelve, came, and with him a great multitude with swords and clubs, from the chief priest and elders of the people.	14:43 Immediately, while he was still speaking, Judas, one of the twelve, came—and with him a multitude with swords and clubs, from the chief priests, the scribes, and the elders.	22:47 While he was still speaking, behold, a multitude, and he who was called Judas, one of the twelve, was leading them.	18:2 Now Judas, who betrayed him, also knew the place, for Jesus often met there with his disciples. 18:3 Judas then, having taken a detachment of soldiers and officers from the chief priests and the Pharisees, came there with lanterns, torches, and weapons.

26:48 Now he who betrayed him gave them a sign, saying, "Whoever I kiss, he is the one. Seize him."	14:44 Now he who betrayed him had given them a sign, saying, "Whoever I will kiss, that is he. Seize him, and lead him away safely."	He came near to Jesus to kiss him.	
26:49 Immediately he came to Jesus, and said, "Hail, Rabbi!" and kissed him. 26:50 Jesus said to him, "Friend, why are you here?"	14:45 When he had come, immediately he came to him, and said, "Rabbi! Rabbi!" and kissed him.		
			18:4 Jesus therefore, knowing all the things that were happening to him, went forth, and said to them, "Who are you looking for?"
			18:5 They answered him, "Jesus of Nazareth."
			Jesus said to them, "I am he." Judas also, who betrayed him, was standing with them.
			18:6 When therefore he said to them, "I am he," they went backward, and fell to the ground.
			18:7 Again therefore he asked them, "Who are you looking for?"
			They said, "Jesus of Nazareth."
			18:8 Jesus answered, "I told you that I am he. If therefore you seek me, let these go their way,"

			18:9 that the word might be fulfilled which he spoke, "Of those whom you have given me, I have lost none." [John 6:39]
Then they came and laid hands on Jesus, and took him.	14:46 They laid their hands on him, and seized him.		
		22:49 When those who were around him saw what was about to happen, they said to him, "Lord, shall we strike with the sword?"	
26:51 Behold, one of those who were with Jesus stretched out his hand, and drew his sword, and struck the servant of the high priest, and struck off his ear.	14:47 But a certain one of those who stood by drew his sword, and struck the servant of the high priest, and cut off his ear.	22:50 A certain one of them struck the servant of the high priest, and cut off his right ear.	18:10 Simon Peter therefore, having a sword, drew it, and struck the high priest's servant, and cut off his right ear. The servant's name was Malchus.
26:52 Then Jesus said to him, "Put your sword back into its place, for all those who take the sword will die by the sword.			18:11 Jesus therefore said to Peter, "Put the sword into its sheath. The cup which the Father has given me, shall I not surely drink it?"
		22:51 But Jesus answered, "Let me at least do this"—and he touched his ear, and healed him.	
26:53 Or do you think that I couldn't ask my Father, and he would even now send me more than twelve legions of angels? 26:54 How then would the Scriptures be fulfilled that it must be so?"			

26:55 In that hour Jesus said to the multitudes, "Have you come out as against a robber with swords and clubs to seize me? I sat daily in the temple teaching, and you didn't arrest me. 26:56 But all this has happened, that the Scriptures of the prophets might be fulfilled."	14:48 Jesus answered them, "Have you come out, as against a robber, with swords and clubs to seize me? 14:49 I was daily with you in the temple teaching, and you didn't arrest me. But this is so that the Scriptures might be fulfilled."	22:52 Jesus said to the chief priests, captains of the temple, and elders, who had come against him, "Have you come out as against a robber, with swords and clubs? 22:53 When I was with you in the temple daily, you didn't stretch out your hands against me. But this is your hour, and the power of darkness."	
		22:54 They seized him,	18:12 So the detachment, the commanding officer, and the officers of the Jews, seized Jesus and bound him,
		and led him away, and brought him into the high priest's house.	
			18:13 and led him to Annas first, for he was father-in-law to Caiaphas, who was high priest that year.
Then all the disciples left him, and fled.	14:50 They all left him, and fled.		
	14:51 A certain young man followed him, having a linen cloth thrown around himself, over his naked body. The young men grabbed him, 14:52 but he left the linen cloth, and fled from them naked.		

Event 125: Jesus' Jewish trial before Caiaphas
Time: April 3, 33 A.D. (Friday)
Place: Jerusalem, Judea

MATTHEW 26:57-66	MARK 14:53-64	LUKE 22:54-71	JOHN 18:13-24
26:57 Those who had taken Jesus led him away to Caiaphas the high priest, where the scribes and the elders were gathered together.	14:53 They led Jesus away to the high priest. All the chief priests, the elders, and the scribes came together with him.	22:54 They seized him, and led him away, and brought him into the high priest's house.	18:12 So the detachment, the commanding officer, and the officers of the Jews, seized Jesus and bound him, 18:13 and led him to Annas first, for he was father-in-law to Caiaphas, who was high priest that year.
			18:14 Now it was Caiaphas who advised the Jews that it was expedient that one man should perish for the people.
26:58 But Peter followed him from a distance, to the court of the high priest, and entered in and sat with the officers, to see the end.	14:54 Peter had followed him from a distance, until he came into the court of the high priest.	But Peter followed from a distance.	18:15 Simon Peter followed Jesus, as did another disciple.
			Now that disciple was known to the high priest, and entered in with Jesus into the court of the high priest;
			18:16 but Peter was standing at the door outside.
			So the other disciple, who was known to the high priest, went out and spoke to her who kept the door, and brought in Peter.

		22:55 When they had kindled a fire in the middle of the courtyard, and had sat down together, Peter sat among them.	
			18:17 Then the maid who kept the door said to Peter, "Are you also one of this man's disciples?"
			He said, "I am not."
			18:18 Now the servants and the officers were standing there, having made a fire of coals, for it was cold. They were warming themselves. Peter was with them, standing and warming himself.
			18:19 The high priest therefore asked Jesus about his disciples, and about his teaching.
			18:20 Jesus answered him, "I spoke openly to the world. I always taught in synagogues, and in the temple, where the Jews always meet. I said nothing in secret. 18:21 Why do you ask me? Ask those who have heard me what I said to them. Behold, these know the things which I said."
			18:22 When he had said this, one of the officers standing by slapped Jesus with his hand, saying, "Do you answer the high priest like that?"

			18:23 Jesus answered him, "If I have spoken evil, testify of the evil; but if well, why do you beat me?"
			18:24 Annas sent him bound to Caiaphas, the high priest.
26:59 Now the chief priests, the elders, and the whole council sought false testimony against Jesus, that they might put him to death; 26:60 and they found none.	14:55 Now the chief priests and the whole council sought witnesses against Jesus to put him to death, and found none.		
Even though many false witnesses came forward, they found none.	14:56 For many gave false testimony against him, and their testimony didn't agree with each other.		
But at last two false witnesses came forward,	14:57 Some stood up, and gave false testimony against him, saying,		
26:61 and said, "This man said, 'I am able to destroy the temple of God, and to build it in three days.'"	14:58 "We heard him say, 'I will destroy this temple that is made with hands, and in three days I will build another made without hands.'		
	"14:59 Even so, their testimony did not agree.		
26:62 The high priest stood up, and said to him, "Have you no answer? What is this that these testify against you?"	14:60 The high priest stood up in the midst, and asked Jesus, "Have you no answer? What is it which these testify against you?"		
26:63 But Jesus held his peace.	14:61 But he stayed quiet, and answered nothing.		

The high priest answered him, "I adjure you by the living God, that you tell us whether you are the Christ, the Son of God."	Again the high priest asked him, "Are you the Christ, the Son of the Blessed?"		
26:64 Jesus said to him, "You have said it.	14:62 Jesus said, "I am.		
Nevertheless, I tell you, after this you will see the Son of Man sitting at the right hand of Power, and coming on the clouds of the sky."	You will see the Son of Man sitting at the right hand of Power, and coming with the clouds of the sky."		
26:65 Then the high priest tore his clothing, saying, "He has spoken blasphemy! Why do we need any more witnesses? Behold, now you have heard his blasphemy. 26:66 What do you think?"	14:63 The high priest tore his clothes, and said, "What further need have we of witnesses? 14:64 You have heard the blasphemy! What do you think?"		
They answered, "He is worthy of death!"	They all condemned him to be worthy of death.		
26:67 Then they spit in his face and beat him with their fists, and some slapped him, 26:68 saying, "Prophesy to us, you Christ! Who hit you?"	14:65 Some began to spit on him, and to cover his face, and to beat him with fists, and to tell him, "Prophesy!" The officers struck him with the palms of their hands.		
	14:66 As Peter was in the courtyard below, one of the maids of the high priest came, 14:67 and seeing Peter warming himself, she looked at him, and said, "You were also with the Nazarene, Jesus!"	22:56 A certain servant girl saw him as he sat in the light, and looking intently at him, said, "This man also was with him."	18:25 Now Simon Peter was standing and warming himself. They said therefore to him, "You aren't also one of his disciples, are you?"

	14:68 But he denied it, saying, "I neither know, nor understand what you are saying."	22:57 He denied Jesus, saying, "Woman, I don't know him."	He denied it, and said, "I am not."
	He went out on the porch, and the rooster crowed.		
	14:69 The maid saw him, and began again to tell those who stood by, "This is one of them."	22:58 After a little while someone else saw him, and said, "You also are one of them!"	18:26 One of the servants of the high priest, being a relative of him whose ear Peter had cut off, said, "Didn't I see you in the garden with him?"
	14:70 But he again denied it.	But Peter answered, "Man, I am not!"	18:27 Peter therefore denied it again,
			and immediately the rooster crowed.
	After a little while again those who stood by said to Peter, "You truly are one of them, for you are a Galilean, and your speech shows it."	22:59 After about one hour passed, another confidently affirmed, saying, "Truly this man also was with him, for he is a Galilean!"	
	14:71 But he began to curse, and to swear, "I don't know this man of whom you speak!"	22:60 But Peter said, "Man, I don't know what you are talking about!"	
	14:72 The rooster crowed the second time.	Immediately, while he was still speaking, a rooster crowed.	
	Peter remembered the word, how that Jesus said to him, "Before the rooster crows twice, you will deny me three times." When he thought about that, he wept.	22:61 The Lord turned, and looked at Peter. Then Peter remembered the Lord's word, how he said to him, "Before the rooster crows you will deny me three times." 22:62 He went out, and wept bitterly.	

		22:63 The men who held Jesus mocked him and beat him. 22:64 Having blindfolded him, they struck him on the face and asked him, "Prophesy! Who is the one who struck you?"	
		22:65 They spoke many other things against him, insulting him.	
27:1 Now when morning had come, all the chief priests and the elders of the people took counsel against Jesus to put him to death:	15:1 Immediately in the morning the chief priests, with the elders and scribes, and the whole council, held a consultation,	22:66 As soon as it was day, the assembly of the elders of the people was gathered together, both chief priests and scribes,	
		and they led him away into their council, saying,	
		22:67 "If you are the Christ, tell us."	
		But he said to them, "If I tell you, you won't believe, 22:68 and if I ask, you will in no way answer me or let me go.	
		22:69 From now on, the Son of Man will be seated at the right hand of the power of God."	
		22:70 They all said, "Are you then the Son of God?"	
		He said to them, "You say it, because I am."	
		22:71 They said, "Why do we need any more witness? For we ourselves have heard from his own mouth!"	

27:2 and they bound him, and led him away, and delivered him up to Pontius Pilate, the governor.	and bound Jesus, and carried him away, and delivered him up to Pilate.	23:1 The whole company of them rose up and brought him before Pilate.	18:28 They led Jesus therefore from Caiaphas into the Praetorium.

Event 126: Judas commits suicide
Time: April 3, 33 A.D. (Friday)
Place: Jerusalem, Judea

MATTHEW 27:3-10
27:3 Then Judas, who betrayed him, when he saw that Jesus was condemned, felt remorse, and brought back the thirty pieces of silver to the chief priests and elders, 27:4 saying, "I have sinned in that I betrayed innocent blood."
But they said, "What is that to us? You see to it."
27:5 He threw down the pieces of silver in the sanctuary, and departed.
He went away and hanged himself.
27:6 The chief priests took the pieces of silver, and said, "It's not lawful to put them into the treasury, since it is the price of blood."
27:7 They took counsel, and bought the potter's field with them, to bury strangers in. 27:8 Therefore that field was called "The Field of Blood" to this day.
27:9 Then that which was spoken through Jeremiah the prophet was fulfilled, saying, "They took the thirty pieces of silver, the price of him upon whom a price had been set, whom some of the children of Israel priced, 27:10 and they gave them for the potter's field, as the Lord commanded me." [Zechariah 11:12-13; Jeremiah 19:1-13; 32:6-9]

Event 127: Jesus' Roman trial before Pilate
Time: April 3, 33 A.D. (Friday)
Place: Jerusalem, Judea

MATTHEW 27:2, 11-31	MARK 15:1-20	LUKE 23:1-25	JOHN 18:28-19:16
27:2 and they bound him, and led him away, and delivered him up to Pontius Pilate, the governor.	and bound Jesus, and carried him away, and delivered him up to Pilate.	23:1 The whole company of them rose up and brought him before Pilate.	18:28 They led Jesus therefore from Caiaphas into the Praetorium.
			It was early,
			and they themselves didn't enter into the Praetorium, that they might not be defiled, but might eat the Passover.

			18:29 Pilate therefore went out to them, and said, "What accusation do you bring against this man?"
			18:30 They answered him, "If this man weren't an evildoer, we wouldn't have delivered him up to you."
		23:2 They began to accuse him, saying, "We found this man perverting the nation,	
			18:31 Pilate therefore said to them, "Take him yourselves, and judge him according to your law."
			Therefore the Jews said to him, "It is not lawful for us to put anyone to death,"
			18:32 that the word of Jesus might be fulfilled, which he spoke, signifying by what kind of death he should die.
		forbidding paying taxes to Caesar, and saying that he himself is Christ, a king."	
27:11 Now Jesus stood before the governor:			18:33 Pilate therefore entered again into the Praetorium, called Jesus,
and the governor asked him, saying, "Are you the King of the Jews?"	15:2 Pilate asked him, "Are you the King of the Jews?"	23:3 Pilate asked him, "Are you the King of the Jews?"	23:3 Pilate asked him, "Are you the King of the Jews?"
Jesus said to him, "So you say."	He answered, "So you say."	He answered him, "So you say."	18:34 Jesus answered him, "Do you say this by yourself, or did others tell you about me?"

			18:35 Pilate answered, "I'm not a Jew, am I? Your own nation and the chief priests delivered you to me. What have you done?"
			18:36 Jesus answered, "My Kingdom is not of this world. If my Kingdom were of this world, then my servants would fight, that I wouldn't be delivered to the Jews. But now my Kingdom is not from here."
			18:37 Pilate therefore said to him, "Are you a king then?"
			Jesus answered, "You say that I am a king. For this reason I have been born, and for this reason I have come into the world, that I should testify to the truth. Everyone who is of the truth listens to my voice."
			18:38 Pilate said to him, "What is truth?"
		23:4 Pilate said to the chief priests and the multitudes, "I find no basis for a charge against this man."	When he had said this, he went out again to the Jews, and said to them, "I find no basis for a charge against him.
	15:3 The chief priests accused him of many things.		
27:12 When he was accused by the chief priests and elders, he answered nothing.			

27:13 Then Pilate said to him, "Don't you hear how many things they testify against you?"	15:4 Pilate again asked him, "Have you no answer? See how many things they testify against you!"		
27:14 He gave him no answer, not even one word, so that the governor marveled greatly.	15:5 But Jesus made no further answer, so that Pilate marveled.		
		23:5 But they insisted, saying, "He stirs up the people, teaching throughout all Judea, beginning from Galilee even to this place."	
		23:6 But when Pilate heard Galilee mentioned, he asked if the man was a Galilean. 23:7 When he found out that he was in Herod's jurisdiction, he sent him to Herod, who was also in Jerusalem during those days.	
		23:8 Now when Herod saw Jesus, he was exceedingly glad, for he had wanted to see him for a long time, because he had heard many things about him. He hoped to see some miracle done by him.	
		23:9 He questioned him with many words, but he gave no answers.	

		23:10 The chief priests and the scribes stood, vehemently accusing him.	
		23:11 Herod with his soldiers humiliated him and mocked him. Dressing him in luxurious clothing, they sent him back to Pilate.	
		23:12 Herod and Pilate became friends with each other that very day, for before that they were enemies with each other.	
		23:13 Pilate called together the chief priests and the rulers and the people, 23:14 and said to them, "You brought this man to me as one that perverts the people, and see, I have examined him before you, and found no basis for a charge against this man concerning those things of which you accuse him.	
		23:15 Neither has Herod, for I sent you to him, and see, nothing worthy of death has been done by him.	
		23:16 I will therefore chastise him and release him."	

27:15 Now at the feast the governor was accustomed to release to the multitude one prisoner, whom they desired.	15:6 Now at the feast he used to release to them one prisoner, whom they asked of him.	23:17 Now he had to release one prisoner to them at the feast.	18:39 But you have a custom, that I should release someone to you at the Passover.
27:16 They had then a notable prisoner, called Barabbas.	15:7 There was one called Barabbas, bound with those who had made insurrection, men who in the insurrection had committed murder.		
	15:8 The multitude, crying aloud, began to ask him to do as he always did for them.		
27:17 When therefore they were gathered together, Pilate said to them, "Whom do you want me to release to you? Barabbas, or Jesus, who is called Christ?"	15:9 Pilate answered them, saying, "Do you want me to release to you the King of the Jews?"		Therefore do you want me to release to you the King of the Jews?"
27:18 For he knew that because of envy they had delivered him up.	15:10 For he perceived that for envy the chief priests had delivered him up.		
27:19 While he was sitting on the judgment seat, his wife sent to him, saying, "Have nothing to do with that righteous man, for I have suffered many things this day in a dream because of him."			

27:20 Now the chief priests and the elders persuaded the multitudes to ask for Barabbas, and destroy Jesus.	15:11 But the chief priests stirred up the multitude, that he should release Barabbas to them instead.	23:18 But they all cried out together, saying, "Away with this man! Release to us Barabbas!"— 23:19 one who was thrown into prison for a certain revolt in the city, and for murder.	18:40 Then they all shouted again, saying, "Not this man, but Barabbas!" Now Barabbas was a robber.
27:21 But the governor answered them, "Which of the two do you want me to release to you?"	15:12 Pilate again asked them, "What then should I do to him whom you call the King of the Jews?"	23:20 Then Pilate spoke to them again,	
		wanting to release Jesus,	
They said, "Barabbas!"			
27:22 Pilate said to them, "What then shall I do to Jesus, who is called Christ?"			
They all said to him, "Let him be crucified!"	15:13 They cried out again, "Crucify him!"	23:21 but they shouted, saying, "Crucify! Crucify him!"	
27:23 But the governor said, "Why? What evil has he done?"	15:14 Pilate said to them, "Why, what evil has he done?"	23:22 He said to them the third time, "Why? What evil has this man done? I have found no capital crime in him.	
		I will therefore chastise him and release him."	
But they cried out exceedingly, saying, "Let him be crucified!"	But they cried out exceedingly, "Crucify him!"	23:23 But they were urgent with loud voices, asking that he might be crucified.	
			19:1 So Pilate then took Jesus, and flogged him.

			19:2 The soldiers twisted thorns into a crown, and put it on his head, and dressed him in a purple garment.
			19:3 They kept saying, "Hail, King of the Jews!" and they kept slapping him.
			19:4 Then Pilate went out again, and said to them, "Behold, I bring him out to you, that you may know that I find no basis for a charge against him."
			19:5 Jesus therefore came out, wearing the crown of thorns and the purple garment. Pilate said to them, "Behold, the man!"
			19:6 When therefore the chief priests and the officers saw him, they shouted, saying, "Crucify! Crucify!"
			Pilate said to them, "Take him yourselves, and crucify him, for I find no basis for a charge against him."
			19:7 The Jews answered him, "We have a law, and by our law he ought to die, because he made himself the Son of God."
			19:8 When therefore Pilate heard this saying, he was more afraid.
			19:9 He entered into the Praetorium again, and said to Jesus, "Where are you from?"

			But Jesus gave him no answer.
			19:10 Pilate therefore said to him, "Aren't you speaking to me? Don't you know that I have power to release you, and have power to crucify you?"
			19:11 Jesus answered, "You would have no power at all against me, unless it were given to you from above. Therefore he who delivered me to you has greater sin."
			19:12 At this, Pilate was seeking to release him,
			but the Jews cried out, saying, "If you release this man, you aren't Caesar's friend! Everyone who makes himself a king speaks against Caesar!"
			19:13 When Pilate therefore heard these words, he brought Jesus out, and sat down on the judgment seat at a place called "The Pavement," but in Hebrew, Gabbatha."
			19:14 Now it was the Preparation Day of the Passover, at about the sixth hour. [12:00 pm]
			19:15 They cried out, "Away with him! Away with him! Crucify him!"
			Pilate said to them, "Shall I crucify your King?"

			The chief priests answered, "We have no king but Caesar!"
27:24 So when Pilate saw that nothing was being gained, but rather that a disturbance was starting, he took water, and washed his hands before the multitude, saying, "I am innocent of the blood of this righteous person. You see to it."			
27:25 All the people answered, "May his blood be on us, and on our children!"			
		Their voices and the voices of the chief priests prevailed.	
27:26 Then he released to them Barabbas, but Jesus he flogged and delivered to be crucified.	15:15 Pilate, wishing to please the multitude, released Barabbas to them, and handed over Jesus, when he had flogged him, to be crucified.	23:24 Pilate decreed that what they asked for should be done. 23:25 He released him who had been thrown into prison for insurrection and murder, for whom they asked, but he delivered Jesus up to their will.	19:16 So then he delivered him to them to be crucified. So they took Jesus and led him away.
27:27 Then the governor's soldiers took Jesus into the Praetorium, and gathered the whole garrison together against him.	15:16 The soldiers led him away within the court, which is the Praetorium; and they called together the whole cohort.		
27:28 They stripped him, and put a scarlet robe on him. 27:29 They braided a crown of thorns	15:17 They clothed him with purple, and weaving a crown of thorns, they put it on him.		

and put it on his head, and a reed in his right hand;			
and they kneeled down before him, and mocked him, saying, "Hail, King of the Jews!" 27:30 They spat on him, and took the reed and struck him on the head.	15:18 They began to salute him, "Hail, King of the Jews!" 15:19 They struck his head with a reed, and spat on him, and bowing their knees, did homage to him.		
27:31 When they had mocked him, they took the robe off of him, and put his clothes on him,	15:20 When they had mocked him, they took the purple off of him, and put his own garments on him.		
and led him away to crucify him.	They led him out to crucify him.		19:17 He went out, bearing his cross,
			to the place called "The Place of a Skull," which is called in Hebrew, "Golgotha," 19:18 where they crucified him, and with him two others, on either side one, and Jesus in the middle.

Event 128: Jesus is executed by crucifixion
Time: April 3, 33 A.D. (Friday)
Place: Jerusalem, Judea

MATTHEW 27:31-56	MARK 15:21-41	LUKE 23:26-49	JOHN 19:16-30
and led him away to crucify him.	They led him out to crucify him.		19:17 He went out, bearing his cross,
			to the place called "The Place of a Skull," which is called in Hebrew, "Golgotha," 19:18 where they crucified him, and with him two others, on either side one, and Jesus in the middle.

27:32 As they came out, they found a man of Cyrene, Simon by name, and they compelled him to go with them, that he might carry his cross.	15:21 They compelled one passing by, coming from the country, Simon of Cyrene, the father of Alexander and Rufus, to go with them, that he might bear his cross.	23:26 When they led him away, they grabbed one Simon of Cyrene, coming from the country, and laid on him the cross, to carry it after Jesus.	
		23:27 A great multitude of the people followed him, including women who also mourned and lamented him.	
		23:28 But Jesus, turning to them, said, "Daughters of Jerusalem, don't weep for me, but weep for yourselves and for your children. 23:29 For behold, the days are coming in which they will say, 'Blessed are the barren, the wombs that never bore, and the breasts that never nursed.' 23:30 Then they will begin to tell the mountains, 'Fall on us!' and tell the hills, 'Cover us.' [Hosea 10:8] 23:31 For if they do these things in the green tree, what will be done in the dry?"	
		23:32 There were also others, two criminals, led with him to be put to death.	
27:33 They came to a place called "Golgotha," that is to say, "The place of a skull."	15:22 They brought him to the place called Golgotha, which is, being interpreted, "The place of a skull."	23:33 When they came to the place that is called The Skull,	

		they crucified him there with the criminals, one on the right and the other on the left.	
		23:34 Jesus said, "Father, forgive them, for they don't know what they are doing."	
27:34 They gave him sour wine to drink mixed with gall. When he had tasted it, he would not drink.	15:23 They offered him wine mixed with myrrh to drink, but he didn't take it.		
27:35 When they had crucified him, they divided his clothing among them, casting lots, [TR adds "that it might be fulfilled which was spoke by the prophet: 'They divided my garments among them, and for my clothing they cast lots'] 27:36 and they sat and watched him there.	15:24 Crucifying him, they parted his garments among them, casting lots on them, what each should take.	Dividing his garments among them, they cast lots.	
	15:25 It was the third hour [9:00 am], and they crucified him.		
27:37 They set up over his head the accusation against him written, "THIS IS JESUS, THE KING OF THE JEWS."	15:26 The superscription of his accusation was written over him, "THE KING OF THE JEWS."		19:19 Pilate wrote a title also, and put it on the cross. There was written, "JESUS OF NAZARETH, THE KING OF THE JEWS."
			19:20 Therefore many of the Jews read this title, for the place where Jesus was crucified was near the city; and it was written in Hebrew, in Latin, and in Greek.

			19:21 The chief priests of the Jews therefore said to Pilate, "Don't write, 'The King of the Jews,' but, 'he said, I am King of the Jews.'"
			19:22 Pilate answered, "What I have written, I have written."
27:38 Then there were two robbers crucified with him, one on his right hand and one on the left.	15:27 With him they crucified two robbers; one on his right hand, and one on his left.		
	15:28 The Scripture was fulfilled, which says, "He was numbered with transgressors."		
27:39 Those who passed by blasphemed him, wagging their heads,	15:29 Those who passed by blasphemed him, wagging their heads, and saying,	23:35 The people stood watching.	
27:40 and saying, "You who destroy the temple, and build it in three days, save yourself! If you are the Son of God, come down from the cross!"	"Ha! You who destroy the temple, and build it in three days, 15:30 save yourself, and come down from the cross!"		
27:41 Likewise the chief priests also mocking, with the scribes, the Pharisees [TR lacks "the Pharisees], and the elders, said,	15:31 Likewise, also the chief priests mocking among themselves with the scribes said,	The rulers with them also scoffed at him, saying,	
27:42 "He saved others, but he can't save himself.	"He saved others. He can't save himself.	"He saved others. Let him save himself,	

If he is the King of Israel, let him come down from the cross now, and we will believe in him.	15:32 Let the Christ, the King of Israel, now come down from the cross, that we may see and believe him." [TR lacks "him"]	if this is the Christ of God, his chosen one!"	
27:43 He trusts in God. Let God deliver him now, if he wants him;			
for he said, 'I am the Son of God.'"			
		23:36 The soldiers also mocked him, coming to him and offering him vinegar,	
		23:37 and saying, "If you are the King of the Jews, save yourself!"	
		23:38 An inscription was also written over him in letters of Greek, Latin, and Hebrew: "THIS IS THE KING OF THE JEWS."	
27:44 The robbers also who were crucified with him cast on him the same reproach.	Those who were crucified with him insulted him.		
		23:39 One of the criminals who was hanged insulted him, saying, "If you are the Christ, save yourself and us!"	
		23:40 But the other answered, and rebuking him said, "Don't you even fear God, seeing you are under the same condemnation? 23:41 And we indeed justly, for we receive the due reward for our deeds, but this man has done nothing wrong."	

		23:42 He said to Jesus, "Lord, remember me when you come into your Kingdom."	
			19:23 Then the soldiers, when they had crucified Jesus, took his garments and made four parts, to every soldier a part; and also the coat.
			Now the coat was without seam, woven from the top throughout.
			19:24 Then they said to one another, "Let's not tear it, but cast lots for it to decide whose it will be,"
			that the Scripture might be fulfilled, which says, "They parted my garments among them. For my cloak they cast lots." [Psalm 22:18]
			Therefore the soldiers did these things.
			19:25 But there were standing by the cross of Jesus his mother, and his mother's sister, Mary the wife of Clopas, and Mary Magdalene.
			19:26 Therefore when Jesus saw his mother, and the disciple whom he loved standing there, he said to his mother, "Woman, behold your son!"

			19:27 Then he said to the disciple, "Behold, your mother!"
			From that hour, the disciple took her to his own home.
27:45 Now from the sixth hour [12:00 pm] there was darkness over all the land until the ninth hour. [3:00 pm}	15:33 When the sixth hour [12:00 pm] had come, there was darkness over the whole land until the ninth hour. [3:00 pm]	23:44 It was now about the sixth hour [12:00 pm], and darkness came over the whole land until the ninth hour [3:00 pm].	
27:46 About the ninth hour [3:00 pm] Jesus cried with a loud voice, saying, "Eli, Eli, lima [TR has instead "lama"] sabachthani?" That is, "My God, my God, why have you forsaken me?" [Psalm 22:1]	15:34 At the ninth hour Jesus cried with a loud voice, saying, "Eloi, Eloi, lama sabachthani?" which is, being interpreted, "My God, my God, why have you forsaken me?" [Psalm 22:1]		
27:47 Some of them who stood there, when they heard it, said, "This man is calling Elijah."	15:35 Some of those who stood by, when they heard it, said, "Behold, he is calling Elijah."		
			19:28 After this, Jesus, seeing [TR and NU have "knowing" instead of "seeing"] that all things were now finished,
			that the Scripture might be fulfilled,
			said, "I am thirsty."
27:48 Immediately one of them ran, and took a sponge, and filled it with vinegar, and put it on a reed, and gave him a drink.	15:36 One ran, and filling a sponge full of vinegar, put it on a reed, and gave it to him to drink,		19:29 Now a vessel full of vinegar was set there; so they put a sponge full of the vinegar on hyssop, and held it at his mouth.

27:49 The rest said, "Let him be. Let's see whether Elijah comes to save him."	saying, "Let him be. Let's see whether Elijah comes to take him down."		
			19:30 When Jesus therefore had received the vinegar,
			he said, "It is finished."
		23:45 The sun was darkened, and the veil of the temple was torn in two.	
27:50 Jesus cried again with a loud voice, and yielded up his spirit.	15:37 Jesus cried out with a loud voice, and gave up the spirit.	23:46 Jesus, crying with a loud voice, said, "Father, into your hands I commit my spirit!" Having said this, he breathed his last.	He bowed his head, and gave up his spirit.
27:51 Behold, the veil of the temple was torn in two from the top to the bottom.	15:38 The veil of the temple was torn in two from the top to the bottom.		
The earth quaked and the rocks were split.			
27:52 The tombs were opened, and many bodies of the saints who had fallen asleep were raised; 27:53 and coming out of the tombs after his resurrection, they entered into the holy city and appeared to many.			
27:54 Now the centurion, and those who were with him watching Jesus, when they saw the earthquake, and the things that were done, feared exceedingly	15:39 When the centurion, who stood by opposite him, saw that he cried out like this and breathed his last,	23:47 When the centurion saw what was done,	
saying, "Truly this was the Son of God."	he said, "Truly this man was the Son of God!"	he glorified God, saying, "Certainly this was a righteous man."	

		23:48 All the multitudes that came together to see this, when they saw the things that were done, returned home beating their breasts.	
		23:49 All his acquaintances,	
27:55 Many women were there watching from afar, who had followed Jesus from Galilee, serving him.	15:40 There were also women watching from afar,	and the women who followed with him from Galilee, stood at a distance, watching these things.	
27:56 Among them were Mary Magdalene, Mary the mother of James and Joses, and the mother of the sons of Zebedee.	among whom were both Mary Magdalene, and Mary the mother of James the less and of Joses, and Salome; 15:41 who, when he was in Galilee, followed him, and served him;		
	and many other women who came up with him to Jerusalem.		

Event 129: Jesus is buried
Time: April 3, 33 A.D. (Friday)
Place: Jerusalem, Judea

MATTHEW 27:57-66	MARK 15:42-47	LUKE 23:50-56	JOHN 19:31-42
27:57 When evening had come,	15:42 When evening had now come, because it was the Preparation Day, that is, the day before the Sabbath,		19:31 Therefore the Jews, because it was the Preparation Day, so that the bodies wouldn't remain on the cross on the Sabbath (for that Sabbath was a special one), asked of Pilate that their legs might be broken, and that they might be taken away.

			19:32 Therefore the soldiers came, and broke the legs of the first, and of the other who was crucified with him;
			19:33 but when they came to Jesus, and saw that he was already dead, they didn't break his legs.
			19:34 However one of the soldiers pierced his side with a spear, and immediately blood and water came out.
			19:35 He who has seen has testified, and his testimony is true. He knows that he tells the truth, that you may believe.
			19:36 For these things happened, that the Scripture might be fulfilled, "A bone of him will not be broken." [Exodus 12:46; Numbers 9:12; Psalm 32:20] 19:37 Again another Scripture says, "They will look on him whom they pierced." [Zechariah 12:10]
a rich man from Arimathaea, named Joseph, who himself was also Jesus' disciple came.	15:43 Joseph of Arimathaea, a prominent council member who also himself was looking for the Kingdom of God, came.	23:50 Behold, a man named Joseph, who was a member of the council, a good and righteous man 23:51 (he had not consented to their counsel and deed), from Arimathaea, a city of the Jews, who was also waiting for the Kingdom of God:	19:38 After these things, Joseph of Arimathaea, being a disciple of Jesus, but secretly for fear of the Jews,

27:58 This man went to Pilate, and asked for Jesus' body.	He boldly went in to Pilate, and asked for Jesus' body.	23:52 this man went to Pilate, and asked for Jesus' body.	asked of Pilate that he might take away Jesus' body.
	15:44 Pilate marveled if he were already dead;		
	and summoning the centurion, he asked him whether he had been dead long.	and summoning the centurion, he asked him whether he had been dead long.	
Then Pilate commanded the body to be given up.	15:45 When he found out from the centurion, he granted the body to Joseph.		Pilate gave him permission.
			He came therefore and took away his body.
			19:39 Nicodemus, who at first came to Jesus by night, also came bringing a mixture of myrrh and aloes, about a hundred pounds. [100 Roman pounds of 12 ounces each, or about 33 kilograms or 72 pounds]
27:59 Joseph took the body, and wrapped it in a clean linen cloth,	15:46 He bought a linen cloth, and taking him down, wound him in the linen cloth,	23:53 He took it down, and wrapped it in a linen cloth,	19:40 So they took Jesus' body, and bound it in linen cloths with the spices, as the custom of the Jews is to bury.
			19:41 Now in the place where he was crucified there was a garden.
27:60 and laid it in his own new tomb, which he had cut out in the rock,	and laid him in a tomb which had been cut out of a rock.	and laid him in a tomb that was cut in stone, where no one had ever been laid.	In the garden was a new tomb in which no man had ever yet been laid. 19:42 Then because of the Jews' Preparation Day (for the tomb was near at hand) they laid Jesus there

and he rolled a great stone to the door of the tomb, and departed.	He rolled a stone against the door of the tomb.	.	
		23:54 It was the day of the Preparation, and the Sabbath was drawing near	
27:61 Mary Magdalene was there, and the other Mary, sitting opposite the tomb.	15:47 Mary Magdalene and Mary, the mother of Joses, saw where he was laid.	23:55 The women, who had come with him out of Galilee, followed after, and saw the tomb, and how his body was laid.	
		23:56 They returned, and prepared spices and ointments.	
		On the Sabbath they rested according to the commandment.	
27:62 Now on the next day, which was the day after the Preparation Day, the chief priests and the Pharisees were gathered together to Pilate,			
27:63 saying, "Sir, we remember what that deceiver said while he was still alive: 'After three days I will rise again.'			
27:64 Command therefore that the tomb be made secure until the third day, lest perhaps his disciples come at night and steal him away, and tell the people, 'He is risen from the dead;' and the last deception will be worse than the first."			

27:65 Pilate said to them, "You have a guard. Go, make it as secure as you can."			
27:66 So they went with the guard and made the tomb secure, sealing the stone.			

Event 130: Various women, Peter and John at the empty tomb and Jesus appears
Time: April 5, 33 A.D. (Sunday)
Place: Jerusalem, Judea

MATTHEW 28:1-15	MARK 16:1-11	LUKE 24:1-12	JOHN 20:1-2
		23:55 The women, who had come with him out of Galilee, followed after, and saw the tomb, and how his body was laid.	
		23:56 They returned, and prepared spices and ointments.	
		On the Sabbath they rested according to the commandment.	
28:1 Now after the Sabbath, as it began to dawn on the first day of the week,	16:1 When the Sabbath was past,	24:1 But on the first day of the week, at early dawn,	20:1 Now on the first day of the week,
Mary Magdalene and the other Mary came to see the tomb.	Mary Magdalene, and Mary the mother of James, and Salome, bought spices, that they might come and anoint him. 16:2 Very early on the first day of the week, they came to the tomb when the sun had risen.	they and some others came to the tomb, bringing the spices which they had prepared.	Mary Magdalene went early, while it was still dark, to the tomb,

28:2 Behold, there was a great earthquake, for an angel of the Lord descended from the sky, and came and rolled away the stone from the door, and sat on it.			
28:3 His appearance was like lightning, and his clothing white as snow.			
28:4 For fear of him, the guards shook, and became like dead men.			
	16:3 They were saying among themselves, "Who will roll away the stone from the door of the tomb for us?" 16:4 for it was very big.		
	Looking up, they saw that the stone was rolled back.	24:2 They found the stone rolled away from the tomb.	and saw the stone taken away from the tomb.
	16:5 Entering into the tomb,	24:3 They entered in,	
		and didn't find the Lord Jesus' body. 24:4 It happened, while they were greatly perplexed about this,	
	they saw a young man sitting on the right side, dressed in a white robe, and they were amazed.	behold, two men stood by them in dazzling clothing.	
		24:5 Becoming terrified, they bowed their faces down to the earth.	

28:5 The angel answered the women, "Don't be afraid, for I know that you seek Jesus, who has been crucified. 28:6 He is not here, for he has risen, just like he said. Come, see the place where the Lord was lying.	16:6 He said to them, "Don't be amazed. You seek Jesus, the Nazarene, who has been crucified. He has risen. He is not here. Behold, the place where they laid him!	They said to them, "Why do you seek the living among the dead? 24:6 He isn't here, but is risen.	
		Remember what he told you when he was still in Galilee, 24:7 saying that the Son of Man must be delivered up into the hands of sinful men, and be crucified, and the third day rise again?"	
		24:8 They remembered his words,	
28:7 Go quickly and tell his disciples, 'He has risen from the dead, and behold, he goes before you into Galilee; there you will see him.' Behold, I have told you."	16:7 But go, tell his disciples and Peter, 'He goes before you into Galilee. There you will see him, as he said to you.'"		
28:8 They departed quickly from the tomb with fear and great joy, and ran to bring his disciples word.	16:8 They went out, and fled [TR adds "quickly"] from the tomb, for trembling and astonishment had come on them.	24:9 returned from the tomb,	
	They said nothing to anyone; for they were afraid.		
28:9 As they went to tell his disciples, behold, Jesus met them, saying, "Rejoice!"			

They came and took hold of his feet, and worshiped him.			
28:10 Then Jesus said to them, "Don't be afraid. Go tell my brothers that they should go into Galilee, and there they will see me."			
28:11 Now while they were going, behold, some of the guards came into the city, and told the chief priests all the things that had happened.			
28:12 When they were assembled with the elders, and had taken counsel, they gave a large amount of silver to the soldiers, 28:13 saying, "Say that his disciples came by night, and stole him away while we slept. 28:14 If this comes to the governor's ears, we will persuade him and make you free of worry."			
28:15 So they took the money and did as they were told. This saying was spread abroad among the Jews, and continues until this day.			
	16: 9 Now when he had risen early on the first day of the week, he appeared first to	24:10 Now they were Mary Magdalene, Joanna, and Mary the mother of James.	20:2 Therefore she ran and came to Simon Peter, and to the other disciple whom

	Mary Magdalene, from whom he had cast out seven demons.	The other women with them told these things to the apostles.	Jesus loved, and said to them, "They have taken away the Lord out of the tomb, and we don't know where they have laid him!"
	16:10 She went and told those who had been with him, as they mourned and wept.	and told all these things to the eleven, and to all the rest.	
	16:11 When they heard that he was alive, and had been seen by her, they disbelieved.	24:11 These words seemed to them to be nonsense, and they didn't believe them.	
		24:12 But Peter got up and ran to the tomb.	20:3 Therefore Peter and the other disciple went out, and they went toward the tomb.
			20:4 They both ran together. The other disciple outran Peter, and came to the tomb first.
		Stooping and looking in, he saw the strips of linen lying by themselves, and	20:5 Stooping and looking in, he saw the linen cloths lying, yet he didn't enter in.
			20:6 Then Simon Peter came, following him, and entered into the tomb.
			He saw the linen cloths lying, 20:7 and the cloth that had been on his head, not lying with the linen cloths, but rolled up in a place by itself.
			20:8 So then the other disciple who came first to the tomb also entered in, and he saw and believed.

			20:9 For as yet they didn't know the Scripture, that he must rise from the dead.
		he departed to his home, wondering what had happened.	20:10 So the disciples went away again to their own homes.
			20:11 But Mary was standing outside at the tomb weeping. So, as she wept, she stooped and looked into the tomb,
			20:12 and she saw two angels in white sitting, one at the head, and one at the feet, where the body of Jesus had lain.
			20:13 They told her, "Woman, why are you weeping?"
			She said to them, "Because they have taken away my Lord, and I don't know where they have laid him."
			20:14 When she had said this, she turned around and saw Jesus standing, and didn't know that it was Jesus.
			20:15 Jesus said to her, "Woman, why are you weeping? Who are you looking for?"
			She, supposing him to be the gardener, said to him, "Sir, if you have carried him away, tell me where you have laid him, and I will take him away."

			20:16 Jesus said to her, "Mary."
			She turned and said to him, "Rhabbouni!" which is to say, "Teacher!"
			20:17 Jesus said to her, "Don't touch me, for I haven't yet ascended to my Father; but go to my brothers, and tell them, 'I am ascending to my Father and your Father, to my God and your God.'"
			20:18 Mary Magdalene came and told the disciples that she had seen the Lord, and that he had said these things to her.

Event 131: Jesus appears to 2 disciples on the road to Emmaus
Time: April 5, 33 A.D. (Sunday)
Place: road to Emmaus, Judea

MARK 16:12-13	LUKE 24:13-35
16:12 After these things he was revealed in another form to two of them, as they walked, on their way into the country.	24:13 Behold, two of them were going that very day to a village named Emmaus, which was sixty stadia [about 11 kilometers, 7 miles] from Jerusalem.
	24:14 They talked with each other about all of these things which had happened.
	24:15 It happened, while they talked and questioned together, that Jesus himself came near, and went with them.
	24:16 But their eyes were kept from recognizing him.
	24:17 He said to them, "What are you talking about as you walk, and are sad?"
	24:18 One of them, named Cleopas, answered him, "Are you the only stranger in Jerusalem who doesn't know the things which have happened there in these days?"

	24:19 He said to them, "What things?"
	They said to him, "The things concerning Jesus, the Nazarene, who was a prophet mighty in deed and word before God and all the people; 24:20 and how the chief priests and our rulers delivered him up to be condemned to death, and crucified him.
	24:21 But we were hoping that it was he who would redeem Israel. Yes, and besides all this, it is now the third day since these things happened.
	24:22 Also, certain women of our company amazed us, having arrived early at the tomb; 24:23 and when they didn't find his body, they came saying that they had also seen a vision of angels, who said that he was alive.
	24:24 Some of us went to the tomb, and found it just like the women had said, but they didn't see him."
	24:25 He said to them, "Foolish men, and slow of heart to believe in all that the prophets have spoken! 24:26 Didn't the Christ have to suffer these things and to enter into his glory?"24:27 Beginning from Moses and from all the prophets, he explained to them in all the Scriptures the things concerning himself.
	24:28 They drew near to the village, where they were going, and he acted like he would go further.
	24:29 They urged him, saying, "Stay with us, for it is almost evening, and the day is almost over."
	He went in to stay with them.
	24:30 It happened, that when he had sat down at the table with them, he took the bread and gave thanks. Breaking it, he gave to them.
	24:31 Their eyes were opened, and they recognized him, and he vanished out of their sight.
	24:32 They said one to another, "Weren't our hearts burning within us, while he spoke to us along the way, and while he opened the Scriptures to us?"

16:13 They went away	24:33 They rose up that very hour, returned to Jerusalem,
and told it to the rest.	and found the eleven gathered together, and those who were with them, 24:34 saying, "The Lord is risen indeed, and has appeared to Simon!" 24:35 They related the things that happened along the way, and how he was recognized by them in the breaking of the bread.
They didn't believe them, either.	

Event 132: Jesus appears to the disciples in Jerusalem absent Thomas
Time: April 5, 33 AD (Sunday)
Place: Jerusalem, Judea

MARK 16:14-18	LUKE 24:36-39	JOHN 20:19-23
16:14 Afterward he was revealed to the eleven themselves as they sat at the table,		20:19 When therefore it was evening, on that day, the first day of the week, and when the doors were locked where the disciples were assembled, for fear of the Jews,
	24:36 As they said these things, Jesus himself stood among them, and said to them, "Peace be to you."	Jesus came and stood in the midst, and said to them, "Peace be to you."
	24:37 But they were terrified and filled with fear, and supposed that they had seen a spirit.	
and he rebuked them for their unbelief and hardness of heart, because they didn't believe those who had seen him after he had risen.	24:38 He said to them, "Why are you troubled? Why do doubts arise in your hearts?	
	24:39 See my hands and my feet, that it is truly me. Touch me and see, for a spirit doesn't have flesh and bones, as you see that I have."	
	24:40 When he had said this, he showed them his hands and his feet.	20:20 When he had said this, he showed them his hands and his side.

	24:41 While they still didn't believe for joy, and wondered, he said to them, "Do you have anything here to eat?"	
	24:42 They gave him a piece of a broiled fish and some honeycomb.	
	24:43 He took them, and ate in front of them.	
	24:44 He said to them, "This is what I told you, while I was still with you, that all things which are written in the law of Moses, the prophets, and the psalms, concerning me must be fulfilled."	
	The disciples therefore were glad when they saw the Lord.	
	24:45 Then he opened their minds, that they might understand the Scriptures. 24:46 He said to them, "Thus it is written, and thus it was necessary for the Christ to suffer and to rise from the dead the third day, 24:47 and that repentance and remission of sins should be preached in his name to all the nations, beginning at Jerusalem.	
	24:48 You are witnesses of these things. 24:49 Behold, I send forth the promise of my Father on you.	
16:15 He said to them, "Go into all the world, and preach the Good News to the whole creation.		20:21 Jesus therefore said to them again, "Peace be to you. As the Father has sent me, even so I send you."
	But wait in the city of Jerusalem until you are clothed with power from on high."	20:22 When he had said this, he breathed on them, and said to them, "Receive the Holy Spirit!

16:16 He who believes and is baptized will be saved; but he who disbelieves will be condemned.		20:23 Whoever's sins you forgive, they are forgiven them. Whoever's sins you retain, they have been retained."
16:17 These signs will accompany those who believe: in my name they will cast out demons; they will speak with new languages; 16:18 they will take up serpents; and if they drink any deadly thing, it will in no way hurt them; they will lay hands on the sick, and they will recover."		

Event 133: Jesus appears to the disciples with Thomas
Time: April 13, 33 A.D. (Monday)
Place: Jerusalem, Judea

JOHN 20:24-29
20:24 But Thomas, one of the twelve, called Didymus, wasn't with them when Jesus came.
20:25 The other disciples therefore said to him, "We have seen the Lord!"
But he said to them, "Unless I see in his hands the print of the nails, and put my hand into his side, I will not believe."
20:26 After eight days again his disciples were inside, and Thomas was with them.
Jesus came, the doors being locked, and stood in the midst, and said, "Peace be to you."
20:27 Then he said to Thomas, "Reach here your finger, and see my hands. Reach here your hand, and put it into my side. Don't be unbelieving, but believing."
20:28 Thomas answered him, "My Lord and my God!"
20:29 Jesus said to him, "Because you have seen me, [TR adds "Thomas"] you have believed. Blessed are those who have not seen, and have believed."
20:30 Therefore Jesus did many other signs in the presence of his disciples, which are not written in this book; 20:31 but these are written, that you may believe that Jesus is the Christ, the Son of God, and that believing you may have life in his name.

Event 134: Jesus appears to the disciples in Galilee
Place: Galilee
Time: sometime between April 13 and May 11, 33 A.D.

JOHN 21:1-25
21:1 After these things, Jesus revealed himself again to the disciples at the sea of Tiberias. He revealed himself this way.
21:2 Simon Peter, Thomas called Didymus, Nathanael of Cana in Galilee, and the sons of Zebedee, and two others of his disciples were together.

21:3 Simon Peter said to them, "I'm going fishing."
They told him, "We are also coming with you."
They immediately went out, and entered into the boat. That night, they caught nothing.
21:4 But when day had already come, Jesus stood on the beach, yet the disciples didn't know that it was Jesus.
21:5 Jesus therefore said to them, "Children, have you anything to eat?"
They answered him, "No."
21:6 He said to them, "Cast the net on the right side of the boat, and you will find some."
They cast it therefore, and now they weren't able to draw it in for the multitude of fish.
21:7 That disciple therefore whom Jesus loved said to Peter, "It's the Lord!"
So when Simon Peter heard that it was the Lord, he wrapped his coat around him (for he was naked), and threw himself into the sea.
21:8 But the other disciples came in the little boat (for they were not far from the land, but about two hundred cubits [200 cubits is about 91 meters or 100 yards] away), dragging the net full of fish.
21:9 So when they got out on the land, they saw a fire of coals there, and fish laid on it, and bread.
21:10 Jesus said to them, "Bring some of the fish which you have just caught."
21:11 Simon Peter went up, and drew the net to land, full of great fish, one hundred fifty-three; and even though there were so many, the net wasn't torn.
21:12 Jesus said to them, "Come and eat breakfast."
None of the disciples dared inquire of him, "Who are you?" knowing that it was the Lord.
21:13 Then Jesus came and took the bread, gave it to them, and the fish likewise.
21:14 This is now the third time that Jesus was revealed to his disciples, after he had risen from the dead.
21:15 So when they had eaten their breakfast, Jesus said to Simon Peter, "Simon, son of Jonah, do you love me more than these?"
He said to him, "Yes, Lord; you know that I have affection for you."
He said to him, "Feed my lambs."
21:16 He said to him again a second time, "Simon, son of Jonah, do you love me?"
He said to him, "Yes, Lord; you know that I have affection for you."
He said to him, "Tend my sheep."
21:17 He said to him the third time, "Simon, son of Jonah, do you have affection for me?"
Peter was grieved because he asked him the third time, "Do you have affection for me?" He said to him, "Lord, you know everything. You know that I have affection for you."
Jesus said to him, "Feed my sheep.
21:18 Most certainly I tell you, when you were young, you dressed yourself, and walked where you wanted to. But when you are old, you will stretch out your hands, and another will dress you, and carry you where you don't want to go."
21:19 Now he said this, signifying by what kind of death he would glorify God.
When he had said this, he said to him, "Follow me."

21:20 Then Peter, turning around, saw a disciple following. This was the disciple whom Jesus sincerely loved, the one who had also leaned on Jesus' breast at the supper and asked, "Lord, who is going to betray You?"
21:21 Peter seeing him, said to Jesus, "Lord, what about this man?"
21:22 Jesus said to him, "If I desire that he stay until I come, what is that to you? You follow me."
21:23 This saying therefore went out among the brothers, that this disciple wouldn't die. Yet Jesus didn't say to him that he wouldn't die, but, "If I desire that he stay until I come, what is that to you?"
21:24 This is the disciple who testifies about these things, and wrote these things. We know that his witness is true.
21:25 There are also many other things which Jesus did, which if they would all be written, I suppose that even the world itself wouldn't have room for the books that would be written.

Event 135: Jesus delivers the great commission
Time: May 11, 33 A.D.
Place: Jerusalem, Judea

MATTHEW 28:16-20
28:16 But the eleven disciples went into Galilee, to the mountain where Jesus had sent them.
28:17 When they saw him, they bowed down to him, but some doubted.
28:18 Jesus came to them and spoke to them, saying, "All authority has been given to me in heaven and on earth. 28:19 Therefore go, and make disciples of all nations, baptizing them in the name of the Father and of the Son and of the Holy Spirit, 28:20 teaching them to observe all things that I commanded you. Behold, I am with you always, even to the end of the age."
Amen.

Event 136: Jesus appears and ascends to heaven
Time: May 15, 33 A.D.
Place: Jerusalem area, Judea

MARK 16:19-20	LUKE 24:50-53	ACTS 1:9-12
		1:1 The first book I wrote, Theophilus, concerned all that Jesus began both to do and to teach, 1:2 until the day in which he was received up, after he had given commandment through the Holy Spirit to the apostles whom he had chosen.

		1:4 Being assembled together with them, he commanded them, "Don't depart from Jerusalem, but wait for the promise of the Father, which you heard from me. 1:5 For John indeed baptized in water, but you will be baptized in the Holy Spirit not many days from now."
		1:6 Therefore, when they had come together, they asked him, "Lord, are you now restoring the kingdom to Israel?"
		1:7 He said to them, "It isn't for you to know times or seasons which the Father has set within his own authority. 1:8 But you will receive power when the Holy Spirit has come upon you. You will be witnesses to me in Jerusalem, in all Judea and Samaria, and to the uttermost parts of the earth."
	24:50 He led them out as far as Bethany, and he lifted up his hands, and blessed them.	
16:19 So then the Lord Jesus, after he had spoken to them, was received up into heaven, and sat down at the right hand of God.	24:51 It happened, while he blessed them, that he withdrew from them, and was carried up into heaven.	1:9 When he had said these things, as they were looking, he was taken up, and a cloud received him out of their sight.
		1:10 While they were looking steadfastly into the sky as he went, behold, two men stood by them in white clothing, 1:11 who also said, "You men of Galilee, why do you stand looking into the sky? This Jesus, who was received up from you into the sky will come back in the same way as you saw him going into the sky."

16:20 They went out, and preached everywhere, the Lord working with them, and confirming the word by the signs that followed. Amen.	24:52 They worshiped him, and returned to Jerusalem with great joy, 24:53 and were continually in the temple, praising and blessing God. Amen.	1:12 Then they returned to Jerusalem from the mountain called Olivet, which is near Jerusalem, a Sabbath day's journey away. 1:13 When they had come in, they went up into the upper room, where they were staying; that is Peter, John, James, Andrew, Philip, Thomas, Bartholomew, Matthew, James the son of Alphaeus, Simon the Zealot, and Judas the son of James. 1:14 All these with one accord continued steadfastly in prayer and supplication, along with the women, and Mary the mother of Jesus, and with his brothers.

A BIBLIOGRAPHY

Abrahams, I. *Studies in Pharisaism and the Gospels* (University Press, Cambridge, 1924)

Albright, W.F. and Mann, C.S., *The Anchor Bible: Matthew* (Doubleday, New York, 1971)

Aland, K. and Aland, B., *The Text of the New Testament* Trans. E.F. Rhodes (William B. Eerdmans Publishing Company, Grand Rapids, 1989)

Anderson, H., *The New Century Bible Commentary: The Gospel of Mark* (William B. Eerdmans, Grand Rapids, 1976)

Anderson, N., *Jesus Christ: The Witness of History* (Inter-Varsity Press, Downers Grove, 1985)

--------, *A Lawyer Among the Theologians* (William B. Eerdmans Publishing Company, Grand Rapids, 1973)

Archaeology and the Bible: Volume 2 Archaeology in the World of Herod, Jesus and Paul Edit. H.Shanks and D.P.Cole (Biblical Archaeology Society, Washington, 1990)

Argyle, A.W., *The Cambridge Bible Commentary on the New English Bible: The Gospel according to Matthew* (Cambridge University Press, London, 1963)

A Theological Word Book of the Bible Edit. A. Richardson (Macmillan Publishing, New York, 1950)

Authenticating the Activities of Jesus, Edit. B. Chilton and C.A. Evans (Brill Academic Publishers, Boston, 2002)

Authenticating the Words of Jesus, Edit. B. Chilton and C.A. Evans (Brill Academic Publishers, Boston, 2002)

Baez-Camargo, G., *Archaeological Commentary on the Bible* (Doubleday, Garden City, 1986)

Bailey, J.L, and Vander Broek, L.D., *Literary Forms in the New Testament* (John Knox Press, Louisville, 1992)

Baker Enclyclopedia of Bible Places: Towns & Cities, Countries & States, Archaology & Topography Edit. J.J.Bimson (Inter-Varsity Press, Downers Grove, 1995)

Barbet, P., *A Doctor at Calvary: The Passion of Our Lord Jesus Christ as Described by a Surgeon* Trans. The Earl of Wicklow (P.J.Kenedy & Son, New York, 1950)

Barclay, W., *Introduction to the First Three Gospels* (The Westminister Press, Philadelphia, 1975)

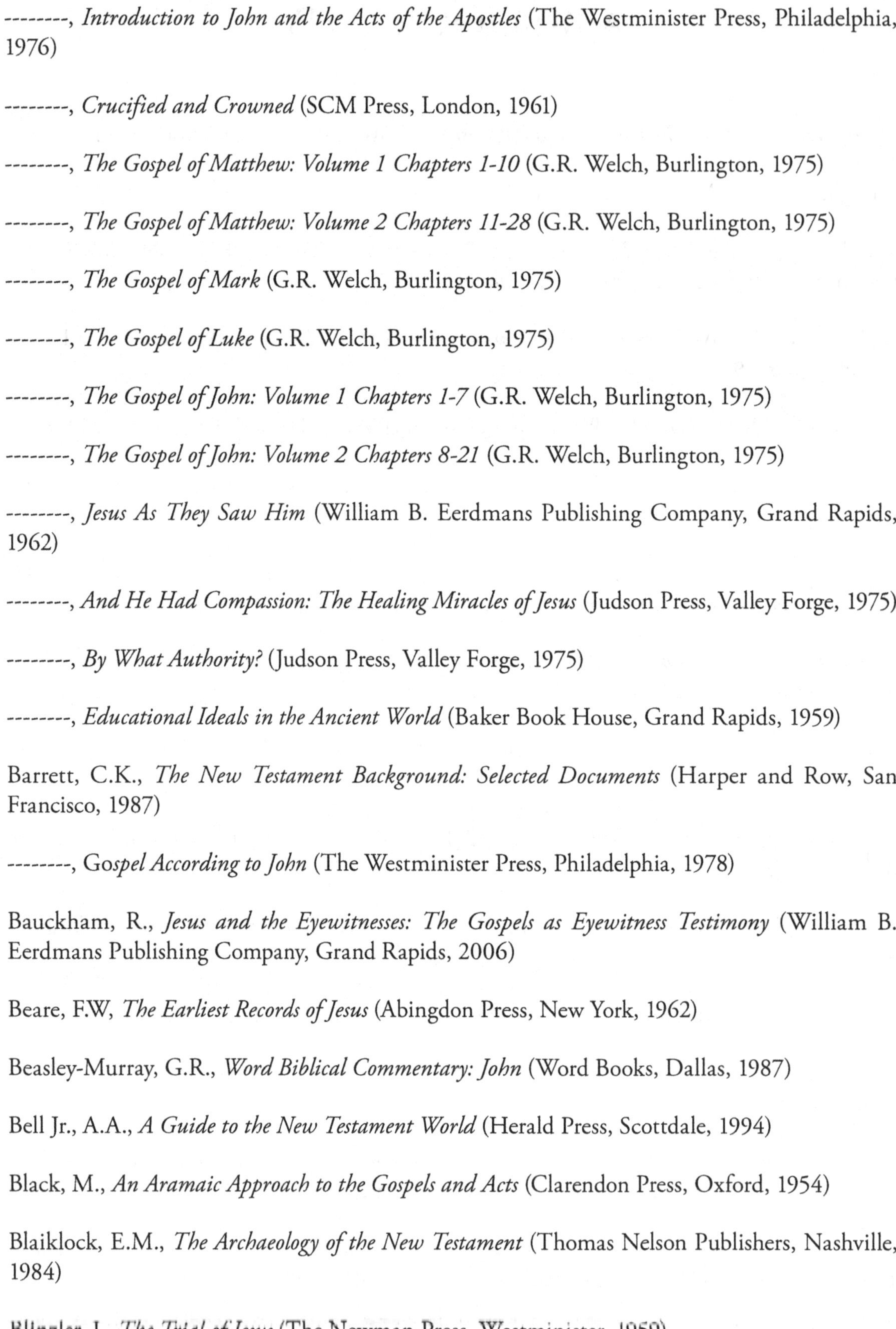

--------, *Introduction to John and the Acts of the Apostles* (The Westminister Press, Philadelphia, 1976)

--------, *Crucified and Crowned* (SCM Press, London, 1961)

--------, *The Gospel of Matthew: Volume 1 Chapters 1-10* (G.R. Welch, Burlington, 1975)

--------, *The Gospel of Matthew: Volume 2 Chapters 11-28* (G.R. Welch, Burlington, 1975)

--------, *The Gospel of Mark* (G.R. Welch, Burlington, 1975)

--------, *The Gospel of Luke* (G.R. Welch, Burlington, 1975)

--------, *The Gospel of John: Volume 1 Chapters 1-7* (G.R. Welch, Burlington, 1975)

--------, *The Gospel of John: Volume 2 Chapters 8-21* (G.R. Welch, Burlington, 1975)

--------, *Jesus As They Saw Him* (William B. Eerdmans Publishing Company, Grand Rapids, 1962)

--------, *And He Had Compassion: The Healing Miracles of Jesus* (Judson Press, Valley Forge, 1975)

--------, *By What Authority?* (Judson Press, Valley Forge, 1975)

--------, *Educational Ideals in the Ancient World* (Baker Book House, Grand Rapids, 1959)

Barrett, C.K., *The New Testament Background: Selected Documents* (Harper and Row, San Francisco, 1987)

--------, Go*spel According to John* (The Westminister Press, Philadelphia, 1978)

Bauckham, R., *Jesus and the Eyewitnesses: The Gospels as Eyewitness Testimony* (William B. Eerdmans Publishing Company, Grand Rapids, 2006)

Beare, F.W, *The Earliest Records of Jesus* (Abingdon Press, New York, 1962)

Beasley-Murray, G.R., *Word Biblical Commentary: John* (Word Books, Dallas, 1987)

Bell Jr., A.A., *A Guide to the New Testament World* (Herald Press, Scottdale, 1994)

Black, M., *An Aramaic Approach to the Gospels and Acts* (Clarendon Press, Oxford, 1954)

Blaiklock, E.M., *The Archaeology of the New Testament* (Thomas Nelson Publishers, Nashville, 1984)

Blinzler, J., *The Trial of Jesus* (The Newman Press, Westminister, 1959)

Blomberg, C.L., *The New American Commentary: Matthew* (Broadman and Holman Publishers, 1992)

--------, *The Historical Reliability of the Gospels* (Inter-Varsity Press, Downers Grove, 1987)

--------, *The Historical Reliability of John's Gospel: Issues and Commentary* (Inter-Varsity Press, Downers Grove, 2001)

Bock, D.L, *Blasphemy and Exaltation in Judaism: The Charge Against Jesus in Mark 14:53-65* (Baker Books, Grand Rapids, 2000)

--------, *Studying the Historical Jesus: A Guide to Sources and Methods* (Baker Academic, Grand Rapids, 2002)

--------, Jesus According to Scripture: Restoring the Portrait from the Gospels (Baker Academic, Grand Rapids, 2002)

Bonsirven, J., *Palestinian Judaism in the Time of Jesus Christ* Trans. W. Wolf (Holt, Rinehart and Winston, New York, 1964)

Borchert, G.L., *The New American Commentary: John 1-11* (Broadman and Holman Publishers, 1996)

--------, *The New American Commentary: John 12-21* (Broadman and Holman Publishers, 2002)

Bowker, J., *Jesus and the Pharisees* (Cambridge University Press, Cambridge, 1972)

Brandon, S.G.F., *Jesus and the Zealots* (Manchester University Press, Cambridge, 1967)

--------, *The Trial of Jesus of Nazareth* (Dorset Press, New York, 1968)

Brooks, J.A., *The New American Commentary: Mark* (Broadman and Holman Publishers, 1991)

Brown, R.E., *The Death of the Messiah: Volume 1* (Doubleday, New York, 1994)

--------, *The Death of the Messiah: Volume 2* (Doubleday, New York, 1994)

--------, *The Anchor Bible: John 1-X11* (Doubleday, New York, 1966)

--------, *The Anchor Bible: John X11-XX1* (Doubleday, New York, 1970)

--------, *An Introduction to New Testament Christology* (Paulist Press, New York, 1994)

--------, *The Churches the Apostles Left Behind* (Paulist Press, New York, 1984)

--------, *The Critical Meaning of the Bible: How a Modern Reading of the Bible Challenges Christians, the Church and the Churches* (Paulist Press, New York, 1981)

--------, *Biblical Exegesis and Church Doctrine* (Paulist Press, New York, 1985)

--------, *Responses to 101 Questions on the Bible* (Paulist Press, New York, 1990)

--------, *Recent Discoveries in the Biblical World* (Michael Glazier Inc., Wilmington, 1983)

Brown, R.E. and Meier, J.P., *Antioch and Rome: New Testament Cradles of Catholic Christianity* (Paulist Press, New York, 1983)

Bruce, F.F., *New Testament History* (Doubleday, New York, 1969)

--------, *Jesus & Christian Origins Outside the New Testament* (William B. Eerdmans Publishing Company, 1974)

--------, *The Gospel of John* (William B. Eerdmans Publishing Company, Grand Rapids, 1983)

--------, *The Canon of Scripture* (Inter-Varsity Press, Downers Grove, 1988)

--------, *The Books and the Parchments: How We Got Our English Bible* (Fleming H. Revell Company, Old Tappan, 1984)

--------, *Second Thoughts on the Dead Sea Scrolls* (Wm. B. Eerdmans Publishing Company, Grand Rapids, 1961)

--------, *Jesus and Paul: Places They Knew* (Thomas Nelson, Nashville, 1983)

Buchler, A., *Studies in Sin and Atonement in the Rabbinic Literature of the First Century* (Ktav Publishing House, New York, 1967)

Carnley, P., *The Structure of Resurrection Belief* (Clarendon Press, Oxford, 1987)

Carson, D.A., *Matthew* in *The Expositor's Bible Commentary: Volume 8* (Zondervan Publishing House, Grand Rapids, 1984)

Carson, D.A., Moo, D.J. and Morris, L., *An Introduction to the New Testament* (Zondervan Publishing House, Grand Rapids, 1992)

Cartlidge, D.R. and Dungan, D.L., *Documents for the Study of the Gospels* (Collins, New York, 1980)

Catchpole, D.R., *The Trial of Jesus: A Study in the Gospels and Jewish Historiography from 1770 to the Present Day* (E.J. Brill, Leiden, 1971)

Charlesworth, J.H., *Jesus within Judaism: New Light from Exciting Archaeological Discoveries* (Doubleday, New York, 1988)

Chilton, B.D., *A Galilean Rabbi and His Bible: Jesus' Use of the Interpreted Scripture of His Time* (Michael Glazier Inc., Wilmington, 1984)

--------; Evans, C.A.; Neusner, J., *The Missing Jesus: Rabbinic Judaism and the New Testament* (Brill Academic Publishers, Boston, 2002)

Cohn, H., *The Trial and Death of Jesus* (KTAV Publishing House, New York, 1977)

Cole, A., *Tyndale New Testament Commentaries: The Gospel according to St. Mark* (William B. Eerdmans Publishing Company, Grand Rapids, 1961)

Comfort, P.W., *Early Manuscripts and Modern Translations of the New Testament* (Tyndale House Publishers, Wheaton, 1990)

--------, *The Quest for the Original Text of the New Testament* (Baker Book House, Grand Rapids, 1992)

Crossan, J.D., *The Historical Jesus: The Life of a Mediterranean Jewish Peasant* (Harper Collins, New York, 1992)

--------, Who Killed Jesus? Exposing the Roots of Anti-Semitism in the Gospel Story of the Death of Jesus (Harper Collins, San Francisco, 1995)

Crossan, J.D. and Reed, J.L., *Excavating Jesus: Behind the Stones, Behind the Texts* (Harper, San Francisco, 2001)

Daniel-Rops, H., *Daily Life in the Time of Jesus* Trans. P.O. Brian (Servant Books, Ann Arbour, 1962)

Daube, D., *The New Testament and Rabbinic Judaism* (Hendrickson Publishers, Peabody, 1956)

Davies, W.D., *Jewish and Pauline Studies* (Fortress Press, Philadelphia, 1984)

--------, *Paul and Rabbinic Judaism: Some Rabbinic Elements of Pauline Theology* (Fortress Press, Philadelphia, 1980)

Derrett, J.D.M., *Law in the New Testament* (Darton, Longman & Todd, London, 1970)

DeVaux, R., *Ancient Isreal: Its Life and Institutions* (Darton, Longman & Todd, London, 1965)

Dictionary of Jesus and the Gospels: A Compendium of Contemporary Biblical Scholarship Edit. J.B. Green, S. McKnight and I.H. Marshall (Inter Varsity Press, Downers Grove, 1992)

Dictionary of Judaism in the Biblical Period 430 BCE to 600 CE, Edit. J. Neusner and W.S. Green (Hendrickson Publishers, Peabody, 1996)

Dictionary of New Testament Background: A Compendium of Contemporary Biblical Scholarship Edit. C.A.Evans and S.E.Porter (Inter Varsity Press, Downers Grove, 2000)

Donahue, J.R. and Harrington, D.J., *Sacra Pagina: The Gospel of Mark* (The Liturgical Press, Collegeville, 2002)

Dood, C.H., *The Interpretation of the Fourth Gospel* (Cambridge University Press, Cambridge, 1953)

Downing, F.G., *Cynics and Christian Origins* (T and T Clark, Edinburgh, 1992)

Edersheim, A., *The Life and Times of Jesus the Messiah: Volume 1* (Wm.B. Eerdmans Publishing Company, Grand Rapids, 1945)

--------, *The Life and Times of Jesus the Messiah: Volume 2* (Wm.B. Eerdmans Publishing Company, Grand Rapids, 1945)

--------, *Sketches of Jewish Social Life in the days of Christ* (Wm.B. Eerdmans Publishing Company, Grand Rapids, 1985)

--------, *The Temple: Its Ministry and Services As They Were in the Time of Christ* (Wm. B. Eerdmans Publishing Company, Grand Rapids, 1982)

Edwards, J.R., *The Pillar New Testament Commentary: The Gospel According to Mark* (William B. Eerdmans Publishing Company, Grand Rapids, 2002)

Ellis, E.E., *The New Century Bible Commentary: The Gospel of Luke* (William B. Eerdmans, Grand Rapids, 1974)

Evans, C.A., *Word Biblical Commentary: Mark 8:27-16:20* (Thomas Nelson Publishers, Nashville, 2001)

--------, *Jesus and His Contemporaries: Comparative Studies* (Brill Academic Publishers, Boston, 2001)

--------, *Noncanonical Writings and New Testament Interpretation* (Hendrickson Publishers, Peabody, 1992)

--------, *Jesus and the Ossuaries: What Jewish Burial Practices Reveal about the Beginning of Christianity* (Baylor University Press, Waco, 2003)

--------, *Assessing the New Testament Evidence for the Historicity of the Resurrection of Jesus* (The Edwin Mellen Press, Lewiston, 1989)

--------, *Fabricating Jesus: How Modern Scholars Distort the Gospels* (Inter Varsity Press, Downers Grove, 2006)

Exegetical Dictionary of the New Testament, Edit. H. Balz and G. Schneider (William B. Eerdmans Publishing Company, Grand Rapids, 1982-1983)

Falk, H., *Jesus the Pharisee: A New Look at the Jewishness of Jesus* (Paulist Press, New York, 1985)

Farmer, W.R., *The Synoptic Problem: A Critical Analysis* (Western North Carolina Press, Dillsboro, 1976)

Ferguson, E., *Backgrounds of Early Christianity* (William B. Eerdmans Publishing Company, Grand Rapids, 1993)

Finegan, J., *The Archeology of the New Testament: The Life of Jesus and the Beginning of the Early Church* (Princeton University Press, Princeton, 1992)

--------, *Handbook of Biblical Chronology: Principles of Time Reckoning in the Ancient World and Problems of Chronology in the Bible* (Hendrickson Publishers, Peabody, 1998)

Finkel, A., *The Pharisees and the Teacher of Nazareth* (E.J. Brill, Leiden, 1964)

Finkelstein, L., *The Pharisees: The Sociological Background of their Faith Volume 2* (The Jewish Publication Society of America, Philadelphia, 1962)

Fitzmyer, J.A., *The Anchor Bible: Luke 1-1X* (Doubleday, New York, 1981)

--------, *The Anchor Bible: Luke X-XXIV* (Doubleday, New York, 1985)

Flusser, D., *Jesus* Trans. R.Walls (Herder and Herder, New York, 1969)

Foreman, D., *Crucify Him: A Lawyer Looks at the Trial of Jesus* (Zondervan Books, Grand Rapids, 1990)

Freyne, S., *Galilee from Alexander the Great to Hadrian 323 BCE to 135 CE: A Study of Second Temple Judaism* (Michael Glazier Inc., Wilmington, 1980)

Frommer's Isreal (Simon and Schuster Inc., New York, 1996)

Funk, R.W., Hoover, R.W. and the Jesus Seminar, *The Five Gospels: The Search for the Authentic Words of Jesus* (Macmillan Publishing Company, New York, 1993)

Funk, R.W. and the Jesus Seminar, *The Acts of Jesus: What Did Jesus Really Do?* (Harper Collins, San Francisco, 1998)

Geldenhuys, N., *The New International Commentary on the Old Testament: The Gospel of Luke* (William B. Eerdmans Publishing Company, Grand Rapids, 1983)

Gerhardsson, B., *Memory and Manuscript: Oral Tradition and Written Tradition in Rabbinic Judaism and Early Christianity* (Ejnar Munksgaard, Copenhagen, 1961)

Gilmore, S.M., *The Gospel of Luke* in *The Interpreter's Bible: Volume 8* (Abingdon Press, Nashville, 1954)

Goodacre, M., *The Case Against Q: Studies in Markan Priority and the Synoptic Problem* (Trinity Press International, Harrisburg, 2002)

Gospel Parallels: A Synopsis of the First Three Gospels Edit: B.H. Throckmorton Jr. (Thomas Nelson Publishers, Nashville, 1979)

Goulder, M.D., *The Evangelists' Calendar: A Lectionary Explanation of the Development of Scripture* (SPCK, London, 1978)

Gower, R., *The New Manners and Customs of the Bible* (Moody Press, Chicago, 1987)

Grant, F.C., *The Gospel of Mark* in *The Interpreter's Bible: Volume 7* (Abingdon Press, Nashville, 1954)

--------, *The Economic Background of the Gospels* (Oxford University Press, London, 1926)

Greenleaf, S., *The Testimony of the Evangelists: The Gospels Examined by the Rules of Evidence Administered in Courts of Justice* (Kregel Classics, Grand Rapids, 1995)

Grelot, P., *What are the Targums?* Trans. S. Attnasio (The Liturgical Press, Collegeville, 1992)

Guelich, R.A., *Word Biblical Commentary: Mark 1-8:26* (Word Books, Dallas, 1989)

Guignebert, C., *The Jewish World in the Time of Jesus* (University Books, New York, 1959)

Guilding, A., *The Fourth Gospel and Jewish Worship: A Study of the Relation of St. John's Gospel to the Ancient Jewish Lectionary System* (Clarendon Press, Oxford, 1960)

Gutherie, D., *New Testament: Introduction* (Inter Varsity Press, Downers Grove, 1990)

Habermas, G.R., *The Verdict of History: Conclusive Evidence for the Life of Jesus* (Thomas Nelson Publishers, Nashville, 1984)

Hagner, D.A., *Word Biblical Commentary: Matthew 1-13* (Word Books, Dallas, 1993)

--------, *Word Biblical Commentary: Matthew 14-28* (Word Books, Dallas, 1995)

Harrington, D.J., *Sacra Pagina: The Gospel of Matthew* (The Liturgical Press, Collegeville, 1991)

Harrington, W., *Mark* (Michael Glazier Inc., Wilmington, 1979)

Havener, I., *Q: The Sayings of Jesus* (The Liturgical Press, Collegeville, 1987)

Hengel, M., *The Zealots: Investigations into the Jewish Freedom Movement in the Period from Herod 1 Until 70 AD* Trans. D. Smith (T&T Clark, Edinburgh, 1989)

--------, *The 'Hellenization' of Judaea in the First Century after Christ* Trans. J. Bowden (Trinity Press International, Philadelphia, 1989)

--------, *Victory over Violence: Jesus and the Revolutionists* Trans. D.E. Green (Fortress Press, Philadelphia, 1973)

--------, *Crucifixion in the Ancient World and the Folly of the Message of the Cross* Trans. J. Bowden (Fortress Press, Philadelphia, 1977)

--------, *Judaism and Hellenism: Studies in their Encounter in Palestine during the Early Hellenistic Period Volume 1* Trans. J.Bowden (Fortress Press, Philadelphia, 1974)

--------, *Judaism and Hellenism: Studies in their Encounter in Palestine during the Early Hellenistic Period Volume 2* Trans. J. Bowden (Fortress Press, Philadelphia, 1974)

Herford, R.T., *Christianity in Talmud & Midrash* (KTAV Publishing House, New York, 1975)

Hill, D., *The New Century Bible Commentary: The Gospel of Matthew* (William B. Eerdmans, Grand Rapids, 1972)

Hillel and Jesus: Comparative Studies of Two Major Religious Leaders Edit. J.H. Charlesworth and L.L. Johns (Fortress Press, Minneapolis, 1997)

Hilton, M. and Marshall, G., *The Gospels and Rabbinic Judaism* (SCM Press, London, 1988)

Hoehner, H.W., *Chronological Aspects of the Life of Christ* (Zondervan Publishing House, Grand Rapids, 1975)

Horsley, R.A., *Galilee: History, Politics, People* (Trinity Press International, Valley Forge, 1995)

Hoskyns, E.C., *The Fourth Gospel* (Faber and Faber Limited, London, 1947)

Howard, W.F., *The Gospel of John* in *The Interpreter's Bible: Volume 8* (Abingdon Press, Nashville, 1954)

Irwin, W.A., *Job* in *Peake's Commentary on the Bible* (Thomas Nelson and Sons Ltd., New York, 1962)

Jeremias, J., *Jerusalem in the Time of Jesus: An Investigation into Economic and Social Conditions during the New Testament Period* (Fortress Press, Philadelphia, 19690

Jesus and Faith: A Conversation on the Work of John Dominic Crossan Edit. J. Carlson and R.A. Ludwig (Orbis Book, Marykoll, 1994)

Jesus and His Times Edit. K. Ward (The Reader's Digest Association, Pleasantville, 1987)

Jesus' Jewishness: Exploring the Place of Jesus within Early Judaism Edit. J.H. Charlesworth (Crossroad, New York, 1991)

Jesus Under Fire, Edit. M.J. Wilkins and J.P. Moreland (Zondervan Publishing House, Grand Rapids, 1995)

Jewish Writings of the Second Temple Period: Apocrypha, Pseudepigraphra, Qumram Sectarian Writings, Philo, Josephus Edit. M.E. Stone (Fortress Press, Philadelphia, 1984)

Johnson, L.T., *Sacra Pagina: The Gospel of Luke* (The Liturgical Press, Collegeville, 1991)

--------, *The Real Jesus: The Misguided Quest for the Historical Jesus and the Truth of the Traditional Gospels* (Harper Collins, San Francisco, 1992)

Johnson, S.E., *The Gospel of Matthew* in *The Interpreter's Bible: Volume 7* (Abingdon Press, Nashville, 1954)

--------, *Jesus and his Towns* (Michael Glazier, Wilmington, 1989)

Jones, A.H.M., *Studies in Roman Government and Law* (Basil Blackwell, Oxford, 1960)

Kee, H.C., *Understanding the New Testament* (Prentice Hall, Englewood Cliffs, 1993)

--------, *Jesus in History: An Approach to the Study of the Gospels* (Harcourt Brace Jovanovich, New York, 1977)

Keener, C.S., *A Commentary on the Gospel of Matthew* (William B. Eerdmans Publishing Company, Grand Rapids, 1999)

Klausner, J., *Jesus of Nazareth: His Life, Times, and Teaching* Trans. H. Danby (Menorah Publishing Company, New York, 1925)

--------, *The Messianic Idea in Israel from Its Beginning to the Completion of the Mishnah* Trans. W.F. Stinespring (George Allen and Unwin Ltd., London, 1956)

Lachs, S.M., *A Rabbinic Commentary of the New Testament* (KTAV Publishing House Inc., Hoboken, 1987)

Lane, W.L, *The New International Commentary on the Old Testament: The Gospel of Mark* (William B. Eerdmans Publishing Company, Grand Rapids, 1974)

Liefeld, W.L., *Luke* in *The Expositor's Bible Commentary: Volume 8* (Zondervan Publishing House, Grand Rapids, 1984)

Lightfoot, J., *A Commentary on the New Testament from the Talmud and Hebraica: Volume I Place Names in the Gospels* (Hendrickson Publishers, Peabody, 1859 reprinted 1989)

--------, *A Commentary on the New Testament from the Talmud and Hebraica: Volume II Matthew-Mark* (Hendrickson Publishers, Peabody, 1859 reprinted 1989)

--------, *A Commentary on the New Testament from the Talmud and Hebraica: Volume III Luke-John* (Hendrickson Publishers, Peabody, 1859 reprinted 1989)

Lindars, B., *The New Century Bible Commentary: The Gospel of John* (William B. Eerdmans, Grand Rapids, 1972)

Linnemann, E., *Is there a Synoptic Problem: Rethinking the Literary Dependence of the First Three Gospel* Trans. R.W. Yarbrough (Baker House Books, Grand Rapids, 1992)

Lord, A.B., *The Singer of Tales* (Harvard University Press, Cambridge, 1960)

Maccoby, H., *Early Rabbinic Writings* (Cambridge University Press, Cambridge, 1988)

--------, *The Myth Maker: Paul and the Invention of Christianity* (Harper San Francisco, San Francisco, 1986)

--------, *Paul and Hellenism* (Trinity Press International, Philadelphia, 1991)

Mack, B.L., *The Lost Gospel: The Book of Q and Christian Origins* (Harper Collins, San Francisco, 1993)

MacKenzie, R.A.F. and Murphy, R.E., *Job* in *The New Jerome Biblical Commentary* (Prentice Hall, Englewood Cliffs, 1990)

Malina, B.J. and Rohrbaugh, R.L., *Social-Science Commentary on the Synoptic Gospels* (Fortress Press, Minneapolis, 1992)

Mann, C.S., *The Anchor Bible: Mark* (Doubleday, New York, 1986)

Mason, S., *Josephus and the New Testament* (Hendrickson Publishers, Peabody, 1992)

Matthews, V.H. and Benjamin, D.C., *Old Testament Parallels: Laws and Stories from the Ancient Near East* (Paulist Press, New York, 1991)

McBirnie, W.S., *The Search for the Twelve Apostles* (Tyndale House Publishers, Wheaton, 1973)

McCall, H., *Mesopotamian Myths* (University of Texas Press, Austin, 1990)

McNamara, M., *Palestinian Judaism* (Michael Glazier Inc., Wilmington, 1983)

Meeks, W.A., *The Moral World of the First Christians* (The Westminister Press, Philadelphia, 1986)

Meier, J.P. *Matthew* (Michael Glazier Inc., Wilmington, 1980)

--------, *A Marginal Jew: Rethinking the Historical Jesus- Volume 1: The Roots of the Problem and the Person* (Doubleday, New York, 1991)

--------, *A Marginal Jew: Rethinking the Historical Jesus- Volume2: Mentor, Message and Miracles* (Doubleday, New York, 1994)

--------, *A Marginal Jew: Rethinking the Historical Jesus- Volume 3: Companions and Competitors* (Doubleday, New York, 2001)

Metzger, B.M., *The New Testament: Its Background, Growth and Content* (Abingdon Press, Nashville, 1983)

--------, *The Text of the New Testament: Its Transmission, Corruption and Restoration* (Oxford University Press, New York, 1968)

--------, *The Early Versions of the New Testament: Their Origin, Transmission and Limitations* (Clarendon Press, Oxford, 1977)

Midrash Rabbah, Trans. H.Freedman and M.Simon (The Soncino Press, New York, 1983)

Millard, A., *Discoveries from the Time of Jesus* (Lion Publishing, Oxford, 1990)

Miller, M.S. and Miller J.L, *Harper's Encyclopedia of Biblical Life* (Harper and Row, San Francisco, 1978)

Moloney, F.J., *Sacra Pagina: The Gospel of John* (The Liturgical Press, Collegeville, 1998)

Montefiore, C.G., *Rabbinic Literature and Gospel Teachings* (Macmillan and Company, London, 1930)

--------, *The Synoptic Gospels: Volume 1* (KTAV Publishing House, New York, 1968)

--------, *The Synoptic Gospels: Volume 1* (KTAV Publishing House, New York, 1968)

Montefiore, C.G. and Loewe, H., *A Rabbinic Anthology* (The Jewish Publication Society of America, Philadelphia, 1963)

Moore, G.F., *Judaism in the First Centuries of the Christian Era: The Age of Tannaim Volume 1* (Harvard University Press, Cambridge, 1955)

--------, *Judaism in the First Centuries of the Christian Era: The Age of Tannaim Volume 2* (Harvard University Press, Cambridge, 1955)

--------, *Judaism in the First Centuries of the Christian Era: The Age of Tannaim Volume 3* (Harvard University Press, Cambridge, 1955)

Morris, L., *The New International Commentary on the Old Testament: The Gospel of John* (William B. Eerdmans Publishing Company, Grand Rapids, 1971)

--------, *The Gospel according to Matthew* (William B. Eerdmans Publishing Company, Grand Rapids, 1992)

--------, *Tyndale New Testament Commentaries: The Gospel according to St. Luke* (William B. Eerdmans Publishing Company, Grand Rapids, 1974)

--------, *Studies in the Fourth Gospel* (William B. Erdmans Publishing Company, Grand Rapids, 1969)

--------, *The New Testament and the Jewish Lectionaries* (The Tyndale Press, London, 1964)

Mowinckel, S., *He That Cometh* Trans. G.W. Anderson (Abingdon Press, New York, 1954)

Neusner, J., *The Rabbinic Traditions About the Pharisees before 70: Part I The Masters* (E.J.Brill, Leiden, 1971)

--------, *The Rabbinic Traditions About the Pharisees before 70: Part II The Houses* (E.J.Brill, Leiden, 1971)

--------, *The Rabbinic Traditions About the Pharisees before 70: Part III Conclusions* (E.J.Brill, Leiden, 1971)

--------, *The Mishnah: Introduction and Reader* (Trinity Press International, Philadelphia, 1992)

--------, *Christian Faith and the Bible of Judaism: The Judaic Encounter with Scripture* (William B. Eerdmans Publishing Company, Grand Rapids, 1987)

--------, *Messiah in Context: Isreal's History and Destiny in Formative Judaism* (Fortress Press, Philadelphia, 1984)

--------, *Judaism in the Beginning of Christianity* (Fortress Press, Philadelphia, 1984)

New Testament Apocrypha Volume 1: Gospels and Related Writings Edit. W. Schneemelcher Trans. R.M.Wilson (John Knox Press, Louisville, 1991)

New Testament Apocrypha Volume 2: Writings Relating to the Apostles; Apocalypses and Related Subjectss Edit. W.Schneemelcher Trans. R.M.Wilson (John Knox Press, Louisville, 1992)

Nickelsburg, G.W.E. and Stone, M.E., *Faith and Piety in Early Judaism: Texts and Documents* (Trinity Press International, Philadelphia, 1991)

Nolland, J., *Word Biblical Commentary: Luke 1-9:20* (Word Books, Dallas, 1989)

--------, *Word Biblical Commentary: Luke 9:21-18:34* (Word Books, Dallas, 1993)

--------, *Word Biblical Commentary: Luke 18:35-24:53* (Word Books, Dallas, 1993)

Oakman, D.E., *Jesus and the Economic Questions of His Day* (The Edwin Mellen Press, Lewiston, 1986)

O'Collins, G., *Interpreting Jesus* (Paulist Press, Mahwah, 1983)

Patai, R., *The Messiah Texts* (Wayne State University Press, Detroit, 1979)

Perkins, P., *The Gnostic Dialogue: The Early Church and the Crisis of Gnosticism* (Paulist Press, New York, 1980)

Pesikta de-Rab Kahana: R. Kahana's Compliation of Discourses for Sabbaths and Festival Days, Trans. W.G.Braude and I.J.Kapstein (Jewish Publication Society of America, Philadelphia, 1975)

Pfeiffer, C.F. and Vos, H.F., *The Wycliffe Historical Geography of Biblical Lands* (Moody Press, Chicago, 1967)

Robinson, J.A.T., *Redating the New Testament* (Westminister Press, Philadelphia, 1976)

--------, *The Priority of John* (Meyer Stone Books, London, 1985)

--------, *Can We Trust the New Testament?* (Wm.B. Eerdmans Publishing Company, 1977)

Rousseau, J.J. and Arav, R., *Jesus and His World: An Archaeological and Cultural Dictionary* (Fortress Press, Minneapolis, 1995)

Rudolph, K., *Gnosis: The Nature and History of Gnosticism* Trans. R.M.Wilson (Harper and Row, San Francisco, 1987)

Russell, D.S., *Between the Testaments* (Fortress Press, Philadelphia, 1965)

Safrai, Z., *The Economy of Roman Palestine* (Routledge, London, 1994)

Saldarini, A.J., *Pharisees, Scribes and Sadducees in Palestinian Society: A Sociological Approach* (Michael Glazier, Wilmington, 1988)

Sanders, E.P., *Jesus and Judaism* (Fortress Press, Philadelphia, 1985)

--------, *Jewish Law from Jesus to the Mishnah* (SCM Press, London, 1990)

--------, *Judaism: Practice and Belief 63 BCE- 66 CE* (SCM Press, London, 1992)

--------, *Paul, the Law and the Jewish People* (Fortress Press, Philadelphia, 1983)

--------, *Paul and Palestinian Judaism: A Comparison of Patterns of Religion* (Fortress Press, Minneapolis, 1977)

--------, *The Historical Figure of Jesus* (The Penguin Press, London, 1993)

Sanders, E.P. and Davies, M., *Studying the Synoptic Gospels* (Trinity Press International, Philadelphia, 1989)

Sandmel, S., *Judaism and Christian Beginnings* (Oxford University Press, New York, 1978)

Schechter, S., *Aspects of Rabbinic Theology: Major Concepts of the Talmud* (Schocken Books, New York, 1961)

Schurer, E., *A History of the Jewish People in the Time of Jesus Christ- Division 1: Political History of Palestine from BC 175 to AD 135, Volume 1* Trans. J. MacPherson (T&T Clark, Edinburgh, 1910)

--------, *A History of the Jewish People in the Time of Jesus Christ- Division 1: Political History of Palestine from BC 175 to AD 135, Volume 2* Trans. J. MacPherson (T&T Clark, Edinburgh, 1910)

--------, *A History of the Jewish People in the Time of Jesus Christ- Division 2: The Internal Condition of Palestine and of the Jewish People in the Time of Jesus Christ, Volume 1* Trans. S.Taylor and P.Christie (T&T Clark, Edinburgh, 1910)

--------, *A History of the Jewish People in the Time of Jesus Christ- Division 2: The Internal Condition of Palestine and of the Jewish People in the Time of Jesus Christ, Volume 2* Trans. S. Taylor and P.Christie (T&T Clark, Edinburgh, 1910)

--------, *A History of the Jewish People in the Time of Jesus Christ- Division 2: The Internal Condition of Palestine and of the Jewish People in the Time of Jesus Christ, Volume 3* Trans. S.Taylor and P. Christie (T&T Clark, Edinburgh, 1910)

Sherwin-White, A.N., *Roman Society and Roman Law in the New Testament* (Clarendon Press, Oxford, 1963)

Smith, G.A., *The Topography, Economics and Historical Geography of Jerusalem* (Ariel Publishing House, Jerusalem, 1907)

Smith, M., *Tannaitic Parallels to the Gospels* (Society of Biblical Literature, Philadelphia, 1951)

Stein, R.H., *The Synoptic Problem: An Introduction* (Baker Book House, Grand Rapids, 1987)

--------, *The New American Commentary: Luke* (Broadman and Holman Publishers, 1992)

--------, *Jesus the Messiah: A Survey of the Life of Christ* (Inter-Varsity Press, Downers Grove, 1996)

--------, *Gospels and Tradition: Studies on Redaction Criticism of the Synoptic Gospels* (Baker Book House, Grand Rapids, 1991)

--------, *Studying the Synoptic Gospels: Origin and Interpretation* (Baker Academic, Grand Rapids, 2001)

Steinsaltz, A., *The Essential Talmud* (Basic Books Inc., New York, 1976)

Stemberger, G., *Jewish Contemporaries of Jesus: Pharisees, Sadducees, Essenes* Trans. W.W. Mahnke (Fortress Press, Minneapolis, 1995)

Stephens, W.H., *The New Testament World In Pictures* (Broadman Press, Nashville, 1987)

Stott, J.R.W., *The Cross of Christ* (Inter Varsity Press, Downers Grove, 1986)

Strack, H.L., *Introduction to the Talmud and Midrash* (Harper Torchbooks, New York, 1931)

Strack, H.L. and Stemberger, G., *Introduction to the Talmud and Midrash* Trans. M. Bockmuehl (Fortress Press, Minneapolis, 1992)

Stambaugh, J.E. and Balch, D.L., *The New Testament in Its Social Environment* (The Westminister Press, Philadelphia, 1986)

Tacitus, *The Annals of Imperial Rome* Trans. M. Grant (Penguin Books, Middlesex, 1956)

Tasker, R.V.G., *Tyndale New Testament Commentaries: The Gospel according to St. Matthew* (William B. Eerdmans Publishing Company, Grand Rapids, 1961)

--------, *Tyndale New Testament Commentaries: The Gospel according to St. John* (William B. Eerdmans Publishing Company, Grand Rapids, 1960)

Tenny, M.C., *New Testament Times* (Wm.B. Eerdmans Publishing Company, Grand Rapids, 1965)

--------, *John* in *The Expositor's Bible Commentary: Volume 9* (Zondervan Publishing House, Grand Rapids, 1981)

The Anchor Bible Commentary Edit. D.N. Freedman (Doubleday, New York, 1992)

The Antiquities of the Jews in *The Works of Josephus* Trans. W. Whiston (Hendrickson Publishers, Peabody, 1987)

The Archaeological Enclyclopedia of the Holy Land Edit. A. Negev (Thomas Nelson Publishers, Nashville, 1986)

The Babylonian Talmud: Volume 1 Sabbath Trans. M.L. Rodkinson (The Talmud Society, Boston, 1918)

The Apocryphal New Testament Trans. M.R. James (Clarendon Press, Oxford, 1924)

The Babylonian Talmud: Volume 3 Festivals Trans. M. Rodkinson (The Talmud Society, Boston, 1918)

The Dead Sea Scriptures Trans. T.H. Gaster (Anchor Books, Garden City, 1976)

The Gnostic Scriptures Trans. B. Layton (Doubleday, Garden City, 1987)

The Jewish People in the First Century: Historical Geography, Political History, Social, Cultural and Religious Life and Institutions Volume 1 (Fortress Press, Philadelphia, 1974)

The Jewish People in the First Century Volume 2 (Fortress Press, Philadelphia, 1976)

The Literature of the Sages- First Part: Oral Tora, Halakha, Mishna, Tosefta, Talmud, External Tractates Edit. S. Safrai (Fortress Press, Philadelphia, 1987)

The Mishnah Trans. H.Danby (Oxford University Press, Oxford, 1933)

The Nag Hammadi Library in English Trans. J.M. Robinson (Harper and Row, San Francisco, 1988)

The New Oxford Annotated Bible, New Revised Standard Version with the Apocryphal/ Deuterocanonical Books, Edit. B.M. Metzger and R.E. Murphy (Oxford University Press, New York, 1991)

Theological Dictionary of the New Testament: Abridged in One Volume, Edit. G.Kittel and G.Freidrich and Trans. G.W.Bromley (Wm.B.Eerdmans Publishing Company, Grand Rapids, 1985)

The Other Gospels: Non-Canonical Gospel Texts Edit. R. Cameron (The Westminister Press, Philadelphia, 1982)

The Oxford Companion to the Bible Edit. B.M. Metzger and M.D. Coogan (Oxford University Press, New York, 1993)

The Social World of Luke-Acts: Models for Interpretation, Edit. J.H. Neyrey (Hendrickson Publications, Peabody, 1991)

The Tosefta: Volume 1, Trans. J. Neusner (Hendrickson Publishers Inc., Peabody, 2002)

The Tosefta: Volume 1, Trans. J. Neusner (Hendrickson Publishers Inc., Peabody, 2002)

The Trial of Jesus, Edit. E.Bammel (SCM Press, London, 1970)

The Works of Josephus Trans. W. Whiston (Hendrickson Publishers, Peabody, 1987)

The Works of Philo Trans. C.D. Yonge (Hendrickson Publishers, Peabody, 1993)

The Wycliffe Bible Commentary Edit. C.F. Pfeiffer and E.F. Harrison (Moody Press, Chicago, 1962)

Thompson, J.A., *Handbook of Life in Bible Times* (Inter-Varsity Press, Downers Grove, 1986)

Tinsley, E.J., *The Cambridge Bible Commentary on the New English Bible: The Gospel according to Luke* (Cambridge University Press, London, 1965)

Tinsley, E.J., *The Cambridge Bible Commentary on the New English Bible: The Gospel according to Luke* (Cambridge University Press, London, 1965)

Tomson, P.J., *Paul and the Jewish Law: Halakha in the Letters of the Apostle to the Gentiles* (Fortress Press, Minneapolis, 1990)

Twelftree, G.H., *Jesus the Exorcist: A Contribution to the Study of the Historical Jesus* (Hendrickson Publishers, Peabody, 1993)

Understanding the Dead Sea Scrolls: A Reader from the Biblical Archaeology Review Edit. H.Shanks (Vintage Books, New York, 1992)

Urbach, E.E., *The Sages: Their Concepts and Beliefs* Trans. I. Abrahams (Harvard University Press, Cambridge, 1987)

Vermes, G., *Jesus the Jew* (Fortress Press, Philadelphia, 1973)

--------, *The Religion of Jesus the Jew* (Fortress Press, Minneapolis, 1993)

--------, *Jesus and the World of Judaism* (Fortress Press, Philadelphia, 1983)

Walker, B., *Gnosticism: Its History and Influence* (The Aquarian Press, Wellingborough, 1983)

Weesel, W.W., *Mark* in *The Expositor's Bible Commentary: Volume 8* (Zondervan Publishing House, Grand Rapids, 1984)

Wenham, J., *Redating Matthew, Mark and Luke: A Fresh Assault on the Synoptic Problem* (Inter-Varsity Press, Downers Grove, 1992)

Whittaker, M., *Jews and Christians: Graeco-Roman Views* (Cambridge University Press, Cambridge, 1984)

Wilkinson, J. *The Jerusalem Jesus Knew: An Archaeological Guide to the Gospels* (Thomas Nelson Publishers, Nashville, 1978)

Winter, P., *On the Trial of Jesus* Edit. T.A. Burkill and G. Vermes (Walter de Gruyter, New York, 1974)

Witherington III, B., *Jesus the Sage: The Pilgramage of Wisdom* (Fortress Press, Minneapolis, 2000)

---------, *Jesus the Seer: The Progress of Prophecy* (Hendrickson Publishers, Peabody, 1999)

Wright, N.T., *Jesus and the Victory of God* (Fortress Press, Minneapolis, 1996)

--------, *The New Testament and the People of God* (Fortress Press, Minneapolis, 1992)

--------, *The Resurrection and the Son of God* (Fortress Press, Minneapolis, 2003)

--------, *Who Was Jesus?* (William B. Eerdmans Publishing Company, Grand Rapids, 1992)

Wycliffe Bible Encyclopedia Edit. C.F. Pfeiffer, H.F. Vos and J. Rea ((Moody Press, Chicago, 1975)

Young, B.H., *Jesus: The Jewish Theologian* (Hendrickson Publishers, Peabody, 1995)

--------, *Jesus and His Jewish Parables: Recovering the Roots of Jesus' Teaching* (Paulist Press, New York, 1989)

Zeitlin, I.M., *Jesus and the Judaism of His Time* (Polity Press, Cambridge, 1988)

Printed in the United States
By Bookmasters